BIOGRAPHY OF PIR-O-MURSHID INAYAT KHAN

M. H. Thurburn.

کنایت خان

BIOGRAPHY OF PIR-O-MURSHID INAYAT KHAN

Revised Edition

Sulūk Press
Richmond, Virginia

© 2020 by the Nekbkaht Foundation

Previous volumes in this series:

Biography of Pir-o-Murshid Inayat Khan (1979)
Complete Works of Pir-o-Murshid Hazrat Inayat Khan, Original Texts:
Sayings, Part I (Gayan, Vadan, Nirtan, 1982, rev. ed. 1989)
Sayings, Part II (Bowl of Saki, Aphorisms, Unpublished Sayings, 1982, rev. ed. 1989

Lectures on Sufism:
1922 I: January-August (1990)
1922 II: September-December (1996)
1923 I: January-June (1989)
1923 II: July-December (1988)
1924 I: January-June (2004)
1924 II: June-December (2010)
1925 I: January–June (2013)
1925 II: 14 June–22 November (2017)
1926 I: December 1925–May 12 (2010)
1926 II: March 14–May 28 (2012)
Published by the Nekbakht Foundation;
the Complete Works are downloadable from
nekbakhtfoundation.org
© 2020 by the Nekbakht Foundation

This book and website are copyrighted under the Berne Convention. Enquiries should be addressed to Fondation Nekbakht, 34 rue de la Tuilerie, 92150 Suresnes, France.

No part of this book may be reproduced in any form, by print, photoprint, microfilm, electronic reproduction, or by any other means without written permission from the copyright holder. Permission is given to download this document from nekbakhtfoundation.org, and part or all of it may be printed for personal use.

Printed on acid-free paper that meets ANSI standard X39-48.
Editorial and production services by Suluk Press/Omega Publications Inc.
Manufactured in the United States of America.

Inayat Khan (1882–1927)
Biography of Pir-o-Murshid Inayat Khan
1. Inayat Khan 1882-1927 2. Sufis-India-biography

Library of Congress Control Number 2020935843

ISBN 978–1–941810–36–1

Contents

List of photographs of Pir-o-Murshid Inayat Khan   7
Introduction   9
Editor's note to the 2019 Edition   13

Biography of Pir-o-Murshid Inayat Khan:

    Part I.   *Biography:*   15

        India   17
        Baroda   18
        Maula Bakhsh   19
        Rahmat Khan   28
        Khatidja Bibi   30
        Infancy   33
        Childhood   35
        Ladhood   41
        Boyhood   45
        Youth   53
        Maheboob Khan   102
        Musharaff Khan   103
        Ali Khan   104

    Part II.   *Autobiography:*   105

        America, 1910-1912   107
        England, 1912-1913   113
        France, 1913   114
        Russia, 1913-1914   115
        France (again), 1914   123
        England (again), 1914-1920   123
        Switzerland, 1920   133
        France (again), 1920   138
        Holland, 1921   138
        Belgium, 1921   141

Germany, 1921   **143**
Switzerland (again), 1922   **144**
America (again), 1923   **150**
France (again), Suresnes, 1923   **159**
Switzerland (again), Geneva, 1923   **159**

Personal Account   **161**

Diary, 1923-1926   **173**

Part III.   *Journal*:   **193**

Review of Religions   **195**
Organization   **211**
East and West   **217**
Music   **229**

Anecdotes   **235**

Epilogue   **245**

Illustrations   **247**

Biographical sketches of principal workers   **341**

Family Tree   **379**

Maps: **385**

India   **386**
United States of America   **388**
Europe   **390**
Switzerland   **392**
United Kingdom   **394**
Belgium, Netherlands   **396**

Notes and Glossary   **399**

Index   **439**

List of Photographs

Frontispiece – portrait painted by M.H. Thurburn, Paris 1913   2
1. Childhood portrait, Baroda, India, c.1894   34
2. Playing the Jalatarang, Baroda, India, c.1898   80
3. With garland of flowers and gold medal, Madras, India, c.1902   82
4. Hyderabad, India, c.1905   84
5. Professor Inayat Khan with gold medals, India, c.1910   86
6. Performing the Tiger Dance, c.1910   88
7. Calcutta, India, c.1908   92
8. Calcutta, India, c.1909   94
9. San Francisco, USA 1911   96
10. Pittsburgh, USA 1910   98
11. San Francisco, USA 1911 (Taber Stanford Studio)   108
12. Published in Paris, November 1912, in the Journal de la Société Unitive   116
13. Published in Paris, November 1913, in the Journal de la Société Unitive   117
14. In meditation, London, UK 1914   118
15. London, UK April 1915   120
16. Moscow, Russia 1913   122
17. London, UK 11th December 1914 (J. Russell & Sons)   124
18. London, UK October 1917 (Beresford Studio)   126
19. Playing the vina, London, UK April 1915   128
20. London, UK October 1917 (Beresford Studios)   130
21. London, UK October 1917 (Beresford Studio)   132
22. London, UK November 1918 (Beresford studio)   134
23. Leaflet for a vina recital, London, UK 31st January 1920   135
24. Geneva, Switzerland 18th February 1921 (Boissonnas Studio)   137
25. Geneva, Switzerland 18th February 1921 (Boissonnas Studio)   139
26. London, UK May 1921 (Beresford Studio)   140
27. Leerdam, Netherlands, with child called Cochius, 5th February 1921   142
28. Jena, Germany October 1921 (Alfred Bischoff Studio)   145
29. In Cherag's robe, c.1922   146
30. Jena, Germany October 1921 (Alfred Bischoff Studio)   147
31. Berlin, Germany October 1924 (Press Photo News Service)   148
32. Katwijk Beach, Netherlands September 1922   149

8 LIST OF PHOTOGRAPHS

33. Entering the gate of Fazal Manzil, Suresnes, France c.1926   151
34. New York, USA 28th February 1923
    (Underwood & Underwood Studios)   152
35. New York, USA 28th February 1923
    (Underwood & Underwood Studios)   153
36. New York, USA Spring 1923
    (Underwood & Underwood Studios)   156
37. New York, USA 1923 (Underwood & Underwood Studio)   163
38. With his wife Amina Begum in the Sufi Garden,
    Suresnes, France, 1926   164
39. Birthday celebration in the Sufi Garden, Suresnes,
    France, 5th July 1926   168
40. Conversation with a mureed in the Sufi Garden,
    Suresnes, France, 1926   171
41. New York, USA, 28th February 1923   175
42. London, UK May 1921   177
43. Palace of Arts, San Francisco, USA 1923   179
44. London, UK May 1921   181
45. USA, 1926   183
46. In the garden of Fazal Manzil, Suresnes, France c.1926   185
47. On SS Majestic New York to Cherbourg, June 1926   187
48. Grand Canyon, Arizona, USA, 14 April 1926 (Fred Harvey)   188
49. Suresnes, France 13th September 1926   189
50. New York, USA December 1925 (Muray Studios)   223
51. Playing the vina, London, UK June 1919 (Beresford Studios)   228
52. Jena, Germany, October 1921 (Alfred Bischoff Studios)   231
53. Haarlem, Netherlands with the Van Meerwijk children,
    10th September 1921   239

Introduction

The age-old mystic philosophy known today in the East mainly in the different Sufi Orders, was given to the world by Pir-o-Murshid Inayat Khan as the Sufi Message. A very short outline of the Sufi Message, where possible in his own words, may be appropriate here.

Pir-o-Murshid Inayat Khan explained that Sufism is the ancient School of Wisdom from which have sprung many cults of a mystical and philosophical nature such as the ancient School of Egypt. In this same school Abraham received his initiation. Traces of Sufism are to be found in different parts of the world and in all periods of history. To the ancient Greeks this wisdom was known as *sophia*, from the word *sophos*, meaning wise. But the Arabic word *saf* (pure) could be the origin of the word Sufi, for there was a time when Sufis were known as *Brothers of Purity*. The Prophet Muhammad called them the *Knights of Purity*. Although Sufism is in reality the essence and spirit of all religions, several Sufi Orders representing the esoteric side of Islam came into existence when this religion was spreading. As the Sufis expounded their free thought in Persia there was much opposition and persecution from the then current religions. So in that part of the world Sufism found its outlet in poetry and music through such great poets as Hafiz, Rumi, Shams Tabriz, Sa'adi, Nizami, Attar and others, giving in this way its wisdom to the world.

He explained furthermore that although the Sufism he represented in the West was different in nature and character from Sufi Schools in the East, he used the same name, as both considered wisdom as a means towards the end. By pointing to wisdom, that same wisdom which is present in the various faiths and beliefs, Sufism makes men rise above the boundaries of creed, race, caste and nation. It is the discovering of the essential Truth underlying all religions and beliefs which is the aim of the Sufi. In his search for what is behind things as they appear to be, in his search for the cause behind the cause, the Sufi not only comes nearer to that Ultimate Truth at every step he takes, but at the same time he becomes more loving and understanding towards his fellowmen. It is a harmonious development of the vertical and of the horizontal line: of one's inner being and of the feeling of brotherhood.

In his Biography Pir-o-Murshid Inayat Khan describes the two periods of his life. The first part, called *Biography*, covers his life in India from childhood to manhood, showing his character and interests. From the very beginning this period can be seen as a preparation for the task awaiting him: the spreading of the Sufi Message. The second part he calls his *Autobiography*. In this he relates his experiences in studying the Western mentality, the Western way of life, his encounters and his work of delivering the Sufi Message, also the establishment of the Sufi Movement in the West.

The text of the *Biography*, as presented here, is his final version. Previous to this, two short biographical sketches had been published. The first one appeared as an article in the *Bulletin Mensuel de la Société Unitive*, Paris, of April 1913. It was rewritten as an introductory chapter to the book *A Sufi Message of Spiritual Liberty* and signed by Tserclaes. The other was a booklet written by Regina Miriam Bloch entitled *The Confessions of Inayat Khan*. This was published in London in 1915. Some passages of *The Confessions* have been copied from the Introduction signed by Tserclaes. Pir-o-Murshid Inayat Khan himself had long had the idea of producing an autobiography but the decisive push came from H.H. the Maharaja of Baroda. The Maharaja had encouraged Inayat in his musical career when he was a boy, and when many years later the two met in London, shortly after the first world war, His Highness suggested that Inayat should write his autobiography. From then on he began to record in his pocket notebooks his various observations, notes and short anecdotes.

Part of the Indian period of his life, was dictated by him during 1919 and 1920 to some of his first mureeds in England among whom were Miss Khatidja Young[1], Mrs. Hanifa Sheaf, Murshida Sophia Saintsbury-Green and Murshida Sharifa Goodenough, from notes about the situation in India at that time and about his family and childhood. These notes had been sent to him at his request by his brother-in-law Mehr Bakhshe and probably also by his uncle Dr. Pathan. Other notes were added in 1922 and 1923 at the time of the Summer School in Suresnes, France. Pir-o-Murshid Inayat Khan dictated a large part of the *Biography* to his secretary, Miss Sakina[2] Furnée, who took his words down in shorthand. This part, besides the extra papers about his brothers and cousin, included his musical tour throughout Southern India, Ceylon, Burma and Calcutta. The encounter with his Murshid, Sayyed Abu Hashim Madani, the meeting of the dervishes at Ajmer and a few other passages included in the *Biography* have been taken from *The Confessions of Inayat Khan*.

The second part of the book, called *Autobiography*, begins with Pir-o-Murshid Inayat Khan's departure from India to the United States of America. Between the summer of 1922 and the autumn of 1925 he dictated the events he wished to put on record to Miss Sakina Furnée and arranged them in the sequence given here in the text. The account of his lecture tour through the

---

1. A few words should be said here regarding an Eastern custom of a Murshid giving a new name, a Sufi name to mureeds in order to help them in their spiritual progress. The vibration of the sound and the meaning of the word itself make this name an instrument for the spiritual development of the pupil and an aid towards the fulfilment of a given purpose in the life of that pupil.
2. Later, Nekbakht, this is not further noted

United States in 1925-1926, which ends the book, was dictated to Miss Kismet Stam. The passage dealing with the attitude of the Press and its influence upon the public, referred to in both the chapters *America again (1923)* and *East and West*, has been taken from questions and answers recorded after a lecture titled *The Purpose of Life* given in the summer of 1924. Other parts of the chapter *East and West* had formerly been published in the magazine *Sufism*, March and June 1922. Minor events and considerations, although included in the text, were indicated by him as notes; they have therefore been shown in italics. The anecdotes in the last chapter were collected by Murshida Sharifa Goodenough, Miss Sakina Furnée and Miss Kismet Stam; some of these were taken from his notebooks.

It was his wish that biographical sketches of the *pioneers of the Message* as he used to call them, should be published with his biography. He considered as such those mureeds on whom he had bestowed the higher initiations of Sheikh(a), Khalif(a) and Murshid(a) and those whom he had appointed to the higher offices in the International Headquarters, together with those who carried out the function of National Representative. The ranks mentioned in these sketches are those conferred on them by Pir-o-Murshid Inayat Khan himself. Some of these persons wrote their own biographies for him, others submitted some data, while details on still others were missing altogether. Their names have also been included, with the little information available from the records of the Nekbakht Foundation or with the help of other mureeds.

Pir-o-Murshid Inayat Khan entrusted Miss Sakina Furnée with all these notes, manuscripts and documents. She guarded them most carefully, then copied and arranged them according to his instructions. The greater part of the text was then submitted to Murshida Sharifa Goodenough for correction of the English language to ensure that it conveyed the appropriate meaning, although the typical style and rhythm of his language has been faithfully maintained. In a statement in Miss Sakina Furnée's handwriting it is said that she had to read the entire text two or even three times to him and that he made modifications or additions each time. The final text of the *Biography* was lastly completed and the version presented in this book is a true copy.

His mureed and secretary Miss Kismet Stam has made a beautiful calligraphic copy of this Biography, a treasure which is kept among the records of the Nekbakht Foundation. Engraved in gold on the leather binding of this copy is the Sufi emblem – the winged heart – with other designs which, with her kind permission, have been used for this first publication of the *Biography*.

The following must be said about the system of transliteration adopted in this *Biography*. Eastern names are generally written as they are pronounced in India. Not all details of the pronunciation of foreign words are marked, but the sound 'tsj' is rendered by 'ch', 'kh' stands for the sound 'ch' as in the Scottish 'loch' or German 'ach', 'gh' is its voiced or soft counterpart (as 'Z' is of 'S'). Long vowels are indicated by a dash over them (a)[3]. Sometimes a consonant has been doubled for the sake of correct pronunciation.

It was the author's wish that the words *Mr., Mrs.* and *Miss* should be written in the language of the nationality of the person mentioned in his Biography, e.g. *Frau, Herr, Fröken, de Heer, Mevrouw* and *Mejuffrouw*.

An asterisk after a word in the text shows that an explanation can be found in the Notes and Glossary[4].

In preparing this biography for final presentation, every care has been taken to avoid inaccuracy, and to make it as complete as possible. Should anything, however, have been overlooked or any errors have been made, we ask to notify the publisher, so that corrections can be made in a subsequent edition.

On the whole this book differs from the usual Western concept of a biography. The last time Pir-o-Murshid Inayat Khan referred to the proposed publication of the Biography was in Delhi in December 1926 at the end of his life, to Miss Kismet Stam. She says about this subject: 'Murshid wished the Biography to be published exactly as it is'. But, Murshid said, 'people do not like it, they find it too simple'. Then Murshid spoke about the possibility of a committee to be formed to choose from different biographies written on the example of the original one by intelligent mureeds who would be capable of doing it. After a while Murshid added, 'But that would not be the thing to do'. And Murshid's last words about it were these, 'Who could write it better than Murshid himself?'

Suresnes, August 1977

        Elise Guillaume-Schamhart
        Munira van Voorst van Beest
        Staff members of the Foundation, the Nekbakht Stichting

---

3. For this edition the diacritical marks have been omitted
4. For this edition the asterisks have been omitted

Editor's Note to the 2019 Edition

This is a new edition of the Biography of Pir o Murshid Hazrat Inayat Khan which has been out of print for many years. The biography was originally published by East-West Publications in 1979.

The text of the biography remains intact, with minor changes to correct spellings, dates, typographical errors from the first edition, and some errors of translation from Dutch to English. It was decided to take out the diacritical marks (marks or accents above or below a letter to indicate a particular pronunciation) and the asterisks marking inclusion in the Notes and Glossary as it was felt that these marks impeded the reader rather than helping. Nor does this edition include the reference section. The Foundation has made a scan of all these documents and they are now available on the website (www.nekbakhtfoundation.org).

An extensive search of the archives in Suresnes has been made but we have been unable to find originals of all the photographs included at the end of the biography under the heading List of Illustrations. It is possible that for the first edition individuals were asked to provide a photograph of themselves and that this was then returned to them. The reader will therefore notice a difference between the photographs which are a mixture of scans from the first edition and actual photographs held within the archive collection.

Finally when using the Index, please note that in India surnames are not used in the same way as in Europe. For this reason Indian individuals are listed by their first name, ie Sayyed Muhammed Abu Hashim Madani is listed under M for Muhammed and not M for Madani (Sayyed being a title); Murshid Ali Khan is listed under A, etc.

The Nekbakht Foundation apologizes sincerely and is happy to correct the error on page 406 of the first edition where a picture of Moulana Sayyed Muhammed Hashmi was erroneously identified as Sayyed Muhammed Abu Hashim Madani. We are grateful to Khursheed Ali of Hyderabad for informing us of this error.

Sincere thanks go to Shaikh al Mashaik Mahmood Khan who gave his time unstintingly to the editor in checking facts, translation anomalies, and in updating the Family Trees; to Pir Zia Inayat Khan for updating the phonetic transcription of certain Arabic or Farsi phrases; to Hamida Verlinden, Sufi Movement archives for helping in the search for photographs and for correcting Dutch names; to Ger Stok of ImageSoft for his patience in correcting the proofs, and to Jeremy Foster for redesigning the maps and family trees.

This edition came about through the vision, energy and determination of Jos van den Heuvel, secretary of the Nekbakht Foundation. When he joined the Board, he was surprised to learn that this book about the life of Pir o Murshid Inayat Khan was not available to all who count him as their teacher.

Suresnes, July 2019

> Anne Louise Wirgman
> Editor, Nekbakht Foundation

PART I
Biography

India in 1882

Towards the middle of the latter half of the 19th century, a desire for religious and social reform was awakening in India among Hindus and Muslims alike. Centuries earlier, Shankaracharya had turned the tide of religious feeling towards a greater spirituality. Both Nanak, the great Guru of the Sikhs, and Kabir, the poet, had created and left in the land a living spirit of tolerance in religion and of spiritual purity. A fresh fire was given to religious life by the great sages Dadu and Sundar. More recently the religious association Arya Samaj had been founded by Dayananda Saraswati, the religious reform of Swami Narayan had been made, Devendranath Tagore had lighted a new flame of religion in Brahmo Samaj. Then Mirza Ghulam Hussein Qadiani[5] had set on foot the Ahmadia Movement, the Christian missionaries were endeavouring to propagate Christianity and the Theosophical Society had established itself as The Hindu College at Benares.

The dark clouds that had hung over the land in the years following the Mutiny, were breaking. On the one hand Sir Sayyed Ahmad Khan was working to induce the Muslims to make the best of existing conditions, in particular by the foundation of Aligarh College and to arouse in the Muslim youth a spirit of enterprise, energy and self-dependence, and on the other hand the British Government was setting to work at reform in law, education and administration.

Such was the condition of India in 1882

---

5. The full name is Mirza Ghulam Hussein Ahmad Qadiani

Baroda[6]

Nowhere was social reform carried on with more energy than in the State of Baroda. The Maharaja Sayaji Rao Gaekwar (Ill. 1), and before his accession, the Prime Minister Sir T. Madhari Rao recognized clearly the necessity of overstepping the barriers that stood in the way of progress, and saw that means must be taken to bring to the country a measure of prosperity, for lack of which it was sinking to a depressed and dependent state. On the initiative of the latter, schools were opened and education encouraged. The aims of Maharaja Sayaji Rao can best be given in his own words: 'India must cease to be an agricultural country and must make her place among the commercial and manufacturing nations. I can conceive of no loftier mission than this, to teach philosophy to the West and learn its science, to impart purity of life to Europe and attain to her loftier political ideal, to inculcate spirituality to the American mind and acquire the business ways of her merchants.'[7] Schools were opened, and attendance was encouraged, so that by 1904 education could be made compulsory. Encouragement was given to agriculture and to the mechanical arts, the greater part of the revenue being spent on this. The Baroda College was opened in 1882, the Kala Bhawan, the Temple of Art, had been founded earlier. The hopes of renaissance and projects of reform that were coming to men's minds in India in those years found welcome in Baroda, where also men of talent and worth (Ill. 2) were sure of recognition.

---

6. Now known as Vadodara, this is not further noted
7. Conclusion of the inaugural address, delivered in Calcutta in 1906 at the Industrial Conference

Maula Bakhsh (1833-1896)

Maula Bakhsh (Ill. 3,8) the grandfather of Inayat Khan came from a family of Zamindars. Left an orphan, he was brought up by his uncle. Little is known of his boyhood, except that he was a well-built, athletic boy, good at wrestling and fond of riding, and sociable and friendly towards all.

It was when he was about fifteen years of age that he befriended a holy pilgrim, a wandering ascetic, who was passing through the town – an act that marked a turning point in his life. This dervish belonged to the sect of the Chishtis, that is to say he expressed his devotion to, and meditation upon the divine by means of music; and after he had experienced the hospitable help and friendship of the boy, he said to him: 'My soul longs for music, would you sing to me?' The boy answered: 'I have no skill in singing, but I will sing what I can to you.' And after he had sung his song, the dervish thanked him, saying: 'I am a poor man and a pilgrim upon the face of the earth, nevertheless it is in my power to give you a treasure. I will baptize you with a new name: Maula Bakhsh, God-gifted, shall be your name and this name shall be known throughout this land of India and your music shall make it famous.' The boy listened attentively and received the blessing of the holy pilgrim with reverence and locked this saying in his heart. From that day he changed his name to Maula Bakhsh.

He appears, however, to have shown no marked alteration in his behaviour, although his interest in music was heightened, until some three years later, when he came to a decision to study seriously.

His grandfather Anvar Khan had been a successful singer and the family generally had an inclination towards music; so, with his uncle's consent Maula Bakhsh set out to travel from place to place in order to hear different musicians and to instruct himself in their art.

Ghasit Khan was at that time one of the most accomplished singers of India and the most considered and talented in Gujerat.

It must be remembered that in India, where science and art are considered sacred and hereditary possessions, it is not usual for an artist to part with his knowledge to any chance pupil. An artist will consider his art in the same light as his family honour and will pass it on to his heir, or failing an heir, will allow it to die with him. Moreover, in India the great artist will not display his talent before large and mixed audiences; he reserves his art for a discriminating few.

Ghasit Khan was a wealthy man and though acclaimed in Gujerat as a master, he had never had a pupil. The young Maula Bakhsh, unknown though he was, without money, a beginner, leading a hand to mouth existence and on the very threshold of his career, felt an overwhelming desire to hear the music of this famous man and cast about in his mind how he should approach him. He hung about his house and as always, friendly and sociable, soon made friends with the porter; then he found, as he sat in the porter's little shelter, that from there he was able to hear every note, every variation of the Master's voice as he practised and composed and improvised. And so, day after day Maula Bakhsh came to the porter's lodge and talked to him and amused him with stories and jokes until the opium-sodden servant would doze off, trusting to the boy to wake him should occasion arise, and then Maula Bakhsh would give himself up to listening to the voice that issued from the house. In this way, for many months Maula Bakhsh studied, and each day after listening and noting all he heard, he would practise, modelling his own singing upon that of Ghasit Khan.

One day it happened as he was practising industriously that Ghasit Khan passed his house and stopped to listen. It seemed to him that it was one of his own compositions that he heard and moreover, one that he had not as yet sung to anybody. He listened, and his curiosity was so aroused that he entered the house where Maula Bakhsh lodged and spoke to the young singer. 'Continue your singing,' he said to him, but Maula Bakhsh was dumbfounded. 'May I ask who your teacher is, young man?' 'My teacher is great, truly,' said Maula Bakhsh, 'but if I reveal his name to you, then indeed my hope of progressing further under him must be given up.' 'Whoever heard of such a teacher!' said Ghasit Khan impatiently, 'what teacher forbids his pupil to speak of him?' 'Since you urge it, I will tell you; it is yourself, you are my teacher.' 'I? Why, I have never seen you before.' Then Maula Bakhsh explained what he had done and as Ghasit Khan listened and stood there wondering at such perseverance and patience[8] the young musician continued: 'But now what chiefly grieves me is the thought that when I leave – for now I cannot go on listening to you as I did before – I must say that it is from you that I have learned; for indeed I have not yet studied long enough nor gained enough of your knowledge to be worthy of being called the pupil of such a master as yourself.'

It was this point of view that interested and pleased Ghasit Khan and he invited Maula Bakhsh to learn from him.

This anecdote illustrates many sides of the character of Maula Bakhsh but suggests perhaps more than anything else that there was in him an irresistible personality, which indeed his life seems to prove, that neither misfortune nor difficulty ever was able to diminish. That the proud and reserved man should accept the tuition of this unknown lad was in itself a matter of surprise; and what a teacher did he prove himself!

---

8. An older version has it that Maula Bakhsh studied in this way for two years

There was nothing of his art which the master withheld from Maula Bakhsh, the only pupil he had ever accepted. When he died, Maula Bakhsh, who stayed with him until his death, was a living record of his accomplishments.

After the death of Ghasit Khan, Maula Bakhsh travelled from court to court in what seemed to the young man a triumphal procession – for everywhere he met with praises and rewards, such as filled his ardent spirit with a contentment and joy in existence and the pursuit of his chosen art. At Mysore[9], the land in which he was destined to reap his greatest success in life, he settled for some time, attached to the court. And while there, he came to know the daughter of the Rajbhakshi, the court chamberlain, who was expert in the music of the Karnatic. Maula Bakhsh, an accomplished performer, but as yet unlearned in the theory of music, became very anxious to study this ancient science of the Karnatic, pure as it was from any foreign influences of the Moghul schools. But the learned lady told him that her art belonged to the Brahmans alone, that it was their property, as sacred to them as their religion. 'If you wish to learn', she said to him, 'then you must learn when you are born a Brahman, you must wait until a future reincarnation.' This answer seemed to him so hard and this point of view so inhuman, since he himself was such a devoted disciple of music, that Maula Bakhsh felt that he could not tolerate the atmosphere of the court any longer. And so once more he set out on his wanderings.

It was in Malabar that he met with Subramani Ayar, the most honoured musician among the Brahmans of his time. This Brahman took such care of his shastras, his manuscripts, that he was never parted from them, not even at the time of ablutions. As he bathed, he would hold them now in his hand and now under his armpits. So devout was he and so orthodox, that he felt compelled to purify himself with a bath if only the shadow of a non-Brahman fell upon him. Nevertheless, he developed an attachment for Maula Bakhsh and taught him all he knew of his science besides the ancient classical music and Sanskrit songs and the harmonies of Tyagaraja and Dikshitar. Maula Bakhsh was not yet thirty when he returned to the Court of Mysore. There he seems to have enjoyed the personal friendship of the monarch who wished to bestow upon him the highest marks of honour that it is possible to give in India, which is the Kalaggai or gold circlet; the Sarpachi, a chaplet of pearls for the turban; the Chatri or gold canopy, which is held over the head by a foot servant as the owner walks or rides; the Chamar or baton of honour which a servant carries before; and the Mashal, the torch that is carried before and lighted at night. But the Brahmans pointed out to the Maharaja that these honours should be reserved for one acknowledged to be without an equal in his art; and that there was no reason why Maula Bakhsh should be regarded as having attained that position. At the insistence of the Brahmans therefore

---

9. Now known as Mysuru, this is not further noted

a contest of musicians, mainly Brahmans, took place and lasted ten months; and at the end of it Maula Bakhsh was acknowledged by the pandits, i.e. the learned in music, to have surpassed all the other performers. And so he was duly honoured by the Maharaja with these marks of distinction and the conferring of them was made the occasion of a stately procession.

It was about this time that Maula Bakhsh married the daughter of an ancient house.

It must be remembered that since the risings against the British, the survivors of the families of the Moghuls had lived in hiding. They had chosen concealment not only through fear of the terrible political situation, but the contrast between their present and past fortunes was such a bitter one, that they naturally preferred to withdraw themselves from every kind of publicity and to escape the common gaze. This girl had been protected by two devoted adherents to her house, with whom Maula Bakhsh became acquainted and after his marriage he took these two loyal and devoted guardians as part of his household, and even after their death their families lived under his roof. His marriage was of great importance in his life. Although his wife maintained the strictest seclusion, her influence pervaded the household. Strangers spoke of the courtesy and charm with which they were received, and which marked even the manners of the servants. This lady who held herself aloof even from visits from the ladies of Baroda, felt so deeply the tragedy of life as she knew it in the history and fate of her house, that she impressed her daughter, the mother of Inayat Khan with her own attitude and feeling, and that same mystery that surrounded the mother seemed to envelop the daughter also. If they were conscious of their high birth, they were conscious also of the obligations and duties that should attend it. No doubt the presence of the two guardians who knew her history heightened the atmosphere of mystery and tragedy that surrounded her, but so far as her grandchildren knew, her ancestry was never referred to in words and they never heard the full story of her life. Nevertheless, her daughter's children were conscious of the fact that they were expected to hold themselves with dignity and to show courtesy and gentleness in manners and to maintain a high standard in life, even as if they were maintaining the noble traditions of an ancient and great line.

Maula Bakhsh was now enjoying a period of great prosperity. Several ruling princes invited him to their Courts and he at last accepted the invitation of the Maharaja Khanda Rao of Baroda.

Arrived at Baroda, he found, however, to his disappointment that the Maharaja was less interested in music than in the fact that he had attached the greatest singer of the day to his Court. And Maula Bakhsh had to face the opposition of the courtiers, who could not brook the fact that this singer expected to be treated on an equality with themselves, and the Maharaja on his side was disappointed in Maula Bakhsh, who did not feed his vanity with the subservience which he expected from those around him. At the Court ceremonials, and at the processions of state Maula Bakhsh would appear with the marks of honour that he had received – the gold canopy held above his head, the baton of honour carried before him, and wearing the chaplet of pearls and circlet of gold. The Court officials having pointed out that this musician gave himself almost royal rank, the Maharaja sent an ironical word to him, saying: 'If you wear crown and sceptre, what shall Rajas wear?' And Maula Bakhsh answered with a quotation from the Sanskrit:

Sva deshe pujita raja,	*The king is honoured in his country,*
Sva grame pujita prabhu,	*a chief is honoured in his district,*
Sva grahe pujita murkha	*a fool is honoured in his home but a*
Vidvana sanvatra pujayat.	*genius is honoured everywhere.*

'Your Highness, my kingdom is everywhere', was the answer that Maula Bakhsh sent.

And now it remained for Maula Bakhsh to prove that he was a genius, for the Maharaja who had called him to the Court on account of his fame, now wished to humble him; and so a musical congress was arranged to which the celebrities of India were bidden. There came Kanhai, the acknowledged master of dance and rhythmical movement, and Ali Hussain, the great vina player, and Nasir Khan, a master of rhythm and pakhawaj player, and Khadim Hussain, the great singer. And Maula Bakhsh competed with each and showed himself superior to each one in turn. The upshot of it was that Maula Bakhsh was accused of hypnotizing his opponents and of hypnotizing his audience – and finding that the Maharaja was prepared to give credence to such a suggestion, he left Baroda and at the request of Sir Salar Jung, Prime Minister to the Nizam, he settled for a time at the Court of Hyderabad.

But the ordeal that he had lately passed through, had made such an impression upon him that it marked a turning point in his career. The congress had opened his eyes to the greatness of Indian music, and also to its defects. Each performer had shown a highly developed art, but not one had been conversant with its theory and science, and one and all had sacrificed system and order to fantasy. He himself was naturally gifted with what is called in India the quality of *laya*, that is the sense of time and rhythm. He possessed a natural tenor voice of an extraordinary lyrical beauty, tender and appealing, and to his natural gifts were added the skill acquired through many years of patient work and training. Yet he saw that it would have been difficult, perhaps impossible for him to have held his own against so many specialists, if it had not been for his knowledge of Karnatic music, of the system preserved by Southern India. His position was thus perhaps unique, and his music reflected the skill of the North together with the depth of the South.

Kanhai was a great dramatic artist of such talent that his every movement seemed instinct with meaning. His very hands seemed to speak. Undoubtedly a master of this ancient Eastern branch of musical art, he was yet unable to compare with Maula Bakhsh in his knowledge of that psychology, of that theory of drama, so carefully taught in the Karnatic school. Nasir Khan, who alone of the competitors on this occasion became his lifelong friend, was also defective in technique and so it was with the others. He saw how one-sided was the work of these different artists. It was brought home to him with renewed force that the art of the North, which bears the stamp of Persian and Arabian music and also of the music of ancient Greece, full of grace and beauty as it is, rich in charm and fantasy, is yet inferior in many ways to the more austere music of the South, which has ever been held sacred and as a part of religion.

At Hyderabad Maula Bakhsh spent months that were fruitful in work and experience; and after the death of the Maharaja Khanda Rao he returned to Baroda. The new Maharaja Malhar Rao very soon incurred the displeasure of the British.

It happened that the daughter of the British Resident was interested in music and she began to take lessons from Maula Bakhsh, who thus made acquaintance with the Resident, and a friendship sprang up between them. In the eyes of Maula Bakhsh, the ruling prince was not only foolish but evil; but he made every effort to assist him and to keep him on his throne from a sense of that loyalty which is expressed in the phrase *true to salt*. He obtained a promise from the Resident that the British would not molest the prince if he altered his ways; and to this effect Maula Bakhsh continually advised and warned him. In this way a responsibility of State fell on him. But this position became gradually untenable, not only on account of the blindness and folly of the prince, but because of the suspicion which was spread about by the obsequious courtiers, that he was actually in the service of the British. And he became disheartened at the construction put on his efforts to guide this young man.

He left Baroda and took the opportunity to travel to many parts of India, to make known his ambition about the future of Indian music and the system of notation which he was evolving, in which he hoped to combine the theory and practice of the North with that of the South.

For all this time Maula Bakhsh, with much patience and thought, was thinking out methods of reform. With great perseverance he was endeavouring to perfect a system of notation which should be acceptable to all India. At Calcutta[10] he was the guest of Maharaja Jotindra Mohan Tagore and that family, so capable of artistic devotion and expression, was keenly interested in his enthusiasm and ambition. Surendra Mohan Tagore, who was later to prove himself so great in the world of music, was not a little inspired by the genius of Maula Bakhsh.

About this time, he was introduced to the Viceroy and he prepared him-

---

10. Now known as Kolkatta, this is not further noted

self for this occasion by diligently studying Western music. He was anxious to prove to the English that the musical art of India was indeed an art; and he felt that the only means of making Eastern art intelligible to an alien ear, was by studying the Western principles. Thus he took every means that he could, to raise his art in the eyes of those with whom he came into contact and to kindle enthusiasm for it.

Two incidents which took place at this period of his life stand out as having had a great influence on him. On one occasion he visited Vajad Ali Shah, the imprisoned king of Oudh, a visit that proved a revelation, for the king was himself a composer, a connoisseur of music; steeped in his love for it, he showed the greatest appreciation and understanding as Maula Bakhsh sang, and played, and discussed with him. And the idea came to Maula Bakhsh that music could become as potent a force for the destruction of man as for his elevation. The king, when in power, had been a great patron of music and had named the musicians attached to his court *arbab-i nishat*, that is to say the *companions of pleasure* and here, so it seemed to Maula Bakhsh, the king had at once struck the false note which was to prove not only his undoing but the degradation of the art which he professed to honour. To link music with the amusement of life must, it seemed to him, result in a degeneration and the idea began to strengthen in his mind that music should be regarded as an essential part of education.

Another occasion that gave him much food for thought was when, at the invitation of the Maharaja Ram Singh of Jaipur, he met the Guni Jan Khana, or the staff of the talented of Jaipur. At this association, which had been formed by the Maharaja, he was warmly welcomed, and it gave him a great pleasure to be able to meet there many artists from all parts of the vast empire of India, who had made a mark both as composers and performers. But he could not help regretting that no association of the kind existed for teaching and for advancing musical education generally.

He returned to Baroda after Malhar Rao had been deposed. From that time dates his close friendship with Sir T. Madhari Rao, who deserves the credit of having prepared the young Maharaja Sayaji Rao Gaekwar (Ill. 1) for his brilliant career and for having laid the foundation of the future successful reign. This brilliant young ruler recognized talent of whatever kind. It was his distinction that he was always ready to help and foster reforms – social and educational, and it was he who at last made it possible for Maula Bakhsh to realize the dream of his life, for he founded the Academy of Music at Baroda and appointed Maula Bakhsh its first director.

Thereafter, Maula Bakhsh devoted the remainder of his life to the formation of the Academy and to the organization of the courses of instruction. His younger son Alaoddin (Ill. 7) went to London to the Royal Academy of Music, where he studied for five years and obtained the degree of Doctor of Music and thus carried out his conviction that it is necessary for the musicians of the East to learn Western art if they would interpret their art to a foreigner. His eldest son Murtaza Khan (Ill.6), took up the study of Eastern music and followed in his father's footsteps so closely as to take, so to speak, the very form and mould of his father's genius. Representatives of every musical school were welcomed at the Academy and instruction was not refused to any caste or creed, and was open to boys and girls alike. He strove to spread the idea that the knowledge, which hitherto had been considered a hereditary possession, should be collected and given out again freely and generously. He wished to spread his conviction that music should form the basis of the education of every child; not that he wished to make all musicians, but because of the influence which music exerts upon the character, upon the rhythm of thought, upon movement and gait, and action and speech.

He introduced into the School of Music, the study of the great poets, of Kabir, of Nanak and of Sundar, feeling that the beauty of their words and thoughts must animate the minds of the students and inspire them with a sense of the divine in life and so form a fitting accompaniment to instruction in the divine art.

The interest of the Maharaja Gaekwar in social and educational reform drew the best minds of India to Baroda, and the house of Maula Bakhsh became a meeting-place for philosophers and poets as well as musicians. Maula Bakhsh had never lost that gift of sociability to which he owed his well-found name.

Although he was friendly and accessible to all, his life was marked throughout by that same independence of spirit which he had displayed at the Court of Khanda Rao.

There is a story told by friends with whom Maula Bakhsh lodged at Hyderabad. He returned late one night to their house after playing at the Court and the servant who had waited to attend him, helped him down from the elephant on which he was riding, and taking his vina from him, asked what it was and said how much he wished that he could hear it played. Maula Bakhsh displayed the instrument to the servant, answering all his ignorant questions and although wearied out, played and sang to him. The next day the host having heard the story through the servants asked him: 'O, Maula Bakhsh, how did you rest last night?' and Maula Bakhsh recounted how he had played again and again at the request of the company at the Court and that on coming home and seeing the curiosity of this poor servant, who in comparison with the wealth of the Court had so little in life, he had been touched by his ignorance and poverty and felt that to refuse to play to him would be even as refusing to play to God. And so he had sat and played to him through the night, explaining all that he could to him.

The death of Maula Bakhsh in 1896 was a blow to many hearts and at his funeral gathered Hindus and Muslims alike. Himself brought up an orthodox Muslim, and one who never missed one of the five daily times of prayers, he was a freethinker, of broad views that recognized beauty in all religions and a great number of his pupils were Brahmans. His was a life of success and the circle of his family and friends was a happy one. From his earliest years he had enjoyed success and recognition; in his day he was recognized not only by his own people but by the British, by whom he was asked to play at the Delhi Darbar. Of a commanding presence, endowed with remarkable gifts, a man of upright character, he had a tremendous sense of the value of life, of the dignity of the human being, of the beauty of the world.

It was always said in Baroda that 'the best horse in Baroda is certain to be Maula Bakhsh's horse', and such a detail as this, shows how his standard of excellence applied to all things. But if he wished for beauty, his was no selfish and exclusive nature and throughout his life he was devoted in service to his fellow-beings and to India. After his death, once a camel-driver spoke to one of his sons in terms of such sorrow that it seemed he must be a great friend of Maula Bakhsh; but no, he had only spoken to him once and then Maula Bakhsh had talked to him on music in terms of such perfect equality, with no hint of the attitude of patronage, but with such immense interest that the man had never forgotten it. It would be possible to give many stories of this kind of him. It was this sense of the dignity of the human being, combined with his sense of the value and beauty of life, that gives the keynote of his career.

As he grew older he developed a greater sensibility to the deeper emotions, as with every year his interest in music grew and with it his understanding of life. When he was aged it was often seen that as he played or sang or listened to others, he would be caught up by some feeling or thought of exquisite emotion and tears would fall from his eyes. To his students he showed the same tenderness of heart in his sympathy and interest and friendship.

The last years of his life were filled with a new interest in his hopes of his eldest grandson, Inayat. There seemed a special connection between these two, as close as that which exists between an old plant and the shoot that springs from its roots. It was as if the hungering and thirsting child drew into himself the whole soul of his adored grandfather, and as if the grandfather fostered and watched the child in the belief that here was the most complete fruit of an existence spent in the pursuit of the ideal.

The great musicians before Maula Bakhsh left songs that were handed down by tradition. He was perhaps the first artist to leave to India an inheritance that can be judged on its own merits by coming ages, in his many published compositions, in the system of notation which he strove to perfect, so that it might be an acceptable one for all India and which has inspired much fresh work along this line, also in the ideals which are enshrined in the first founded Academy of Music of India.

Rahmat Khan (1843-1910)[11]

Rahmat Khan (Ill. 4), Inayat's father, came from a family of musicians and poets, in which, according to a family tradition, in every generation there was one mystic. His father, Bahadur Khan, had been known for a bravery that matched his name. Bahadur Khan's father, Nyamat Khan, was a musician. His brother was revered in Punjab as a great saint, mystic and ascetic, possessor of great spiritual power. Rahmat Khan became a pupil of the greatest composer of Punjab, one recognized as a holy man, Saint Alias, by whom he was trained in the ancient, classical music of India. This saint was a Sufi and led the life of an ascetic.

Saint Alias had not more than five things in his hut: a mat, a brick that served as a pillow, a walking stick, an earthen bowl for water, and a broom. His habit was that every offering brought to him by friends or pupils was used on the same day, that nothing of the world might be left for the morrow. And when he did not receive any offering, he would go without meals, but would never ask anyone for food.

Once a Maharaja of Kashmir paid him a visit and left as an offering a large sum of money and when he went away his disciples asked him: 'What may be done with this money?' Saint Alias said: 'Use it as usual.' 'But,' they said, 'this is so large a sum, it will last for the whole year.' He said: 'Not one penny of this must be kept overnight, call the poor of the neighbouring villages, and let us all have a feast to finish it.'

The saint's character brought Rahmat Khan to a deeper understanding of life and this gave him a regard for every soul, in whatever garb it might be.

Rahmat Khan, leaving his home, set out on his travels. His mother, when she had no news of him for some length of time, travelling being at that time difficult and unsafe, grew distressed and anxious and thus drew death nearer; her only wish was to find her son. The elder son, Jafar Khan, went in search of his brother and not knowing where to search for him, he being a visionary and mystically minded, went first to the tomb of a saint, a place of pilgrimage, and there asked the saint's guidance. He had a dream that night, and next morning he found Rahmat Khan, who returned with him. Before they could reach their home, however, the mother had died and this was a wound to Rahmat Khan's heart that troubled him all through his life. In pain and trouble only one word would come to his lips, 'Mother'.

---

11. According to an old manuscript, probably by a family member, he died aged 80 which would make this date 1830

He then left Punjab, undecided where to go. As he was passing by a place where a saint was standing and had stood for many years, untiring, unprotected from sun and rain, save for a roof which the state had lately caused to be built over him, it came to Rahmat Khan's mind to ask the saint where he should go. He did so, and he saw the saint wave his hand in a certain direction. Rahmat Khan went in the direction in which that movement seemed to point and so he came to Baroda.

There he met Maula Bakhsh, who took a liking to him. A friendship was formed which in time became a close one, and Maula Bakhsh married his eldest daughter, Fatima Bibi, to Rahmat Khan, and after her death gave him his second daughter, Khatidja Bibi, in marriage.

Rahmat Khan helped Maula Bakhsh in his work at the Academy of Music and was the great musician's staunchest support and defender. He himself was the greatest singer of the classical music, *dhrupad*, and highly esteemed by those who understood the music, though never in a general sense popular. He gave the true image of *ragas*, so much sought after in India and so hard to be found. He guarded his knowledge as a treasure, had few pupils and barely taught his music even to Inayat, whose attention in his childhood was so riveted upon the brilliant music and fascinating personality of his grandfather that he scarcely thought of his father until after the latter's death. Rahmat Khan proved himself throughout his life self-sacrificing, diligent and utterly devoted. He was by temperament austere, strict, expecting others to be as he was; with his children he was strict to the point of severity although most loving and kind, always granting their wishes at whatever sacrifice. He was unassuming, honest and sincere, and it is no exaggeration to say that he never in his life told a lie. He was a philosopher with little love for book learning. Kind actions and courtesy he held to be the chief thing in life, and he took pains and every care to spare the feelings of others.

What Inayat learned from his father in philosophy, became the foundation of his whole life. Inayat received it gratefully. Rahmat Khan lived a long life, was a true friend and a help to students of music. He died in 1910 at the age of eighty.

He saw in a dream in his last days on earth Ali's funeral passing on a camel's back, a great many people with it and he saw himself among the spectators who were standing on both sides of the way. To his great surprise the door of the coffin was opened, and Ali raised his head from it and said: 'Come along, without any fear or anxiety, for this is the way for every soul born on earth.' Next morning as he arose he called Mehr Bakhshe (Ill. 5), his son-in-law, and told him not to trouble more about his cure but to prepare for his departure from this earth, for he had heard the call.

Khatidja Bibi (1868-1902)

Khatidja Bibi, the second of Maula Bakhsh's three daughters, had a retiring disposition. She had a keen interest in learning. She was trained in household duties, but yet had more learning than the daughters of a family were usually allowed. She was acquainted with Arabic, Persian and Urdu. Her nature was devout and loving and gentle. She was liked by all. At the age of fifteen she was given in marriage to Rahmat Khan, who had previously married her elder sister, Fatima Bibi, who had died, leaving him with one daughter, Jena Bibi, who was married to a cousin Mehr Bakhshe.

She loved her four children, Inayat, Maheboob, Karamat and Musharaff so devotedly that it seemed extraordinary, even on the part of a mother. She was as kind to the servants in the house as to the children. No one ever heard a cross word from her. If anyone hurt or annoyed her, she would be silent, believing that for the sake of the welfare of those dear to her she must keep a harmonious atmosphere, even if she had to endure lack of consideration. Her special love was for Inayat.

Once, when told about her share in the division of the property of her father Maula Bakhsh, she said: 'I do not care about my father's property, my wealth is in my children, and as God has granted me this wealth, I do not wish for other wealth or anything greater.' 'But', they said, 'for your children.' She replied: 'May God bless my children; if they inherited the great quality of my father, rather than a share of his property, that is quite enough. How long will that earthly property last? That which is dependable in life is only one thing and that is the quality of their grandfather; that they can inherit.' So she, who was born in a rich house, remained poor all her life, with her children, in whom she placed all her hopes.

Inayat's mother, before his birth had dreams, in which she saw Christ coming and healing her and sometimes Muhammad appeared and blessed her, sometimes she found herself in the midst of prophets and saints, as though they were taking care of her, or receiving her, or were waiting for something coming or preparing for a time which they had foreknown.

She was by nature very devout, most modest, humble and unassuming. She told of her dreams to no one except Bima, her grandmother, who also was very pious and at that time very aged. The grandmother said: 'It is good tidings and yet a great burden and responsibility for you as the mother and also for who will be coming. Do not tell anyone about it but ask the protection of God and the help of those you see.' Khatidja Bibi was rather confused, frightened and yet resigned to the will of God. She was careful to ask the protection of God and help of every saint and prophet that she knew. She addressed them saying:

> As-salam 'alaika ya Ibrahim Khalil Allah
> As-salam 'alaika ya Musa Kalim Allah
> As-salam 'alaika ya 'Isa Ruh Allah
> As-salam 'alaika ya Muhammad Rasul Allah.

which means:

> Hail to Thee, O Abraham, the Friend of God,
> Hail to Thee, O Moses, the Word of God,
> Hail to Thee, O Jesus, the Spirit of God
> Hail to Thee, O Muhammad, the Prophet of God.'

Infancy

Inayat was born in Baroda, a city in Gujerat Presidency, on Wednesday the 5th of July at 11.35p.m. in 1882 in the house of Maula Bakhsh.

The aunt of this infant child, Inayat Bibi, always held the ideal that the world should become a better and higher place. She had suffered for this ideal and was dying for its sake. On her deathbed she was told of the birth of a child in her home and she said: 'He is born with the ideal for which I am dying, and my only satisfaction in the hour of my death will be that this child should be called by my name, Inayat', which means loving kindness[12].

One evening Inayat's father brought him home some sweets, but finding the child asleep, put them aside till morning. During the night Inayat had a vision in which he saw exactly what his father had done. As soon as he awoke, the child called out for the sweets, but his mother, not knowing what the father had done, said there were none. Inayat persisted till at last his mother asked him: 'Where?' 'Over there,' he replied, pointing with his hand. His mother went, thinking to pacify the child, but to her great surprise found he was right, there were some sweets where he had said. On inquiry she learned what had occurred. 'But,' said his father, 'Inayat did not know, for he was fast asleep.'

---

12. Translated as Benignity in first edition

Photograph 1. Baroda, India c.1894

Childhood

From earliest childhood Inayat showed great gentleness of disposition and nobility of character. He found the greatest joy in sharing every cake or sweet he had with his brothers or playmates, however little it might be he had. When he received any fruits or flowers, his greatest joy was to offer the gift to his mother.

In the family of Inayat there was not much belief in superstition and yet the idea of the evil eye still existed. Whenever little Inayat was indisposed, his mother would prepare a cotton wick.

One day Inayat was bitten by a scorpion. His limb became swollen and discoloured and the pain increased frightfully as the poison spread. His father carried him to a doctor and on the way, greatly alarmed and distressed at the sight of his suffering child, asked him if he were in great pain. Inayat, seeing his father so troubled, could not bear to be the cause of such distress and though suffering intense pain, restrained his moans and replied: 'Not much father.'

On one occasion his elder sister, Jena Bibi, was playing with several dolls and Inayat picked up one of them, tucked it under his arm and ran off with it. His sister ran after him, caught him and gripped his arm, making him cry with pain. His father, hearing the cry, called Inayat and asked the cause. On being told he said: 'Well, fetch your sister and I'll scold her.' When she came, her father said: 'Did you hurt your brother?' Inayat, thinking she would be punished, answered quickly: 'No, she did not!'

Once, while ill, when a bitter and most nauseous medicine was given him, again and again he refused to take it, until at last someone present said: 'Drink it, Inayat, for brave boys never refuse to take any medicine, however bitter.' He only asked: 'Is it brave to drink bitter medicine?' They said: 'Yes.' He said: 'I will drink it and be brave,' and then drank it without hesitation and without making a wry face. From that time he never hesitated to take any medicine given him, however bitter or distasteful.

One of Inayat's favourite occupations was to gather together all his toys and, giving a certain personification to each, to arrange them in the order of a grand procession, each toy occupying its own appointed place.

It was a pleasure to Inayat to obey his parents in spite of all inclination to playfulness. However, he would not keep away from those things that he was told not to do. One thing was climbing the guava tree. He would venture even if he saw one pear ripe. His father asked him to remain in his room studying at noon when the sun burns and scorches in the zenith and the fiery wind blows through the summer day. But often he was found on a tree in the garden, on the guava tree, a kind of pear-tree, the pear of which is called *amrut*, the fruit of life. What would alarm his parents most was his love for walking through the streams and canals when the country was flooded after a heavy rain. He most loved to jump from great heights and to do all sorts of acrobatics.

Frequently Inayat would play at circus. Assembling as many children as he could, he made each represent some animal, which was to jump high or low, walk, trot, run or stand still, as occasion required. Whip in hand he would stand in the midst and direct the movement of each child most accurately by the dexterous use of his whip.

He was always pleased to buckle on a boy-sword and to drill a group of boys. When once someone asked: 'Whose head are you going to cut off with this sword?' 'No one's,' he said, 'rather than cutting off another person's head, I would cut off my own.'

Inayat often took the part of a doctor. He would get a few glasses and any kind of white powder and mix a dose and then invite the sick of the household to come and be cured. And often it happened that some of the simple maids and servants in the house were cured instantly.

On one occasion Inayat visited the house of an old man, a Hindu. Here he saw a picture representing a most beautiful man and woman. This attracted him greatly, for the two seemed to be playing a game he had often seen children play, in which two stand facing each other, their toes meeting, their hands tightly clasped and then leaning back as far as possible, spin round and round, their heads describing a circle. Inayat, being curious, asked about the picture. 'That is Krishna,' said the old man. 'Krishna, Krishna, who is he?' inquired the child. 'Krishna is our God,' replied the Brahman. 'Your God? Has your God a playmate?' 'Yes.' 'And does your God dance?' continued Inayat, 'Oh, yes,' came the reply. Inayat gazed at the picture, thought for a moment and then said: 'I like your God.'

Inayat and some companions were one day playing on an open space, where there was a pond round which were placed many Hindu idols. The boys who were Muslims, felt little regard for these objects, sacred to the Hindus. They began to jump on them and to play about them. 'Do not do that!' called out Inayat. 'What does it matter?' cried they, 'they are not our Gods.' 'No,' replied he, 'but they are somebody's Gods.'

Inayat loved listening to stories of heroes, of men of great ideals and virtues. He never tired of listening to the same stories no matter how often told him. As he had a remarkably good memory, he would repeat these stories to other people, never failing to make the account interesting.

Inayat as a child was great friends with his father, and every evening he used to ask his father to tell him some story. His father after finishing all the stories he knew, had to read in order to tell him more. But the demand was greater than the supply. In the end his father began to make up stories to tell him and such stories that would be an education for Inayat in his life. Inayat was not satisfied by hearing these stories only, but would want an explanation of different points in the story. Sometimes he would argue so much that his father would say: 'Please keep it until tomorrow.' Inayat would not forget and next day he would raise the same point and would not be satisfied until it had been made clear. In all this Inayat's father found in his little son a great thirst for knowledge and a deep understanding which gave him great satisfaction. Inayat, under his father's training was told many things that made an everlasting impression upon him.

Inayat once saw a boy among his companions treating his mother very insolently[13]. He was shocked at it and said to the boy: 'You have treated your mother so insolently! Now, remember, you will never be happy, and you must meet with a bad end!' This prophecy came true, for the boy to whom he had said this came to a terrible end.

Inayat was an extraordinarily sensitive child and this manifested not only in his love of beauty and refinement of thought, but also in his great sympathy with the sorrows and woes of the people around him. He was wide awake to see the conditions of his surroundings and always inclined to sympathize with the weak and sorrowful. He was a keen observer of human nature and he saw in life more pain than pleasure, and more falsehood than truth. This would sometimes work intensely in his thoughts and even as a child he would go into solitude and be there by himself, silent, doing nothing, just pondering over things, sitting in a restful attitude with a serious expression on his face.

At the age of five Inayat was sent to school. There was a discussion in his family to which school he should be sent, whether to the school for Muslim boys or to the Hindu school. As the Hindu boys are less playful, it was decided he should go to the Hindu school and there he began his schooling in the Marathi language. The system of education at that time and the way the teachers drove everyone with the same cane, was somehow against Inayat's nature and he would rather be playing in the open, and give freedom to his imagination and the thoughts that came to him, than sitting amongst children of his age, in a school where the teacher ruled all with the cane. Inayat used to be depressed in the school and often would be caught drawing pictures on a slate, when everybody was supposed to be learning lessons. After being much scolded and often whipped on his bare legs, he would be most thankful to leave the school in the evening and come home. He was promoted as he grew from one class to another, although he did not always pass his examinations.

Once Inayat's father visited his school, enquiring the reason of his being

---

13. An older version has it that one day Inayat saw a boy fighting with his mother, and that he beat and kicked her till she cried.

backward in his studies. The teacher said: 'In no way does he lack intelligence, yet he is playful and neglects his studies.' After some talk on the subject they found that in mathematics, history, geography and grammar Inayat was placed last, but in poetry and its interpretation or in composition he was first, to the surprise of the whole class, as that seemed an unusual place for him. This teacher was wise. He said: 'There is something wonderful in him, he has expression and gives out what is in him. He is, by nature, not a pupil but a teacher.' This was the one teacher who refrained from whipping him for not learning his lessons, but used to talk to him, so that he would feel ashamed of himself. All the teacher's efforts were in vain, for Inayat would not give his thoughts to the studies he did not care for and only gave thought to the subjects which interested him.

For his parents, Inayat was the greatest problem. Inayat wakened to sympathy, ready to be friends with anybody, willing to take interest in everything that attracted his curiosity, emotional besides, with love of beauty in form and colour and everything that attracted him, was open to all influences. Therefore, his parents' responsibility increased, together with their anxiety, with his growth.

The ordinary games of other children had but little attraction for him and he much preferred donkey-riding.

The first drama that Inayat saw in his life was a most ancient play of India, *Harish Chandra*, the drama of renunciation, which brings out the moral of keeping one's honour. It made such an impression on young Inayat that for years he craved to see the drama. He saw it three times, but it was never enough; then, he enacted it himself at home.

Many times Inayat would make up a play and get the other children to act it. To each child he would give a part and teach him how to perform it. When the time came for giving the play, the children would forget; but as often as one forgot and could not think how to act, Inayat would stand behind, speak the words and tell the player how to act. So in reality the whole play was performed by himself.

One day late in the evening, Inayat had not yet come home and everyone became anxious and people were sent out in search of him. In the end he was found at a lecture given by Jinsi Wali, a great social reformer. Inayat was so absorbed in what Jinsi Wali said, that he had lost all idea of time. Seeing his interest in things of learning, his parents excused the fault of his not being at home when he ought to have been.

His parents wondered at times what could be the matter with the child. Thinking that he did not act always as a child, they did everything to satisfy his fancies; gave him ponies and other playthings and tried their utmost to provide him with everything, but nothing would keep him continually interested. Very often in the midst of great activity or excitement, among his relations and friends, Inayat would be quite tranquil and he would seem above all things around him. Some people or conditions or subjects which he noticed would give him the inclination to scrutinize them deeply within himself. So in this way he was a mystery to his parents.

Inayat's father taught him many wise things; he produced in him, even in childhood, a spirit of self-respect. He taught him not to show too great enthusiasm or excitement on seeing things beautiful or rich, to retire when he saw friends or even relations enjoying or amusing themselves, that he might not, uninvited, intrude on enjoyment of others, or even desire to share it. He taught him not to go where he was not wanted, never to frequent a place where he was not welcome, not to visit anyone too often, but only to see friends when it was proper, not to intrude upon anybody's time, nor to interfere with anybody's privacy, not to be very friendly to those who don't care to reciprocate. He said: 'Do not pursue friends who like to avoid you. Do not seek association with those who prefer being left alone. Do not make yourself a burden upon anyone. Rather starve and die a death in pride than live a life of humiliation.'

He taught him to refrain from desiring comforts that could only be obtained at the expense of the comfort of others, to renounce a comfort rather than obtain it by asking a favour of another, to restrain or rather to crush every desire that would bring humiliation upon him.

This teaching became so natural to Inayat that it seemed as if he were told just what he himself innately desired.

He was taught to sit quietly among elder people, to greet others first and if others greeted him first, to be sorry to have lost the opportunity; not to belittle the talk of others, however simple it might be; to avoid all inquisitiveness and to withdraw without being asked, if he felt a conversation taking place was private; to keep his own secret and those of others; not to interrupt, but to wait until a talk was finished; to avoid anything rude, rough or abrupt in thought, speech and action; not to contradict his elders, even if he thought what was said was not true, for, he was told, it was not the words only that count but the time and conditions which caused the necessity for saying a certain thing, which, even if not true from one point of view, might be true from another. And he was taught never to speak boastfully, nor presumptuously.

To Inayat, with his inborn love of beauty, beauty of manner appealed so much that he never found it difficult to abide by the principles taught him by his father. But this opened up to him the reason why he liked some people and did not like others. He always recalled a saying: *Ba adab ba nasib; be adab be nasib*, which means: 'Good manner, good fortune; ill manner, ill fortune.' Inayat's father taught him to offer the better seat to an elder person. Not to retort in speech with people; not to show annoyance by word or frown or by looking cross. He told him not to ask his parents for anything they could not provide and not to ask in the presence of others, which would embarrass them, if they could not provide what he asked and also lest it should give to the others any suggestion of getting it for him, which would be just as bad.

He was told not to excite himself in laughter or crying and to have full control over these emotions. He was told not to give too much expression to his affections, that affection was in the heart, not in touching, or embracing or kissing. And he was told not to speak disrespectfully about religion, the Prophet and the God-ideal, but always to have the most respectful tendency toward all that is sacred and holy.

Inayat's father believed in the influence of the presence of the *Majzubs*, Yogis and sages and used to take him to them for their blessing.

Ladhood

Inayat attracted friends, he was as a magnet and was capable of great attachment to those whom he drew.

In any game or pursuit Inayat was always the leader.

When quite a small boy Inayat had his own little private room where he studied. Whatever he got for this room showed good taste and everything in it was arranged artistically. The room was kept spotlessly clean and tidy and it was his pride that, no matter how early visitors might arrive, none should enter his sanctum and find it in the least unprepared. To accomplish this he would often himself dust the room long before it could be done for him.

His grandfather Maula Bakhsh always took Inayat with him when he went to visit the sages. They were all fascinated by him at the first glance and he sat so still, an unusual thing in one so young. He sat before them, hearing their discourse and seeing all that went on. He used to be as absorbed as if he understood everything that passed. He preferred sitting with grown-up people and would listen to their talk, discourse and argument with great interest. He would sit with his grandfather, who received in his house all those eminent in learning and culture. At these receptions Inayat was allowed to be in the reception room and this he preferred to playing with children of his own age and he tried to listen and understand and took interest in all that was going on. His grandfather respected this tendency so much that he always had Inayat sit on a corner of his own seat. The young child looked up to him as to his ideal, watched every move he made, listened to every word he said to his friends and accompanied them in their drives in the gardens.

Every morning Maula Bakhsh went to wake his little grandson and Inayat's first impression at daybreak was his grandfather coming to wake him after his morning prayers. Inayat then spent the morning with Maula Bakhsh, who practised his singing and taught Inayat music. Young Inayat used to hum or sing to himself, making up words of his own and he would form different rhythms and phrases of music and would amuse himself by repeating them. He had a good ear for music and remembered every song he heard.

Inayat spent his evenings in Gayanshala, the Academy of Music, which had been established as the first music school in India and had been founded by his grandfather Maula Bakhsh and also was under his direction. The house of Maula Bakhsh was practically a temple of talent. All the talented people, musicians, poets, the artistic and literary, came to him for several reasons: some to learn from him, some to be benefitted by his company and others to show their art in order that they might be presented by him at the Court. Some came to benefit by the opportunity of seeing and hearing many people of great talent. Little Inayat was always to be found sitting quietly in some corner of the room, always wholly attentive to all the conversation and everything that went on. In this way, in his early age, he heard and learned more music, poetry and other arts, than many people could learn in their whole life. The joy of Maula Bakhsh was boundless seeing that his little grandson was born with the hunger and thirst for knowledge, and that he was eagerly ready to learn and practise all that was taught him. He also understood Inayat's great desire to see the mystics and to hear about mysticism. From childhood Inayat was curious about every faqir or dervish he saw. Their lives would interest him and by nature he was attracted to them. Maula Bakhsh was a great friend of the wise and godly, being himself a great lover of God and a seeker after truth.

He often took Inayat with him to Narsiji, a sage, whose dwelling he always frequented and the sage recognized the spirit of this lad and told Maula Bakhsh to take special care of his grandson. He said: 'You do not yet know with what he has come into the world.' Maula Bakhsh thenceforward gave still more attention to his little grandson. He exempted Inayat from the obligation in the East, that the young should wait upon the elder in the family and instead of the least place, he was always given the best seat, a thing contrary to the custom of Orientals. And Inayat's response to his grandfather was such that he absorbed the charm of personality that Maula Bakhsh possessed and inherited from him all that was good, beautiful and of value.

Inayat read the newspaper to his grandfather and afterwards discussed different topics of the news of the world and showed his interest in every side of the questions in the world.

Inayat's grandfather bought him a book on morals, called *Vidurniti*. It interested him very much and he could not read it too often.

Inayat wrote a dialogue between fate and free will, picturing them as persons. He showed it to his grandfather, asking him to suggest any alterations. Maula Bakhsh was so pleased that he took his grandson's manuscript to his friend, a great literary man, a Brahman named Govind Vishnu Dev, who was a lawyer. The Brahman was most astonished and wanted to see Inayat and told his grandfather to wait and see what would come from this promising youth, that some very wonderful incarnation was the spirit of Inayat.

One day Inayat heard his grandfather promising some author a short sketch of his own biography. Inayat heard it and remembered and asked: 'What is meant by the word biography?' His grandfather said: 'An account of a life.' After some time he asked his grandfather if the biography had been sent. His grandfather said: 'No, I am sorry, but I have not had the time to write.' Inayat asked if he would be allowed to try. His grandfather instantly said yes. Inayat asked him some questions about his life and set to work.

After three days he came with a short sketch in his hands and asked his grandfather if it was worth sending. His grandfather was much pleased and allowed the biography to be sent to the editor of *Mahajan Mandal*.

He especially studied poems in school, and one poem, of heartfelt gratitude to the mother, he preferred to all others. He had a great liking for the poems of Dayananda Saraswati, whose life and philosophy he read with great admiration. The poetry of Kabir and Nanak also interested him very much and he sang with great feeling the songs of Dadu and Sundar. He loved the poems of Ram Das and sang to himself and others the verses Ram Das addressed to the mind. He was very fond of the *Abhangas* (poems) of Tukaram. Inayat loved best of all to study the *Bhagavad Gita*, the words of Krishna to Arjuna and he took great interest in all the mystical legends of the Hindus, in prose or poetry.

Inayat learned the language of the Brahmans, Marathi, as well as a Brahman and spoke it at nine years old; and from his manner and speech no Brahman could ever imagine that he was a non-Brahman and people were astonished when they heard his name. But the Brahmans did not like him to be called by his own name, therefore they called him Vinayak, which is a name of Vishnu.

Inayat's parents were troubled at his interest in poetry. They thought the life of a poet and dreamer was a life of constant misery and that as a poet is not a practical man, he must therefore of necessity suffer in an era of commercialism and competition. Young Inayat did two things, either he drew pictures, or he wrote poems and his people snatched the papers from his hands and wanted to impress him by saying that to write poems brought bad luck.

His father once spoke before him a verse of a fable in which a wolf approaches a lion, finding him in a difficult position, and challenges him. The lion says: 'I am a lion and thou art a wolf. There can never be a match between us. If I won, then it would not add to my honour and if I were defeated it would dishonour my whole ancestry.' Also his father quoted before him sayings of Sa'adi, such as: *Akhira gurbazada gurba shavad, lek ba adami buzurgi shavad.* (In the end a kitten proves to be a kitten, though by the contact of human beings it may sit on the sofa against cushions in dignity.) And also, the well-known saying: *Kunad hamjins ba hamjins parwaz; kabutar ba kabutar, baz ba baz.* (Like flies with like, pigeon with pigeon, eagle with eagle.)

Hearing different things from thinkers, seers and fortune tellers, some of which they would perhaps believe and some they could never believe to be true, Inayat's parents were rather confused and watched and guarded him constantly and tried to keep him away from mysticism or philosophy, or even from poetry, but in spite of all their watching they could not keep Inayat away from that for which he was born on earth. His attempts at writing poetry without any training in the art of metre and form, compelled his parents to place him under the tutorship of Kavi Ratnakar, the great Hindustani poet.

One day his uncle Murtaza Khan, said to him: 'Are there not enough songs in the world that you must needs add to the number?' Inayat said in answer: 'No uncle, not enough, if there were enough songs, God would not have created me.' His uncle had nothing more to say but was amused.

Murtaza Khan, (Professor Murtaza Khan) the eldest son of Maula Bakhsh, was like his father. Simple and happy by nature, he was quite fit to carry on the line of his father as a singer. He was a great help to Maula Bakhsh, for he sang duets with him. Murtaza Khan, with his commanding look, was most sociable. He was always kind in helping his nephews, especially Inayat in his musical advancement, until he saw Inayat had already gone too far. He had a most wonderful voice, so as to deserve the place of the chief among the Court singers and to be most in favour of H.H. the Maharaja Gaekwar. His voice, with his most imposing appearance, would make such an impression upon people at his recitals, that they would carry with them that impression; and no singer, after his song, could ever succeed in making an impression upon the audience. Murtaza Khan held the position of his father after him at the Court as the principal singer and as professor in the Gayanshala, the Academy of Music, founded by his father in Baroda. He had a son, called Alla Bakhsh (i.e. Allahdad Khan). He took the place of his father at home and outside. He died in December 1924.

Once Inayat and his companions heard a Christian missionary teaching his religion to any who would listen. Many interruptions came from the bystanders in the form of questions and arguments and soon Inayat's friends joined with the opponents. When Inayat showed his surprise at his friends' conduct, they said: 'Why should he wish to teach us that religion?' 'He is not doing wrong, he is teaching his own religion; if he is doing it with goodwill, what does it matter?' replied Inayat.

Wrestling is a national sport of India, and the State of Baroda is especially known for it. Everyone in Inayat's family was more or less interested in wrestling, also his brothers and cousin. On holidays when public wrestling takes place, people gather from all parts of the city to watch the wrestling with the same interest with which a boxing match is followed in the West. Young Inayat was once taken among that crowd, where he saw nothing but two people, each trying hard to get the other down, and in the end the rejoicing of the one who had won, and the disgrace of the other. The only impression made upon Inayat was that of the stupidity of human nature. Inayat saw how childish man is, to rejoice at seeing such a thing. He looked with great pity at the cruel side of it, that the one who does not win suffers disgrace. He pictured himself in the position of him who had failed to win and thought how useless was both winning and not winning. He never again went to see that sport and this attitude always astonished those around him[14].

---

14 First edition has 'his surroundings' a Dutch rendition

Boyhood

Inayat was grown-up for his age and people called him *Buddhi Arwah*, the Old Soul.

In his family he preferred to be in the company of older people rather than with children of his own age. He was by nature playful, but his interest in any childish play never lasted. When his playmates were playing with kites or pigeons, he would be sitting talking to his grandmother or some older person of things beyond his age.

Inayat was always curious to know about the life of the people of the West and he was very much interested to hear about it. He read books on the subject, and also heard lectures concerning it. His uncle, Dr. Alaoddin Khan, was being sent to England to study music and there was talk of one or two students being sent together with him. Inayat was most eager to be one of them although nobody thought him old enough to make that journey. Inayat silently continued in his desire of journeying to Europe, but did not know when it would be.

Dr. Alaoddin Khan (Dr. A.M. Pathan), the younger son of Maula Bakhsh, Inayat's maternal uncle, was the hope of his father. Most intelligent, at the same time obstinate by nature, he was studious and enthusiastic. He always was opposed to become an artist, seeing the degeneration of the life of the artists and art in India and seeing how shamefully they were treated. He therefore, being of a proud nature, wished to strike out another line through his life, which was so different to the line of India where every profession is learned by virtue of family tradition. Every rank, position and work remained in the families in India for thousands of years, so he could not very well give up the line of music, nor could he be an artist, so he first helped his father Maula Bakhsh at the Academy of Music. He was most inclined to learn European music and his wish was granted at last and he was sent to England by the State of Baroda to learn European music. He studied for five years in London at the Royal Academy of Music and took the first place among many candidates, to their great surprise, in obtaining the degree of Doctor of Music. Also at the Guildhall he passed his examination of Band Master. He acquired a great qualification in the theory of music and had several degrees given to him by the London College of Music of Licentiate and Associate and also from Germany and other places. He then travelled throughout Europe, in France, Germany and Italy, to gain more experience of European music before he returned to India. On his return to Baroda, Maharaja Gaekwar appointed him as superintendent of all the different departments of the State of Indian and European music, including the military bands and orchestras, which took away his thought from art to administration, for which also he was most efficient by temperament. Inayat was from childhood very fond of his uncle and copied his modern ways readily. He was affectionate and kind towards his nephews, yet his way of managing them sometimes seemed hard to sensitive and independent Inayat, although it all helped him towards the purpose for which Inayat was being prepared. His coming to Baroda brought a great change to all the young men in the family. For they all, to the distress of the old people of the family, under his influence turned against the Indian musical profession, for which they had been trained from childhood and which was the only art they knew. Inayat was too enthusiastic in anything he did, and this troubled his uncle very much. He often could not keep a proper control upon Inayat; besides there was much which was not in common between Inayat and his uncle. Maheboob (Ill.11), being wholeheartedly responsive to his influence, was his uncle's favourite. Ali Khan (Ill. 10, 23) was closely attached to him.

Alaoddin Khan was a genius in music and a most efficient organizer and administrator, also a wonderful teacher of music. He was sociable, yet proud and would not have anyone walk over his head, whatever be his power or position. After some years' service in Baroda State, Dr. Alaoddin Khan retired from his post and was called away by the State of Nepal, where he is still working as director of music.[15]

Inayat's love for the West was the token of his work there in the future. Inayat was very much inclined to learn English, although he never liked to study. When he began to speak a little, he was eager to talk with foreigners. He would go and talk to a soldier or to a missionary. Once he met English travellers, Mr. and Mrs. Cotton, who were looking for the State Library and they became friends with him and he took them to the Library and invited them to see the School of Music where he was a student. They were very much impressed by their enthusiastic little friend and when after many years Inayat visited England meeting them again, he reminded them of that incident and they remembered it.

In 1893 there was some talk of Maula Bakhsh, his grandfather, going to Chicago to represent Hindu music at the exhibition to be held there. Inayat was wondering in his mind with much eagerness whether his grandfather would think him old enough to accompany him. No occasion occurred for Inayat to make the journey to Europe, but much later the return of his uncle Dr. Pathan from England brought a new stimulus to his desire of going to the West. Inayat asked endless questions about the West and the life there and every day his interest grew greater and greater.

When the occasion of the Paris exhibition came, there was talk of some

---

15. Dictated summer 1922

students being sent from Baroda State to study different things and Inayat was most inclined to be among them. He went to his mother and said that he had for so long desired to go and that seemed to be the opportunity for him to travel to the West; would she mind if he went. His mother, who was always kind and wise, said to him: 'Child, if it is for your good I have nothing to say in the matter. I will bear all for your happiness in life and whatever seems best for you, you may do, I shall never oppose it. But as to me, the pain of separation I am afraid will be unbearable and I should not be surprised if you would not find me living on your return.' Hearing this Inayat said: 'There is nothing in the world, however profitable and attractive, that will take me away from you and I could never be happy wherever I went, not even in Paradise, if I had the slightest thought that you were unhappy on my account. Therefore, mother, be at rest, I am ready to sacrifice all my prospects in life if it were necessary to keep you happy, which I hold to be my first duty.'

Inayat was very much interested in the Sanskrit language, although in school he was taught Sanskrit as a second language. He made friends with Professor Kaushik Ram, who was very well versed in Sanskrit, from whom he learned.

Inayat was fond of speaking and when eleven years old he formed a children's association and called it *Bala Sabha*, he being the youngest among all the members. Inayat spoke with great interest on topics concerning home life and school life and life in general. Many boys were invited in this Sabha from his school, but among them the most willing speaker was Inayat himself.

Once Inayat's father met in the street an aged Brahman, a well-known and learned man, a *Shastri*, and the Brahman asked Inayat's father how his friend was. The father wondered whom he was inquiring after and looked with a smile of surprise at the Brahman, The Brahman said: 'Your little son, he is a wonder to me and he has been a consolation to me, especially since I have lost my own son. Your son and I have talked about life and death and we have had such interesting times together. Remember me kindly to him. May God bless him.'

Inayat talked with his father very often about woman's rights and on religion and in spite of his father's always trying to avoid discussions on delicate subjects such as these, Inayat always dragged them from him by his great eagerness in these questions.

Inayat was always first in his studies and practices in music at the Gayanshala, the Academy of Music and he worked as one of the foremost students and was the first to take part in every concert given at the school. There he learned and advanced more quickly than anyone could imagine and in his ear-training, in his improvisation, he surpassed all in the class.

Once a great musician of Karnatic, Subramani Ayar, was visiting the school and asked different questions of the students and tested their voices and ear. Inayat's turn came and the musician sang a phrase and asked him to tell the notes. Inayat sang the phrase in notes, in *sa ra gam*. The musician then gave him a more difficult phrase and he sang that correctly also, and as they went on, the musician gave him more and more difficult phrases, until they arrived at the point of rivalry and Inayat answered his very last question. The musician struck his hands on the table with pleasure and surprise and asked who this lad was. They said: 'He is the grandson of Maula Bakhsh.' The musician then said: 'Now I am not surprised.'

A guest was one day expected at the palace in Baroda and Maula Bakhsh was speaking with his friends about arranging a musical programme and making a song in his honour. Inayat heard it somehow and before anyone thought of composing the song, Inayat had already composed it and brought it before his grandfather to sing and asked him if it was worth singing before the guest. His grandfather very much appreciated his talent and enterprise and always tried to encourage him.

Inayat very much liked to tease a singer who had come from Jaipur, who used to smoke hashish and was very sensitive to teasing. And he did it in this way: whenever this musician sang a new song and said it was by his great Guru, Vallabha Charya, immediately after hearing it Inayat went into another room and composed exactly the same form of song with new words and coming back to the musician said: 'Will you sing it again? Do you call it a new song I have not heard? Here I have known it for many years.' Everyone looked with great surprise and the musician would become very confused and annoyed and when he said: 'Show me if you know it,' Inayat would readily sing the song which he had just composed, and it would surprise everyone, and a roar of laughter would arise on every side at seeing the musician so confused. Inayat did this often for amusement, and once when he was going into the other room to compose, after hearing one of the songs, the musician caught hold of him and made him sit before him, not letting him go away. Inayat immediately took the pencil in his hand and said: 'Wait, let me call it to mind, I think I know this song also.' He then and there composed and sang in answer to the musician's song. The musician said: 'This young fellow is a *Jinn*; no sooner do you repeat a word than he knows it already.' Then Inayat told him that he did not doubt for one moment that it was a new song, but he was in fun and liked to tease him. Then the musician told his master about Inayat and the latter became very anxious to meet him. When later Inayat went to Jaipur, the Guru gave him a very warm welcome and said to his friends: 'Here is the divine gift,' pointing to Inayat, 'a thing that can never be learned and it is the very thing that gives man the belief in God.'

Inayat was taken to Patan when eleven years of age, by his uncle Murtaza Khan, who had been invited by a well-known citizen of the town, Bhartiji, in whose house sages from different places and of different mystical orders met. And to Inayat this was the most congenial association he ever had in his life. Every sage there was most attracted to the lad and Inayat became friends with all. The impression of this meeting always remained with him and from this time he began to study comparative religions.

In order to make a diversion in Inayat's life, his father took him and Maheboob both with him to Idar in Kathiawar (Gujarat), to the Court of the Raja Kesri Singh. Inayat enjoyed this journey very much, and travelling for part of the journey on the back of a camel through hot sand, especially interested him. Raja Kesri Singh was very much impressed by the youth, who readily answered questions about the music of India before it was necessary for his father to utter a word. This visit gave Inayat some insight into the kind of life that the Rajas live, which revealed to him the main cause of the downfall of India. His father observed that every day Inayat looked more and more behind the surface of things.

Inayat happened to hear that there was a Yogi lecturing in his town. He hastened to attend these lectures and was very much interested in all the Yogi said. This was Swami Hamsasvarupa. Inayat thought that life was only worth living if man arrived at the stage of such an understanding of life. Yet he could not link the religion of the Hindus with that of his own people, the Muslims. Inayat personally was more inclined to Hinduism than to Muslim faith, as was also his grandfather Maula Bakhsh. His father also took interest in the philosophy of Hinduism, being always in the society of Hindus. Having learnt his first lesson in the Hindu school, naturally Inayat was more inclined to Hinduism, but nevertheless he was as interested in hearing the wise *wa'iz*, the preaching of the Muslim Maulavi and was regular in his prayers and had an inborn love for Muhammad.

One day, Inayat was praying on the roof of the house, offering his prayers and he thought to himself that there had not been an answer yet to all the prayers he had offered to God, and he did not know where God was to hear his prayers, and he could not reconcile himself to going on praying to the God whom he knew not. He went fearlessly to his father and said: 'I do not think I will continue my prayers any longer, for it does not fit in with my reason. I do not know how I can go on praying to a God I do not know.' His father, taken aback, did not become cross lest he might turn Inayat's beliefs sour by forcing them upon him without satisfying his reason and he was glad on the other hand to see that, although it was irreverent on the child's part, yet it was frank, and he knew that the lad really hungered after Truth and was ready to learn now, what many could not learn in their whole life. He said to him: 'God is in you and you are in God. As the bubble is in the ocean, and the bubble is a part of the ocean and yet not separate from the ocean. For a moment it has appeared as a bubble, then it will return to that from which it has risen. So is the relation between man and God. The Prophet has said that God is closer to you than the jugular vein, which in reality means that your own body is farther from you than God is. If this be rightly interpreted, it will mean that God is the very depth of your own being.' This moment to Inayat was his very great initiation, as if a switch had turned in him, and from that moment onward his whole life Inayat busied himself, and his whole being became engaged in witnessing in life what he knew and believed, by this one great Truth. It was like a word that was lost, and he found it again.

The intensity of the call Inayat felt even in his early age. He used to get a feeling of despair at the falsehood of all things and it would manifest as a depression with the spirit of indifference and independence which can be explained in one Oriental word: *vairagya*. Although this feeling was not clear either to himself or to his surroundings, yet once it manifested to the great astonishment of his people.

With all the love Inayat had for his people, he was most drawn to solitude. He loved the stories of the ascetics who lived in the mountains and forests and he longed to go there. And a feeling every now and then showed in him the nature of the deer which retreats from the crowd, though on the other hand he had also the most sociable tendency. He attracted others about him and was pleasant to others and he derived pleasure from association with people. These two contradictory moods came and went like the ebb and flow of the tides.

Inayat one day set out on a journey with the idea of leaving home for good for the sake of devoting his life to contemplation, study and solitude. He told nobody at home, except his brother Maheboob, who was most attached to him and did not like to leave him for one moment, and two friends very devoted to him. Maheboob tried his best to keep him from leaving home, but it was all in vain and Inayat refused to take Maheboob with him for he thought it would mean the loss of two sons to the family instead of one. There was boundless pain in the heart of Maheboob, who had a dreadful task before him, namely to conceal his feelings from his parents and to allow his brother to leave home. When Inayat separated from him he was most touched by his brother's unhappiness. His two devoted friends also tried to stop his going, but they could not influence him against his wishes. In the end they decided they would not let him go alone and would follow him wherever he went. Inayat said that since he was not clear about the purpose of his going away and as he would be travelling without any means and not knowing why and whither, it was better for his friends to let him go alone and answer his call. The friends would not listen, and they followed Inayat; but after walking a few miles away from the city, one of them felt drawn towards home and he influenced the other, who they supposed knew the way and so they took a route which instead of taking them farther away from the city, would bring them closer to it. There was a panic in Inayat's home and people were sent all about the city to find him. One of them at length found Inayat and brought him home against his wishes. On coming home Inayat learned how much pain his absence would have caused his parents and he resolved that however deep the impulse, he would always resist it, so as not to cause pain to his parents whom he loved most.

Once Inayat was with his grandfather at a religious ceremony in honour of Ganesh, the God of Luck, and during the ceremony he sang the well-known hymn to Ganesh, in the raga *Hamsadhvani*, composed by Dikshitar. It created such an atmosphere on that occasion that the Maharaja Sayaji Rao Gaekwar of Baroda gave him a reward and granted him a scholarship, to encourage him in his studies in music.

The access to the palace of Baroda from childhood, was the great education for Inayat, to become acquainted with all the functions which took place there, which he loved very much, being by nature inclined to refinement.

The administrative efficiency of Maharaja Gaekwar, who was the unique ruler, Inayat observed keenly, which became useful to him later in his work of organizing his Movement.

Together with his love of beauty and response to all that is good and beautiful, Inayat saw the futility of all things, which strike the young mind and attract young souls. His father was often amazed to see his love of beauty and at the same time his ascetic indifference.

Inayat's father disclosed to him some part of his own experience of life. He showed him how dependent the life of man is on woman and that of woman on man. He showed him how much more a child is indebted to his mother than to his father. He told him how impossible it was for any soul to be happy in life, who, when grown-up, proved ungrateful to his parents, after he had received all kindness, and love, and tender care from them.

He taught him how worthless was the path of asceticism and that mastery lay alone in being in the world and yet above the world. Inayat's father saw that he had a great tendency towards *vairagya*, a solitary and ascetic life in the forests or caves of the mountains and that he always longed for that, and by showing the great importance of the life in the world, he brought about that balance in Inayat's thought which prepared him for his work in the future. He told him that the man who thought deeply on life and helped his fellowmen, was greater than the one who dwelt in the forest and thought deeply for himself. He showed Inayat how much more beautiful it was to love one's fellowman, to accommodate him, to serve him, to be united with him, than to leave the world and go away into a cave in the mountain. He said the world was created for some purpose and that purpose can best be fulfilled by living for one's fellowman and loving him and in this way living for God and loving God. He taught him that family life was an attribute of the Creator and it brought all blessings, in this way expanding in loving others so that the whole humanity may become for him one family. He said to him: 'You must give proof of your love for your fellowmen by loving your brother first. Be sincere and true to everyone and try to fulfil your duties to everyone, in whatever relation you stand to him.'

Inayat's father taught the lesson of speaking the truth and of living a pure life, not only by words but by the example of his own life. Besides this moral, he taught Inayat faith and trust in God, that those who trust God, were always provided for in their need; however great the need was, the Divine Providence was greater still. This teaching went through the very depths of Inayat's being.

It was as though something that was in his nature was brought to the surface.

His father taught him the blessing of a simple life and of sharing one's good with another. He taught contentment in all conditions of life and he taught him to hide one's difficulties in life from others. He said that no poverty, however great, must ever be told even to friends or relations, for God alone must know of it. It is only happiness that we must make others share with us.

He taught Inayat to take care of his brothers, and taught them that their strength in life was in standing by each other in all times of hardship and difficulty. He taught him that no poverty was worse for man than dishonour and he warned him constantly to have regard to honour at the cost of anything in life.

Inayat was very much impressed by a moral his father taught by quoting to him a saying: *Neki kar pani me dal, badi kar pallu me bandh.*[16] (Forget all the good you do, but remember your every fault.) His father held this principle very firmly, that dignity is man's honour and not necessarily pride, and he pointed out to young Inayat the beauty of dignity in all walks of life and the moral degradation of the undignified. He taught him to realize that man's honour was his dharma, and his self-respect his virtue. Modesty, he said, was the best thing in life, but humiliation was the worst.

---

16. Literally: Good that you have done, put that in the water; Bad that you have done, tie that in the border of your sari

Youth

Though but a young lad, Inayat was always anxious to do all the work he could when it was such as he liked. He would go to the different teachers at the music school and say: 'May I explain to your class the lesson on music I learned yesterday?' The teacher would be most glad to give Inayat some work to do and get into the open air, away from the heat he felt sitting in the class. He would go to another teacher and say: 'May I finish the teaching of the song which you have begun in your class?' To the third he would say: 'May I teach a song which I feel your class will like very much?' In this way, he did almost the work of all the teachers in the school, who were most pleased to let him do it. There was no assuming on his part, he only did it out of enthusiasm to serve and be useful.

At the students' gathering at the High School of Baroda, Inayat was once invited to give a programme of music, and taking that occasion as a good opportunity to tell people what he thought of the present condition of Indian music, he of his own accord, offered to speak on the subject. Before the professors and students, he spoke earnestly explaining the importance of musical education. Those who heard him there, invited him to speak at the temple of Narsiji. Inayat accepted the invitation most willingly and spoke to them, giving with his lecture different kinds of music and illustrating the scientific and religious aspects of the subject. When next day the lecture was printed in the Baroda newspaper, his people knew about it and it was a shock and surprise to them.

Inayat felt keenly about the lack of female education, especially amongst Muslims. There was hesitation amongst Muslims, especially at that time, to teach music to girls, for they considered gaiety of any kind a thing forbidden, not only for women, but for men also. In order to give girls an education in real music, Inayat wrote a textbook of music, *Balasangitmala*, in Hindustani and tried to bring it before the leaders of the Muslim community, though he was too young for his voice to be heard by the educational authorities.

The very first blow that Inayat received in his early youth, was the death of his grandfather Maula Bakhsh, under whose shelter Inayat had grown as a little plant under the shade of a large tree. A grandfather so great as Maula Bakhsh, so kind, with a magical personality, the only one in the world who had really understood the lad, who was most gentle with him in all his doings. Besides, he was an ideal for Inayat to look up to, and a companion and a friend, and at the same time his teacher. It seemed to Inayat as if both heaven and earth were shaken, but at the same time this great pain of separation, so to speak, opened his heart wider to the question of birth and death. Everyone saw a change come to Inayat. People began to see in the youth the expression of the mature. His parents regarded this change in him with no little anxiety and tried whether by making some change in his environment they could turn the mind of the lad from brooding over his loss.

Providence changed Inayat's environment. H.H. the Maharaja Bhim Shamsher of Nepal had called an assembly of all the eminent musicians of the land, and the invitation had reached all the well-known schools of music, which are known as *khandan* (families). From the school of Maula Bakhsh, Rahmat Khan, Inayat's father, was proposed to attend the function and on Inayat's persistent request to accompany him, his father agreed to his doing so. Although this was the first time Inayat was to go away from his mother's tender care and from the comfort of home, nevertheless his joy in making this long journey from Baroda to Nepal was great.

He had the opportunity of staying on the way at Gwalior, where his father took him to the tomb of Tansen, to pay homage to India's most celebrated singer. According to the custom of the place, the leaves of the tree that sheltered the tomb of Tansen Inayat took as *tabarruk*, a sacrament. Here in Gwalior, which has been a city well-known for its great musicians, Inayat had the opportunity of hearing the successors of the eminent singers Hadu, Hasu Khan as well as Tanras Khan and was much impressed and helped by the expert execution of *Khayal* songs by the singers there.

When the journey was broken at Benares[17], the state of Inayat's spirit became inexplicable. He felt exalted and experienced a feeling as though his spirit was going through an initiation; and his visit there he felt as being for a purpose which his soul alone knew. He walked gently through the streets of Benares, he walked along the banks of the Ganges, around the sacred shrines of the Hindus with a deeply felt worshipful attitude. This visit for Inayat was not the breaking of the journey, it was to his heart the first and great pilgrimage in his life.

From Sigoli, where the train journey ends, they had six days' journey through the forest. This was a new experience to a soul who wanted to breathe a breath of freedom from the crowd, and to whom nature was not only appealing but uplifting. Chairs that four people carry on their shoulders were sent to them by the State to carry them through the forest, but Inayat did not at all like the idea of a person in good health being carried on the shoulders of others. Besides, a respect for human beings was inborn in this youth, who regarded these human beings who carried the chairs with the same attitude with which he regarded everything in nature.

He regarded nature all around him, which expressed to him from all sides the sublimity of the divine manifestation. He at the same time did not let others know his point of view in this, trying not to give the others the idea that his attitude was any better than that of those who were sitting in the

---

17. Now known as Varanasi, this is not further noted

chairs and enjoying the journey through the forest. He showed to all that he preferred to walk, because he enjoyed walking more than sitting. So he journeyed on foot, walking from morning till evening through woods and valleys, enjoying the beauty of nature all about him, observing the effect of the sunrise and sunset, enjoying the little showers coming now and then after the hot sun, and listening to the blowing and cooing of the wind. Certainly the path was full of dangers. They were threatened now and then by tigers, lions, elephants, bears and rhinoceroses and the wild animals of all sorts living in the forest. They stopped each evening at a grass hut, made to afford shelter to travellers.

Inayat's enjoyment was boundless. For the first time in his life there came to him the realization of the saying: 'The city was made by man and the country was made by God.'

The solitude of the forest, the sounds of the birds that one never feels nor hears in the crowd, the trees standing in stillness for hundreds of years, a place never occupied by man, gave him a feeling of that calm and peace that every soul longs for, consciously or unconsciously. This journey was a kind of answer to the cry of his soul. He felt in the sphere a welcome and blessing given by the long-standing trees, venerable in age and appearance. He saw the hand of God blessing in every bending branch. He pictured his hands in the branches that stretched upwards, hands constantly praying and asking for blessing from above.

It happened that at that time the Maharaja Dhiraja of Nepal was hunting in the forest with a troop of five hundred elephants. This brought before him a sight of uncommon grandeur and he noticed with great interest the arrangement and the manner in which the elephants were trained to surround the tiger and bring it to bay. The intelligence and the obedience of the elephants, how they stood close to each other, side by side, brought vividly to his mind the thought that unity can stand against any power, however great. It is through lack of unity that the same elephant, when alone, with all his gigantic form and monstrous strength, becomes a prey to the tiger.

He saw there not only tiger-hunting but the way in which the wild elephants are caught. Out of the trained group of elephants one, chosen for its magnetic force, was sent into the interior of the forest. There it made friends with a wild elephant, and kept that elephant there till it had grown friendly enough to walk about with him. Then one other elephant was sent and the two got one on either side of the wild creature. Then the rest of the group was sent to surround the three. The wild elephant then wanted to get free, but was powerless to do so, as he was wedged in between the first two, who held him as in a vice. With all the enjoyment and interest that this offered to Inayat, he could not help feeling pity for the poor wild elephant. And this suggested to him how much more capable man is of getting his fellowman into his grip by means of his strength and clever ways and that it is man who deprives his fellowman of his happiness and freedom in life. Inayat as a rule had no liking for sport. He always had an aversion to a rough game, even where one could hurt another, or be proud of his conquest over another, shooting or killing apart.

From Mount Akdanta they had to take a journey. The way was so steep that it was difficult for a man who had not learned how to climb mountains. Therefore, men were sent to carry the travellers on their backs in a kind of cane chair, shaped like a basket. Although the men are so accustomed to taking heavy loads on these mountains, a man's weight being as nothing, Inayat still refused to be on another person's back. Although all the other travellers were sitting on the backs of these men, he proceeded on his journey across the mountains in the same way as through the forest, though it was very difficult. In the first place he had never before seen such high mountains, and then walking on the steep paths was difficult. He had nearly finished the hard journey, when drawing near to Kathmandu, the capital of Nepal, his foot slipped, and he was somewhat hurt, but everyone was thankful that a greater mishap had been avoided.

Inayat's mother had never been separated from her child before and her thoughts dwelt constantly upon her beloved son, and on that night she dreamt that Inayat came to her, showing her his hurt knee. That same night, in a dream, Inayat saw his mother sympathizing with him in his pain. There could not have been a greater proof than this for Inayat to realize that space cannot separate truly attached hearts, and this gave him the greatest proof of the singleness of life.

On arriving at Kathmandu, the capital of Nepal, Inayat had what he wished. He had the opportunity of listening to all the great singers of India, who were invited to that assembly, which was a great help to the youth, who was constantly advancing in the science and art of music. Besides that, it was a great study from a psychological point of view for Inayat to come into contact with all these personalities. Inayat learned not only the best execution of classical singing, but how music sweetened the personality, and how harmonious the thought, speech and action of a musician becomes, emitting the atmosphere of music. He saw that during their conversations their gestures were graceful, their words and phrases poetical, their voices sweet, the expression of their countenance pleasant. He noted their high ideals, their tender hearts, their kind attitude and their natural leaning towards God. He learned more than ever before to regard music as sacred, and to respect a musician, so won was he by the beauty of their art, and by their harmonious personality. He saw also that those who were not yet deepened in music were on the contrary more inclined toward amusement and frivolity, more drawn toward the gaiety and merriment of life, uncontrolled in their affections, and inconsiderate in passion. That explained to him why the Prophet forbade music to his followers. His Message was an all-reviving force and his first followers, who founded the nucleus of the brotherhood of Islam, were naturally taught not to indulge in anything that led to frivolity and gaiety. Inayat saw that the best part of music that rises in its perfect development can surely not be *haram*, forbidden.

Inayat was much impressed by the grandeur of the martial life of Nepal, but was always against the tendency of the musicians to bow and bend to their utmost before the Rajas, and to make every effort in praising and flattering them in order to gain their favours. He saw that this, the degeneration of India's music, was due to this method, and that it naturally reacted upon the musicians of India, most of whom were placed in the category of entertainers or flatterers. He would often feel humiliated when among them, and he saw that the diamonds are few and the pebbles many. So the really great ones are few, and the few have to fall in with the custom and conventions of the majority, and thus the sin of some involves all. He saw at the same time that the effect of their praise and flattery was detrimental to the Rajas themselves, who thought that they knew more of music than they really did, and the musicians, by pleasing them and satisfying their fancies, kept them ignorant of the real music, and by falling in with their fancies they brought their music from bad to worse.

Often musicians incited and urged them on to a life of gaiety and therefore, during the reign of the Moghuls, the staff of musicians was called *arabab-i nishat*, the company of pleasure.

This in no way made any difference to the great ideal of music that Inayat had; he felt the sacredness of music so much; but it kept him rather aloof from the musicians, while at the same time he was full of respect and admiration for their art. Although reluctant to associate with them, he was ever eager and ready to learn music from them. The difference of Inayat's nature from that of the other musicians, and the independence of his spirit, attracted to him both the rich and the poor with whom he came in contact. Among them Prince Chandra Vikram Shah, and Bahujangi Raja became his friends.

In Kathmandu lived a very old Sufi, a faqir, who was spiritual guide to the Raja Bhim Shamsher. This Sufi was from Punjab and he had a most beautiful personality. His presence was mercy and compassion itself. Inayat was greatly drawn to him and this Sufi, in return, was much attracted by Inayat. Inayat frequently visited his dwelling and conversed with him on human life. Inayat's contact with him was most helpful. Inayat observed all he did, listened to all he said and thought and pondered over his visit to this Sufi, and always felt in his soul the exaltation of the blessing he received there. This was all training toward the fulfilment of the purpose of his life.

Inayat's father was employed in teaching music at the palace of the Maharaja, and therefore Inayat's time was all his own. Much of this time he spent in singing practice and the rest of the time he went on horseback into the Himalayan regions nearby and remained there in solitude, which was what he most desired, and was a healing to his soul and a necessary preparation for his future work.

One day, while travelling over the hills and dales, he saw at a distance someone sitting in a place where scarcely anyone would ever be seen. On arriving there he found the man was a Mahatma, sitting in silent meditation in that lonely spot, perhaps for ages. In the meeting of glance Inayat was filled with a feeling of exaltation, and the calm and peace and the atmosphere that the Mahatma had created there were beyond expression. It seemed as if there all the trees, even every leaf, was standing respectfully, motionless before the Mahatma. It seemed as if the ever-blowing wind was in abeyance under the reign of perfect stillness, caused by the peace of his soul. Inayat sang to that Mahatma and received in return a blessing through his inspiring glance. After that, Inayat frequented the place, sometimes with his vina, and won the favour of the Mahatma. The light, strength and peace that Inayat received from him, designed the career which was destined for him.

After one year's stay in Nepal, Inayat's father took leave of the Maharaja and left Nepal for Baroda, his home. Inayat's mother, not having seen her son for a whole year, was very eager to see him. When she heard the most exciting news of her son's arrival from Nepal after the long separation, Khatidja Bibi, instead of going to the door to receive him, went first to her room, to offer thanks to God for having brought him back. And on seeing him she found an immense change in the youth. Inayat had become gentler and more patient and many of his boyish traits were subdued. This separation had taught Inayat to value his mother and motherhood more than ever before. From his early age Inayat was a most affectionate son, but now came the time that his affection was expressed by manner and action.

A time came when, owing to famine in the country, household expenses were increased, and seeing his parents in need, Inayat of his own accord offered to go and work for them. He taught music to the children of Dewan Srinivasa Raghava Ayangar, the Prime Minister of Baroda State. Besides these, he taught music to other pupils. This wise Dewan, a Brahman by caste and not only a great statesman, but a great reader of human nature, took a great liking to Inayat and told the Maharaja how promising he thought him.

At this time Inayat's uncle, Dr. Alaoddin Khan, had returned from England, where he had studied music and taken his degrees as Doctor of Music. His return was an answer to Inayat's great yearning to know about Europe. Inayat took great interest in learning all he could about European music, and in following his uncle's advice in many directions, Inayat played the violin for some time, and studied the theory of European music. He heard military band and orchestra, and on some occasions conducted himself, thereby entering into the spirit of Western music. Inayat discussed with his uncle the difference between Eastern and Western music. They had talks together about human nature in general and life in the world, sometimes touching upon philosophical and religious thoughts. They were drawn to each other, and at the same time Inayat's way was his own.

Inayat's interest in the music of the West and his neglect of Eastern music, brought dismay to the family. But Inayat's answer to all his people was that whatever he took up, he took up wholeheartedly. It was a passing phase, the music of the East was too deeply ingrained in him that he could ever give it up.

In every musical activity in Baroda State some important part was always undertaken by him, and it was invariably successfully carried out. He composed songs and wrote the words in four languages: Urdu, Hindi, Marathi and Gujarati. He composed a book of these songs and called it *Sayaji Garbawali*, and dedicated it to the Maharaja of Baroda. They were sung at a festival, called *Navarat*, at the Lakshme Vilas Palace before H.H. the Maharaja. This made known his talent not only as a singer, but as a composer and teacher of music throughout the State of Baroda.

Between Inayat and his mother understanding grew greater day by day, making their lives more wrapped up in each other; and it was a sudden blow to Inayat when his mother passed away after a very brief illness. Then once again the world appeared to him in a new light. It seemed to him as if there had been a shelter under which he had taken refuge from every hurt and harm coming from the world; and now that this shelter was removed and he found himself deprived of it, he realized by this two things: that with all love and kindness the father cannot fill the place of the mother; and that true love, unlimited, self-sacrificing and above all passion, is the mother's love, which cannot be compared with any other; and that the mother's love is a divine blessing, and if there be any sign of God's mercy and compassion, it is truly in the love of the mother.

This despair made it necessary for Inayat to go away from the environment of home, which seemed to show him every moment of his life the absence of his mother, who had been the centre of his home.

He went, alone, on a visit to Madras[18], where the Right Hon. Mr. Anandacharlu took great interest in the youth's talent. Khan Bahadur Hadi Pasha and Khan Bahadur Walji Lalji became admirers of his talent. He won the friendship of many people during his short visit there, and they, as citizens of Madras, presented him with an address and a gold medal in token of their admiration. Becoming through this incident better known in the Southern part of India, Inayat was invited to Mysore, where his grandfather had won such great renown. He was invited by the State to the installation of the Maharaja Krishna Raja Vodyer.

Once he was waiting at a junction for the next train. He was in some despair for his purse was empty. While he was fighting bravely his appetite, sitting at the junction, and perplexed what would happen when he arrived at his destination, a Brahman came near with a hot dish of *bhajia*, a dish which Inayat had always liked, and offered it him. Inayat, so young and proud, said: 'I do not want it, thank you.' The man said: 'No, you must eat, you will make

---

18. Now known as Chennai, this is not further noted

me unhappy if you refuse. It is right that you do not want it, but it is true that you need it. You have a long journey before you.' Inayat thankfully accepted and ate, and yet was wondering what would happen at his destination. This Brahman who waited upon Inayat all the time while he was eating, was a seer. He said: 'Do not be worried, all will be well.' He said: 'You are going to a place where you will be received with open arms and a warm heart. You will be honoured at the Court of the Maharaja, and from the moment you step on the soil of Mysore, you will be received as a royal guest.' And so it happened. He was also warmly received at the Darbar where he sang and played with much success.

Inayat met the great Shaishanna, Shamanna and Subanna, the well-known musicians of the Court of Mysore.

Hearing the music of Karnatic so well performed, brought most vividly to his memory the happiest moments that he had spent with his grandfather. People in Mysore were glad to see Inayat, who represented to them Maula Bakhsh, whose memory was so dear to all there. Inayat was, after Maula Bakhsh, the first musician to go from the North to the South, and to sing before the people of the South their own music, as if to the manner born. Inayat once heard a song of Tyagaraja's and after hearing it once, he was able the next time to join with the singer in singing it, and did so without a mistake. He sang *Pallavi*, which is peculiar to the people of the South alone, with the same singer, and he improvised in so masterly a manner that the assembly marvelled greatly at his talent. After a very successful visit to Mysore he returned home. Inayat brought with him that atmosphere of success to which all his family had been accustomed during the time of his grandfather. This journey proved to his people how successful Inayat was in every way, and thenceforward he acted as the foremost worker in the State Musical Department, both in art and in education, although his two uncles, Murtaza Khan and Alaoddin Khan (Dr. A.M. Pathan), were the figureheads.

However, with all his enthusiasm and talent and his desire to do some good work, there was not scope enough for him in Baroda State, since the best positions in music were occupied by his two uncles. He began to feel uncomfortable at the lack of opportunity to exercise his ability, and he therefore left Baroda for Hyderabad. He visited Bombay[19] on his way and learned through this visit to what extent the Indian music was becoming degraded. Several dramatic companies had been playing on the stage, casting aside the riches and beauty of music which the different modes and ragas give. There was a general inclination for light music, most songs there being like the ragtime in the West. To Inayat, born and brought up in the very home of music, who had heard almost all the well-known musicians, it was agony to hear in his land from all sides a fantastic music with no soul in it. He discovered the reason for this state of things, and that was that for ages the real music had

---

19. Now known as Mumbai, this is not further noted

only been sung chiefly in palaces and rarely in temples, and the public was always kept ignorant of it. Especially in a crowded city like Bombay, where commercialism reigns, people cared little for any serious music, but were willing to enjoy whatever appealed to their senses at the moment. When he began his career as a singer, he used to feel the lack of response or the lack of understanding in his audience, and it used to depress him, so that he was not able to sing in a way at all equal to his powers. And therefore, there was rarely an occasion when he sang wholeheartedly, and the most satisfactory time was that when he sang by himself. That was a great drawback to his progress in life, and in the life before him, where he must depend upon himself for his living. It was hard. The only way that he found was from that moment when he decided never to feel that he was singing for others, but only that he was singing to himself. With open eyes he looked only at himself in the crowded audience and from that time on he was successful.

The most painful thing for Inayat was to see the art of music in common hands. Women, whose occupation was generally entertainment, made music their profession, and besides, music was considered as nothing more than an amusement or a pastime. He saw the profession of music so much degenerated; musicians being at the mercy of the commercial people, most of whom knew nothing but how to buy and sell. These engaged musicians to play and sing for the whole night. The audience forming into groups, one group would enjoy the music at the first part of the night; this group would then retire and send another group in its place, thus treating the talent of the artist as the task of a labouring man. They enjoyed the singing and dancing of the artists, making fun all the time. Inayat found another class of people who may be called Europeanised Indians, who treated the fine art of their land as a secondary recreation, their talking, smoking and jollity – amidst the strains of music – occupying their minds the most. He found yet another set of people who rightly regarded theatrical music as trivial, but considered other music as *ustadi*, or best music, which was in reality not any better than the most ordinary. It was a great pain to Inayat to feel the music of India was so little understood by the well-to-do people of the country.

He had an amusing experience one day when he was invited by a Parsi family in Colombo, and was requested to sing. First, he was introduced to some people there, who were said to be not only very fond of music, but connoisseurs of the art. Inayat was glad to know that, and therefore he chose some really good songs to sing. But as he began, the connoisseur said that it was very good but not what he had expected to hear. Inayat asked: 'What would you like me to sing?' He said: 'Something still more ustadi,' meaning superior. Inayat sang a song of still greater weight, but he seemed not to like it at all. So Inayat thought, perhaps the man is pretending to be a connoisseur, and he chose a lighter song, and as soon as he began, the face of the so-called connoisseur became most cheerful. It seemed his whole body responded to its rhythm. Inayat, seeing this, began to sing a still lighter song of a more popular kind and the delight of the pretended connoisseur and of all who sat there was boundless. Inayat was very much amused at this, especially at hearing from him that this was the ustadi. Though it amused him, still he went home with a heavy heart, pondering upon the condition of his people and the state in which the art of music was.

Among those who knew something about music he found many tyrants, whose every wish was to prove their little knowledge of ragas as the touchstone of music. They, instead of allowing the musician to show his best, and enjoying his talent, tried to examine him, whether he knew this or that raga. They themselves often knew no more than the name of a raga. The one who was the most headstrong and the boldest, generally seemed victor to the spectators, who hardly knew the real merit. Another cruelty Inayat saw on the part of the music lovers, was that they took delight in setting a match going between two musicians, and instead of enjoying the beauty of music, they enjoyed the competition between them. Few perhaps knew who really won, but the pleasure of seeing the victory of one over another was the only aim, which seemed altogether void of harmony to Inayat. Mr. Bhatkhande, a student of music, asked Inayat according to what *shastra* (science) he proved his ragas true. Inayat said: 'According to my shastra; it is man who has made shastra, it is not shastra that has made man.'

At seeing this degenerated condition of India and its music, he broke down and invoked the name of the deity and prayed for the protection of the sacred art of India, and he said: 'Lord, if our people had lost only its wealth and power, it would not have been so grievous to bear, since these temporal things are ever changing hands in the mazes of *maya*. But the inheritance of our race, the Music of the Divine, is also leaving us through our own negligence, and that is a loss my heart cannot sustain!'

From Bombay Inayat went to Hyderabad, where he knew none. On his arrival there he made some acquaintances, to whom he made known the reason of his visiting Hyderabad, which was to render his music before H.H. Mir Maheboob Ali Khan, the Nizam of Hyderabad. So difficult was it for anyone to approach H.H. that every friend was astounded at such a request being made, and each one was certain he would be disappointed. To Inayat, however, there seemed no difficulty; the only thing that did surprise him was the pessimistic view. From that day on he never spoke of his intentions to anyone. Six months passed by, during which time he practised music and wrote a book on music in Hindustani, called *Minqar-e-Musiqar*. By this time, he had made acquaintances who later became his great friends, and he was surrounded by the most loving of friends. A friend, Raja Din Dayal, one day took Inayat for a drive to the Mount of Maula, where the Nizam and his chief of staff were camping, celebrating some festival. The Raja happened to visit Lukman ud Dawlah, the Court physician, who was a Sufi, and who was engaged at that time in writing a commentary on the works of Rumi. At first sight he was impressed by Inayat, and felt drawn to him, and he suggested unasked that it would be a good thing if this young musician could be introduced to the Maharaja. He immediately sent word to H.E. Maharaja Kishan Pershad, who was also Prime Minister of the State, and was camping nearby. On receiving the message, the Maharaja immediately sent for Inayat.

Madar ul Maham, the Prime Minister, was sitting greatly depressed. Those about him said he was not well. When Inayat saw him, he found that he was on the verge of collapse. The Maharaja felt that there was some hidden meaning in Inayat being sent to him. As they conversed the countenance of the Maharaja began to change every moment, and a kind of joy beamed forth, which was a pleasant surprise to those around him. To see the Maharaja smile again after so long was a great relief and delight to them. Speaking of music Inayat said: 'Sirkar, there was a time when music in the land of India was held most sacred, and the great teachers of ancient times, such as Nardar and Tumbara, were great musicians. Although at the present time music is so cast aside in India, still it is the same precious cordial. My work in music on the soil of India is to raise music to its pristine glory, that it may intoxicate those souls whose destiny it is to be exalted by the power of music. Among the Sufis of the Chishtia Order, music is still the source of elevation, by which means they attain to that ecstasy which culminates in the revelation of truth.' That which made the greatest impression on the Maharaja was what Inayat said further: 'Sirkar Ali, there are four intoxications: the intoxication that comes from physical power, the intoxication which wealth gives, the intoxication of rule, and the intoxication which comes from knowledge. But there is one intoxication superior to these aforesaid intoxications, which is that produced by music.' The sincerity with which Inayat spoke and the effect of what he said, working not only upon himself but upon all who heard him, greatly raised him in their estimation. He felt that there was in Inayat's conversation something sacred hidden in the realm of art, and he felt greatly drawn to him.

In the midst of that talk, which was taking place between the Maharaja and Inayat, word came from the Nizam that H.H. would visit the camp of the Maharaja that night. This was an excellent news for the Maharaja, who had been for some time out of favour with the Nizam, and in his mind he at once associated Inayat's visit with the coming of his august master. He requested Inayat to stay in his camp that evening, and Inayat most gladly accepted.

A most joyful atmosphere was spread in the Maharaja's camp, each one saying to the other with great enthusiasm: *Huzur bar amad* (H.H. is coming). Every kind of preparation was made and message after message came at intervals about each movement of the Nizam, until the arrival. This created still greater enthusiasm in the camp and one could feel the very atmosphere anticipating the royal visit. At last midnight passed and now the people began to be uneasy, and upon the sun of hope the clouds of fear began to hover. Still the hope was there. And at about two o'clock in the morning definite news came that H.H. had already left the camp and might be expected any moment. At last he appeared amidst the sound of bugles and the beat of drums, dispersing the gloom which had fallen on the camp. The Nizam was seated on an elephant, while Arabs sang and sword-danced around him and the whole procession moved in the light of thousands of torches. The elephant walked gently, raising its head as though proudly conscious of his master's dignity. It was a picture that one's eyes could scarcely believe real, that time of early morn making it seem a vision. The elephant, covered with yellow plush trappings, arrived at the Maharaja's gate. There were also the mounted courtiers surrounding the elephant, Afsar-ul-Mulk, the most in favour Aide-de-Camp, leading the elephant.

The Maharaja received and welcomed H.H. who entered the room, followed by his courtiers and the presentation of *nazar*, the old custom of Hyderabad, began. The Maharaja then spoke of Inayat with great enthusiasm, which aroused the Nizam's interest so that he at once expressed a desire to see him and hear him sing. When Inayat arrived in the Nizam's presence, the first meeting of glance created an understanding between them. The harmonious influence of Inayat was brought to bear on the Nizam, who continued to stand, while permitting Inayat to sit, for three hours, and he did not know whether he was sitting or standing, so absorbed was he in listening to Inayat sing and to all that Inayat had to say. The Nizam was often moved by the high ideal of music Inayat had and by the songs of devotion he sang, of symbolical philosophy. The Nizam, himself a poet and a musician, felt the call that came through Inayat in the realm of music. Inayat at the same time was impressed by the simplicity and kindness, and by the unique understanding of human nature that the Nizam had. The Nizam sensed that the musical talent shown by Inayat, was but an outer garb, covering some wonderful secret, which he sought to fathom.

He asked Inayat to tell him the secret of the magical effect of his music. 'Huzur,' said Inayat, 'as sound is the highest source of manifestation it is mysterious in itself. And whosoever has the knowledge of sound, he indeed knows the secret of the universe. My music is my thought and my thought is my emotion. The deeper I dive into the ocean of feeling, the more beautiful are the pearls I bring forth in the form of melodies. Thus my music creates feeling within me even before others feel it. My music is my religion, therefore worldly success can never be a fit price for it and my sole object in music is to achieve perfection.'

A deep impression was made on the Nizam which nothing among his royal environment could remove; all night it remained with him and he could not rest for six hours till he sent for Inayat. He felt that a message had come to him in the realm of music and he wished to receive that message in private, away from his usual environment, dressed in simple garments, and sitting on the ground without either courtiers nor Aide-de-Camp in attendance. First Inayat performed his music and when he sang his own song, the meaning of which was that behind all this play of the universe, continually going on, there is one single power, perfect in its wisdom, which every moment is working through all, this moved the mystical soul of the Nizam to great ecstasy and he heaved a deep sigh on hearing it. Then he asked if he might know Inayat's object in life and whether there was any particular motive in his leaving his country to come there. Inayat replied: 'Huzur, all outward motives which manifest through various people have behind them inward motives, and if one would think of all causation, one would find that there is one principle cause behind it all; and therefore it would not be wrong if I only said in answer to your question: 'I am sent here by God. What I have brought to you is not only music merely to entertain, but the appeal of harmony which unites souls in God.' Some in the Court of the Nizam wondered and asked if some *mansub* (service) might not be given to Inayat. With unconcealed surprise the Nizam said: 'Service, to whom? To Inayat?' As if to say: 'What are you saying?' There seemed no apparent justification for that deep regard with which the Nizam treated young Inayat, except that inner recognition he had of him. After that he always spoke of Inayat to his courtiers in terms of great esteem and appreciation. The Nizam named Inayat 'Tansen', after the eminent Tansen, one of the nine jewels of the great Akbar's Court, at the same time placing a magnificent emerald ring upon his finger. Inayat was further rewarded with a purse full of *ashrafis* and from that time he had access to the Nizam's Court.

This incident made Inayat known throughout the whole of India, as the Court of the Nizam was the foremost in the land. The nobility, the Rajas and Nawabs of Hyderabad State then began to invite Inayat to come to their houses, but his loyalty to the Nizam did not allow him to accept any invitation and so he sang to the Nizam solely.

This interview of the Nizam gave Inayat such a heart-revealing idea of the act of God, something about which he could not talk to his friends during his stay in Hyderabad, and he spoke of it to no one but to God; thus to see his desire granted in a brief time, without a single effort on his part, could give belief in God to the greatest unbeliever.

Pondering on this thought, he remembered a thought that he had given to the idea of meeting Nizam, once when nine years old he was looking at a map of India at school, and when he saw Hyderabad on the map, asked about the place and about its ruler of his friend who was sitting next to him; and one moment he had a vision after his speaking then to his friend, of being one day at the Court of the Nizam and in this interview he saw that fulfilled exactly, which he had then seen for one moment.

While here he made many acquaintances. He was the friend of Maulawi Abdul Qadir, the Subedar of Gulbarga and of Maulawi Yusuf Ali Subedar, who was his Murshid's friend. He made acquaintance with Raja Shivaraj Bahadur and his brother Raja Morsi Manoher; he became acquainted with Maulawi Sayyed Hassan Bilgrami, Nawab Imad-ul-Mulk, Nawab Maheboob Yar Jung, Nawab Wazir Jung, Nawab Sultan-ul-Mulk, Maulawi Habib-ud-Din,

Mr. Hydari and many others of the Hyderabad nobility. Maulana Hashmi (Ill. 89) was his great friend and *ustad*, who taught him the Persian and Arabic literature of the ancient Sufis and being a great mystic, recognized in Inayat what other friends of his (Ramyar (Ill. 9) and Hafiz Khan), though his great friends and admirers, were at a loss to understand. But Hashimi knew that something was being prepared in Inayat for the years that were in store for him, which was beyond words or imagination. Through his friendship with Ramyar he came in touch with many Parsis of Secunderabad, of whom many became his pupils in music. He saw Sirdar Dastur Hoshang, the high priest of the Parsis, the most saintly man of the most ancient religion of the Zoroastrians. Dastur was most impressed by what he heard from young Inayat and was most enchanted, not only by the music he brought to him but by the idea that Inayat, who was not of their own religion, rendered their sacred chants into ragas with the same enthusiasm and reverence as he would have his own.

His stay in Hyderabad made Inayat see and appreciate all the good to be found in the Muslim people, especially in manner and personality, also in their dignity and hospitality which is an outcome of the high teachings of the Prophet of Islam,

During his travels throughout India, it often happened that Inayat either saw in a dream or vision, or he felt, that his father was ill or unhappy and he went back home without any sign having been made from there and found his impression true.

Inayat used to wake for night vigils at midnight. Sleep during youth was so overwhelming that it would come upon him as a sympathetic friend, telling him: 'Sleep on, as everybody just now is sleeping; you are young, you have a long time before you to worship, it is cruel indeed to be so hard on yourself. Even God Himself will not be inclined to listen to you at this time of the night.' And his ascetic soul, with the power of determination, would answer: 'Away devil, do not whisper in my ears, I will rise and attend to the service of God.' So he would pass most of the night in night vigils. And at dawn it was too beautiful to go to sleep, after his exaltation that he would receive with the rising of the sun. He used to spend the early morning in singing divine lyrics and so built the foundation for the whole day of spiritual joy.

In Hyderabad, when in solitude, Inayat devoted most of his time to contemplation. He began to feel that the room in which he sat was illuminated and wherever he moved he found a radiant light around him. He first thought it came from somewhere outside, until he was told by a wise friend, that it all came from within, that the light was in every soul, and yet it remained buried; but he who rises up from his grave, experiences his resurrection, and this was the sign, and it was this sign which was the second birth.

Following upon this came a voice which Inayat often heard while asleep: *'Allahu akbar! Allahu akbar!* God is great! God is great!' which awoke him from his sleep. Wondering what it was and what it could mean, Inayat spoke of it to his wise friend, who replied: 'When He calls His servants, He calls them aloud and those hear, the ears of whose heart are open. There is no soul to whom the voice within does not speak, but the pity is that not every soul hears. I am sure that you are one whom a call from within could reach. Further than this I cannot say, for trying to explain more would be like plunging into deep waters; one would lose one's foothold. It is beyond me, I can only advise that the best thing would be to waken when the call comes, and give attention to what follows, as it is the duty of obedient servants to answer the call of the master.' From that day onward Inayat rose from his bed, every time he heard the call, and devoted himself to contemplation. He sat in silence for hours during the night and one day saw with closed eyes a figure rising before him and beheld a most beautiful face. Next day Inayat spoke of his inner experience to his friend, who told him: 'Now you have reached a point where you should look for a Murshid.'

Inayat had never had that idea, for he had always felt the guidance from within every day wakening in his own spirit, which was sometimes most amazing to those around him. And at the same time he was quite willing to give himself into guidance of someone whom he considered his superior. To obey someone, to look up to someone, was Inayat's natural tendency. He begged his friend to be his guide, but the friend said: 'Pray, do not ask me such a thing. I would hold it a privilege to do you service, but if you wish to follow someone as your guide, I will gladly take you to one.'

So one day Inayat went with his friend to the house of Maulawi Umar, who was the cynosure at that moment in the spiritual world of Hyderabad. He welcomed Inayat and his friend cordially, but on being asked if he would undertake to guide Inayat, he said: 'No, I beg your pardon, I cannot imagine taking this young man as my mureed. I regret it very much, but I feel there is someone, whom I do not know, who may be the one for him.' So the search for the guide continued, the guide who was so sorely needed at that period of Inayat's life.

A faqir lived in a village at some distance from Secunderabad and he avoided all those who went to him as adherents so as to bring him publicity. And the manner he adopted to accomplish his object was very amusing; for everyone who went to him, rich or poor, whatever their rank, he insulted to their face. In this way he turned many away from coming to him, but some came in spite of all insults. A friend of Inayat's took Inayat with him when he went, looking forward with curiosity to seeing how he would be treated by the faqir. He did not tell Inayat beforehand about his manner, thinking perhaps he would refuse to go. But when they arrived there, to his very great surprise the faqir acted in a manner quite contrary to his usual custom. He rose from his seat to welcome Inayat and offered him the best place, sitting before him in silence, seeking a silent contact with him. But he treated the man who had taken Inayat there in his usual manner, or with even more insults and the man was much disappointed to find himself in the same position in which he had hoped to see Inayat placed.

In Secunderabad, Inayat was staying in a little bungalow and always had friends about him, who were very fond of him and of his music. One day he sent for a faqir who used to walk through the city with a bag full of money, all of which he would spend for the children and at night none was left. And in the morning he would come again with a bag full of money. The police watched him constantly to see from where he got that money, but they could not find any key to the mystery. In order to shield himself from the glance of many wondering souls, he used to hold a bottle of liquor and a glass in his hand almost all the time. Inayat sent for him, promising to sing before him. It was that which attracted him, and he came. Inayat gave him the best seat in the room and he began to speak. He told everyone in the room things about their lives and every word he said was true. It was more than surprising to everyone present. When he had talked to them all he greeted Inayat with folded hands and said: 'Mahatma, I ask for thy blessing,' and then went his way. This surprised all present still more and Inayat had a hard time clearing away the seriousness which had spread through the atmosphere.

One day they chanced to visit a great sage of Hyderabad, who was a most learned man, Maulana Khair-ul-Mubin. To hear this man preach the Nizam would go and stand with all reverence in any corner where he could find a place. With all his greatness it was the extreme humility of the Maulana which appealed to Inayat very much. When he was told by the friend that Inayat was seeking for guidance in the spiritual path, he said: 'I? I do not deserve that privilege. I am not worthy.' He saw in Inayat's eyes what the latter did not express in words, a feeling of reverence, answering which he said: 'I am your servant, your slave.'

By a most wonderful coincidence he received a telepathic message, whereupon he called a boy to open the door and prepare a seat and turning to his visitors he said: '*Hazrat* (Master) is coming.'

In a moment there appeared, entering in at the door, a personality which seemed as of one who had dropped from heaven and was now gently stepping on the earth, that was not his place. Yet Inayat felt that the face was not unknown to him. On further thought it flashed into his mind that it was the same face which he used to see in his meditation. After the Master had seated himself in the seat prepared for him, he looked at Inayat and it seemed as if he could not take his eyes away from him.

Their glance meeting awakened in an instant, so to speak, an affinity of thousands of years. 'Who is this young man? He attracts my soul very intensely,' said the Master. Maulana said: 'Your Holiness, this young man is a musical genius and is desirous of submitting himself to your most inspiring guidance.' The Master instantly granted the request and initiated Inayat then and there.

Inayat wrote a song to his Murshid, the meaning of which was:

Thou hast my hand, my revered initiator,
Now my pride is in Thy hand.
The heart, my only treasure, I gave Thee,
Now nothing is left with me, I am glad.
The bowl Thou gavest me made me drunken.
Now I ask not for nectar.
As Joseph Thou didst win my heart,
As Christ Thou raisest me from the dead,
As Moses Thou didst give me the Message,
As Muhammad Thou gavest me the bowl,
By Thy favour Inayat hath all he desired,
Hallowed be Thou, Saviour, my Lord.

He sang it to his Murshid, who was very deeply impressed by it. Thereupon he placed his hands upon Inayat's head and blessed him, saying: 'Be thou blessed by the Divine Light and illuminate the beloved ones of Allah.'

Inayat went as often as he could to see his Murshid, who lived at a distance of about seven miles and he regarded his Murshid as one would regard his king. The link between Inayat and his Murshid increased every moment of the day. The Murshid saw in him his life's purpose, to which even Inayat himself was not yet awakened. Neither did his Murshid try to awaken it, except that he prepared him and led him along the road of his destiny in his most gracious way of mercy and compassion. The Murshid was very fond of Inayat, not only for his talent in music, which he much admired, being a great lover of music, but also for the music expressed in his personality, which endeared Inayat to the Murshid more and more every moment.

Inayat used to go and sit in the presence of the Murshid with open heart, as an empty cup, into which might be poured the illuminating words, the intoxicating glance and the uplifting atmosphere with which the whole surroundings of his Murshid were charged.

After his initiation by the hand of his Murshid, Inayat went to the Murshid's house for six months during which not one word was spoken to him by his Murshid on metaphysics. At last Murshid told him about *tanzih* and *tashbih* (transcendence and immanence), also about *wujud* and *shuhud* (manifestation and consciousness) and explained to him the different aspects of these ideas which interested Inayat immensely, for he had a natural inclination towards metaphysics. This was greatly appreciated by his Murshid, who spoke of him to others with pride.

In connection with this, an incident of an amusing nature occurred as for the first time in his life Inayat heard his Murshid's words on metaphysics. He became so keenly interested and filled with enthusiasm about what was being said that he took a notebook from his pocket, intending to take notes of it. But as soon as the Murshid saw the pencil and notebook in his hand, he instantly began to speak of an altogether different subject. Inayat realized by this that his Murshid meant that his words must be engraved on the soul, they were not to be written with a pencil on the pages of a notebook.

He would return home silent and remain speechless for hours, pondering over the words which had fallen upon his ears. His friends began to wonder what could have happened to him in such a short time, that his whole life should be so changed. He had now become quite a different person in his speech, actions, ways, expression, in his attitude and in his atmosphere. In all these, he showed a marked and definite change. It seemed to them as if, while a traveller walking at a certain rate of speed should have journeyed a mile, Inayat had suddenly made such an advance as to cover a hundred miles in the same space of time.

Inayat's singing changed, his voice and the effect that was produced by it showed quite a different charm. The Nizam and his surroundings began to marvel at it, yet not knowing what was the reason. The more they tried to hold him fast, the more he wished to be let loose.

Freedom seeking which was his innate desire, then became awakened and expressed itself in a form of independence which enhanced his dignity while at the Court of Hyderabad. That silent vairagya, which was his very nature, now and then urged him to turn his back upon all that was interesting in worldly life and showed itself in many ways.

The prosperity at the Court of the Nizam did not for a single moment delude Inayat and he had now found something in life which was much greater in comparison with all the stately grandeurs which surrounded him and that was the presence of his Murshid, Sayyed Muhammad Abu Hashim Madani. He had now two sovereigns before him, one the sovereign of the earth, the other the heavenly blessed Master of life, here and in the hereafter. Therefore, his everyday life lessened the importance of earthly grandeur and raised in his eyes the value of spiritual greatness.

Inayat made two visits to Baroda during his stay in Hyderabad to see his father and family there. His father, who always had a great influence on him and who was a very great knower of Inayat's nature, began to feel that something which was told to him by different people at different times was now on the point of springing. He saw that the great energy and spirit of activity was now stilled and calmed down in Inayat's nature and all Inayat said and did moved him so much that once his feelings overcame him and he exclaimed: 'I wish I were young just now to sit by you and receive reverently all you give.' Inayat said: 'Father, you must not say that, you make me abashed.'

Once an orthodox friend of Inayat was visiting his Murshid and told him how very unorthodox Inayat was. He said to the Murshid that he should teach him the ways of the faithful and also their customs and manner of life, for he seemed to know nothing of these things. He said: 'The clothes he wears are not such as we wear, and he scarcely goes to the Mosque. Among his friends are people of other religions, Hindus, Parsis and Christians and Jews, and with them he feels at home. I should have thought that by coming in contact with your Holiness he would have altered, but he seems to be just the same.' Inayat's Murshid said to him: 'While you see the outward person of Inayat, I see his inner being, I cannot very well tell you what Inayat is and what he is to me, except that he is my beloved mureed and I am proud of him.' This answer made the man silent.

Inayat always believed that the greatest and best expression of love and devotion was respect, and to him to give respect was not only to fulfil a duty, but it was an impulse of his soul that, expressed in the form of respect, gave him great joy and satisfaction, and he saw in his Murshid the most deserving among all living beings on this earth. To him, therefore, the right place for the expression of such respect was the presence of his Murshid. One day the Murshid sent him word by a messenger, an old servant of his house, who, when he arrived at Inayat's house, was kept waiting by the gatekeeper, who, considering him of little importance, did not show him to the house. Inayat was seen at a distance coming, but his appearance so impressed the man that he wondered if Inayat would speak to him civilly, even if he would deign to speak at all. But when Inayat drew near he asked the man whence he had come and received the reply: 'From Madani Sahib' (his Murshid). No sooner did Inayat hear the name of his Murshid, than he bowed low and kissed the hands of that Arab, and seemed so moved by the message that no homage appeared to him adequate to express his feelings. The man was so much touched by this unexpected reception, that his feelings overcame him, and the occasion was unforgettable to him.

One day Inayat heard that his Murshid was coming to visit him and this brought him unspeakable joy. He thought out and planned all sorts of ways of giving his Murshid an unparalleled reception. But nothing seemed good enough to satisfy the longing he felt to honour his Murshid. At last an idea occurred to him which pleased him greatly. He thought of standing at a considerable distance from his home awaiting his Murshid's carriage and then keeping step with the horses and running by its side. On the appointed day, however, this was not carried out, as his Murshid had chosen to come by a different road from what Inayat had expected.

Inayat always remembered the words his Murshid said: 'There are many ties which make people friends in this world, but there is one tie which is the closest of all and that is the relation between Murshid and mureed, which is a friendship that never ends, for it is in the path of God and Truth and is eternal.'

The Murshid was fond of music to an unusual degree and greatly enjoyed Inayat's proficiency in music. As his heart was that of the true Chishti, which constantly longs to hear music, his feelings were always deeply stirred whenever he heard Inayat sing.

For this reason many times he denied himself the pleasure, for he took every means to avoid exposing his emotion before others. But with all the great longing he had to hear some music from Inayat, he would never ask him to sing to him, for even that he deemed to be too much of the nature of a command or an intrusion upon Inayat's free will, although he knew that nothing would give Inayat greater pleasure than to carry out his Murshid's orders and especially to bring him some joy by his music. When he felt a very great longing to hear music, on seeing Inayat he would only say: 'Please tell me about that raga, what are the notes in it?' Then Inayat would know that his Murshid desired to hear music and he would begin to sing in illustration of his explanation. Murshid would be filled with spiritual joy, which is called *hal* (ecstasy).

The Murshid was an ascetic within, but a man of the world without. He had a large family, sons and daughters, and a home where love and culture reigned, and which was always hospitably thrown open to all comers. He used to dress simply, in white muslin garments and sometimes wore a pale yellow turban, which would blend nicely with his white beard. He had a most beautiful, venerable appearance with commanding, lustrous eyes and a spiritual expression radiating wherever he went a heavenly atmosphere.

He used to wear shoes embroidered with gold. One day, when Inayat's eyes strayed to these shoes, a thought arose in his mind: why Murshid with all his simplicity should wear such costly shoes? At once his conscience pricked him, he felt so guilty that such a thought of one who was above question should have entered his mind, that instantly his face turned pale. But the Murshid knew all about it and only said with a smile: 'The wealth of this earth is only worth being at my feet.'

At whatever distance Inayat might be, he would feel his Murshid's call and would immediately respond to it.

Most frequently it happened that on arriving at the Murshid's house, someone among the servants or the members of the family would say: 'Today Murshid wanted you, he spoke about you, he was expecting to see you.' On coming into the presence of the Murshid he found that he was already expected there, and this was the greatest proof to both that this was the living link established between them. All telephones, telegraphs and the invention of wireless telegraphy seemed superfluous with this realization.

Another most wonderful thing that was vouchsafed to Inayat was that all he had thought during the week, or as he journeyed to see his Murshid, or whilst sitting in his presence, came out in some way or other in the course of conversation on the part of Murshid and all problems were solved without Inayat having to ask about anything. Inayat found that words were not necessary, the presence of the Murshid was itself light which illuminated the minds of those in his presence. All that seemed difficult and obscure became simple and most clear. It seemed as if all were known to him, yet veiled from his eyes and that all became unveiled in the presence of his Murshid.

One day, Inayat was both amused and embarrassed, when his Murshid told him that he might leave. Inayat had been thinking of taking leave earlier than usual in order to call on some friends and yet he was most reluctant to tear himself away. But the Murshid had read his thought and at once granted the unspoken request.

His Murshid used to bless him at the time of departing, saying: 'May God strengthen your faith.' At that moment he did not realize the full value of it. The realization of this came to him afterwards, namely that once faith is developed in man, all he wishes is granted.

One day, when the Murshid was nearing the end of his earthly life, he became rather unwell. It was a heavy burden of sorrow for Inayat to bear, with all his tenderness and sympathy and devotion he had for his Murshid.

When in his presence a thought came to Inayat: 'Why even to such exalted beings illness should come?' The moment the thought came, Inayat held his tongue between his teeth thinking it sacrilege to hold such a thought, regarding his Murshid whom he revered most in the world. Murshid saw from his eyes and expression the trend of his question and immediately answered: 'Bandagi becharagi,' which means: 'Life on earth is poor, subject to nature's laws.' It was so touching and so true. Then he quoted a Hindustani verse: 'Aish to hamne kiya tha ab musibat pai kaun,' meaning: 'If man shall experience only pleasure, who is left to experience the pain?'

This last illness showed in every stage of its development that the Murshid was nearing the end of his life on this earth. This gnawed into the very heart of Inayat, and yet it was a marvel to him to see someone with a human body able to bear all pain with such fortitude and patience. There was not one moment when Murshid was unconscious of his spiritual realization. Everything he said and did, every move he made, even the atmosphere there, all showed that although God is All-pervading, yet there He made His special abode. One could hear from every corner of the house the name of God, and feel in the presence of Murshid the presence of God.

The day of which he had told his wife six months before, when Murshid was to depart, arrived. He, on that day, asked all who were near to come to him and said to them a word of consolation and advice. He next asked for the servants in the house, to bid them farewell and asked all those around him if ever he had spoken a word, or committed a deed that was hurtful and asked forgiveness of them. Then he prayed for all, gave them blessing and begged to be left alone in the room, where he continued his *Zikr* and through the same *Zikr* he passed from this life of limitation to the sphere of freedom.

To Inayat the passing of his Murshid left an aching void, which nothing on this earth could ever fill. Receiving visits from friends became irksome and all things in life distasteful. The Court of the Nizam with all its grandeur no longer had any attraction for Inayat. The association with Maharaja Kishan Pershad and his poetical surroundings no longer drew him. The fertile soil of Hyderabad was to him now a barren desert. The old craving, which from childhood had possessed him, that desire for solitude and the renunciation of all worldly life revived. Therefore, without saying one word to anyone at the Court, he went away.

Now, instead of going home to Baroda, which had no more any call for him, he started on a pilgrimage to the holy men of India. First, he went to the tomb of Bandanawaz at Gulbarga and from there a three days' journey in a bullock cart to the temple of Manek Prabhu, the great Guru of the Brahmans, whither many went to worship.

When travelling in a bullock cart from Gulbarga to Manekpur, Inayat had a most wonderful experience. In that region none would travel during the day, owing to the strong sun. All travellers therefore, journeyed by night, in small caravans. At this time Inayat travelled with the smallest caravan, consisting of only three bullock carts, the last of which conveyed him. The people in the caravan said there was great danger from robbers on the path, who would not hesitate to deprive one of every scrap of clothing, besides all else they could lay hands on. He was not in the least perturbed by this warning, but kept awake, lest he might encounter the danger unawares. As the night passed and while darkness still prevailed, a misty figure arose, which became more and more concrete to his view. The figure walked by the side of the cart, holding a staff in his hand as he went. It seemed as if someone had taken charge of the cart and was walking along with it, to guard and guide it.

Inayat's heart almost burst within him when he saw this misty figure develop into the form of his Murshid. His gratitude was boundless, and this vision brought him the fullness of trust he had in the idea, which he had always believed, that Murshid was always with his sincere devotee and at any time of difficulty even more. This gave the heart of Inayat peace. Drowsiness now to some extent overcame him and he fell into a light slumber. A loud shouting suddenly aroused him, and he became aware of a great horror spread throughout the caravan. 'What is the matter?' he asked of the driver of the cart. 'Robbers have come and robbed those two wagons in front, but they have left our wagon unmolested,' he was told. Here was the proof and the result of the vision Inayat had just seen; for there was every reason that the first and last carts should be attacked and that the middle cart should escape, if any did, since it was protected by the other two. Instead of that it was Inayat's cart that was left untouched.

The people, whose duty it was to receive the guests, owing to their caste distinction gave Inayat a room near the stable, a place swarming with insects and above which was a *roshan chauki* where a band of musicians played at intervals of three hours, both day and night, their flutes making the most screeching sounds, accompanied by the noise of drums. Inayat waited with patience the pleasure of seeing the Guru, and did not in the least mind where he was put. On the contrary, he was happy to have been so cast away, for he was spared the notice of others and joyfully accepted the noise of the band, as an alarm to rouse him from sleep for his night vigils. One day, after a morning's bath in the river, Inayat was returning to his lodging, when he chanced to see the son of the Guru looking out from his verandah. His eyes fell on Inayat and no sooner did their glance meet, then the young man felt instinctively drawn to him and sent for him. Inayat went to see him, the one who was so adored by the followers of Manek Prabhu. As he saw Inayat, he rose from his seat, offered it to him and apologized for having intruded upon his time, but said that he had felt drawn to him and desired much to know him. 'What has brought you here?' said he and Inayat replied: 'I have heard that the home of Manek Prabhu is not only a religious temple, but a centre of music also and as I have taken this tour to pay homage to the holy men living on the soil of India, I first chose to visit this place.' 'But I am very surprised that you have chosen our place, instead of choosing the place of some Muslim Saint,' remarked the astonished youth. To this Inayat replied: 'Muslim or Hindu are only outward distinctions, the Truth is one, God is one, life is one. To me there is no such thing as two. Two is only one plus one.' This reply struck a chord in the heart of the Guru's son, which vibrated through his whole being. He asked Inayat to speak further of his belief, but Inayat replied that he had no such belief that could be distinguished as his own belief; he believed in all that was true and saw everywhere the immanence of Truth. The Guru's son was greatly impressed by all Inayat had to say and asked if he might know his name. On Inayat's telling him his name, the young man said: 'The other day I read in the newspaper of your having been highly rewarded by the Nizam' 'Yes,' replied Inayat simply. 'Who would have thought of your coming here to our remote temple?' exclaimed the astonished youth. Inayat replied: 'For me the temple has much more attraction than a palace.' The Guru's son could not forgive those in charge for having relegated Inayat to the background; his face paled and he became greatly abashed. He said: 'Will you please wait a while, I will go and speak to my father, the Guru.' With sadness in his tone Inayat replied: 'Now you have taken from me my shield; I was most happy at the way I was received. My blessing would have been ten times greater if no one had known who I was, or from whence I had come. If I had only seen your revered father and asked in silence for his blessing.' The youth was so touched by all that he heard from Inayat that he could not wait one moment longer without telling his father of his extraordinary visitor. On hearing from his son, the Guru became most interested and was filled with curiosity to see Inayat. At last they met and he at once asked Inayat the purpose of his coming. Inayat said: 'When I had the presence of my Murshid on this physical plane, I was most happy with my privilege; since he has passed from this world I have taken this tour to see his image in various forms and especially to recognize his countenance in the faces of the holy ones'. The Guru then told Inayat that he had a great respect for the Sufis and was most interested in Sufism and the proof of this interest was that he had kept the flagstaff of Khwaja Abdul Qadir Jilani, the great Saint. 'But,' he said: 'I should like to know something more of the Sufis and Sufism.' Inayat said: 'Call it Sufism or Vedantism, it is the one and only Truth, perhaps given in different forms, but as it all comes from one source, it cannot be different, it is all the same.' The Guru was extremely struck with this idea and by the sincerity with which Inayat had expressed his broad outlook. He went on to say: 'There seems to be one small difference and that is, there is so much spoken about reincarnation in our faith, but no Sufi seems to have expounded that idea: one would have thought they had never grasped the idea and therefore that accounted for its absence from Sufi writings and yet I cannot understand how such great and perfect beings as are among Sufis, known and recognized by the spiritual world, could not understand this idea which is known by us all, young and old alike. Will you please tell me if there exists among Sufis any belief on the subject?' 'There is,' answered Inayat, 'it is known to Sufis as *tanasukh*, meaning reincarnation. But the principal thing for a Sufi is to deny his limited personality and to affirm the sole existence of God, that the false ego, which is subject to births and deaths, may fade away and the true ego, which is the divine hidden in man, may rise and discover itself. In this lies the fulfilment of the main object of the creation. The Sufi thinks that what is past and unknown to him is of little use for him; what is coming and not known is an unnecessary worry for the present time. He thinks that all that is important is 'just now' and if this 'just now' is made to be as he wishes it to be, he desires nothing better. Among the Hindus,' continued Inayat, 'the belief of reincarnation is prevalent, and they make the most of it. Yet the greatest principle of the Vedanta, from which all different beliefs of Hindus are derived, is *Advaita* that means 'no duality', in other words 'unity'. May I, therefore ask if this principal teaching of the Vedanta is better promulgated by belief in the doctrine of reincarnation, or by leaving it alone?' The Guru was speechless and saw the truth in Inayat's argument. Proceeding further in his conversation with the Guru, Inayat said: '*Mukti* (liberation) is the ideal of life; it is the rising above the various births and deaths, rather than being involved in the eternal wheel of births and deaths, which is continually running by the ever-changing battery of *karma* (action).' The Guru was deeply impressed by all that fell from Inayat's lips and showed his appreciation by bestowing on him an apricot-hued shawl, a sign of great distinction, and then he blessed Inayat. In apt terms Inayat expressed his deep gratitude to the Guru for his kind and benign reception.

When returning in the waggon, Inayat had another very wonderful experience. It so happened that, having kept watch during the greater part of the night, drowsiness overcame him. He began to nod and during that little sleep he had a dream. He thought a robber came and thrust his hand into the cart, but before the robber could take anything, he rushed at him and the man fled empty-handed. While actually dreaming this, a robber was at that moment searching the waggon to see what was worth taking. Instantly the driver shouted and Inayat awoke and rushed at the man, who fled immediately. Inayat pursued him till he was lost to view. His fleeing was profitless, for Inayat had no intention of punishing him, he only wanted him to understand.

On arriving at the tomb of Bandanawaz, at Gulbarga, the weariness of the night's journey, with the attendant excitement on the way, had given Inayat fever; and it came at that time when the plague was prevalent in India and preventive measures were being taken to suppress it. Some doctors, through fear that the plague might spread, deliberately put an end to the lives of many people, who showed only the slightest sign of the plague. A medical inspection awaited Inayat, but an hour before the inspection he paid a visit to the tomb of Bandanawaz, rubbing the dust at the gate of the tomb on his forehead. His faith was so great that the dust, like the white powder of the alchemists, healed him instantly. When he came out from the tomb, he was as fresh, healthy and energetic as ever before. To the ordinary mind this incident was merely imagination, but to the faith of Inayat it was a miracle.

He broke his journey at Baroda, where all his family was impressed by the great change that had come to his personality. For he had risen, so to speak, not above the desire of acquiring wealth, for that had never been in his nature, but he seemed to be above the desire of power or position, or anything belonging to this world. His tranquillity was a proof of the stillness of his mind and the way that he won the affection of all who came to meet him, of his friends and his relations, and joined the broken threads, showed to all at home the seedling of something, the promise of which they had partly recognized in him in his childhood. It was then that the people of Baroda offered him an address and a medal.

On his way to Ajmer he visited the place of pilgrimage of Miran Datar, to which the sick and obsessed go from all parts of the country to be cured. There he saw how many illnesses are of the spirit rather than of the mind, and how little is known to the physician of such illnesses and that these diseases can only be cured by one of exalted spirit. Besides, it gave him proof that he who dies before death, and so becomes spiritual, certainly lives after the death of his mortal self. He went to see the people there and spoke to them, discovering their different complaints and seeing how they were spiritually healed. It was a most marvellous experience for him to find himself among thousands of obsessed people, showing their disease in different forms. Any impressionable person would certainly lose his mind, if he were in these surroundings, constantly seeing the obsessed. This helped Inayat very much in his natural gift of analysis of human life and character.

From there he went to Ajmer and visited the tomb of Khwaja Moinuddin Chishti, the most celebrated Sufi Saint of India. The atmosphere of his last resting place was within itself a phenomenon; a sense of peace and calm pervaded it and among all that throng of pilgrims he yet felt as if he were the only one present. At nightfall he went home and said *tahajjud*, the midnight prayer. And lo! at the end of his prayers there came to him a voice, as though in answer to his invocations. It was the voice of a faqir, calling the people to prayer before sunrise, and he sang: 'Awake, o man, from thy fast sleep! Thou knowest not that death watcheth thee every moment. Thou canst not imagine how great a load thou hast gathered to carry on thy shoulders and how long the journey is yet for thee to accomplish. Up! Up! The night is passed, and the sun will soon arise!' The unearthly quiet of the hour and the solemnity of the song moved Inayat to tears. Sitting on his rug with a rosary in his hand, he reflected that all the proficiency and reputation which he had achieved were utterly profitless in regard to his *najat* or salvation. He recognized that the world was neither a stage set up for our amusement, nor a bazaar to satisfy our vanity and hunger, but a school, wherein to learn a hard lesson. He then chose quite a different path to the track which he had followed until then, in other words he turned over a new page in his life. The morning broke and the birds commenced their hymn of praise to Allah. Inayat heard men and women pass by below, some going to the mosque, others to the temples and the general masses to the toil that yields the daily bread. Then he too fared forth and lost in his thought, not knowing his destination, made his way towards the jungle.

He had an inner yearning to be apart from the world, and give an outlet to the thoughts and emotions wherewith his mind was so occupied. He arrived at a cemetery where a group of dervishes sat on the green grass, chattering together. They were all poorly clad, some were without shoes and others without coats, one had a shirt with only one sleeve and another lacked them both. One wore a robe with a thousand patches and the next a hat without a crown. This strange group attracted Inayat's attention and he sat there for a time, noticing all that was passing, while yet feigning to be utterly indifferent. Presently their Pir-o-Murshid or Master came towards them, even more scantily clad than they and with a group of dervishes circling round him as he approached. Two of the latter led the odd procession and with each step they cried out loudly: '*Hosh dar dam, nazr bar qadm, khilwat dar anjuman!*': 'Be conscious of your breath and watch every step you take and thus experience solitude in the crowd!' When the Murshid arrived at the assembly of his disciples, each one greeted the other, saying: '*Ishq Allah, Mahbub Allah!*': 'God is Love, and God is Beloved.' It was this very greeting which later unveiled to Inayat the Bible words that: 'God is Love' and also the verse of the Arabian poet Abu'l-Ala, who sayeth:

> A church, a temple or a Kaaba stone,
> Qur'an or Bible or a martyr's bone,
> All these and more my heart can tolerate,
> Since my religion now is love alone.

The solemnity of the sacred words they uttered, found their echo in Inayat's soul and thereupon he watched their ceremonial with still greater attention. Naturally at first sight their dire poverty was puzzling, but then he had learned ere he saw them how the holy Prophet had ever prayed to Allah to sustain him in his life among the *miskin* or dervishes, who voluntarily choose this humble way of living. The queer patches on their garments reminded him of the words of Hafiz: 'Do not befool thyself by short sleeves full of patches, for most powerful arms are hidden under them.' The dervishes first sat lost in contemplation, reciting charms one after the other, and then they began their music. Inayat forgot all his science and technique while listening to their simple melodies as they sang to the accompaniment of Sitar and Dholuk, the deathless words of the Sufi Masters such as Rumi, Jami, Hafiz and Shams Tabriz. The rhapsody which their ecstasies conjured up, seemed to him so strong and vital, that the very leaves of the trees seemed to hang spellbound and motionless. Although their emotions manifested themselves in various forms, they were regarded with silent reverence by all that strange company. Each one of them revealed a peculiar mood of ecstasy; some expressed it in tears and others in sighs, some in dances and yet others in the calm of meditation. Although Inayat did not enjoy the music as much as they, still it impressed him so deeply that he felt as if he were lost in a trance of harmony and happiness. But the most amazing part of the proceedings came when the assembly was about to disperse. For one of the dervishes arose and while announcing *bhandara*, or dinner, addressed them in the following terms: 'O Kings of Kings, O Emperors of Emperors!' This amused Inayat greatly at the time, while he regarded their outward appearance. His first thought made them merely kings of imagination, without throne or crown, treasury, courtiers, or dominions, those natural possessions and temporal powers of kingship. But the more he brooded upon the matter, the more he questioned whether the environment or the imagination made a king. The answer came at last: the king is never conscious of his kingship and all its attributes of luxury and might unless his imagination is reflected in them and thus proves his true sovereignty. For instance, if a baby were crowned and seated upon a throne, he would never comprehend his high position until his mind evolved sufficiently to realize his surroundings. This shows how real our surroundings seem to us and yet how dead they are in the absence of imagination. And it also reveals how the fleeting of time and the changes of matter make all the kings of the earth but transitory kings, ruling over transitory kingdoms, owing to their dependence upon their environment, instead of their imagination. But the kingship of the dervish, independent from all external influence, purely based on his mental perception and strengthened by the forces of the will, is much truer and at once unlimited and everlasting. Yet to the materialistic view his kingdom would appear as nothing, while to the spiritual conception it is an immortal and exquisite realm of joy. Thus Inayat compared our deluded life with their real life and our artificial being with their natural being, as one might compare the false dawn to the true. He realized our folly of attaching undue weight to matters wholly unimportant and how apt we are to laugh at the dreamer, building his lovely castles in the air. He saw how our momentary affairs are blown about as chaff is blown in the wind, while the imagination is difficult to alter. 'It is possible for the land to turn into water and for water to turn into land, but the impression of an imagination can never change.'

Inayat thought: 'Now, what shall I do next? Shall I become a dervish and live

Photograph 2. Playing the Jalatarang, Baroda, India c. 1898

on the alms offered to me? If I did so,' he thought, 'I would only be a burden on those who earn their livelihood.' He thought, 'If I went to earn my livelihood in the world and sold my music for money, it would be worse than slavery; besides it would be throwing pearls before swine.' To see the music and his profession so badly treated by the rich in his country, wounded his heart. He thought that the best use he could make of this wound was to try to raise, by his independent spirit, the music of India to its pristine glory.

While on his pilgrimage to the saints of India, he made up his mind that he would live the life of an adept, hidden in the guise of a musician, and live such a simple life that with very little money he could live and give most of his time to giving lectures on music, illustrated by his singing and playing, and by that, raising the idea of music in the heart of his people.

People were surprised to know of a musician's using his music only for the sake of art and not for any material benefit. Those who had the greatest contempt for the art of music and for the artists began, by one interview, to look upon the art of music from quite a different point of view.

Inayat, always attracted by the South of India, started on a tour from Madras, where he was received by the Prince of Arcot. He became a friend of Chitti Babu, a great admirer of Indian music, who gave him a decoration. He gave a musical performance at the Cosmopolitan Club, where his melodious voice and scientific singing were highly appreciated. He made the acquaintance of Ghulam Mahmud Khan and of Nawab Sayyed Muhammad, of Sultan Muhidin, of Habibuddin, of Tiruswam Hayra Naidu, who all showed much esteem for his singing. He met there a great musician of the South, Trikuti Kavel Krishna Ayar, a violinist of great repute, who was called the king of rhythm. Seeing that Inayat was so young, he first took no notice of him. But on hearing Inayat, the musician was so moved that he came and embraced him after his singing as Inayat got up from his chair and when he knew of Inayat's mission and his ideal, he felt very much drawn to him.

Inayat wished to visit Mysore once again, but this time his purpose was quite different. There was something drawing him toward it which he himself did not know.

While travelling, he met in the train Captain Baker, Ali Khan by name. They became great friends and Inayat was this man's guest in Mysore. At that time many musicians from all countries had assembled at the Court. It was during the festival of Dasei, during which he had the opportunity of hearing a great many musicians, among them Sheshena, the great vina player. Inayat saw the Maharaja once again and saw how the conventionalities of the monarchies make the Rajas stiff as statues. They are no longer Rajas but statues. One can hardly find in them a trace of living personality. It seems as if they were in their grave. He thought: 'Although the Rajas have kept alive the flame of India's best music, still the very source is a cause of the downfall of the art. For music, which is a celestial art, is made by the great artists of the country an offering to merriment.'

He spoke in public on that subject, on the condition of Indian music and

Photograph 3. Madras, India c. 1902

his talent was marvelled at and highly esteemed and expression was given to this in the address that was presented to him by the citizens of Mysore, together with a gold medal.

But Inayat discovered that that was not the cause why he had been sent to Mysore. He met Pir Jemat Ali Shah, a Sufi sage, travelling at that time in that country. No sooner they saw each other, than they became most drawn to each other. Inayat visited his dwelling every day and the sage felt more and more drawn to Inayat every day. Thousands of people were interested in his call and followed him, but it was to Inayat alone that the sage was drawn. So the purpose of the visit to Mysore manifested.

Inayat went to Bangalore[20], which is not far from Mysore. The influence of the sage stimulated in him that Sufi feeling which was the main joy of his life. A public concert had been arranged. Those who were to accompany him in his singing and playing were not there at the appointed time. He found later that, after taking a little draught of liquor, his accompanists, instead of going to the concert hall, perhaps went home. He was glad for them, but sorry on his own account and still more sorry for the audience, then anxiously awaiting. It was already late, but Inayat's coming and the lecture he gave, picturing the music and the musicians of India, impressed the audience very much and then he sang without accompanist, keeping the chord on the tambura, so that it ended in the whole audience being spellbound. The audience presented him with an address and a gold medal.

However, the times when he sang at home were much greater and more wonderful as compared with the public performances. He used to practise singing after sunset, this being his service and devotion. Friends used to come and would feel exalted, for often during his singing he used to rise to the state of *wajd*.

A pedlar, who also used to come, thinking that he might not be allowed to sit in the house, was wont to stand behind a tree in the courtyard, fearing that he might be driven away. And he attended Inayat's music regularly. One day a friend saw him in the courtyard and told Inayat of him. Inayat said: 'Let him come in.' When he came in, Inayat saw him full of ecstasy and the light that was shining in his eyes proved him to be a Master. He sat there silent and listened to the song through ecstasy. He then held Inayat's hands, kissed them and pressed them to his eyes and said: 'I have ever longed to meet you in the flesh and now my sympathies are with you. I know you and I know what you will have to go through, but be sure that the sympathy of my heart will follow you wherever you go.' Then they took a warm farewell of one another and all present were deeply impressed but could not in the least understand what it was all about.

Here in Bangalore he met a real Sufi, a sage to whom all religions were nothing but different paths to God, whose eyes were inspiring, whose atmos-

---

20. Now known as Bengaluru, this is not further noted

Photograph 4. Hyderabad, India c.1905

phere was uplifting, love gushing from his heart at every moment of the day. Once he had begun his preaching, crowds of people, Hindus or Muslims, whatever their castes, would flock around him and sit listening to his words, even if he spoke the whole night. Inayat went to pay him a visit and was very much struck by his great power and piety. As a rule, he always attracted sages. This sage also instantly became his friend. 'In this,' said Inayat, 'the purpose of my coming to Bangalore is fulfilled.'

At the request of Trikuti Kavel Krishna Ayar, Inayat went to Kumbakonam, a town which is the home of the Karnatic musicians, where none but expert musicians dared to sing, for the audience was extremely critical and consisted chiefly of musicians. And once a musician had passed his examination there, he was welcomed everywhere in the South. Besides making impression upon his audience in this town by his execution of both Hindustani and Karnatic music, Inayat spoke before them of what was needed for the revival of the art of music in India, giving them the example how in the Western world music advanced with the continual progress there; and this won for him the greatest admiration.

How like attracts like was seen in the life of Inayat continually. When in Kumbakonam no Brahman would give room to anyone who was not of his caste. This awakened Inayat in unhappy wise to the cause of India's degeneration, which is caste distinction. For him it was most painful to find that he could not be taken as a brother by his own countrymen. He pitied those who are considered pariahs, the classes who are not touched, and thought what a dreadful thing it is to be for generations in a caste which is looked down upon as not fit to touch. Inayat, in whom respect for the human being was the chief sentiment and held by him as his religion, felt sore at heart and yet self-pity was ever the last thing he would allow to make him miserable and so looking at the same from Brahmanic point of view, he soon got over that feeling. In the end he came to a house of a Cholia, whose mind had never been touched by art or science, only absorbed in his business, who had only a shed to offer him, far from the town and not fit even for cows to live in. Inayat went and as was his habit, made the most of what he had. And as the holes in the ground were many and he could not very well sleep there comfortably, he watched and passed the night in meditation. Before dawn, he heard a voice speaking to him: '*Salam aleikum!*' 'Good morning!' Inayat opened his eyes and looked to see who was there and saw that it was a dervish. The dervish said: '*Subhan Allah!*' 'Hail to God!' 'How much I have enjoyed your nightlong vigil, beautiful, beautiful! You are certainly blessed.' Inayat asked him how he happened to come there. The dervish said: 'I have taken shelter under this roof from storm and wind and come and spend my nights here for twenty years.' Inayat thought in his mind: 'Here was I trying to endure this one night's trial and the true lovers of God do not feel it a trial after having passed twenty years under this roof.' He saw to what degree in the search of Truth one has to journey through the path of continual endurance and found that after all

Photograph 5. India c.1910

that strain on his patience he had not gone very far along that road.

Inayat went from there to Negapatam, to do homage at the tomb of a great saint at Nagore. He was the guest of a friend there, Qutbuddin and there he saw how this saint, who had then passed away, had inspired the community of Cholias, living in that province, in the development of their commercial and industrial qualities, so that a community so backward as that had been, had become the wealthiest and most advanced, so as to represent the prosperity of Sumatra. He realized by this that spiritual culture is the yeast which has come down for ages and will always inspire mankind to reach perfection in every direction of life.

He went from there to Tanjore and was received as a guest in the old royal house. The young Raja Shivaji Rao and the Dewan and the Queen Mother were all impressed at seeing a young artist in a musician's garb, but with a kingly spirit, who passed three days with them. To Inayat this was another experience of the human race, to see the beauty of an aristocratic family, with their traditions and culture, albeit worn out, that fineness, that gentleness, modesty, that gracious manner they showed, which proved their aristocracy much more than did their palaces and stately environments.

Inayat was happy to visit Tanjore, this well-known centre of music in the South of India, where lived most of the celebrated musicians of Karnatic. With his tender feeling toward them and their work, he walked gently, with reverence on the land of Tanjore and admired all the little tokens of their work to be seen there. He sang at the Tanjore Union Club and the citizens of Tanjore gave him a manuscript address, signed by the best professional musicians, to show their gratification.

He proceeded next to Trichinapoli and was received there by Sayyed Mustapha Khan Bahadur, who had devoted his life to the education of the poor orphans among his people and showed the example of a true worker for humanity. Not only did Inayat by his music and personality win his heart, but he awakened in Inayat the virtue that lies in the service of one's fellowmen. Inayat began to see that it is not enough to make oneself spiritual, for that is of no benefit or perhaps little benefit to others. It is not the flower, it is the fruit which is most useful. The people of Trichinapoli gave Inayat warm welcome and read an address in an open meeting to welcome their talented guest.

From there he went to Madura, a place well-known for its ancient temples. Moving about in the town, going from one temple to another, he thought: 'Is it idolatry or is it something else?' In every temple he visited, he felt that he was in the house of God and these temples, with their carved pillars and engraved walls and their thousand idols, became for him sacred scriptures. As he walked alone from one temple to another, his mind pondered upon the meaning of all that he saw. He felt that these temples were nothing other than an education in human life and nature, given to the unlettered man of the past and this was so clear to Inayat's sight, that every symbol suggested

Photograph 6. India c.1910

to him a meaning, as every sound of music always held some significance for him.

He entertained the members of the Union Club and sang at the Theosophical Society, whose members wished him success in his tour round the world.

From there he went on to Coimbatore, where he was received by the Anjuman Islam. It made him happy to think how the Muslims of this part of the world were awakening for the betterment of their race, how a new consciousness was coming to the Muslim people, which was making them more united and more progressive. Inayat's talent was very much appreciated and welcomed there, he was presented with a gold medal and an address was read to him.

He looked forward to visiting Malabar, of which he had heard all his life. On visiting that region, he saw that it was quite a different India, and felt it was a place first inhabited by the Aryans, who chose it, not for worldly life, but solely for a meditative life. The simplicity of the women's clothing gave him the idea how nature's beauty shines out in its most glorious form when it is not crushed by the artificiality of human attire and how much less toil and expense there is when one lives quite a natural life.

The watery land of Cochin, with little islands here and there, where people visited their neighbour's house in tiny boats, was very interesting and enjoyable for Inayat. The travelling by boat through the moonlight nights of the summer months, green before the eyes, right and left, occasionally stopping at a village of ten or twenty houses, where the coconut milk and some fruits of the forest were brought by the peasants to sell to those travelling in the boats; this all, the sight of nature, was once again a vision of paradise to Inayat, as he had once before experienced it on his journey to Nepal.

He was very much appreciated in Ernakulam. He made the acquaintance of Pattabhirame Ran, who was struck by his sweet voice.

He went to Trichur and gave a performance to the great satisfaction of the people there.

From Ernakulam he took a boat to row across the narrow stream of water to Travancore, where he was received by Raja Kopal Chari, the Dewan of the State and he was there a state guest. He gave a recital of vocal music at the Maharaja's College, where everyone was delighted and enjoyed listening to his music. He had an interview with the Maharaja and after a conversation with him Inayat felt how the princes and potentates of India, upon whom depends the welfare of the country, are unaware of the progress of the world in general, absorbed only in their little narrow groove and conscious of their little kingship. He thought it was a great misfortune for the land. The presence of Inayat overpowered the Maharaja; he could not very well make out what Inayat was striving after, and yet he could not help feeling regard for someone who had dedicated his youth to the upliftment of the music of India. Raja Kopal Chari, the wise Dewan, was much impressed by Inayat, to whom he presented a gold medal in remembrance of the place and his visit there.

Inayat then for the first time in his life sailed from Tuticorin to Ceylon[21], again quite another India, unlike the Central India or the North. Among the people there, he found Singhalese, who have some idea of Southern Indian music and among Muslims, Markias, who only know that there exists some such thing as music somewhere, but most restricted by their faith and afraid to go where there was a danger of hearing music. He made the acquaintance of Mahamudalyar Bhandara Nayak of Colombo and of Haji Muhammad Macan Markar, the Consul for Turkey and was a guest of Jelaluddin Markia and made acquaintance with the younger Muslims, who were trying hard to come out of their old restrictions and who besides their appreciation of Inayat as a musician found in him a young reformer. They enjoyed his music and his personality. Inayat visited Kandy and Nuralja. In Kandy he had taken a room and during the hours of his meditation in the evening, whilst he was engaged in the sacred practices, he felt very restless and wrathful and he could not fix his mind on his meditation for a single moment. He became cross with himself and went to bed. The uneasiness increased still more. Then he got up and wanted to look in the cupboards. He did not know why he was doing so. He thought perhaps his inner self wanted to guide him to the reason of such an unusual experience with himself. He found there, to his surprise, a bunch of black hair, looking as if some woman had collected combings of hair there for a long time. He spent a bad night and in the morning the first thing he did was to ask the landlady who had lived in this room before him. She said: 'Sir, don't remind me of her. The thought of her takes my breath out of me. A woman lived here for some time. She never paid me rent, called me bad names, fought with the men and quarrelled every day without fail, driving away every other tenant who came to live in this house. Now my heart is at rest since she has left this house.' Inayat said: 'What a shame that you gave me such a room to live in.' She said: 'Sir, I gave you that room on purpose, because you seem from your looks to be a godly man, so that I was sure that this room will be purified by your good influence.' Inayat had no answer for her but a smile.

What impressed Inayat in Ceylon was nature rather than personalities, but his respect for human nature made him take all things patiently.

After a short stay there, he took ship for Burma[22] and was most delighted to arrive at Rangoon. He found the people of Burma quite unlike his countrymen, both in appearance and nature and yet he was impressed by them. What appealed to him in them was the simplicity of the Burmese nature. Their womenfolk, as busy as the men, perhaps more occupied in business and in the affairs outside their home. Generous and humble as he found them to be, he saw in the life of Burmese his ideal of human brotherhood. For they consider no-one, whatever be his faith or belief, in any way inferior to themselves. They celebrate their weddings silently and funerals grandly,

---

21. Now known as Sri Lanka, this is not further noted
22. Now known as Myanmar, this is not further noted

especially those of the spiritual persons, in that way recognizing the spiritual individuality and the eternal life of the spiritual soul. They go to the temple of Buddha with their simple devotion, with no pride of religion and with no desire to force their belief on others. Inayat pondered upon the subject and felt what is it in these harmless souls that has kept them behind what is called civilization? And the answer came: they are over-civilized, so the others cannot understand them.

In Rangoon there are so many rich merchants who, hearing of Inayat's fame and his talent, asked him to sing at their houses to their friends. Inayat, as always sacrificing his material gains for the upraising of the dignity of the art of music in his land, refused. Very often it was very hard for him to subsist; yet he would rather starve than sell his art for money.

Once a servant boy in the house took away every penny that Inayat had in his box. In the morning Inayat dreamed, before getting up, that every penny that was in the box had been stolen by somebody. When he got up he saw the trunk actually open and to his great horror, when he went near, he saw that there was nothing in it. He asked the servant what had happened, and the servant denied all knowledge. After that Inayat went without food for days together, meeting with his rich friends who took him for a drive in the carriages and who would have been only too glad to have sent him the needed money. In the end that servant who had taken the money, felt so sorry for him that he offered to lend him some money for food, but Inayat would not accept anything from him. After three days of this fasting and at the same time meeting his friends with a smiling face, the servant on the fourth day gave him back all he had taken.

Inayat went to one wealthy man, only when he could not help going, to a man in Rangoon, called Masiti, who was the head of all gambling and drinking that went on in the town and who had made so much money that he had even the police under his orders. He was almost the uncrowned king of that place, under whose direction all the murders and thefts done in the country were carried out.

In the middle of the night, while Inayat was asleep, he heard a bang at the door and got up with a shock. What had come at that time in the night? Opening the door, he saw a gigantic man with a thick staff in his hand, who brought him a message from Masiti in these words: 'He has heard your name and is eager to hear you. A carriage is waiting for you downstairs and three men are here with me to escort you.' Inayat saw the evil in that man's glance and the first thought that came to him was the word of Jesus: 'Resist not evil.' He went to that place and saw Masiti, awaiting him, sitting among all his gay surroundings. The first thing Masiti asked his men was: 'Did he make a difficulty in coming?' They said: 'No Sir, he came willingly.' Masiti, full of pride, got up from his seat and embraced Inayat as he came in. Such honour he had never before done to a musician, and he said proudly to those present there: 'See, here is this young artist, whom even the Rajas cannot always have come

Photograph 7. Calcutta, India c.1908

to them at their command. He has accepted my call.' He said to Inayat: 'You have honoured me so much by coming here, that I feel more exalted than a king. Now I do not want you to sing, but only to listen while all these artists play and sing.' Inayat's personality made such an impression upon Masiti, that he felt as a slave before him, and so also he acted toward him. Inayat sat there all night; the time that he usually passed in his vigils was spent in these orgies and yet to him even this was his prayer. He was not out of his spiritual atmosphere, for he had the fountain of this atmosphere within himself, spreading wherever he went. He realized by his own experience that it is we who create our heaven or hell, there is no such place as heaven, nor is there any such place as hell. This experience with Masiti opened before him a vast field of thought. He felt how down the ages power has ruled and wisdom submitted; and justice or injustice in life cannot very well be weighed by observing the external part of life only. It is the vision of all which in the end sums up all justice and injustice in one perfect whole.

In Rangoon Inayat met Mahmad Casim Barucha, a leader of the Muslim community there and a friendship was formed between them.

The Burmese – Hindus and Muslims uniting together – acknowledged the talent in music that Inayat showed, by presenting an address to him on behalf of the citizens of Rangoon.

When he left one place to go to another, Inayat had already made friends who were sorrowing on his leaving them and he, after having made deep attachments in a place, had to depart from there. For them it would be an impression, an impression which was everlasting, but for him it was a dream, a dream which was a picture of life, whose beginning signified birth and the end death. Inayat would say to himself while leaving dear and near friends: 'Such is life, when you are sent you come, when you are called you go. What is left with you and with them is the impression of the love and hate you had for them or they had for you.' To him the joy of that love which he had given would rebound with interest.

From Rangoon Inayat sailed to reach the long desired place of his destiny, Calcutta, and wished to settle there for some time. Though this was against his wishes, yet being advised by his father that he must settle in some place, he stayed there some time. He found the people of Bengal a very peculiar race, lovers of originality and saturated with modernity, yet living the simple life of old India; for, as he saw, the Bengalese are down to earth[23]. For some time, no notice was taken of Inayat, a musician so little known in that part of the world and not supported by any princes or potentates, in a vast city, which at that time was the capital of India. In such a large city as Calcutta, there was a great deal of greed for gain, rivalry and competition among the musicians. Some person, who perhaps had a spite against Inayat's people, on hearing of his coming woke up and tried in every way to spoil Inayat's career

23. First edition has Dutch rendering: 'the Bengalese stand on both their feet'

Photograph 8. Calcutta, India c. 1909

in its beginning, so that the plant might be crushed before it could grow. To Inayat's heart it was very painful, for he was so far from the thought of competition or rivalry, that he was not in the slightest degree conscious of any musicians existing who would have such an attitude toward him, who never did or even thought of causing harm to anyone out of professional jealousy. But that made him realize more and more, one among all other causes which have not only ruined the music of India, but have been the cause of the downfall of the whole country.

After prolonged patience, while for six months he had nothing to do in the city, he became acquainted with Babu Laheri, who was a Sufi in spirit and recognized in Inayat something very wonderful and saw that a jewel was lying among the rubbish. He said: 'The benefit of your knowledge must be given to the students. It must not be brought before the masses, who love to be entertained.' He arranged a series of lectures at the University Hall of Calcutta. One day Sir Guru Das Banerji presided at the lecture so arranged, another day Rabindranath Tagore presided. So every day it was presided over by the venerable members of society. The consequence was that the most intellectual public of Calcutta, who were seeking for something greater than the ordinary music, were present among his audience, which roused such an interest in the country that all the spirit of rivalry and competition of the little musicians around there went down, as dust becomes settled under water.

The Maharaja of Natore, the Raja of Rangpur, the Maharaja Tagore, Lord Sinha, were among those whom Inayat met and they admired his art. The only complaint that remained among the professional people was this: 'Inayat does not associate with the artists of the country.' But those who had known Inayat were ready to answer: 'He is not one of you.' Where there is praise, there is blame. The sons of Mahmud Arif and Babu Samacharan Dutt and Manacharsha became his pupils and so he became known to all the different circles in Calcutta. He also sang and played at the Presidency College, where a gold medal was presented to him. The great musician Mohendra Nath Chaterji of that place, who had known Maula Bakhsh, took sides for Inayat. The musical society, Sangit Sammilani, invited Inayat in order to hear his idea and in the address they presented to him, called him the Morning Star of Indian musical revival.

Music was his external garb. His life was to see all day the faqirs and dervishes and to sit for the greater part of the night in his vigils and to sing at dawn the songs of devotion and to meditate with music in the evenings.

Inayat considered it his great privilege to meet a Sufi who was addressing large gatherings on theosophical subjects, arousing the utmost interest, Maulana Ektadarul Huq. He recognized in Inayat something and exclaimed in reference to Inayat: 'Here is a hidden soul, in whom the divine expression is just now budding.'

A master lived in Calcutta in the guise of a Majzub. He often walked along the road, looking at the sights to be seen there from his own point of view,

Photograph 9. San Francisco, USA 1911

sometimes appearing happy and often most amused at seeing the worldly things going on about him. People who knew, respected him very much, but wherever he would find people who recognized him, he would escape from them. Most of his time was occupied with little children, in playing with them, allowing them to ride on his shoulders and to make of him a horse and if they cried, consoling them. He was always a friend of little children. Once Inayat sent for him, requesting him to come and dine. He refused and ran away with his friends, the children. Next time he was invited by Inayat who said that he would like to sing to him. This brought him at once, and on arriving he talked in the language of the Majzub, speaking of the unknown laws of life and nature and about the way to perfection. In this he gave a short summary of his life's experience on the path during one's journey to the spiritual goal. But except Inayat no one understood his language. After this he came often to the house of Inayat and asked of Inayat's brothers: 'Where is my Lord and Master?' They, not being accustomed to hearing such a thing, were perplexed and yet they had such confidence in this Majzub and respect for him that they were shocked at his speaking like this, and Inayat had to explain to them that all great souls call even undeserving souls great, because of their own greatness.

Inayat's greatest friend there was a Babu Hiran Maya, who was a saintly soul and knew that under the guise of musician was something else hidden. He was an elderly man, but his respect for Inayat was like worship, and Inayat would always honour him, as he always honoured elderly people. He was the Dewan of the Maharaja Saraswati Chandra Bahadur of Belgachia.

Inayat lived in Calcutta for several years and there received the news of the death of his beloved father, which was to him a blow inexpressible in words, though thus his life became free from any duty binding him as a sacred tie, as he had felt his duty toward his parents to be. Soon after this another misfortune befell him, namely the loss of his medals. In a moment of abstraction, the case of medals was left in a train compartment[24], which could not be traced despite all his efforts. But in place of the disappointment which at first oppressed him, a revelation from God touched the hidden chords of his mind and opened his eyes to the truth. He said to himself: 'It matters not how much time you have spent to gain that which never belonged to you, but which you called your own; today you comprehend it is yours no longer. And it is the same with all you possess in life, your property, friends, relations, even your own body and mind. All which you call 'my', not being your true property, will leave you; and only what you name 'I', which is absolutely disconnected with all that is called 'my', will remain.' He knelt down and thanked God for the loss of his medals, crying: 'Let all be lost from my imperfect vision, but Thy true Self, ya Allah!'

This prolonged stay in Calcutta brought about in Inayat's life a kind of

24. First edition has 'car'

Photograph 10. Pittsburgh, USA 1910

regularity, which had not existed before. It gave him more chance of contemplating, of thinking and acting as well. Inayat spoke at the Madrasa College to the Muslim students on music and presented before the government of India a scheme, supported by Mr. Ross, the principal of that College, for introducing the scientific music of India in the schools; so that the children might grow to express music in their life, that their personality might become, so to speak, musical. Of course, such a project had to pass through a great many formalities in the State. Inayat had not the patience nor the time to stay in one place, so before the answer came he had already left Calcutta to make a tour through Bengal.

In Bengal he first visited the Raja of Lalgola, then the Maharaja of Cossimbazar, who being a civilized prince, very much appreciated Inayat's ideas for the cultivation of music.

When he was once visiting Murshidabad, he met with Fizl Rubbee the Dewan of the State, who became a great admirer of Inayat's talent and personality. Inayat was greatly interested to hear Munawar Khan, the most talented vina player. He was staying with some friends who, knowing him as a musician, through his music and personality soon became attached to him.

In Murshidabad he made the acquaintance of the Dewan of H.H. the Nawab Bahadur.

One day, when these friends had assembled, a Brahman came who had a gift of palmistry. He looked at the hands of some of those present and told each one something about his life, saying some funny things which amused all present. He then asked to look at Inayat's palm and Inayat unhesitatingly stretched out his hand. As soon as the Brahman looked at Inayat's palm, he was taken aback. His expression changed and for a moment he became speechless. He then touched Inayat's feet and apologised for having dared to make such an attempt; he showed such a reverential attitude towards Inayat that the friends, whose attitude was that of ordinary friendship, were much impressed. The spirit of mirth seemed to have been dispelled by this occurrence and it cost a great effort on Inayat's part to tune the atmosphere again to its former pitch.

One day Inayat heard of the arrival in Baroda of a Brahman who was said to be a great seer. This Brahman not only read the thoughts of those who came to visit him, but also all about their past, present and future. He was an enormously stout man and when he was sitting cross-legged, he would take up the space of four people. Many people would tremble before him because of his gigantic appearance, but he was friendly and sociable in spite of his loud voice. Inayat went among the rest to visit this Brahman, but for a long time the latter would not look at him or notice him. So Inayat waited until all the others had gone away. When they were alone the Brahman said: 'Welcome, Mahatma! I am sorry I could not speak to you before all the others, but I can do so now. I see you are depressed at this moment and clouds have surrounded your life; but it is the dawn, look forward to the rising of the sun.

You are to go to the Western world.' Inayat asked when that would be. He answered: 'Not now, later, perhaps after a few years. And there you will do a great work which cannot be told to you just now. It will not bring wealth, but it is work which is beyond imagination. Therefore, build up your courage and all clouds will be cleared away.' While telling Inayat this, the Brahman's eyes were wet with tears; whether of joy or sorrow, it is impossible to say, but he felt it all so deeply that he could not speak one word more.

Inayat then went to Decca, where he was received at the Asan Manzil palace by the Nawab of Decca, who had invited most of the princes and potentates of Bengal on that occasion. Inayat was invited to sing. He accepted the invitation on condition that he should be allowed to speak first. The desire of a young man like Inayat was readily accepted by the experienced Nawab, who was full of goodwill, but to his great surprise, when Inayat began, he spoke in the face of all the princes without the slightest hesitation, of how the art of music had been abused by being made merely a pastime and the means of merriment, especially by the princes and potentates of India; how they were flattered by the musicians and how they were pleased, and out of vanity pretended to know what in reality many did not understand. Among them the Maharaja of Dinajpur saw the truth of what Inayat said in his address and all were so surprised at hearing that unexpected talk, and yet none could deny its truth. Afterwards Inayat sang for a while and there made the acquaintance of the Raja of Sylhet, Gopika Ramon Roy, with whom he travelled to his State, Assam, at his invitation. The Maharaja of Sylhet considered him not a musician, he considered him a teacher. He said to him one day: 'I envy you.' And his only wish was that Inayat should stay all his life in his State and he himself did all he could to love him and be his pupil.

Inayat, by that time had reached the state of *Samadhi*. This, which might come after many years of meditation, came to Inayat while so young. He used to rise to that state in an instant. No sooner did he begin his music than he would rise above the spheres of the earth. It developed to such an extent that not only he himself, but those sitting around him would become spellbound and feel exalted, in which Inayat found the fulfilment of his having the talent of music. They did not know where they were, or what they were hearing and could not realize to what sphere they were lifted from the earth. After finishing his music Inayat was drowned in ecstasy and they all seemed as if lost in a mist. As they opened their eyes their attitude towards him changed and he, whom they had at first taken for a singer, then became a mystery.

Inayat now understood why the medals had been lost; it meant to him that music had fulfilled its work in his life; now a new era of his life was to begin. No doubt, it gradually came. First his devotional songs began to move people to tears and would create an atmosphere of great love and devotion and of harmony. Then it created dreams and a kind of absorption in himself and in others, a kind of exaltation, an upliftment which culminated in profound ecstasy. Inayat's career in India had there reached its term. Things began to work so as to change his life. The consciousness of his Murshid's injunction: 'Fare forth into the world, my child and harmonize the East and West with the harmony of thy music. Spread the wisdom of Sufism abroad, for to this end art thou gifted by Allah, the most Merciful and Compassionate,' came more and more to his realization and a way was cleared for him to leave India to fulfil the mission of his life. Nothing could keep him back then.

His uncle, who had formerly travelled in the West told him the life in the West is difficult for an Eastern person. To make a living is still more difficult. He asked: 'Are you backed by anyone, are you supported, have you any definite place to go to?' 'Yes uncle, I have every support that is necessary, my aim is more than definite, my object is clear to me. Do you wish to ask anything more?' He thought Inayat was so determined that nothing would stop him. Inayat said to his uncle: 'The God, who is the support of all, the Protector of all, does not live only in India. He is everywhere, so I shall be safe, uncle, under His providence; you need not be worried.'

There were two friends also going to America. He joined them and had with him his brother Maheboob Khan and cousin Ali Khan, who accompanied him most willingly.

Maheboob Khan

Maheboob, Inayat's younger brother, had always been so attached to him from his childhood and they had always been together. He was much more diligent at school than Inayat and as a child was loved by all. Therefore, he was called Pyaromia, which means beloved. He was a very engaging child. As he was ill when about nine years, he was shown greater attention at home and therefore was brought up rather differently from Inayat. He proved to be most musical, wise and thoughtful and yet most shy and timid of spirit and exclusive by nature. His grandfather, Maula Bakhsh, recognized in him an extraordinary talent in music and a wonderful gift of improvisation and he trained him together with Inayat in music. But later he grew up in quite another atmosphere from Inayat's; for in his youth he opened his eyes to the influence of his uncle Dr. Alaoddin Khan and lived mostly in his atmosphere, which was pervaded by European music. Military bands, and orchestras, and his uncle's circle represented modern India. Maheboob, being impressionable, took all the colour that the atmosphere he was in gave to his life. After his study of English, Maheboob was put in charge of the pupils of Inayat, whom he taught music, when the latter left Baroda and he held that charge most satisfactorily. Maheboob was popular among his pupils. Inayat, during his visits to Baroda, became conscious of this atmosphere, which differed from his own, yet, adaptable as he was, he did not find it difficult to accustom himself to any atmosphere. It took Inayat but a short time first to blend with his brother's atmosphere and then gently to draw his brother unawares into his own. Yet his almost continual absence from Baroda kept Maheboob on the same line of progress that he was, during which he acquired a great deal of knowledge of European music. He conducted orchestras and took some interest in the theoretical side of Western music. In every case his devotion to Inayat was great. He was a favourite son of his father, though his line of thought was altogether different from his father. Inayat's father, before passing away, told Inayat his great desire that he should take care of both his brothers, Maheboob and Musharaff, and though Maheboob was now capable of looking after himself, still that they might have Inayat's influence, which his father esteemed high. Following his father's injunction and also out of his own wish, Inayat took both his brothers under his wing from the time of their father's death and when he left India for Europe, Maheboob accompanied him on his journey.

Musharaff Khan

Musharaff (Ill. 12, 24) was the youngest of Inayat's brothers and was born at the time when Maula Bakhsh was already passing away from this earth and his father too old to direct his life. Therefore, he received comparatively less care and attention from his family than those who had come before. Most drawn to play, as he was in childhood, he cared little for studies, though music ran in his blood all the time.

It was first suggested to put him in a school of electrical engineering, but he did not keep up his enthusiasm as he was not made for anything but music. He was somewhat under the influence of his uncle, Alaoddin Khan, and yet was too young really to benefit by this influence, and he scarcely had the influence of Inayat, which he always sought and whom he loved most. For it was Inayat who understood him, and understanding is the answer to every soul.

No sooner was Musharaff taken to Calcutta, that he might study there under the influence of Inayat, then Inayat was called away to America and Musharaff was left alone, away from all his people, as they were in Baroda. He was most unhappy at being thus separated from his brothers and left alone while so young. His one prayer was some day to meet his brothers again. His joy was boundless when after one year he was called to America to meet Inayat and this was the turning of a new page in his life.

Ali Khan

Ali Khan (Ill. 10, 23) was a second cousin of Inayat. He was the grandson of Maula Bakhsh's sister, a relationship which in the East is considered almost as close as that of brothers.

He was born in the same house in which Inayat also was born, and they were together as babies. This friendship, begun from babyhood, linked them as brothers for their whole life. Ali Khan grew to be a devoted friend of Inayat and kept near him at all times and under all conditions. When as a child he was taken away from Baroda, either remained in the other's thoughts. After nine years, Ali Khan came again to Baroda and found Inayat quite advanced in many directions. Association renewed the old friendship and they became as fond of each other as they had ever been. Inayat had only to tell his cousin *chelo*, which means: let us go, and he, without asking where or why, would take his hat under his arm and follow. The places that Inayat frequented would not always be very interesting for his cousin. For Inayat, young as he was, would visit dervishes, faqirs, philosophers, mystics who passed through his city. No person of Inayat's age would ever think of going to them and Ali, dragging along with Inayat, would be quite happy to go wherever the latter went, only to be with him and so all was interesting. In this way Ali became the shadow of Inayat and everywhere they were seen together.

Ali came at the time when Alaoddin Khan's influence prevailed in the house, the influence of European music and the atmosphere of modern life, all about. In this way to some extent, Ali Khan was pulled from both sides. He received training in European music; he played all the brass instruments, such as euphonium, trumpet, trombone, and added to them all, the bagpipes, which often tried Inayat's patience and annoyed the neighbours. Ali Khan acted as right hand in Alaoddin Khan's military band and he coached many youths in different instruments. With all this commotion going on from morning till evening, his only moment of relief was when Inayat came and said to him in the evening: chelo!

As a contrast to the European music he loved vina most and used to seek the company of the vina players. His greatest hobby in life was physical culture and wrestling, which prepared him to become an iron wall to stand in support of Inayat against many opposing influences. Ali Khan always showed a great religious spirit, with a most loving heart and was kind and serviceable and most devoted and took pleasure in being of service.

PART II

Autobiography

Autobiography

I was transported by destiny from the world of lyric and poetry to the world of industry and commerce, on the 13th of September 1910. I bade farewell to my motherland, the soil of India, the land of the sun, for America the land of my future, wondering: 'perhaps I shall return someday', and yet I did not know how long it would be before I should return. The ocean that I had to cross seemed to me a gulf between the life that was passed, and the life which was to begin. I spent my moments on the ship looking at the rising and falling of the waves and realizing in this rise and fall the picture of life reflected, the life of individuals, of nations, of races, and of the world. I tried to think where I was going, why I was going, what I was going to do, what was in store for me. 'How shall I set to work? Will the people be favourable or unfavourable to the Message which I am taking from one end of the world to the other?' It seemed my mind moved curiously on these questions, but my heart refused to ponder upon them even for a moment, answering apart one constant voice I always heard coming from within, urging me constantly onward to my task, saying: 'Thou art sent on Our service, and it is We who will make thy way clear.' This alone was my consolation.

This period while I was on the way, was to me a state which one experiences between a dream and an awakening; my whole part in India became one single dream, not a purposeless dream, but a dream preparing me to accomplish something toward which I was proceeding. There were moments of sadness, of feeling myself removed further and further from the land of my birth, and moments of great joy, with the hope of nearing the Western regions for which my soul was destined. And at moments I felt too small and little for my ideals and inspirations, comparing my limited self with this vast world. But at moments, realizing whose work it was, whose service it was, whose call it was, the answer which my heart gave moved me to ecstasy, as if I had risen in the realization of Truth above the limitations which weigh mankind down.

When our ship arrived in the harbour of New York, the first land of my destination, I saw before me the welcoming figure of the Statue of Liberty, an idol of rock, which I felt was awaiting the hour to turn into an ideal, awaiting the moment to rise from material liberty to spiritual liberty. Its wings suggested to me that it wanted to spread from national liberty to world liberty.

My first impression of New York, the city of modern grandeur, was that of a world quite other than those I had seen or known before. The grand, high

Photograph 11. San Francisco, USA 1911.

buildings, the illuminations in all the shops, people moving about in crowds, conveyances running on three levels: tramways, subway, and elevators running overhead, people running at the station, each with a leather bag in his hand, and a newspaper. Everything seemed moving, not only the trains but even the stations, every moment filled with the rush of activity, calling to every sense, on the ears and on the eyes. It was removed from the land I had come from by a distance as wide as the expansion of the vast ocean which separated these two lands.

I soon began to try to get accustomed to the people, to the atmosphere, and to the country. And as I came of that people whose principal characteristic is adaptability, it was not too difficult for me to attune myself to the people and the conditions there. As the Message I brought was the Message of unity, it was natural that I should give proof in my own life of unity with people and conditions, however different and far removed. I saw in the people of America the sum total of modern progress. I called it 'the Land of the Day'; that for which Rumi has used in the Masnavi the word *Dunya*, the worldly life, to which the word *Samsara* is equivalent in Hindi, I found there in its fullness.

The first opportunity I had of making the acquaintance of some people in America, was in the studio of Mr. Edmund Russell, who gave a reception where I met with some people among whom I found some responsive persons. I came to America with the Sufi Message, but the only means which I had to carry out my mission was by music, my profession, in which my cousin Ali Khan and my two brothers Maheboob Khan (Ill. 11) and Musharaff Khan (Ill. 12) assisted me. But my music which was most valued and admired as science and art, was put to a hard test in a foreign land, where it was as the old coins brought to a currency bank.

Now before me there was the question: how to set to work and in what direction? For the Message the time was not yet ripe, as I was at that time rather studying the psychology of the people than teaching. In a busy place like America where in the professional world already great competition exists, to have an opening for concerts or an opportunity to sing at the opera seemed for the moment an impossible thing. I met with the well-known singer Emma Thursby who, being a great artist herself, became interested in our music.

My first address to the people of America was arranged at Columbia University in New York by Dr. Reebner, and there I found a great response. Dr. Reebner, the Head of Music at the University, was most interested in Indian music and we became friends. Among the audience was Miss Ruth St. Denis (Ill. 13) who invented Indian dances of her own and was making a speciality of it, and for whom our music became as a colour and fragrance to an imitation flower. She tried to introduce the Indian music in the programme of her performance, which was to me as a means to an end. We had an interesting tour together throughout the States, and yet for the public, which was for amusement, our music became merely an entertainment. This was an amusement for them, and therefore painful for us. Also, it was not satisfactory to combine real with imitation. However, it helped to keep the wolf away from our door.

I once visited the house of Miss Ruth St. Denis after a long time and saw to my surprise that all the Indian things that were in her room as a decoration, had been removed altogether and in their place Japanese things were placed, which amused me. She then entered the room, in a Japanese kimono, which surprised me still more. I said to her, 'Now I have found out the reason why you have not seen us for a long time. It seems you have forgotten India altogether.' She said, 'I am trying to forget it, though I find it difficult to forget. For now that I have to produce a Japanese dance, I do not wish to think of India any longer.' It explained to me what influence the power of concentration makes upon one's life and work, that when the whole surrounding is inspiring a person with one particular idea, it creates in his soul the spirit of the desired object, and in this lies the mystery of life. I found Miss Ruth St. Denis an inventive genius, and I was struck with a witty answer she gave upon hearing my ideas about human brotherhood, uniting East and West. She said, 'Yes, we, the people of the Occident and Orient may be brothers, but not twins.'

Before ending our tour in the States, I spoke at the University of Los Angeles, and to a very large audience at the Berkeley University of San Francisco where I met with a very great response, and where my lectures on, and my representation of Indian music and the presentation of its ideal met with a great interest.

At the end of my tour through the United States, when I arrived at San Francisco, I found the meaning of the scheme of Providence, that I was meant to come to San Francisco, a land full of psychic powers and cosmic currents, and begin from there the work of my Message. It is here that I found my first mureed Mrs. Ada Martin (Ill. 14).

I was welcomed by Swami Trigunatita and his collaborator Swami Paramananda, who requested me to speak on Indian music to their friends at the Hindu temple, and was presented with a gold medal and an address.

I saw among the audience a soul who was drinking in all I said, as the Hamsa, the bird of Hindu mythology, who takes the extract from the milk leaving the water. So this soul listened to my lecture on music and grasped the philosophical points which appealed to her most. She thanked me as everybody came to show their appreciation after the lecture. But I saw that there was some light kindled there in that particular soul. Next day I received a letter near to my time of departure from San Francisco, saying that this lady was immensely impressed by the Message, though it was given under the cover of an address on music, and would most appreciate some further light on the path. I knew that she received the call, and wrote her that I regretted very much that I was leaving, but yet I could be seen at Seattle, a city at a considerable distance from San Francisco. I had a vision that night that the whole room became filled with light, no trace of darkness was to be found. I certainly thought that there was some important thing that was to be done next day, which I found was the initiation of Mrs. Ada Martin, the first mureed on my arrival to the West and, knowing that this soul will spread light and illuminate all those who will come in contact with her, I initiated her and named her Rabia after the name of a great woman Sufi saint of Basra, about whom so much is spoken in the East. Since her initiation she has entirely devoted her life to spiritual contemplation and the service of humanity.

After my return from San Francisco to New York, I stayed a while to be able to do some work and gave a few lectures at the Sanskrit College where I made the acquaintance of Baba Bharati, who preached the love of Krishna to the Americans. I made there the acquaintance of Mr. Bjerregaard, who afterwards wrote on my request the book called *Sufism and Omar Khayyam*. He was the only student of Sufism known in New York, and he helped me to have access to the Sufi literature in the Astor Library, of which he was the head.

Ralph Perish, Miss Genie Nawn and Mrs. Logan were made mureeds, and later Miss Collins and Mrs. Eldering and also Mrs. Morrison (Ill. 15). Among them there was a mureed who showed no end of respect, devotion and interest in the Cause, and yet there was something in him which voiced to me his hidden insincerity. He followed me for a considerable time, till his patience was exhausted. In the end he gave way to his weakness, admitting he could not go on any longer. I then found out that he had been sent by some society which collected the teachings of different secret orders, where initiations were given, its members entering somewhere or the other in every order of inner cult. It made me very sad, more for him than for me, to think how he wasted his time for nothing. He came, trying to steal something which can never be stolen. Truth is not the portion of the insincere ones. Sincerity alone is the bowl that can hold Truth.

I then called Mrs. Martin, who had by then progressed wonderfully – which consoled me – to whom the robe of Murshida was given; and the care of a grain of the Message, which was cast in the soil of America, was entrusted to her before I left the United States for Europe. She represented the Sufi Message at the religious congress in San Francisco at the Panama Canal World Fair.

During my stay in America for more than two years there was not much done in the furtherance of the Sufi Movement. From my stay in America I began to learn the psychology of the people in the West and the way in which my mission should be set to work.

If I can recall any great achievement in America, it was to have found the soul who was destined to be my life's partner (Ill. 16).

With the liberal idea of freedom in all directions of life and in spite of Abraham Lincoln's liberal example and reform, there is still to be found in America a prejudice against colour which is particularly shown to the Negroes who were for a long time in slavery, and since their freedom the prejudice has become still greater. It seems almost impossible to think that in a country which is most up-to-date in civilization, there should be a population so looked down upon. Yes, in India there are shudras, lower castes who are called untouchable. Yet there have been scientific reasons, from a hygienic point of view, for not touching them, and the attitude of the high caste towards them has never been that of hatred. The men and women of that pariah class in India are called by others mehter, which means master. Yes, the people in America have their reason for it. They think Negroes are too backward in evolution to associate with. But to me it seems that the coming race will be the race of Negroes; they are showing it from now. In whatever walk of life, they find an opportunity, they come forward in competition. Not only in wrestling or boxing, but also on the stage the Negroes show their splendour, and the most surprising thing to me was that, conscious of all the prejudice against the Negro from all around, he does not allow his ego to be affected by it. In every position of outward humiliation he is put to, he stands upright with a marvellous spirit, which I only wished the man in the East had, who has become as a soil worn out after a thousand harvests. The spirit in the East seemed to me deadened, being weighed down by autocratic influences, tramped upon by foreign powers, crucified by high moral and spiritual ideals, and long starved by poverty.

An ordinary man in America confuses an Indian with brown skin with the Negro. Even if he does not think that he is a Negro, still he is accustomed to look with contempt at a dark skin, in spite of the many most unclean, ignorant and ill-mannered specimens of white people who are to be found there on the spot. I did not find so much prejudice existing in America against a Japanese, of which so much has been said. Still in answer to the unchristian attitude of theirs, the government of Japan has all along threatened them with the Mosaic law, and is ready to return the same when the Americans visit Japan. Indians, when insulted abroad, can do nothing but bear it patiently. The colour prejudice in some nations of Europe is even more, but it is often hidden under the garb of politeness and not so freely expressed as in America; the difference is between a grown-up person and a child in his expression of prejudice.

An American as a friend is very agreeable and desirable and most sociable. One feels affection, spontaneity in his feelings, although the business faculty is most pronounced in him, yet together with it he is most generous. The American readily responds to the idea of universal brotherhood. He is open to study any religion or philosophy, although it is a question if he would like to follow a certain religion long enough, because freedom, which is the goal, by many in America is taken as the way, and therefore, before starting the journey towards spiritual freedom, they want the way also to be a way of freedom, which is impossible. I have seen among Americans people of a thorough good nature, and their life itself a religion, people of principle and gentleness. The broad outlook of the people in America gave me a great hope and a faith that it is this spirit which in time must bring the universal idea to the view of the world. It is most admirable for a great nation to bring forward the idea of world disarmament, when many other nations are fully absorbed in covetousness, and submerged in their own interests. This idea of disarmament brought out by President Harding, was responded to by the public there. This shows the bent of their mind. Besides, to friends or enemies, in their trouble, whenever the occasion has arisen, America has most generously come first to their rescue.

With all the modern spirit in America I found among the people love for knowledge, search for truth, and tendency to unity. I found them full of life, enthusiasm, and goodwill, which promises that this modern nation, although it is now in its childhood, will become a youth who will lead the world towards progress.

— . — . —

I went to England in 1912 from America, and there I saw the difference between England and America.

First, I met with some musicians, among them Cecil Scott and Percy Grainger, to whom I was introduced by my friend Mr. Strecker of Augener & Co. I met with Dr. King (Ill. 17) of Brighton, who became very much interested in my ideas. Also, I saw Mr. August Holmes of the Royal Academy of Music. I was introduced in literary circles by Miss Beatrice Irwin (Ill. 18) at a reception given at Monico by the Port's Club; especially Lord Dunsany, who was in the chair on this occasion, was very much interested in the symbology of Sufi poetry. I met there a great many poets and writers, among them Sir Henry Newbolt and Mr. Smith. Rabindranath Tagore was in England in those days, and hearing that I had just come from America, he called me to meet his friends. We went to see the London Conservatory of Music of which Dr. Trotter is the head, who has introduced a new musical system in England. There we met Mr. Fox Strangways who was then writing a book on Indian music, whom I told that it is not much use writing books on Indian music; what would be really worthwhile would be to practise and get a fuller insight into Indian music, only by this could one give the true benefit of the music of the East to the West.

I met in England Miss Maud Macarthy and was astonished to see how keenly interested she was in Indian music, and the simple folk songs from the South of India, which she sang, indeed took me home. She made me a present of her vina. I also saw Mrs. Kumar Swami, about whom so much has been spoken, and who professed to be the first European artist who performed Indian music. But in her case, it was an imitation of the Eastern art rather than real. I gave a lecture on music at the Indian Club in Cromwell Road. Most of the officials of the India Office, the gentry of India and students were present. Very little could I do in the way of my mission at that time, although I was really impressed by the English character. In music I found there little response. Mr. Strangways to whom I supplied information about Indian music for his book, said to me: 'Our people do not go in much for art; in art the French are the foremost, you will find much interest in your music in France.'

— · — · —

So I proceeded from there to Paris in 1913. In France, although to begin with I had no acquaintances, still I found some friends on arriving in Paris who really took interest in Indian music, among them the venerable Monsieur Edmond Bailly (Ill. 19), who was a lover of India and its music. He, by the kind help and co-operation of Lady Churchill, arranged our first concert in Paris.

I gave a few lectures on music, with demonstrations, and tried to introduce Indian music in connection with *Kismet*, an Oriental dramatic production; in the end I found it could not take (Ill. 20). However, my visit to France first gave me a desire to sing once more since leaving my country. I met many musicians, among them Mr. Walter Rummel, through whom I came to know Monsieur Debussy (Ill. 21), the great composer of France, who became very much interested in our ragas. The evening when the ragas were played to him, he always remembered and called it 'the evening of emotions'. I met many musicians and artists who showed sympathy with the art and philosophy of India, among them Isadora Duncan whose art I found genuine.

My mureed, Monsieur A.I. Caillet (Ill. 22), arranged several lectures at different places on music and philosophy, which met with success, and the poet Monsieur Jules Bois became my mureed, and Madame de Reutern Barteneff, a descendant of an old family of Russia, who is a musician, showed great interest in my work.

At that time my book, *A Message of Spiritual Liberty*, as yet in manuscript form, was translated by Mlle. Jorys, and the French translation published afterwards by Monsieur Bailly. My portrait in colours (afterwards published in *A Sufi Message of Spiritual Liberty* English edition of 1914) was painted there by my mureed Mr. M.H. Thurburn.

Still all these years I was learning more than teaching. I was studying the Western mind, the mentality of the Occidental people, their attitude towards life, religion and God.

Materialism on one side, commercialism on the other, besides their agitation against their Church, and their interest in the thought of their modern philosophers turned Europeans, if not from God, at least from the God of Beni Israel. I found that a man today in the West is agitated, not only against the Church, but also against the autocrat God, who works without a parliament, and no one before His government has a vote; who judges people and punishes them for their sin; and before whom men are supposed to be presented in the hereafter with their lives' records of deeds. The man in the Western world, who cannot stand even a king over his head, naturally rebels against a God to be considered as an Emperor of emperors. The modern man does not want anyone to be superior to himself; a priest, saviour, or God, none of them he cares for. If there is anything that appeals to him it is to know of the divine character to be found in the innermost nature of man. The man today is absolutely against a spiritual hierarchy, and therefore naturally against the head of the hierarchy, who is God. In France especially, there are many among the most intelligent people who do not believe in God, soul, or hereafter. And the few who think, perhaps there is something which they do not know, they do not openly admit their belief, fearing that they will appear to be illogical and will not be ranked among the intelligent. They are most anxious to know about the Truth which their soul longs to know, and yet most diffident to show themselves in any way interested or to give themselves in the search of that Truth. It is not their fault, it is the mentality of the day. I had the greatest difficulty to modify my teachings, which are of democratic spirit but of aristocratic form, to those quite opposed to the presentation of the God-ideal in religious form. For me, therefore, there was a ditch on one side, and water on the other. The religious man thought he had a religion, I was intruding upon his belief. The unbeliever thought I was interfering with his disbelief, which he continually guarded against any invasions.

This spirit I did not only meet in France, but I found it more or less everywhere, sharing the missionary's fate, while teaching no particular religion, furthering no special creed.

—·—·—

While in France I was offered an opportunity to go to Russia, which I gladly accepted. By every means I saw the divine hand leading my way towards the spread of the Message. I first visited Moscow, and found that the opportunity which had been offered me, to display my music, was an uncongenial one. I found the place I had been told of was a place of gaiety, where people came for the whole night for their merriment, and yet for me it was a sight to observe how the different temperaments change from the everyday pitch at the moment they are engaged in merriment. It was somewhat troublesome for me to stay up all night, and yet it was an opportunity of studying all the different classes of Russia, all the wealthy classes, and it showed me how the

Photograph 12. 1912

Photograph 13. 1913

Photograph 14. London, UK. 1914

dream of life had absorbed so many of them, and where it would lead Russia in the end. It was as though God wanted to show me, before disaster came upon Russia, how even nations are led to destruction when they, of their own will, choose that path. Had I known beforehand what the offered engagement was, I would certainly not have accepted it. However, God's glory is everywhere to be found.

The people there welcomed me at the Ethnographical Museum, where I had the opportunity of speaking to a large audience on music and there met with great response generally. My friend Mr. Ivanov, the poet, showed great interest, and his wife translated my lectures, sentence by sentence most wonderfully. I was invited then to the Imperial Conservatory of Music where I expounded the ideal of Indian music, with musical illustrations. The response was so great that cheers expressed the enthusiasm, not only in the building of the Conservatory, but following us as far as the gate. I made the acquaintance of the principal of the Conservatory, and Princess Sirtolov Lavrovsky (Ill. 25) became a great friend of mine, and introduced me to the musical circles of Russia. I also became acquainted with Madame Switalovsky, the teacher of music, who became my great friend. I was invited to visit the Imperial School of Opera and Ballet, a marvellous institution. The great development that the art of dancing had attained in Tsarist Russia, was something most amazing, it seemed almost to touch perfection.

One evening I was asked for supper to a friend's house, where Chaliapin, the great singer, had been invited to meet us, and it reminded me of India to find that the supper lasted the whole night. We returned home from there in bright daylight. Those present patiently heard all I had to say and responded to it. Russia reminded me of my country, and the warmth that came from the heart of the people, kept us warm in that cold country where snow lies in the streets for days together, where every house is a Mont Blanc.

One day I had several people at my hotel, among them Count Serge Tolstoy, a son of the great Tolstoy. He, being a musician, was most drawn to our music and was taken also by philosophy. I met an officer in the army, Henry Balakin (Ill. 26), who became my mureed and took great interest in translating *A Sufi Message of Spiritual Liberty* into Russian. This translation was published in a place where, even for the printing of a visiting-card, one had to get the permission of the police. Later the book was published in English by the Theosophical Publishing Society.

While in Russia, I was once taken by a Finnish philosopher, Dr. E.W. Lybeck, to talk of my ideals to friends of his, whose names he would not tell. On the appointed day he came to fetch me. We drove in a sleigh, a thing I always enjoyed, especially when the air was dry, and we arrived at a mysterious edifice. When we had entered that house, the large portals were immediately closed. It seemed that I was expected, and there I found myself in the midst of many priests or monks. I do not know, even now, to which order of monks they belonged, or whether they were a group of priests of the Greek Church.

Photograph 15. London, UK. April 1915

I was given no explanation whatever. There was only one woman in the whole audience, and she had been admitted because among the whole assembly she alone knew English, and so she could translate for me. I was requested to speak on my ideas. I accepted the kind offer most thankfully, and gently began to explain my ideas. At times, when I went a little beyond the boundaries of their religious conventionalities in which they were accustomed to talk, I found them slightly chilled, but I have never seen such comprehensive minds, in which all that is spoken as wisdom and truth so easily finds accommodation. They were interested by the idea, and the only wonder to them was, how could the truth exist in such a perfect form, as I did present, outside their Church, which alone they had so far believed to be the centre of all truth. They were wise people, with awakened sympathy, with the love of Christ and appreciation of truth. To me their contact was a wonderful experience. No end of questions were cast at me, but politely, and the answers to those questions, gently given, went straight to their hearts and sank into their souls. No further argument ensued after they had received one satisfactory answer. I took leave of all present after finishing my work, and it seemed I took with me the friendly feelings which I received through their sympathetic glances.

Among the Russians I found many strict followers of their religion, a thing so little to be found in the more civilized parts of the West. In their churches there is an atmosphere quite like in the temples of India. And yet I found minds philosophically inclined. Once I was invited by a philosophical society, where I gave an address and then was asked different questions on philosophical subjects. I was not asked one question which was a worthless one. Every question, it seemed, was rich in its meaning, and deep, and of importance. I found no desire on their part to argue after once they had received a satisfactory answer.

Professor Corsh, the great linguist of Moscow, became a great friend of mine, and at his house I met some Persians. I saw in Moscow the ambassador of Bokhara, who urged me very much to go with him to meet the Amir of Bokhara, but as my work was destined to the West, I could not have gone to the East. I met many Tartars, and some inhabitants of Kazan, and was invited to the house of Bey Beg, the leader of the Muslims in Moscow.

I gave an address at that meeting on the subject of brotherhood which met with great response, and a musical evening was arranged by them which will always remain in my memory as a most remarkable occasion, where Turks, Tartars, Siberians, Bokharians, Persians, all displayed their national art of music, and the hall was crowded by people of every country of the East. It was something that is so rarely seen, and for me, who had come from far away in the East, leaving my country thousands of miles away, this was a vision of home and yet not home. It was something new and yet akin to my nature, something that I did not know and yet that my soul knew, something so far from my knowledge and yet so near to it.

Photograph 16. Moscow, Russia 1913

At the house of the poet Ivanov, I met Scriabin, who is so well-known in the West. I found his personality not only that of a fine artist, but of a thinker and of a mystic. He seemed dissatisfied with the Western music and thought that there was much in the East which could be introduced in the music of the West, in order to enrich it. I agreed with him, I thought if this idea was ever carried out, although it would be most difficult in the beginning, yet in the end such music would become a world music. And what could be a better means for uniting humanity in a universal brotherhood than the harmony of music, which is loved everywhere in the East or West?

Olga Tucki (Ill. 27), a Russian singer, became a devoted mureed. I wrote a play during my stay in Russia, called *Shiva*. My friend Serge Tolstoy collaborated with me in rendering the music which I wrote for that play in Western harmony. It was being arranged that the Message might be carried to Tsar Nicolas in the form of music; only it was a matter of waiting some time which I could not very well do, for I was to represent Indian music at the musical congress of Paris in 1914, and this brought me back to Paris after a short visit to Petersburg.

I had become very much attached to Russia and its people and but for the climate, which is too cold for one born in tropical lands, I would certainly have decided to settle in Russia at least for some years. I so much liked their language which seems so near to Hindustani and on inquiring into the subject I found that it comes from Sanskrit. I saw in the people of Russia religion, devotion, the idealistic temperament. They are hospitable and affectionate people with a tendency to appreciate and enjoy all beauty, they are gifted in art, inclined to mysticism, seekers of philosophy, ready to become friends and minded to let friendship last.

— . — . —

I was a little late for the congress in Paris, yet I got there in time for the last days and presented the music of India at the very end of their programme. Professor Ecorcheville of the Sorbonne, who had organized the congress, was most interested in Eastern music. He suggested that some records should be taken and kept at the University. The German delegates to the congress were most taken with our music, and they invited me to go to Germany, but before I had made up my mind, the most disastrous war showed itself on the horizon, and we had to pack up and go to England.

Owing to the war, the mind of every person in England was taken up by the thought of war, and the voice of peace at that moment was a dissonant chord to the ears of many. In answer to my call for peace I often heard people say: 'Kill or be killed.' Neither could I do much in the way of presenting music, nor could much be done in philosophy. I spoke a few times at the Higher Thought Centre, which was kept alive by Miss Callow and her friend Miss Hope, who became my mureed. By the kind sympathy of Lady de la Warr a series of lectures was arranged at the rooms of the Royal Asiatic Society,

Photograph 17. London, UK, 11th December 1914

where Lady Muir Mackenzie presided. But the war had paralysed people's minds. It seemed as if there was nothing to be heard except war, war, war, the cry of war coming from every side. I cannot forget the time when I spoke for about six months continually to no more than three persons as my audience. Yes, with patience and with hope I carried on my work. Several times I entertained the wounded Indian soldiers by playing and singing to them (Ill. 28).

My first English mureed, Miss Mary Williams (Zohra) (Ill. 29), came to London to assist me in my work and proved her devotion by serving the Cause, at the time when the Order was a quite helpless infant.

In order to publish literature as we liked, we started a Sufi Publishing Society in England, which was given into the charge of Miss Williams, who brought out a book of some ideas from my lectures, called, 'Pearls from the Ocean Unseen'. Besides the work she did as sub-editor of the Sufi Magazine, she has been a sincere and devoted mureed and a most enthusiastic worker for the Cause. By this Publishing Society my poetical works were brought out: 'Diwan', 'Hindustani Lyrics", and the 'Songs of India', which were rendered into English by Mrs. Jessie Duncan Westbrook. My 'Confessions' were published, written by Miss Miriam Bloch, a treatise on the Rubaiyat of Omar Khayyam by Mr. Bjerregaard was also published by this Society.

I found at that time of difficult beginning, a mureed, Miss Goodenough (Sharifa), who stood as a foundation stone for the building of the Order. In Miss Goodenough (Ill. 30), who was afterwards made a Khalifa, and then was promoted to be a Murshida, I found that spirit of discipleship which is so little known to the world and even rarely found in the East. Besides, I traced in her my own point of view.

Miss Goodenough has proved by her career, firmness and self-sacrifice for the Cause, to which she has devoted her life. There is certainly truth in the idea of heredity, which today people seem to ignore. Although in estimating a horse they still give great importance to heredity, yet they do not for man. Though retiring, exclusive and remote by nature, and independent and indifferent in appearance, which has turned many against her and caused many troubles, she has many pearl-like qualities hidden under a hard shell. She has proved worthy of confidence in the working of the Order and has been patient through all difficulties that we had to meet with continuously on our way. She brought out my ideas in the series of books named: 'The Voice of Inayat', three volumes of which are named: 'Life after Death', 'The Phenomenon of the Soul', and 'Love Human and Divine'. But besides this she has collected, preserved and produced the record of my oral teachings and guarded them from all corruptions. She has kept them for the coming generations in the most authentic form, which act of service the sincere followers of the Message will retain gratefully in their memory.

Photograph 18. London UK. October 1917

Miss Janette Steer (Ill. 31), the well-known English actress also took interest. I made the acquaintance of Dr. Wallace. Miss Mabel Thomson. (Ill. 32) interested herself in the Movement for some time. Miss Benton (Ill. 33) became a mureed, and took interest in Indian music.

Thus began the work of the Movement, which gradually grew, some hot, some cold, some warm and some lukewarm. I found the heart of some flaming, some glowing, some flowing, and some frozen; many came and went their way.

Among those who came later was Miss Shirley (Ill. 34), who showed great enthusiasm in the beginning and did much for the Cause for some time before she retired. Miss Margaret Skinner has been helpful in many ways. Miss Khatidja Young (Ill. 34), a most devout and faithful mureed, came afterwards and assisted me enthusiastically in the extra activities of my work. Mrs. Hanifa Sheaf (Ill. 35) has been a devoted mureed, who proved faithful under all circumstances.

A centre was established in Southampton by the help of Miss Williams.

I started the activity of the Movement in the North of England later, where I first spoke at the Theosophical Society, organized by Mr. Clifford Best, whose brother Shahbaz Cecil Best (Ill. 36) became a mureed and showed a great enthusiasm in the work and was ordained a Cherag in 1921, who now[25] represents the Message in Brazil.

In Leeds Miss Aileen Fletcher took great interest in keeping together the group which was founded in the house of Mrs. Brotherton. Mr. Dickson, in Leeds, has assisted the Movement continuously.

Among a great many mureeds in the North Dr. O.C. Gruner (Ill. 37), a scientific genius whose speciality is blood-research, took up the study of Sufism with great interest and showed himself worthy of Khalifship, which was given to him in 1922 in recognition of his great study, patient working and insight into human nature, with his religious outlook on life, which is the most important thing in the path of Sufism.

My books: 'In an Eastern Rose Garden' and 'The Way of Illumination' have come out through the most enthusiastic efforts of Dr. O.C. Gruner.

In the North of England, I extended my activity round Leeds by starting a group at Harrogate, where my mureed, Mr. King, lived, and in Sheffield, where it was organized by an old Theosophist, Mrs. Chappel, under the care of Mr.

---

25. Dictated summer 1922

Photograph 19. London, UK. April 1915

Mitchell. In Sheffield I made the acquaintance of the well-known English writer Edward Carpenter (Ill. 38), who was greatly in sympathy with my ideas.

It is well-known that it is difficult to make one's way in the Court in England. Several times efforts were made by my friends to carry the Message to the Court, but it was always found difficult, even if it had been through music. However, once Queen Alexandra was present at my performance of Indian music, but apart from that there was no way open to bring the Message to the English royalties. I have discovered for myself that the King of England was not interested in India for its art, poetry, philosophy, or music. The Duke of Manchester heard most attentively of my ideas, but took no step further. I always remember the advice of Lord Lamington, that in order really to succeed in England one must do the work quietly. And the more I worked, the more I realized the truth of his good advice. Lady Lamington had inaugurated the anniversary celebration of the Order in 1920. Lady Harding was most interested in the idea of brotherhood that the Sufi Message had to spread. She had greatly thought of the Indian armies who helped in the war, and she wondered what I thought of the attitude of the Indian nationalists. I said: 'Neither can the nationalist grasp the attitude of the internationalist, nor can an internationalist understand the attitude of a nationalist. The ideal of one is like an ocean, that of the other is like a lake.'

> *Lady Cunard gave a reception, to introduce me to present Indian music to the society of England at Lord French's house. Sir Thomas Beecham was present there, but the only opportunity to present the music of India at the Opera was given me in 'Lakmé', at the French-Russian Opera season by the appreciation and enthusiasm of my friend, the well-known Russian singer, Mr. Rosing. We became friends with Madame Emma Nevada (Ill. 39) and her daughter, Mignon Nevada (Ill. 40), a singer with a great future. My cousin, Ali Khan was taken up by Mme. Nevada, who trained him for grand opera, for she saw in his voice a rare quality of tenor.*

So far, the Order had consisted of one mureed here or there, there was no proper organization, nor was there any society formed. But at this time the interest of some mureeds enabled us to take a house where private lectures could be given to mureeds and their friends. A Khankah was established in no. 86 Ladbroke Road (Ill. 41), in Kensington; throughout the war we were there.

Perhaps many think that between 1910 and 1915 there was ample time for the Sufi Order to grow and flourish. But it is not so; during the war it was just like wanting to cultivate a desert. And even after the war it became difficult, for conditions turned from bad to worse. The little warmth that the war had produced in the feeling of humanity, even that vanished, and hearts became cold by the later effect of war. Therefore, the Sufi Order had a difficult time from the beginning of its work until now. However, the seed was not yet sown, all that time was given to the tilling of the ground.

Photograph 20. London, UK. October 1917

It was Madame Gabrielle Strauss (Ill. 42), who went to France after the war, who created interest for the Cause in Paris, and for the first time we were able to form a group in Paris in 1920. Among my mureeds there were Madame Slatov Portier, Colonel Guillon and Professor Frossard.

Among the royalties of India whom I met in England, was the Maharaja of Kishan Gar, Prince of Rampur, and Princess Taraway of Indore. But my great happiness was that of seeing the Maharaja Sayaji Rao Gaekwar of Baroda, whom I saw again after a long separation of twenty years. Seeing our Maharaja brought to my memory my youth in Baroda, and that garden of genius, the gardener therein is the Maharaja himself. The Maharaja was very much interested in hearing about all my travelling and experiences after leaving Baroda. And on his kind suggestion I have taken up this work of writing the autobiography, containing my life-work and experiences in the West.

At that time many were interested in the work of the Order: the Rev. Dr. Walter Walsh, the leader of the Free Religious Movement; Professor H. M. Léon of the Société Internationale de Philologie, Sciences et Beaux Arts; the Rev. Dr. John Pool, Principal of the International College of Chromatics; Mr. Edmund Dulac, the artist; Mr. Pickthall, the well-known writer; Mr. Skrine, I.C.S.; Sir Mirza Abbas Ali Beg; Sir Probha Shankar Patni of Bhavnager; Sir Gupta and Mr. Sen; Shahzade Aftab Ahmad Khan; and Mr. Laszlo, the painter, and Sir Robert Bridges, the poet laureate; Lady Berkley; Lady Towbridge and Lady Constance Stewart Richardson were visitors at the Khankah. Sir Frederick Smith from South Africa was in London then, he became very much interested in the subject and became a mureed, also Mrs. Fitz Simon. We had some more mureeds from South Africa, among them Mr. and Mrs. Gubbins and Mr. and Mrs. Bodmer. Afterwards I met Dr. A. B. Scott (Ill. 43), who showed a great interest in the Sufi teachings. His earnest study and deep understanding of the Message made him worthy of Khalifship, which was given to him in 1923. He was also ordained a Cherag, and helped to spread the Movement in his country.

There came a time that it was necessary to make a Trust, and the Order was legalized and made official.

By the rising wave of enthusiasm of a mureed, we then were situated in Gordon Square in a much more suitable house, more convenient in every way; but at the falling of the wave it was ended.

Differences among my loving friends threatened our Movement with a breakdown, and caused the removal of the Khankah to Geneva. At that critical moment Miss Dowland (Nargis) (Ill. 44), came to its rescue, and our infant Order was given into her arms when leaving England, recognising in her the hand of God.

Miss Dowland is now[26] the National Representative of the Order in

---

26. Dictated summer 1922

Photograph 21. London, UK. October 1917

England. Her capacity in working had made the Order increase in members, in organization much better than ever before.

> The Sufi Publishing Society, which was dying away, was made alive by Miss Dowland, who called it 'the Sufi Book Depot', and brought out 'The Bowl of Saki', 'The Message', 'The Inner Life', 'The Alchemy of Happiness', 'The Mysticism of Sound', 'Notes of the Unstruck Music' and 'The Soul Whence and Whither'. Besides she wrote 'Between the Desert and the Sown' and 'At the Gate of Discipleship'. The self-sacrificing devotion with which Miss Dowland has worked in England will always remain in the history of the work of the Order in England. Those who have assisted Sheikha Dowland in her work concerning the Order are the Misses Wiseman (Ill. 45), Miss Wentworth Sheilds (Cheraga), and Mr. Mitchell (Cherag).

Miss Green (Sophia) (Ill. 46), who was a Theosophist for most of her life, a special pupil of Mrs. Besant, and who through Theosophy came to recognise the Truth sent in the Sufi Message, was made a Khalifa in England, and then was promoted to be a Murshida, who during my absence watered the plant which I had sown in the soil of England, proving thereby worthy of the work entrusted to her. The inspiration and efficiency she has shown in presenting the Message to her people, her sagely character, with her receptivity to the Message, has been of great importance to the Cause. Her assistance in bringing out my works has been of immense value.

> She has been the first to help me in founding the Church of All, the religious activity, which was introduced in England by her. She was ordained the first Cheraga, and carried out the work most satisfactorily. She edited the Magazine 'Sufism', which has succeeded the periodical called 'The Sufi', which had come out before. Her booklet, lately published, is called 'The Path to God'. She wrote a pamphlet called 'Human Personality'.

Before my departure my English mureeds gave me an address. I left England in 1920, and settled in France (Ill. 47).

— · — · —

There were many reasons both for and against establishing the Headquarters in Geneva (Switzerland), yet the reasons for establishing it there weighed heavier in the balance.

> I met in Geneva Mr. Reelfs and his friends, the Selleger family (Ill. 48) and I spoke before a small audience, mostly foreigners, and those who were most impressed were Mr. and Mrs. Hart van Sautter (Ill. 49) and their friends.

Photograph 22. London, UK. November 1918

Photograph 23.

I found in Baron von Graffenried (Ill. 50) a deep response to my call and it became possible to establish in Geneva a small group of the Order which was given for some time in charge of Mrs. van Sautter. I spoke in Geneva at the University for the Society *Vers l'Unité*; the rector of the University presided. I made acquaintance with Pasteur Charles Martin and was surprised at the spirit of tolerance that he showed to a mission like mine, by being present once at a public meeting given in the Salle Centrale, where we first established our Headquarters.

> *I made acquaintance with Lady Bloomfield, a representative of Bahaism, who was very sympathetic to my ideas. I saw Mrs. Bartram and Dr. Netobi from Japan, who is concerned with the international movements on behalf of the League of Nations. Monsieur de Traz, a Swiss writer, also showed some interest in my philosophy.*

I then visited Lausanne, where lectures were arranged by the kind interest shown by Madame Lavanchy and Frau Schroeder and made some mureeds there. I then visited Vevey, where my mureed Miss Nina Mitchell (Ill. 51) had made every effort to open doors for me, and after my address at the Hotel d'Angleterre I met Baroness van Hogendorp (Ill. 52) who became deeply interested and has shown great zeal in forming a group in Vevey. She became one of the most ardent mureeds and an active worker for the furtherance of the Cause. To this group in Vevey many sincere mureeds joined, among them Mr. Fouad Selim Bey Alhigazi, Monsieur Dussaq, Comtesse Pieri, and others.

Not long after, Miss Goodenough who had been away, joined forces with me in Geneva and took charge of the Headquarters as General Secretary and continued working, which relieved me from many responsibilities. Although the Society in Geneva was formed easily and quickly, it has always been difficult to hold it, for most of the members were foreigners and some Genevese[27], who came with difficulty and went away easily.

The Calvinistic spirit in Switzerland certainly stands as a rock against every spiritual movement. Besides, the Swiss minds his own business and is little concerned with the ideas of others, and there is a reason for it: that all different ideas are brought by different people, coming to Switzerland from all parts of the world. Since the Swiss lay their beauty-laden land at the feet of the travellers, they naturally guard their hearts from being caught up in the nets thrown in the lakes of Switzerland by the fishers of men.

> *The attitude of the Swiss toward those who come to their country, is that of a landlord, who gives houseroom to those who wish to have it, in his property, and he is only concerned with his duty towards it; and yet a Swiss is polite and welcomes all. The Swiss nature is kind and of goodwill, and apprecia-*

---

27. Now known as Genoese

Photograph 24. Geneva, Switzerland. 18th February 1921

tive to a certain extent of all that seems to him good. There is an exclusive tendency in the Swiss nature and great love of independence, which is to the credit of the Swiss race. Switzerland is sought not only for the beauty of its land, but also because of its being pure of heart from any territorial ambition. In this quality it stands unique as a nation bestowing respect and sympathy to all. It is for this reason that destiny had prepared it to deserve being the seat of the League of Nations.

— . — . —

I went again to France and gave some public lectures in Paris, which added to the success of our newly formed group. This group formed in Paris flourished as a garden in spring, but in fall the leaves dropped, and it had to be reorganized, and was then founded on a firmer foundation by Colonel Guillon and by the help and enthusiasm of Baroness d'Eichthal (Ill. 53), who succeeded in being the National Representative for France.

We found in our newly formed French group many interested members, among them Madame Detraux, Mlle. de Sauvrezis, Mme. and Mlle. Gélis Didot, etc[28]. Among foreigners in the Society, Monsieur Choumitzky, Monsieur de Roibul, Mme. Frankowska and Mme. Christowsky, who were with us at the starting of the group, took great interest in the work.

In the absence of Colonel Guillon, the Marquis de Breteuil translated a series of lectures given at the Musée Guimet, to the great satisfaction of all present.

On the soil of France I always felt at home, and the sociability, politeness and courtesy of a Frenchman I always admired, for I saw hidden under the surface of democracy some spirit of aristocracy in their nature, although I found in France a tendency against religion. At the same time in the depth of their soul there is a craving for it, but the Frenchman always fights against it, owing to the external conditions. I found in Frenchmen a profound love of music, art and poetry, and I enjoyed speaking to my respondent French mureeds and audience on the subject of morals and metaphysics in allegorical and symbolical forms, and always felt encouraged by their subtle perception of it. A French lady I found to be feminine in quality, refined, and what especially attracted me to France was that it is a home of art. I never felt more inclined to practise my music anywhere than in France, since I left home.

— . — . —

28. First edition has Dutch rendering a.s.o. (and so on), this is not further noted

Photograph 25. Geneva, Switzerland. 18th February 1921

Photograph 26. London, UK. May 1921

I visited Holland in 1921, where a circuit was arranged by a mureed, Mevrouw Corrie Smit. Several societies, among them the Theosophical Society, invited me to speak to their members. Among those who were first interested in the Message were de Heer en Mevrouw van Ginkel and Mejuffrouw Kerdijk who joined for a time, during which they brought out *Een Inleiding tot het Soefisme* and *De Soefi Boodschap van Geestelijke Vrijheid*. Also de Heer Farwerck and de Heer Toeman and de Heer en Mevrouw van Meerwijk joined and then followed Baron van Tuyll van Serooskerken (Ill. 54), who married my mureed Mejuffrouw Willebeek Le Mair (Ill. 54), an artistic genius who also joined forces with her husband. Since then he has constantly endeavoured to further the Cause in his land as the National Representative of the Order for Holland. Among those who joined first was Mejuffrouw Sakina Furnée (Ill. 55) in whose soul I saw the spirit of my Message reflected with my first glance. My teaching once sown in the soil of her heart, brought a seedling in Switzerland as a proof of her ever-growing interest, and she then joined in the formation of the embodiment of the principal workers as Peshkar.

After more than one visit to Holland and after meeting with a great many difficulties, we were at last able to form a Society, which was constituted of four branches, in The Hague, in Arnhem, in Amsterdam and in Haarlem respectively. De Heer Farwerck and de Heer en Mevrouw van Meerwijk, also de Heer Wegelin (Ill. 56) who was made Cherag and was delegated to China to represent the Sufi Message, took an active part in working.

I found a great enthusiasm among the workers in Holland, and a special tendency to systematic working. People in Holland, being of democratic spirit, are open to any ideas which appeal to them and willing to spread them among their circle of friends. Though they are proud, stern and self-willed, I saw in them love of spiritual ideals, which must be put plainly before them. Dutch people I found by nature straightforward, most inclined toward religion, lovers of justice and seekers after truth. They hunger and thirst after knowledge, and are hospitable and solid in friendship.

After my few visits in Holland I made many friends and mureeds whose earnestness, great enthusiasm and sympathy through all conditions kept the Sufi activities lively.

— · — · —

In 1921 I was invited by some friends in Belgium. I spoke in Antwerp and Brussels to the Theosophical Society. Also in Brussels for the Anglo-Belgian Club, and to the circle of Madame Héris (Ill. 57) of the Star Movement. And by the kindness and earnest efforts of Madame Graeffe van Gorckum (Ill. 58) and Madame de Stürler, by the help of Dr. Bommer, by the co-operation of Madame Marcks and the enthusiasm of Monsieur de Bevere a group of the

Photograph 27. Leerdam, Netherlands. 5th February 1921

Order was formed in Belgium. At the house of the Comte and Comtesse de Laka an address was given to people of the upper class in Belgium interested in the subject. Comtesse de Brémond showed great interest and I spoke several times to a large gathering of students at the club of the Society of *Les Amis de la langue anglaise*, and by the sympathy of Monsieur P. Otlet I addressed a very large audience at different times at the Palais Mondial. I found in Belgium a good field to sow wisdom which requires great cultivation. One can draw out from a Belgian person a great deal of sympathy and goodness, if one only knows their psychology. The Message in Belgium no doubt arrived at the right time, when the Belgian spirit needed healing of its wound, which is still sore.

— . — . —

After the war I made a private tour through Germany, and visited Berlin, Frankfurt, Weimar, Jena and Munich. I made acquaintance with the Herzog von Hessen at Darmstadt, who showed a great interest in the thought and music of India. Graf Keyserling is said to have established some centre of thought at Darmstadt. At Jena I was the guest of Herr Dietrich, the publisher, who introduced me to those interested in music, thought and art. I was warmly received as a guest by Frau Förster Nietzsche at Weimar, who really showed a kindred spirit. Many in Germany said it was a great pity that I had not come before the war. I stayed at the house of Frau Springmann at Hagen and was the guest of Herr Ernest Strauss at Frankfurt. I was glad to find in Berlin my old English mureeds Miss Peak (afterwards Frau Triebel), and Miss Oliver (Ill. 59), who kindly helped me there. Also, I received Herr und Fräulein Hengstenberg into the Order. In Munich I met various professors, among them Prof. Scherman, by the kindness of my hostess Frau Arens Leverkus, whose daughter Fräulein Latifa Leverkus has been greatly interested in Sufism for some time. I strongly felt the clouds of depression which cover the heart of Germany after the war, the effect of which bore too heavily upon me. This country which I have always known as a land of musicians and philosophers I saw, to my great disappointment, in its very worst condition. I made the acquaintance of Professor Hedemann and met with the great philosopher Professor Eucken at Jena, who found my idea more akin to his nature than that which he understood as being the idea of Tagore. The young people in Germany seem most responsive to any idea tending towards the unfoldment of the soul, but in the generality a pessimistic spirit seems to prevail just now, as the after effect of the war. People in Germany seem not open, though capable of understanding, but veiling their grief from others. I had rather a difficult time on account of my tour not having been arranged properly. However, in that land of most exquisite beauty of nature, there is always genius to be found. A nation so proud, efficient and capable as Germany would blaze up, if once blown by the word of God.

> *It was a certain professor, who arranged my visit to Germany, who was probably acting as a tool of some party opposed to my Movement, or else was someone who only wanted to take me as a means for his personal propaganda. He wrote a very enthusiastic letter to me after he had arranged the tour with Baron van Tuyll, who had undertaken to arrange a tour for me through Germany. But from his letter I found that no doubt he was not a right-thinking man, for he wrote to me how he was trying to guard me against all philosophical or psychological Societies which were not worth bothering about, which I thought very strange. For I believe it is worthwhile bothering about everyone in the world, however undeserving and unevolved the person may be. On arriving in Germany to my very great distress he had not made any arrangement for my travelling as well as he wrote in his letter, except some certain engagements that he had made for me which also fell off. I found him to be a most nervous man, somewhat abnormal, proud and ill-mannered, which made my position very difficult in Germany. If it had not been for Professor Scherman, it would have been most difficult for me. He told the false professor to his face of his falsehood, and in this way Baron van Tuyll who accompanied me on this tour was able to get rid of him. But this spoiled my whole tour, for what begins wrongly cannot end rightly.*

— · — · —

At the Headquarters at Geneva a change took place in October 1922, when Miss Goodenough was called to help as *Madar-ul-Maham* at Suresnes. Monsieur Talewar Dussaq (Ill. 60) was then appointed as the General Secretary of the Movement, who most worthily filled this place of trust, and his sister, Comtesse Pieri (Ill. 61), who was afterwards made General Treasurer, wholeheartedly rendered her services to the Cause. The beautiful manner with which they both offered a smiling welcome to friends and strangers at the Headquarters won for them the love and affection of all those who came in contact with them.

Then came to us a wonderful worker, thoughtful and wise, Monsieur de Cruzat Zanetti (Ill. 62), who answered the great need of our Movement. He was then given the most responsible charge of administration, he was appointed Executive Supervisor of the Sufi Movement. Monsieur de Cruzat Zanetti carried out his work so ably that he instantly won admiration of his co-workers.

Among some of my male[29] collaborators I saw a spirit of slight contempt toward the woman-workers, as man has always thought that woman is superfluous or too tender, too much devotional and unintelligent; and they have always sought for a man's collaboration in the work. Nevertheless, however

---

29. First edition has Dutch rendering of 'man collaborators'

Photograph 28. Jena, Germany. October 1921

Photograph 29. c. 1922

Photograph 30. Jena, Germany. October 1921

Photograph 31. Berlin, Germany. October 1924

Photograph 32. Katwijk Beach, Netherlands, September 1922

much qualified men proved to be in the work, the valuable service that women have rendered to the Cause has been incomparably greater. The way how some of them have worked unceasingly with sincere devotion and firm faith, has been a marvel to me. If it was not for some women as my collaborators in the Cause, the Sufi Movement would never have been formed. How easily man forgets the place of woman in all walks of life. It is his self that covers his eyes from recognising the importance of woman's collaboration in every work.

— . — . —

I set out on a journey to America again in March 1923, at the invitation of Murshida Rabia Martin, who had continued the re-echo of the Sufi call which I had once struck upon the gong of the heart of America during my first visit to the United States.

I had to leave Europe confronted by a great many difficulties, as I had the care of little seedlings not yet grown to be plants.

In the ship, through the rain and storm, the Message was felt by people travelling from different countries to the States, having different opinions, who became my friends one after another, up to the moment that we arrived at the point of our destination. By this time almost all had become my friends. No wonder my soul would have sought, after seeing for itself, this phenomenon of the spirit of universal brotherhood.

I was unfortunately detained, as the quota of Indians was completed for that month, and had to visit Ellis Island. And I was glad to have had that experience, to see to what extent materialism has affected nations. It seems so contrary to the attitude of the ancients of welcoming a foreigner as a brother and treating him most kindly in every way, that he may not feel that he is in a strange land.

As nothing disappoints me, this reception affected me but little. They would not have me any longer than a few hours only. I was to stand before a tribunal, they asked me many questions in connection with myself and my work. And I, whose nation was all nations, whose birth place was the world, whose religion was all religions, whose occupation was search after truth, and whose work was the service of God and humanity, my answers interested them, yet did not answer the requirements of the law. In the end my mureed Mrs. Marya Cushing (Ill. 67), who was arranging my visit in New York, came to my rescue and answered all their questions to their utmost satisfaction. They seemed in the end much impressed and embarrassed, and immediately exempted me from the law of geographical expulsion.

While coming out of this house of welcome, I saw my old friend Mr. Logan, eagerly awaiting my deliverance. By the time I saw him the whole United States had heard of my arrival through the newspapers, and many sensible people I found were greatly annoyed and embarrassed, detesting this inhos-

Photograph 33. Suresnes, France. c. 1926

Photograph 34. New York, USA. February 1923

Photograph 35. New York, USA. February 1923

pitable and most abominable behaviour of their country to foreigners, especially those from Asia. No doubt, they have their reasons, but there is no good thing or bad one, which has no reason to support it.

On arriving in New York, I began giving a series of lectures in the city of New York for different Societies interested in philosophical subjects and was glad again to see the smiling face of my friend in music, Dr. Reebner. My old mureeds, Mrs. Eldering, Mrs. Logan and Miss Genie Nawn, came to see me, a meeting which was most delightful to us all. As the time was short in which to visit several places in the States, I soon proceeded to Boston and gave some lectures to the Societies interested in metaphysics. I was pleased to see Dr. A. C. Coomaraswami at the Art Museum of Boston, the only Hindu, I think, who occupies a fitting position in the States. Boston seemed to me a miniature of England in the States, the people reserved, cultured, and refined, and yet difficult to get closer to.

After my short visit to Boston I went to Detroit where the Message met with much response.

Then after paying a short visit to Chicago, I went to the West. California in the month of March was a spring queen, heavily laden with nature's beauty. And an automobile drive that my kind friends Mr. and Mrs. Wolff gave me from Los Angeles to San Francisco was a heavenly treat indeed, as if my soul was enjoying its delicious dinner which nature alone can serve. I could hardly say a word, I was so full of it. There were mountains, and there was sea at the same time, and clear sky with smiling sun above it. Nothing better could one wish.

On arriving in San Francisco, I had the longed-for meeting with Murshida Rabia Martin, whose joy in receiving me in her home was boundless.

I had welcome calls from Mr. Martin, Mr. George Baum, Mrs. Rebecca C. Miller (Ill. 63), Miss D. Hepburn, Mr. Samuel Lewis, etc. Many interesting people I met in San Francisco, as Philip Hackett, Mrs. Havens, Mrs. Long and Dr. Barnes.

I gave a long series of lectures at Paul Elder's Gallery, on philosophy, music and poetry to a most appreciative audience.

Murshida Rabia Martin, to whom was the credit of the most successful arrangement, was then made Siraja. Mr. G. Baum was made a Sheikh, Mrs. Miller, Khalifa and Cheraga, and Mr. Baum, Miss Hepburn, Mr. and Mrs. Duffy, and Mr. Willebeek le Mair (Ill. 64) were made Cherags.

The Movement there was charged with a new life, hope and courage. I had a great joy in watching this development.

While in San Francisco I went to Santa Rosa to pay a visit to America's great horticulturist, Luther Burbank (Ill. 65) and was most delighted to see that not only fine arts and spiritual culture, but even the work with the earth can elevate a man to that serenity and simplicity and love which this scientist's soul expressed. This was a proof added to many other proofs I had in my life of seeing glimpses of the divine perfection in the souls who have touched in some form or other perfection in their life's vocation[30], whatever it may be. In conversation I enjoyed hearing him say that 'I treat the plants as human beings, I feel among them as amidst friends.' For this notion, to me, was as a bridge between science and mysticism, at the same time it was a promise that science in its full rise will someday be completed by mysticism. He told me he was busy at the time trying to take away the thorns from the cactus, and asked me what I was doing. I humbly answered: 'My work is not very different from yours, Sir, for I am occupied taking away thorns from hearts of men.' Thus we came to realize how a real work through matter or spirit in the long run brings about the same result which is the purpose of life.

I then visited Santa Barbara on my way to Los Angeles, accompanied by Murshida Martin and Khalif Connaughton (Ill. 66), and was glad to speak before some appreciative audience, and to form a little group in the home of our beloved Khalif Mr. Connaughton.

Mr. and Mrs. Connaughton were made Cherags.

At Los Angeles several lectures were arranged at the Ambassador Hotel. Many people responded to the Message, which is due to the most enthusiastic spirit of Noor Jahan, Mrs. Sarah Wolff.

Mr. and Mrs. Wolff and Mr. Edgar Conrow were made Cherags.

I met there with my friends Mr. Mirza Assad Ullah and his son, Dr. Farid.

It was a great pity that the time was so short, and I had to leave them soon in having only created interest in that place.

I then paid a short visit to Chicago, where I saw Mrs. Durand, and gave a series of lectures to a very small circle of people, where my mureed Mevrouw Eggink-van Stolk had kindly assisted me in my work.

I left there the Misses Bennetts as the friends of our Movement in Chicago.

I was urged by my friends to visit Detroit again, and so I did, and found everyone nice and kind and the fire that I had kindled was flickering.

Among those interested in the Message Mr. and Mrs. Lowe, Mrs. Venable, Mrs. Hurst, Mr. and Mrs. Hobart, and some others helped to form a group to begin the work of our Movement in Detroit. Mr. Bagley was of a great assistance to me during my visit to Detroit.

Mr. and Mrs. Hobart were made Cherags.

---

30. First edition has 'avocation' thought to be a typographical error

Photograph 36. New York, USA. Spring 1923

Once speaking at a club on the problem of the day, I was very much amused to see what attitude the people had in the beginning of my talk, and how it gradually changed, that in the end many of them who were quite against religion or spiritual ideals, were entirely won over.

I had an amusing conversation with an elderly man. He, while paying me compliments for the talk I had given, declared: 'I like Jesus Christ, because he was not a Christian.'

On coming to New York again, I gave a series of lectures at the ending of the season; but, no doubt, to a very appreciative audience. I paid a flying visit to Philadelphia and gave a few lectures to a most crowded audience, full of appreciation. Alas, my stay there was not long enough to accomplish something worthwhile. Mrs. Sitara Coon had arranged my visit in Philadelphia so successfully. A group of the interested students was founded in New York by our Representative Mrs. Marya Cushing, the Cheraga, and the work of the Order was given in the charge of our Sheikh and Siraj, Mr. Shaughnessy. A committee of the above-mentioned two workers and Mr. Crowley was formed to look after the Movement. Mr. Whitehouse was made a Cherag.

I had to leave New York too soon to the great disappointment of my mureeds and friends, in order to carry out Urs, the season at Suresnes. I left New York on 9th June, accompanied by Mr. Fatha Engle (Ill. 68), a mureed who followed me to Europe.

I found America progressing more rapidly upon the lines on which it is active than my friends in the East can ever imagine. If there is anywhere that the international ideal finds response it is in the United States. It does not mean that there is no feeling of nationalism there. The germ of this disease is to be found everywhere in the world just now. In the name of nationalism, it is sectionalism that is being cultivated in the hearts of humanity, unhappily to their great disadvantage in the light of truth. America, in spite of its nationalism, has, so to speak, a natural tendency towards the international ideal. There was a great spirit of antipathy, especially in the West, towards the Japanese. But when they had an earthquake in Japan and many families destroyed, America was the first to help. There was a greater response to their President than could have been anticipated.

For spiritual things their love is growing every day, more and more. There are so many things to attract their attention, right and wrong both, that they cannot always make out which to accept and which to reject. Many therefore, go from one thing to another, and get so accustomed to moving on, that they do not feel contented with one thing. That is where is the contrast between the extreme East and the extreme West. The people of India have their Vedantas, the people in China have Buddhism; for ages they never can get tired of their religions. It is the ever-moving life in America which keeps people so restless that one cannot find peace anywhere. And yet so many different spiritual Movements seem to have been born in the

United States and carried successfully to the ends of the world.

The great difficulty I found in the United States was to make the message audible, for I felt as though blowing a whistle in the noise of a thousand drums. Anything good or bad should be brought before the people in a grand manner, and if one cannot do it, then, however valuable the Message, it will not find any response. The newspapers upon which the publicity of such things depend, first ask in which hall the lecturer is going to speak, before asking on which subject he is going to speak. As the exponents of truth very often lack the goods of the earth, they have always difficulty to present themselves properly. For instance, Coué went there with his most simple idea, which in the East even a man in the street would not stop to hear, for he would say, it is something which we have known for thousands of years. But because his coming was advertised for six months and the halls which cost many dollars were engaged, his voice reached the whole United States. For me, therefore, there was no reason to feel that the Message brought to them was too simple for them to respond to, but on the contrary, it was too deep, in spite of all its simplicity, and without a proper advertisement, which is necessary for that land.

The newspaper plays the most important part in the lives of the people there. A man would rather go without bread than a paper. The world there moves directed by the people before or behind, as it may be. The tendency of the press today seems pessimistic against what may be called good or spiritual.

The attitude that the Press in the United States takes is queer. Everything spiritual is treated by the Press lightly in order to please the multitude. Therefore, the only source by which to reach the public, seems to be almost a closed door for an earnest exponent of truth. Many reporters from the press came to me and had a conversation. My answers which they got to their questions, if they had been put in the papers would have had so much influence upon the mind of the people. The difficulty was that if a reporter happened to be an understanding and appreciative young man, still he had to show his report to someone else at the office before it was accepted. And if he did not spoil the report, then his chief thought it was too serious, for his readers something different must be put in. It is a kind of profession that the press has taken to distort every good thing and to make light of something which is serious. These tactics of the American press are followed more or less by the press in Europe also. After long conversations that the reporters of the press had with me, who seemed so interested and deeply moved by them, when the report in the papers was published, it was as if the flesh of a living person had been carved off and the skeleton were presented before all. In doing so they do not feel that they are doing any harm to the spiritual truth, nor do they mean to do so. They only think that they are doing good to both: bringing the speaker to the knowledge of the people anyway, and amusing the mob at the same time, which is ignorant of the deeper truth.

Their main object is to please the man in the street. The modern progress has an opposite goal to what the ancient people had. In the ancient times the trend of the people's thought was to reach the ideal man. Today the trend of the people's thought is to touch the ordinary man.

I must admit that in spite of all my difficulties I was not disappointed, for I never allow myself to be disappointed, fully convinced in my heart that Truth alone is victorious in the end. The devotion that my mureeds have shown me, the appreciation shown to me by my friends and the response from the thinking souls that I had during my stay in the United States, all encouraged me greatly and made me feel happy.

— · — · —

No sooner had I returned from America than I had to be occupied with the Summer School, which had no time to be organized as it ought to have been. Yet people came from different countries, lectures were continued, and the work went on well.

A question arose of building a hall in Suresnes to facilitate the work of the Summer School, calling it *Universel*. This idea was responded to by all, but the plans remained scattered, owing to diversity of opinions.

— · — · —

I then went to Geneva where our International Council for 1923 was to meet, where Mr. Zanetti succeeded in forming a literary committee, which was of immense importance for our international work. By his efforts our Constitution was revised, and our International Movement was incorporated in 1923 for the first time, according to the Swiss law.

Personal Account

I found my work in the West the most difficult task that I could have ever imagined. To work in the West for a spiritual Cause to me was like travelling in a hilly land, not like sailing in the sea, which is smooth and level. In the first place I was not a missionary of a certain faith, delegated to the West by its adherents, nor was I sent to the West as a representative of Eastern cult by some Maharaja. I came to the West with His Message, whose call I had received, and there was nothing earthly to back me in my mission, except my faith in God and trust in Truth. In the countries where I knew no-one, had not any recommendations, was without any acquaintances or friends, I found myself in a new world, a world where commercialism has become the central theme of life under the reign of materialism. In the second place there was a difficulty of language, but that difficulty was soon overcome; as I worked more, so my command of language improved.

The prejudice against Islam that exists in the West was another difficulty for me. Many think Sufism to be a mystical side of Islam, and the thought was supported by the encyclopaedias, which speak of Sufism as having sprung from Islam, and they were confirmed in this by knowing that I am Muslim by birth. Naturally I could not tell them that it is a Universal Message of the time, for every man is not ready to understand this. Many felt that the idea of universal brotherhood was a sin against the modern virtue, which is called national patriotism. My Message of peace was often interpreted as what they call pacifism, which is looked upon unfavourably by many. Many there are in the West who are prejudiced against anything Eastern, either thinking that it is too foreign to their nature or assuming that the Eastern people, who cannot even take care of themselves, and are backward in the modern civilization, are behind time; though in philosophical and literary circles the philosophy of India is considered to be ancient[31].

Besides, I often felt as an obstacle on my path the colour prejudice that exists in different places in the West. Some separate the religion of the East and West, saying that Eastern religion is for the Eastern people and Christianity the Western religion for the West; for most of the pictures of Jesus Christ are painted in the Western likeness, ignoring the fact that the Master was from the East.

Many in the Western world are afraid of mystic or psychic or occult ideas, for it is something foreign to them, and especially a foreign representative of

---

31. First edition has 'antique'

that is doubly foreign. If music had not been my shield, my task would have become much more difficult for me in the West, and my life impossible. I had to make my living by my profession of music, which has no particular place in the professional world of the West. Most often I had to sell my pearls at the value of pebbles. In the West I could not place my music in its proper place.

During the war, when my musical activities were suspended, patience was the only means of sustenance for me and my family. Yet a smiling welcome was always offered to friends at our table.

In our very worst times I had with me Miss Goodenough's unassuming help and sympathy. She shared with me her loaf, and she shielded me from the hard and soft blows, coming from both my friends and foes, thus proving to be a friend in need.

I always sensed suspicion from all sides, searchlights thrown on me in suspicion whether my Movement were not political, which always made my work difficult, to my great sadness.

When the clouds of the Socialistic Movement were hovering in the sky of England, a sudden change came in the atmosphere of London. When Gandhi proclaimed non-cooperation I heard its silent echo in the heart of Great Britain. Besides, the Khilafet Movement had stirred up the minds of the people there. I felt a hidden influence coming from every corner, resenting[32] any activity which had a sympathetic connection with the East. I then felt that the hour had come to remove the seat of our Movement to a place such as Geneva, which has been chosen as an international centre by all. In spite of all the urging on the part of my kind mureeds to stay on in England, I left there, with my bag and baggage for Switzerland.

Everything Oriental was regarded with suspicion. National feeling at that moment there was on the rise, which could make any international worker feel uncomfortable, and it had a paralysing influence upon my efforts.

I have always refrained from taking the side of any particular nation in my work, and have tried to keep my Movement free from any political shadows. Vast fields of political activity were laid open before me, during and after the war, in which I was quite capable of working at the time when there was a great demand for work of the kind, at the time of great upheaval in India and in the Near East. And if I hesitated to take interest in such activities, it was only that my heart was all taken by the need of a universal brotherhood in the world.

My own people, who found me busy with something quite different from what they would have expected of me, looked at me and my work with antipathy, and from many of them harm came to me, to add to the many difficulties I had to face. Therefore, in my struggle in the West instead of the support of the East, I had to face opposition, which made my life squeezed between two stone walls, and I have borne this pain, consoling myself with the idea that history repeats itself.

---

32. First edition has Dutch rendering 'resenting against'

Photograph 37. New York, USA. 1923

Photograph 38. With his wife Amina Begum, Sufi Garden, Suresnes, France. 5th July 1926

I would have been most happy sitting with my vina in my hand in some corner in the forest, in solitude, and nothing better would I have asked. There came a time when I could not have sufficient time to keep up my musical practice, which was too great a loss for my heart to sustain. Yet I had to bear it, for every moment of my time was absorbed in the work. I especially yearned for the music of India, the fluid with which my soul was nourished from the moment I was born on earth. But for my music the soil of India was necessary, the juice of that soil for me to live on, the air of India to breathe, the sky of India to look at, and the sun of India to be inspired by. It is just as well that I gave up my music when in the West, for if I had kept it up I would have never been fully satisfied with it, although the sacrifice of music for me was not a small one.

During my stay in the West, I longed to see the rising of the sun in my land, the full moon in the clear sky, the peace of the midsummer night, night of vigil, the sunset that calls for the prayers, and the dawn that moves the soul to sing, besides the occasion that a seeker has of meeting souls who can understand, who can heal hearts and kindle souls, enfolding all that comes in the peace of their own being.

In the West I often felt homesick; especially whenever my longing for solitude showed itself I felt very uncomfortable under all conditions, in spite of all in the West that I loved and admired. My brothers being with me in the West gave my longing soul a great consolation, for they represented India to me. But even they, in their interest in Western music gradually lost their own, which completed the absence of Indian music in my life.

I learnt later why a dervish soul like me, indifferent to the life of the world, constantly attracted to solitude, was set in the midst of the worldly life. It was my training. I learnt as a man of the world the responsibilities and the needs of the worldly life; which one standing apart from this life, however spiritually advanced, cannot understand. To feel in sympathy with my mureeds placed in different situations of life, and to be able to place myself in their situation, and look at their life, it was necessary for me. Besides to have to do with different natures and souls in the different grades of evolution, it was necessary to have had the experience of home life, especially with children, with their different stages of development, which gives a complete idea of human nature.

Ora, afterwards Amina Begum, who was born in New Mexico on 8th May 1888[33], came of a family from Kentucky called Baker, whose great uncle Judge Baker is known in Chicago. She became the mother of my four children (Ill. 69): Noorunnisa or Babuli, born on Friday 20th December 1913, (Russian date) English date: Thursday 1st January 1914; Vilayat or Bhaijan, born on Monday 19th June 1916; Hidayat or Bhaiyajan, born on Monday 6th August

---

33. First edition has 1892, but 1900 Washington State census has 1888, see *We Rubies Four*

1917 and Khairunnisa or Mamuli, born on Tuesday 3rd June 1919.

In spite of the vast difference of race and nationality and custom she proved to be a friend through joy and sorrow, proving the idea, which I always believed, that outer differences do not matter when the spirit is in atonement.

The tests that my life was destined to go through were not of a usual character, and were not a small trial for her. A life such as mine, which was wholly devoted to the Cause, and which was more and more involved in the ever-growing activities of the Sufi Movement, naturally kept me back from that thought and attention which was due to my home and family. Most of the time of my life I was obliged to spend out of home, and when at home, I have always been full of activities, and it naturally fell upon her always to welcome guests with a smile under all circumstances. If I had not been helped by her, my life, laden with a heavy responsibility, would have never enabled me to devote myself entirely to the Order as I have. It is by this continual sacrifice that she has shown her devotion to the Cause.

From a child Ora showed great strength of will. Once, when she was very ill, and a physician had given up hope and had told her mother so, not knowing that she heard that, as she lay in bed, she began to say in her childish manner emphatically: 'I will not die, I don't want to die.' And then, to the great surprise of the doctor, she lived, and he gave all the credit of her cure to her strength of determination, the spirit which fought against death. In this she showed a tendency of a relation of hers, Mrs. Eddy Baker, who has spread that idea in the world as Christian Science.

In early youth Ora once saw near her bed a phantom, an Eastern sage, who appeared a moment and passed across. She afterwards had a dream, that an Eastern sage held her in his arms and rose towards the sky, and carried her away overseas.

When Ora saw Inayat, at first sight she felt wholly drawn to him, and thought this was the one after whom her soul had always sought. He then taught her music. Ora thought it too difficult to express her feelings to Inayat, who seemed so reserved and remote from all earthly attachments. But she silently bore in her heart the great power of the attraction she felt. For some time, she was under the guardianship of her brother, who was a physician by qualification, and a leader of an Order in America.

Inayat, so fully absorbed in the mission for which he was sent to the West, had not the least thought of anything else in life except his work. At the same time, with a heart born to admire and respond to everything good and beautiful, a heart, brave to venture anything, however difficult or high if he only desired, and that ever-springing stream of love and affection running from his heart, he was ready to yield to the call for response from the maiden who was destined to be his life's partner. He perceived in his meditation indications of his future marriage, also visions which showed him the one who was meant to be his wife, and visions in which his Murshid suggested to him that the life that was to come was a necessary one towards his life's purpose. Inayat, passive as he was to the inner call, accepted it, in spite of all the difficulties before him, awaiting.

They had only known each other a few days during which their attachment grew most wonderfully and before it reached its blossom Ora had a dream, which she told Inayat, that there came a stream of water between them both, and it spread on until it turned into an ocean, dividing them both. And very soon that dream became a reality. Ora's brother, who was her guardian, on hearing of her love for Inayat, turned against him, and out of prejudice he held back his sister by force from seeing Inayat at the time when Inayat was on the point of leaving America for England. Months passed in this separation, causing endless misery to both. Not knowing about each other especially was the hardest trial for two souls so closely attached. Yet their determination was great. In the end a miracle happened. One day, arranging papers on her brother's desk she happened to find the address of Inayat's home in Baroda, and then was able to communicate with him. It seemed as if everything in life helped Ora to unite again with Inayat, and it all worked out so marvellously that it seemed nothing but a miracle, which brought about the long-desired moment; and they married in London on 20th March 1913[34].

It is not true that my life was always deprived of riches. There occurred several occasions which offered me enormous wealth. Only every time an occasion like this came, it did not fit in with my principle, and I had to renounce that profit for the sake of my principle. I consider it no loss, although it was a loss outwardly. The strength that I gained by standing by my principle was much greater than any riches of this earth.

Nevertheless, poverty proved to be my bitterest enemy. For it always put me in a position that gave my adversaries every facility they desired to cause me harm. With all my mistakes and failings, which I must not disown, I have always tried to avoid dishonour. I was several times in a position which I should have never chosen to be in, but I was constrained by unfortunate circumstances. My pride at the time was very much hurt, and often that has happened. If there are any pages in the book of my life which I would rather be closed than open, they are narrative of my lack of means.

Miss Dowland brought into existence that fund which was intended to be for my maintenance, and continued it for three years, when it was sorely needed. Later the same fund was also subscribed to by the mureeds from Holland, Belgium and Switzerland.

Many wondered if it was beyond the power of a mystic to attract wealth, if he

---

34. First edition has 1912, but marriage certificate dated 20th March 1913, see *We Rubies Four*

Photograph 39. Sufi Garden, Suresnes, France 5th July 1926

sorely needed it as I did in my life. I could not very well answer this question, but I never felt that it was beyond my reach to obtain wealth if I wanted to. But in this respect my life has been that of a bird, who must descend on earth to pick up a grain, but his joy is in flying in the air. If one told the bird, 'There are no grains in the air, stay on the earth and collect grains', he would say, 'No, it is only a few grains which I need. If there be tons of grains lying on the earth, it will not attract me enough to give up my joy of flying in the air.' In the same way I could not sacrifice the real interest of my life, even if all the wealth that the earth can give was offered to me.

After twelve years of wandering and homeless life in the West, with a large family to look after, in addition to having my laudable object to carry out, I was provided at last with four walls (Ill. 70) at Suresnes, thanks to the kind sympathy of my Dutch mureed, Mevrouw Egeling (Ill. 71); that, when going about to preach in the world, I might have the relief of thinking that my little ones are sheltered from heat and cold under a roof. This saintly soul came into my life as a blessing from above, whom I called Fazal Mai, which means Grace of God, and after her name the house was named. Her hand, as a hand of Providence, became my backbone, which comforted me, and raised my head upwards in thanksgiving, the head which so long was hanging in humiliation, owing to the utter lack of means.

In my life-long work in the West I found that in the West there are no disciples; there are teachers. Woman, being respondent by nature, shows a tendency towards discipleship, but that is not every woman. And men in the West, who try to show the disciple-spirit, somehow fail to play this role some time or the other.

Most of my life in the Western world has been spent to prepare those who were attracted to the inner teachings, to grasp the idea of what is called *Guru Shishya Bhau*, which means the relation between the spiritual teacher and the pupil. And I found that where an Eastern teacher began, that was the end that I was to arrive at in the training of my pupils. So my task, compared with that of the spiritual teachers of the East, was quite different to theirs. Most part of my work was given to prepare the minds of mureeds for that ideal which is so little known in the West. It has been my lot, especially in the beginning of my work, that I had to build the whole building with unaccommodating vessels and broken tools. It was like playing on a piano which is out of tune, and blowing upon the horns full of holes. Later things turned for the better. However, my loneliness was ever on the increase, and my only consolation was in the realization of the divine Truth that 'I alone am the only existing being'.

The Christian faith for long ages has made such a deep impression upon the people in the West, that they cannot see a spiritual teacher with a family-setting, knowing Christ in his exclusive being. Even the nearness of a woman seemed strange in their eyes.

Destiny made women understand my message and sympathize with me more readily than men, whose lives are absorbed in their daily occupations, and whose ideal and devotion is almost lost in the modern way of living. This made my life and work most difficult. I found on one hand a ditch, and on the other hand water.

My difficulty was that those of faith in the Western world clung to their own faith, and those of no faith wanted to keep free from any faith; nor could I catch the former ones, because of their faith, nor could I hold the latter ones, for having no faith. Many who were attracted to my free thought, inspired by the ideal of freedom, tried to keep free from me also.

I always considered myself above everything I had to say, think, or do in my life. I thought, 'surely, it is not the real me, it is my outward limited self, the limitation of life, which always kept my heart sore'.

While travelling in the Western countries I was often asked by people if I had the power of clairvoyance, if I could see their auras, if I could tell them their colour or note, if I could read their thoughts, if I had any psychical powers, if I could foretell what will happen, if I was mediumistic, if I spoke under spiritualistic control, if I knew automatic writing, if I was able to magnetize, if I could psychometrize. Firstly, I was most amused with these questions, to which I could neither give an affirmative nor a negative answer. By an affirmative answer I would have been put to the test, and a negative answer would be my defeat; and yet I often preferred defeat, and in some cases I avoided answering. It is something which in the East a sage does not expect. For a real sage, all these powers are outward plays, little things. Some people claim them, and the Theosophical influence made it even more difficult for me to answer people. Some directly asked me if I was a Master. It made me speechless. What could I have said, the truth or a lie? Could I have claimed, and have become one among the various false claimants, as there are so many in this world? Even I was reluctant in saying 'No'. If I ever said anything, I said: 'My good friend, I am your friend, your brother and your servant, if you take me to be so; for it is not any claim, but service which is both my privilege and honour.'

Photograph 40. Suresnes, France 5th July 1926

Diary

October 1923
The response to the Message was as usual in Geneva.

I had great pleasure in making the acquaintance of Paderewsky and his most responsive wife, who has thought on philosophical subjects for a long time. In all the hospitality I received in their home, what I valued the most was Paderewsky's few minutes at the piano in which he gave life to that thought which I always had, that a great soul in the East or West, is great; that music ennobles personality, that music is intoxicating, it brings ecstasy. In Paderewsky I found the example of this.

At Morges, which is more or less a musical place, by the kindness of the friend of India, Monsieur René Morax, a lecture was arranged. I spoke on the power of music and my lecture was attended by music lovers, among them Paderewsky with his family. I spoke at Lausanne to an appreciative audience. My lectures in Basel and Zürich were well attended. Herr Glaser (Ill. 34) in Basel and the Strauss family in Zürich were most helpful in making my lectures successful. I was pleased to see in Switzerland as responsive a mureed as Fraülein Burkhardt (Ill. 72), who arranged lectures at Rapperswil, which were well attended. I met in Rapperswil Frau Hilda Meyer (Ill. 73), who not only responded but became a mureed. Her thoughtfulness and appreciation for all that is good and real, and her great zeal in trying to bring before others what seemed to her good and beautiful, I found to be most valuable.

Since Frau Hilda Meyer has joined the Order she has been a great blessing to the Cause. From the moment she came, the work in Switzerland has really begun to flourish, and we hope that by her worthy collaboration the Message will indeed spread in that land of beauty. We also recognize the important work she has done in bringing out the literature in the German language, the credit of which is due to her. She has generously responded to the call for help from any side of the Sufi Movement. I found in her a promising mureed and a dependable friend.

From Switzerland I proceeded to Italy, accompanied by Murshida Goodenough and my Cherag, Fatha Engle. We were received in Florence by Marchese Gentile Farinola, whose most kind and gentle nature together with the bright intelligence of Marchesa Farinola (Ill. 74) gave me great pleasure.

Besides it made me happy to see the acquaintance the couple had already made with Sufism, which is so rarely to be found in the Western countries. Through these our kind hosts, some lectures were arranged in Florence, where I had small but most appreciative audiences.

> We saw Lady Sybil Scott, in whose house Graf and Gräfin Wurmbrandt were staying, friends of Murshida Goodenough. I was glad to make acquaintance with Contessa Bacciocchi, an educationist and Signorina Giuliani became my mureed.

The nature in Florence was most fascinating for me. I passed my few days of visit in this sunny land with great pleasure. I gave this farm to look after to my faithful mureed Mrs. Hanifa Sheaf, and went to Rome.

> Rome made upon me a great impression. Once, after having seen the Church in its glory in Russia, which I did not think I could see anymore, I witnessed in Rome that glory of the old Church still in existence. I went to see the Church the like of which I have never seen before in its form and beauty, and in its grandeur. The troops of priests to-be, fifteen, twenty or hundred, moving about hither and thither, gave me quite a new sight, which never in my travelling through the Western world I have seen. I attended some services at the Catholic Church, and what I learned from it was that it was all a preparation, which a service is meant to be, a perfectly organized drill by which to learn to respect man, above all a spiritual man, and in the end by bowing and bending to mankind – which represents spirituality – to arrive at worshipping man (the son of God), God's representative. I thought it is the very sentiment that is needed to waken in man, though it is done in a narrow way; and yet in no other way can it be very well done. The present deplorable condition of religion that is to be found in the Western world is owing to the lack of the same principle which, it seemed to me, the service of the Roman Catholic Church taught: the lack of veneration for one's advanced brother. The spirit of the present generation is: 'I am as good as you.' When a soul has nothing to look up to, it drops its wings, and a soul who was meant to be a bird, remains a beast.
>
> I was introduced at the Vatican where I happened to see Monsignor Cascia and through him Cardinale Gasparri, the Secretary of State, who asked me 'What did I mean by wisdom?' From the explanation of my idea and my work, the Secretary of State saw the importance of it by hesitatingly admitting it with consent and half-consent. And in a ceremony where I was kindly invited, my heart felt it was confirmed by the touch of the Pope's blessing hand.

I gave three lectures in Rome, mostly attended by Theosophists, free thinkers and religious people also. The response there which I felt indeed, exceeded

Photograph 41. New York, USA. 28th February 1923

my expectations. Dott. Assagioli kindly translated my lectures in Florence, also in Rome.

> *I was glad to make acquaintance of Professore Formichi, a Sufi in spirit, and through him was glad to make acquaintance of Contessa Spaletti Rasponi. I found in her the ancient manner with modern culture, noble spirit in simplicity. Her enquiry into the work of the Movement and her keen interest in the seeking of truth brought us in a closer touch.*

The group of students of the new mureeds was carried on by my sincere mureed Miss Angela Alt (Ill.84).

On my return from Italy I occupied myself with the work in Paris. Several new persons became interested during this my visit to Paris.

I proceeded to Belgium and was most delighted to see a page in the book of our Movement turning. The credit of this is due to Mejuffrouw Sakina Furnée who by the help of a devotee to the Cause, Mejuffrouw Hayat Rahusen, endeavoured to waken up the Society there. I spoke that time at several places and gave Mejuffrouw Sakina Furnée the charge of acting National Representative.

During my visit to England in January 1924 I met de Heer van Stolk (Ill. 76) from Holland, whose joining forces with me made my heavy burden easier for me to carry. He accompanied me in my journeys.

We first visited Geneva, where we found the work going on smoothly. Baroness van Hogendorp was busy forming a preparatory group for the study of Sufism. I then proceeded to Bern, visiting Lausanne on my way. Herr Baur (Ill. 75) had prepared in Bern for my lectures, and my Message met there with response.
   De Heer van Stolk accompanied me on my second visit to Italy, where I had some work of cultivating the ground for the Message.

I passed then through Belgium to Holland. During my short stay in Belgium I saw members in Brussels, and I found that the old workers, such as Madame Graeffe and Dr. Bommer, had retired and the whole weight of the responsibility and work fell upon the Acting National Representative, Mejuffrouw Sakina Furnée; and the patience and courage with which she has carried out her work impressed me deeply.

On arriving in Holland, I found that the work of the Movement was progressing. The facility for classes, and services, and readings that Baron van Tuyll, the National Representative, had given in his own house was indeed a

Photograph 42. London, UK. May 1921

step forward. On this occasion I stayed in Holland for a short time.

Then de Heer van Stolk helped me greatly in taking upon himself the organizing of the Summer School at Suresnes. Since he has taken this work in hand, the Summer School has flourished splendidly.

I was for a week in Geneva, to attend different Council Meetings, and was glad to see the great zeal shown by the workers of the Cause.
    I also visited Basel, Zürich, Rapperswil and Lausanne.
    It is since the last three months that my wish of establishing a Press Bureau in connection with the Sufi Headquarters has been materialized by the unceasing efforts of Mr. Armstrong (Sheikh) (Ill. 77), a most enthusiastic worker of the Cause and the Cherag who introduced Universal Worship in South America, with the help of Miss van Hogendorp (Ill. 77), whose soul soaked in the Message, always giving me the joy of seeing her gradual unfoldment.

I took a second tour through Germany and met various people, among them Baronin A. von Grünewaldt. I spoke in Munich once at the Park Hotel and twice in the Steinicke Saal, also at Dr. Arthur Ludwig's house, to appreciative audiences, and left a group of mureeds in charge of Mrs. Hoeber (Ill. 78), my American mureed. Then I proceeded to Berlin, staying with Herr and Frau Triebel. I gave my lectures at the Urania Hall. There was no doubt a great response given to my lectures from all sides. Only the difficulty of translation was excessively great. I felt the spirit in Berlin changing; nevertheless the minds of the people are still sensitive. Baron and Baronin von Barany were made Cherags, and I left the group of mureeds in the charge of Miss Oliver.

We then proceeded to Sweden, where Dr. von Reutercrona had kindly arranged some lectures for me, before a small gathering of people.

I greatly enjoyed the beauty of the country and the simplicity of the people there. It seemed to me that Scandinavia was quite a different part of the world compared to Central Europe. The effect that the worldly life has produced in Central Europe and in the United States of America, has made the inhabitants of these regions partly too clever and partly affected morally and physically by too much strain of everyday life. Both these things seem to be less prevailing yet in Scandinavia.

I did not have as satisfactory results as I had expected to have, for the reason that I went before the ground was cultivated for the Cause. Fröken Haglund, my sincere mureed, kindly tried to do all she could to serve the Cause. Herr Nyrop and some other mureeds formed a group, and the work was, however, begun in Stockholm.

Photograph 43. San Francisco, USA. 1923

I had the great pleasure of seeing, the Archbishop Nathan Söderblom from Upsala, and was pleased indeed to know that he was working to bring together all different Christian faiths. And I was glad to hear him say that this was the first step; that showed me that he believed in the second step also. He was busy at the time we went to him with a school in which he is interested. (Sigtuna). Therefore, we had a short meeting; but I left with an impression of his thoughtful personality.

I then proceeded to Norway, and gave some lectures in the University of Christiania[35] and for the Theosophical Society there. Destiny brought me together with a soul who belonged to us; I only had to go to Christiania in order to find her. It was Fröken Susanna Kjösterud (Ill. 79), a soul whose heart was open to the Message. The Message only had to reach there in order to find response in her. Those who became interested in my teaching, including Herr Björset, formed a group in Oslo, which was carried by Fröken Susanna Kjösterud.

I found a different atmosphere in Norway from that I had felt in Stockholm. People there seemed to be of democratic spirit and they responded more readily to the Message. I went from there to Bergen, a beautiful place near mountains. The atmosphere in that place helped my lectures to make a greater and deeper impression upon the people there. Fröken Thistle and some others became mureeds, and the work has been continued there since then. The credit of my success there was mainly due to my mureed Mejuffrouw Morad Rahusen, who by the help of her kind friend Fru Isaachsen, a deep lady of artistic sense and broad views. was able to arrange my visit so splendidly.

I proceeded from there to Denmark, and found in the English Club in Copenhagen an opening to deliver the Message. By the kindness of Herr Jenssen several lectures were arranged. I found that place more open for the work of the Movement than any other place in the North, although I could do little owing to my short visit in this place. There being no one to conduct the group of some few mureeds which was formed at Copenhagen, it was given in the hands of Fru Paula Steven. I visited where my mureed Herr Hermund arranged a lecture. In Herr Hermund I found a promising mureed.

I had to hasten back to Germany on the invitation of Professor Görcke to speak at Urania Hall again, three times, at Berlin.

On our way back Providence brought us together with Dr. Steindamm, in whom I found the spirit of the worker, who inspired me with the hope that the Message will spread rapidly in Germany, if the Movement there were organized on a sound basis.

---

35. Now known as Oslo, this is not further noted

Photograph 44. London UK. May 1921

I visited Holland on my way back and was glad indeed to see the great zeal that Baron and Baroness van Tuyll showed in furthering the Cause in their land. I saw the Society in The Hague flourishing, and was pleased to see that Jonkheer van Spengler had joined forces with the National Representative, to help him in his responsible work. I was touched by the way Mejuffrouw van Braam (Ill. 80) was working in Amsterdam, without many helpers at her side. I was pleased to hear how busy Mevrouw van Ingen (Ill. 81) has been giving lectures and creating interest in her part of the country; and the new step Mevrouw Eggink (Ill. 82) had taken in having rooms in Rotterdam for the work of the Cause, I thought to be splendid. I appreciated very much the service that Salamat Hoyack rendered to the Cause.

On my way back, I stayed in Belgium, and for the first time visited Liège. I valued Mejuffrouw Sakina Furnée's work more and more each time I have visited Belgium, knowing how hard it is to cultivate that ground in absence of any helpers. It would not be an exaggeration if I said that the Movement is alive in Belgium by the living enthusiasm of one person. No words of praise can be adequate for the patient working of Mejuffrouw Sakina Furnée.

January 1925. On my coming to Paris I found our venerable friend and worker Baroness d'Eichthal as busy as ever. The wonderful talks that our most trusted worker Murshida Goodenough gave to mureeds and friends in Paris kept up the rhythm of my Message during my absence. I spoke at the Musée Guimet, at the Sorbonne, and gave lectures at the drawing room of Baroness d'Eichthal. Paris has so many distractions that it is found always difficult to keep the thoughts of the mureeds concentrated on one line. Besides, for many and various reasons, members seemed to be scattered. It is by the most sincere devotion of Mejuffrouw Kismet Stam (Ill. 83) to the Cause that she made unceasing efforts to keep threads together, thus keeping alive that flame which was once kindled, from being blown away by the continual attacks of the sweeping wind.

January 1925. I was delighted as ever to visit Switzerland, the land of beauty and charm. I appreciated the co-operation of Fräulein Burckhardt (Ill. 72) in literature, also the services of Herr Baur in it. It always has, and it always will make me proud to see in Khalif Talewar Dussaq the devotion of a rare quality, the profound understanding of human nature and his firm faith in the Message of God. The kindness and the warmth that he and his sister, Comtesse Pieri, poured out to all those that came to the Headquarters embraced all in the Sufi warmth. I must not let pass without speaking of it, the great enthusiasm that Naqib Mevrouw van Hogendorp has always shown in serving the Cause, having proved faithful in all conditions and circumstances. She has been a voice in the wilderness. In Monsieur Zanetti I saw a growing interest for the Message, which he showed in controlling and carrying out

Photograph 45. USA 1926

the administrative part of the work every day better and better. In Monsieur Zanetti we indeed have a most precious help. I had a greater response in this year in Bern, Lausanne, Zürich, Rapperswil, and Basel. I should think it is because the lectures were organized better, the credit of which is due to our most worthy National Representative, Frau Meyer de Reutercrona (Sheikha).

I went to Italy, where Miss Angela Alt had charge of the Movement, who worked there so wonderfully in a country where discrimination and tact are most necessary. I appreciated very much the desire to help the Cause by Mrs. Sheaf, who settled in Florence with that intention. I saw a great many difficulties that stand in the way of the worker in Italy, but in spite of that Miss Alt did splendidly. I gave lectures at the British Institute, at the Biblioteca Filosofica, and at the Association for Religious Progress, and created some interest before I proceeded to Rome. By the great enthusiasm of Mr. and Mrs. Craig (Ill. 85) several lectures were arranged in Rome. This time there was a greater response than any other time before. Many cultured people joined the group and an interest in the Movement was created in a place where it is not always easy to work. Mrs. Craig I found to be a splendid worker and a mureed with enthusiasm and understanding of the Message.

On my way back from Italy to Paris, accompanied by de Heer Sirkar van Stolk, I visited Nice, where Mejuffrouw Kismet Stam had arranged some lectures in a public hall. I spoke at the house of Comte and Comtesse Prozor, where I was warmly received. The time when I visited Nice being not propitious, nothing much was accomplished, except that Baron von Howen, who took up the work in that part of the country, followed the Message.

I paid a hurried visit to Germany, first visiting Berlin, and gave three lectures there in the month of March in 1925. I found Frau Triebel as kind as ever, and Miss Oliver busy working, Baron and Baronin von Barany carrying the load of responsibility, and Dr. Steindamm, who was made a Sheikh, showing a growing enthusiasm. I met with the same difficulty as before with the translation of my lectures. From there I went to Munich, where Mejuffrouw Kismet Stam was able to gather up mureeds scattered here and there, giving them a new enthusiasm. She arranged a series of lectures for me. I had the same response from people as I always had in Germany.

On my return from Germany I spoke a few times at the Sorbonne.

In the month of April 1925, I visited and spoke at Bournemouth, and also gave addresses to mureeds in Southampton. Circumstances did not permit more to be done in England this time.

I began working at the Summer School, better arranged this time than ever

Photograph 46. Suresnes, France. c.1926

before by de Heer van Stolk. I was glad to notice the generous response of mureeds to secure the piece of land intended to build the 'Universel' (Ill. 86).

Sixteen Cherags were made, and Monsieur Zanetti, Baron van Tuyll and Khalif Maheboob Khan were made Sheikh, and Fröken Kjösterud and Mrs. Hoeber, Sheikha

This time the Summer School was better attended.

Immediately after the Summer School our yearly Council meetings took place in Geneva, earlier than usual, which were much more lively than in the previous years. For those assembled at them showed intense desire for the furtherance of the Cause. I noticed more clearly the present spirit of the people and nations, knocking at our door also, which to me seemed to be a strange psychological phenomenon. In spite of differences which gave the meetings a modern tone, I felt each one taking the welfare of the Movement too much to heart with the best intentions. I marvelled at Monsieur Zanetti working so wisely under all circumstances.

My plan about going to the United States remained indefinite till I heard from de Heer van Stolk that arrangements were being made for a lecture tour beginning from New York. I reached New York on December 6th and had no difficulty whatever with the port authorities as before, thanks to our friends Mr. Cosgrave and Mr. Chase Crowley. I was glad to meet Mr. Shaughnessy at my arrival. I was a guest of Mr. Crowley at the Waldorf Astoria Hotel. For the first week there was a rush of newspaper reporters calling on me, and after I had given all the points which touched my philosophy and work, after even I had won the sympathy of some of the Press representatives, I found that in the papers it was said quite differently, and often quite the opposite to what I had said. In the place of a horse it was a donkey, and in the place of a man it was a monkey. At my first lecture at the Auditorium of the Waldorf Astoria, there was a great crowd. Some of them came from the advertisements, some of them from the reports the newspapers gave, some of them came to see some phenomena performed on the platform, some out of curiosity; and some had the patience to stay there five minutes after they entered the hall. Nevertheless, it was a success. It made me wonder as to what the world wants: truth or falsehood. Souls unconsciously seek for truth, but are delighted with falsehood.

The cause of the following series of lectures not being well-attended, to my mind was that those lectures were given too late after the Press talk. Also, the advertisement was not continued in the same measure as it began. But some of my friends thought that my voice did not reach. They did not mind if my inspiration was blown away by shouting, as long as my voice reached the masses. Others thought that I did not speak quick enough for the

Photograph 47. June 1926

Photograph 48. Arizona, USA. 14th April 1926

Photograph 49. Suresnes, France. 13th September 1926

American mind. I laughed in my mind thinking: how did they expect the weight of Divine inspiration to be carried quickly to the hearts of the mortal world. However, it is the experience of many that New York is a hard field to work (Ill. 87). Nevertheless, many acquaintances were made, much has been accomplished, several mureeds joined the Sufi group there.

I was asked by the Theosophical Society to speak on the coming world Teacher, and on Mrs. Besant's proclamation about it. But I thought that such a lecture must be given by someone more competent on that subject, and so I refused it. I was invited at a dinner of an Occult Club, where I heard everyone talking freely on their occult experiences. I felt diffident to talk before its members, who, each of them, seemed to have their specific opinion on the subject. It seemed to me a democratic Movement toward the investigation of truth, or of falsehood.

I saw Mrs. Otto Kahn, and was pleased indeed with her sympathetic attitude. I met with some most interesting men at the lunch given by Colonel House; the president of the City College, Dr. Turner, the governor of New Jersey, Mr. A. Harry Moore, Dr. Carrel of the Rockefeller Institute, etc.

Mr. Crowley, knowing my interest for writing plays, took me to several theatres, giving me the idea of the modern play. I thought the modern play is a step forward in civilization, but the people who have already lost ideal, are still further removed from it by the help of the modern play.

I saw Bishop Brown, about whom there is so much talk in the papers, and I thought all the greatness that brought him to that reputation was his insolence to his own religion. He said he did not believe every letter of the words in the Bible as they believe in the Church. No one with thought would believe every word in the same way as every simple person believes. If he did something different, it was that he said it. If one says everything one thinks about in a religion followed by millions of people, it only means one has no respect neither for the Church nor for the community. People were trying to take him in hand in order to give a blow to the Church. On the other side I heard of another amusing story[36]: a New York Rabbi[37] had said to his audience that Jesus was 'a great man', and there was a great talk going on about it all in the papers. I then knew what the Press wants, what the public wants: not philosophy, only sensation.

I was very glad to visit the Rockefeller Institute by the kindness of Dr. Carrel. He asked me if it is true that there is a supernatural power. I said, 'There is a power, but I call it a natural power. People call it supernatural because they do not know it to be natural.' He showed me the new electric machines in which is produced a tremendous power of electricity. Also the

---

35. First edition has Dutch rendering 'another fun'
37. Referring to Rabbi S.S. West

solutions which keep the cells of the human body for many years. I told him that there is that electricity in the human body also. But he asked if it can be utilized for a certain purpose. I said, 'To a greater purpose still.' I added that: 'In regard to the cells which you are able to keep so long, there existed a science in the East by which they used to keep bodies undestroyed in the ground for hundreds of years.' Dr. Carrel asked me if it is possible to lift a pen from the table by the power of thought. I said 'Yes, it is possible, there is nothing impossible; only why should a mystic strive to lift a pen, if he can lift the heart of man by his power to a higher ideal.'

In Mrs. Shewan who joined our Movement, I found a very interesting student of life.

I gave some lectures to a small number of audience at the Lenox Theatre, which were much appreciated, and which brought several members to the Sufi Movement.

The enthusiastic collaboration of Mr. and Mrs. Frey impressed me deeply. The centre which was so well taken care of by Mrs. Cushing, was then given in the hands of Sheikh Fatha Engle, to carry on the work in New York. Several Cherags were ordained before I left for Detroit.

My mureeds, Mrs. Venable and Mrs. Hurst, had arranged a series of lectures at the Twentieth Century Club. My lectures were well attended because of good publicity. I was invited by the Woman's Press Club in Detroit to give a lecture there. Dr. Watson from Canada came to Detroit to meet me there. I had a very interesting visit with Mr. Ford. When one compares his simplicity with his great success in the business world, one cannot help thinking that he is a great soul. Mr. Ford intuitively has been believing which has been known to the Sufis for ages: that to some in the time of their distress and at the time when they must accomplish something worthwhile in life, there came invisible forces to help them. It interested me to hear him say that, 'What I have searched after all my life, you have found it.' He added saying that, 'If you were a businessman, you certainly would have made a success, but I am glad that you are as you are.'

I went to San Francisco, and was glad to see there Murshida Martin, the mother of the Sufi Movement in the United States. I spoke at San Francisco at the Fairmont Hotel to a very large audience and was introduced by Mr. Paul Elder. I also gave a series of lectures to a selected audience in the Sufi Centre and spoke at Oakland, and Berkeley, and at Paul Elder's Gallery. I was interested to speak at the Woman's Press Club, where I met with many interesting people. I had the pleasure of visiting the Oriental house of Mrs. Frank Havens, and I heard Mr. Vandernaillen explain in a most interesting manner about the Mayan philosophy. Mrs. Havens asked me the same question about reincarnation which she had asked me, and I had answered in 1910 and in 1923. I repeated the same answer, but I believe that she wished that question to ring around her always vibrating so that an answer may not reach her, but may be drowned in the noise of her question. Murshida took me to show me the Khankah, which is situated in such a beautiful nature. The house is intended to be a place for meditation for mureeds who wish to take a retreat in the solitude. There was a large rock that belonged to the Khankah which was named Pir Dahan.

I was glad to visit Dr. Abrams' Institute where they kindly explained to me about his system. It interested me very much that even scientists come closer to the idea of vibrations.

Several Cherags and mureeds were made.

A devoted mureed, Saladin Reps, drove me to Santa Barbara. Murshida Martin accompanied me on my tour through California. After one lecture before a fair number of audience in the Recreation Centre, and after ordaining some Cherags, I went to Los Angeles. In Beverley Hills I first received Press representatives and then I went to La Jolla and San Diego on a short visit, where I spoke to fairly large audiences. In San Diego I went to see the place made by Mrs. Tingley, and found the spot to be most beautiful. My first lecture near Los Angeles was given in Pasadena, in the Church of the Truth. I felt the Church was already truth, what more have I to say? But still I tried my best to say little, and the audience, including the clergyman, responded very well.

PART III

Journal and Anecdotes

Review of Religions

I came from the East with the idea, which every Eastern person has, that the people in the West are all Christians. But after coming, the more I saw the Western world and the more I knew about the general attitude of the people in the West towards religion, the more I found that this idea of the Eastern people was unfounded.

I saw in the West people of three categories: those who believe in God and hereafter; those who do not believe the same; and those who believe in the Christian Church. Among intellectual and lettered people and among the people of scientific trend of mind I found most very materialistic, who are truthful in confessing their disbelief, who consider it falsehood to profess a belief in something one does not know. They found their faith upon things that are within the grasp of their reason. Many of them consider belief in God, or the soul, or in hereafter as a religious fad. There are others among them who think, there may be something, perhaps, which we do not know, and it is best not to trouble about it. Most of them believe in the phenomenon of science which is the only source on which they depend. Some of them sometimes in their life begin to wonder at life, and show to know something of its source and goal and of its latent power, which remains so far unexplored by science. They take no other method than that of scientific research to explore the phenomena hidden behind life, and as a natural consequence they arrive at no definite result.

There are many in the West who believe that there is some God and perhaps a hereafter, and there is a soul somewhere within or without, but they do not follow a particular religion, though some of them may belong to a certain Church for the sake of conventionality. They are more open to go into the truth, for no Church in particular binds them. Among them there are some who are contented with their belief in God and trouble no more about it, and there are others who are open to listen to any point of view on the subject other than their own. It is in that category of people that there are some who go in search of the God-ideal, the soul and the hereafter and religious truth. For neither does materialism hinder their path, nor a particular faith stand in their way as an obstacle. Then there are those who belong to a certain Church. Some among them only belong to a Church for the sake of conventionality. There are State Churches to which officials must go, who belong to that State. Some belong to the Church because their friends or relations belong to it, and some for other social reasons. Some no doubt go devoutly, most of them being not of the intellectual classes.

There are two principal Christian Churches in the West: the Roman Catholic and the Protestant, besides the Greek Church and the Old Christian Church which are little known in most of the civilized parts of the Western world. However, as a Church there seems to be only one, which is the Roman Catholic Church. If some reminiscences of the religious form of the old, of the moral, of the ancient, of the manner of the Christians, of the ancient philosophical outlook on life, of the old mystical conception can be found anywhere, it is in this Church. In organization there is no Church in the whole world which could be better founded. Its influence, although gradually being diminished, still is greater than that of any other Church. The Church of Rome is the only one that can be called a Church.

There has always been a friendship and enmity between politics and religion. It is politics which have helped religion in its spread and existence, and so it is politics which have fought with the religion, breaking its backbone and pulling it down to nothingness. This has been the case with the Church of Rome. It grew and spread by its political power and it broke down and fell also by political reasons, and was made and marred both by the same.

The Catholic Church is a body which was built for the mind of Saint Paul to make use of as its vehicle, the mind which was truly inspired by the Christ spirit. The stronger the body became, the weaker became the heart. The consequence was that the spirit could no longer use the heart which was its tabernacle, which became merely a receptacle of the juice of the body. The real subsistence of the Church which was once the flesh and blood of Christ, then remained only in form.

The adherents of this faith have the greatest discipline, although many belong to this Church only outwardly; inwardly they are indifferent or even opposed to it. Not only among the followers, but even among priests, one finds some opponents of this Church. Politics in the Western world have continually taken a place of greater importance until they have uprooted religion from the surface of the Western world. One thing, the riches of the Roman Church, and the other thing, its influence on world polities, have made the opponents inclined to slander the lives of the priests. Celibacy being taught in Christian religion and practised by the Catholic priests has made the idea of celibacy a virtue in the mind of the people in the West. Even though it is not practised by the generality still it remains, so to speak, in the subconsciousness of the Western mind as an ideal and it has caused a great confusion in the social morals of the West. Many in the West attack the priesthood and the working of the Roman Church. All the countries in the West which are known as Catholic countries are not necessarily devout Catholics, though some among them, backward in civilization, still maintain their faith devoutly.

I once met a Catholic priest who is a well-known man in Paris: l'abbé Clain. He asked me if I would tell him some ideas of the Eastern thinkers which they get in their meditation. He listened to what I said attentively.

Every word I said seemed not foreign to him, not against his ideas. He was so pleased with all he heard, and with all we spoke together, and with that which we could not speak in words, but can only be exchanged in silence, and in the end he only said: 'What you say is not different from what we believe, except for the difference in terminology.'

Protestantism is a substitute for a faith rather than a religion; it is a protest against the original Christian Church instead of a prophetic Message. One sees that spirit of protest still alive in some countries. Protestantism is the shadow of the outer form of Islam, not necessarily the reflection of its spirit. The Muslim invasion in 1435 which caused a Reformation in the West, is the evidence of this truth. The Western mind which was to some extent revolting against the Roman Church owing to many reasons, chiefly owing to its political influence, was looking for a change, and the impression that the invaders from the East left behind in the West materialized as an outer Islam, not in name, but in sense, and it was still called a Christian Church, but Protestant. What a follower of Islam lacks in the outward show of religion he makes up for it by his faith in God, belief in Qur'an, and devotion to his Prophet.

Protestantism is a religion which is void both of spirit and form, a flower without colour or fragrance. It is a rattle given into the hand of a child to keep him quiet, when he was crying for candy. Their belief is not very different from that of the new sect called among Muslims *Ahl-i-Hadith*, who stick to the letter exclusive of the spiritual personalities; to them the book is more important than a kindled heart.

I was once travelling and met an intellectual gentleman from Switzerland. We were talking together about the present state of the world in general. I said: 'Religion is the foundation of the whole life in the world, and as long as an understanding is not established between the followers of all different religions, it will always be difficult to hope for better conditions.' He said: 'Yes, you are right. But a better understanding among humanity will not be established as long as the whole world does not accept the Bible as the holy book.' I did not argue more with this person, since I was not against the Bible, only I knew the Bible in all its volumes, which are in different names and held in esteem by different people, and besides the living Bible of nature, which is always manifest to my view. I simply asked him to tell me something more about it, that I might be enlightened on the subject. He did so very willingly, and all through the journey he talked to me about it, and I listened.

The Catholics have their saints; in that way they get an ideal of human personality. They have also the pictures and images of Christ's life, which have the effect of melting the heart. This makes the Catholics tuned to a certain pitch. But the Protestant, who has neither anything in his Church to touch his heart, nor saints to hold as an ideal, has only the name of Christ without form and a closed book to hold on to. It would not be an exaggeration if I said that the downfall of the Christian religion was caused, no doubt, by the Catholic Church by the doctrine that Jesus Christ was conceived of the

Holy Ghost, but the Protestants finished it by their belief in the Divinity of Christ, exclusive of manhood, resulting in the materialism which one finds everywhere in the West.

There is the Anglican Church, which still maintains all form and conventionality of the Roman Church, except the supremacy of the Pope. All forms are kept intact, save the adherence that Christians showed to the recognized Representative of Christ. The members of this Church are numerous; many of them seem devoted to their faith and proud of having overthrown the sovereignty of the Pope.

Among these two Churches, the Protestant and the Catholic, there is a great deal of antagonism, sometimes owing to political reasons, among the intellectual people, and owing to simple differences among the people bigoted in faith. Only the Catholic covers it with his religious dignity and the Protestant shows it without any restraint.

The Christian Bible which consists of the Old Testament and the New Testament has been of great interest to me to study and to look at from all sides. To the Old Testament, which was kept intact by the Jews of ancient times, was later added the New Testament. This was written by Saint Paul, who on hearing the legends which were handed down for about 300 years after the time of Jesus, wrote in the form of his mystical knowledge, giving it a philosophical colouring. Therefore these two Testaments, the Old and the New, are quite different one from the other. And as the centre of the Christian Church was formed afterwards in Rome, the New Testament went through a continual changing process, until it has arrived at the state in which it is today, which is much more comprehensible to the mind of the modern European believer in the Christian faith than is the Old Testament. Those who are willing to follow the Christian religion find it easier to believe in the New Testament, as it is just now, than as it was given by Saint Paul. But the legends as they existed before the time of Saint Paul would never have fitted in with modern conception.

The Hindu scriptures, the ideas of which are more philosophical than those of any other scriptures of the world, were long considered as books of heathen religions until Professor Max Müller translated some of them, and other writers, such as Sir Edwin Arnold who brought out some Oriental scriptures, although the translation can never do justice to the original works. The phraseology of the Qur'an was not very different from the terminology of the Old Testament, although the ideas of the Qur'an answer the advanced mind of the latter age more than the ideas of the Old Testament, which was a Message given to the simple minds of that age. However, the terminology of the Qur'an as it is, cannot quite fit in with the modern expression of thought. Therefore I have always seen that a Western person of good intention, who has given up all prejudices against other religions and is trying to overlook all he has heard against Islam, cannot very well comprehend the ideas of the Qur'an as they are put. For he wants the ideas to fit in with the standard of the day and to be expressed in the language of the present time.

The Greek Church, which had its great time of glory during the Tsarist period, has declined. Yet it has a great religious element in it. The difficulties of Russia certainly mean the downfall of the Greek Church. However, the religious spirit of that Church was not only owing to the priests, but was due to the deep religious feeling of the Russians. Its followers did not have a chance to be civilized enough to destroy their religion until the reign of the Tsar. Now the new wave of reform has swept away not only the Church, but also the religious spirit from the hearts of the faithful. Too much suffering turns people against religion.

The Old Christian Church which exists chiefly in Asia Minor has been always in uncivilized hands and has been under the shade, owing to the light of Islam standing next to it. It never had either inner spirit or outer form to really rise in the world and be something. However, the steadiness of the belief of the followers of this Church has kept it so long just alive.

The modern civilization which has made Western nations so great and powerful has materialism and commercialism as its basis. Consequently, the progress in this direction has been made at the cost of religion. In the West patriotism has taken the place of religion. Nationalism has become as the spiritual ideal of the day. No doubt a great, apparent worldly success, has been achieved by this, which compared to spiritual ideals, is nothing. There exist people in civilized nations in most civilized parts of the West who have erased even the name of God from the textbooks of children's schools, who cannot bear to hear the name of God uttered. It may be called 'great force', or, with a great difficulty 'the gods'. It is a spirit of revolt which destroys all good things, while wanting to destroy bad things.

In the revolution, which caused the Reformation in the West, at every rise religion suffered until now the word religion means something horrible to the mind of many. It does not mean that their soul does not crave for religion or that they are not drawn to it. Only that they try to keep themselves away from it, calling it a temptation. There are many who wonder and would very much like to know if there exists anything behind what we see and perceive and yet the name of God, or religion, or prayer, or Church will frighten them away. It seems they are looking for something and yet not in the form of religion. They have a kind of repugnance against religion and this one finds as a rule among the intellectual people living in the countries foremost in civilization. There are some who think they are too advanced to believe or do as their ancestors did formerly. They think it is behind the times to pray or to hold any belief as sacred or to follow any particular religion, and it is up to date to discard all that is religious. They think religion is only for the masses, not for the intellectual people. There are some who think religion is for women, who have time; men are too busy to sacrifice time, which is precious. Time is money and it is not worthwhile to give it to things that do not bring material benefit. There are others who are afraid of their materialistic surroundings; even if they have any religious sentiment they are afraid to show it in any way, for they think they will be laughed at by those with whom they associate.

There was another substitute for religion. As the Protestant religion was given as a substitute for the Catholic faith to those religiously inclined, so Masonry became a substitute for those disinclined to show outwardly their belief, which they observed in secrecy. This kept them free from the blame of their people, friends and relations, for adhering to another faith, and they had their ritual without a priest imposed upon them from a spiritual hierarchy, having had their worshipful master elected from among themselves. They sought exaltation by the masonic ritual supported by a long tradition and avoided any disputes on religious ideals by keeping their lips closed and by a vow of secrecy. The origin of this is not much different from the Protestant origin, the Protestant religion came from the orthodox Islam, Masonry from the secret order of Muslim mystics, to whom all meant the same, whether Christian, Muslim or Jew. Those seekers after truth who pursued these contemplative souls while in the battle, were admitted to be initiated by the possessors of this mystery, but were welcomed with unsheathed swords and doors were fast locked after their admission, and every manner of reception was expressive of a process through which the enemy was received into the circle of friends. So, the secret of the life of the meditative dervishes, expressed symbolically in the form of ritual, was brought to the Western world as a key to the mystery of life.

Woman was not admitted until A.D. 1893, when Mrs. Annie Besant by the order of the Masons in France opened a new Order and brought into it women and men together in sharing this mystery, which was, however, kept apart and has not been recognized by the Scottish Lodge of Masons until now.

There has been so much spoken of the organization of the Catholic Church being so wonderful, but nothing can equal Masonic organization which today exists in the world, embracing the best intellects and most influential personalities of almost all nations. As Masonry has spread wide, so its social and political influence has become greater every day, and has performed wonders in the social and political world. Yet the main object with which the Masonic initiation was given, still remains to be fulfilled: a drill which is meant for battle. That battle is self-realization, which is the central theme of the Sufi Message.

There are many in the West who are looking for some other religion, which gives scope for the rise of all sorts of activities, true and false. The religions of the ancient people which exist in the world, cannot really answer their purpose. It is natural that what is suitable to Eastern mentality cannot easily agree with the mentality of the Western people. Among the existing religions of the world, Islam is the only one which can answer the demand of Western life, but owing to political reasons a prejudice against Islam has existed in the West for a long time. Also the Christian missionaries, knowing that Islam is the only religion which can succeed their faith, have done everything in their power to prejudice minds of the Western people against it. Therefore there is little chance for Islam being accepted in the West. However, those seekers after religious ideals have more or less regard for the religions of the East and those who seek after truth show a desire to investigate Eastern thought.

The hopeless state of affairs which has manifested on the surface as the outcome of this recent war, has made many anticipate the coming of a world teacher to re-establish the affairs of the world. There are some among those who work for the coming of the world teacher who are sure that they themselves will never arrive at being that themselves. Therefore, they are quite content to be his forerunners. Unconsciously, these very people keep the teacher away from coming. And there are others who are most eager for him to come, but they make him so enormous, out of their imagination, that God himself would have great difficulty in creating one.

An old institution which presents some Eastern thought to the West is the Theosophical Society, which was founded principally by Madame Blavatsky, who was from Russia, a visionary and mystically minded person who is said to have worked wonders. It is told that Masters from the Himalaya are the supporters behind[38] the Society, and that the spiritual hierarchy of certain Masters, whose names seem to be derived from Eastern languages, though they are hardly to be found in any sacred tradition of the world, are so to speak the guardians of the Society, which has an esoteric school of its own under the guidance of Mrs. Annie Besant, who is one of the four chief workers of this Movement. These, namely Colonel Olcott and Mr. Leadbeater and the two above-mentioned ladies, established their headquarters first at Benares and now at Adyar and made the Movement worldwide. If it were not for the Theosophical Society, there would not be the tolerance and response to Eastern thought of every kind which is given by people thus inclined in the West. The work of this Society has broken to a great extent the bias of the Christian faith, and the idea that the people in the East are heathens and their religion barbarous, which was prevalent in the West owing to the Christian missionary propaganda. As the Theosophical Society was the first of its kind in the West, its founders had to withstand no end of opposition. The Movement has splendidly established itself throughout Europe in a comparatively short period of time. It has taken as its principal work to break prejudices of caste, creed or colour by the understanding of Truth, and it has placed Truth on the altar as the principal religion. Every exponent of thought from the East who goes to the West, finds the doors of this Society open to welcome him. A warm welcome and a respectful regard is accorded to him on the platform of the Theosophical Society. A great deal of Buddhistic and Hindu

---

38. First edition has Dutch rendering 'at the back of'

literature has been translated into the Western languages by Theosophical writers. Most of the work has been done by Mrs. Annie Besant, who has shown the most wonderful talent as a speaker and as a writer, besides the great power and efficiency she has shown in holding this vast Movement firmly in hand in spite of all difficulties which stood in her way. I personally have not had occasion to converse with Mrs. Besant, although I have heard her speak. There is a book by Mme. Blavatsky, *The Secret Doctrine*, which is held as a mystery by some of the followers of Theosophy, which contains mostly her dreams and visions. If it were not for the theory of karma and reincarnation which the Theosophical Society has brought forward as its special doctrine on which the whole Theosophical theory is based, it would have had great difficulty in touching the Western mind, which wants food for its reason first before accepting any faith. The ideal of reincarnation and karma made a great revolution in the West in the religious world. The backbone of religion in the West had already been broken, and this idea broke its legs, letting Eastern thought rise, introduced in the West in the form of Theosophy.

However, the idea of reincarnation and karma, which came from the race of Hindus, never has given the full satisfaction to that race itself. The influence of Islam, the ideas of the Sufis, made a great change in the Hindu outlook for many centuries, and great Hindu poets like Nanak and Kabir, Sundar and Dadu, Ram Das and Tukaram, and religious reformers of India like Swami Narayan and Babu Keshoba Chandra Sen, Dayananda Saraswathi, Devendranath Tagore, all these although they could not entirely erase this idea from the surface of the Indian mentality, upon which it had been engraved for ages, yet modified it to such an extent that hardly anyone speaks about these things. Especially the wise, the sages, hold as their object in life *mukti*, liberation from the captivity caused by karma. It is a worn out doctrine of the East which was revivified by the Theosophical Society in the West. In the first place it appealed to the people in the West because it answered immediately the question why one is well off in life and why another suffers. The idea of reincarnation gave an answer readily justifying it: 'Because of the actions of the past,' which gave no scope for further argument on the subject. It at once satisfies the intellect, though the answer of Christ was different. When somebody asked him: 'Master, who did sin, this man or his parents, that he was born blind?' Jesus answered: 'Neither hath this man sinned, nor his parents, but that the works of God should be made manifest in him.' It always appeals to the hearts whose treasure is on the earth to think that even if we passed from this earth we shall not be taken away forever, we shall come back again. And those who have not experienced the life of the earth sufficiently, and who have not achieved their desire in this life, they are only content to think that next time they will come and accomplish it. Then there are some who find that there is little time left in life and they have not yet improved themselves. They can hope that perhaps at their next visit to the earth they will finish the task. Some become happy at the thought 'I am not rich this time, it does not matter, before this time I was a king and after I have paid my debts in this life, in the next life I may become an emperor.' For their likes and dislikes in the world some give the reason of reincarnation, past acquaintances or relationship. This gives scope to the play of the imagination, which very often arrives at very funny ideas about it. Once two people thought that they had been husband and wife in the last incarnation, and at this realization their joy was great to have found themselves again on this earth's platform, but at the same time, in the face of this most unfortunate fact, they were most sad, realizing that this time they are not.

Though I have always had a great response from the members of the Theosophical Society, who love the Eastern thought and readily respond to it, still my position became very difficult when people brought me to the question of karma and reincarnation. The doctrine that interested them the most, had the least interest for me, and I have always tried not to encourage people in that idea, and yet not to oppose their belief, which has been a very hard task for me. Hafiz says: 'Sing, O Singer, the new song of the new life every moment.' For a Sufi to think, 'What was I and what shall I be?' takes him away from the vision of the ever-springing stream of life. Many members of the Theosophical Society have taken interest in my work, since Theosophy prepares them to appreciate the deeper knowledge; although it has made the authorities of the Theosophical Society afraid of losing their members and for some time they have taken precautions so as to close their ears to my call.

It is the lack of personal mystical influence and the absence of a prophetic Message that necessitated the Society bringing forward the belief in Masters, that there might be something for the believers to hold on to. Not only belief, but even imaginary pictures of these Masters are given to the adherents for worship. The esoteric school has existed for some time in the Theosophical Society, in which they have tried to introduce Raja Yoga, the philosophy of the Hindus. But the lack of personal guidance has always proved it to be like a clinic without a surgeon. The various demands of the Western mind kept the Society for all these years busy answering the needs of those working for the Movement. When the members of the Theosophical Society thought that it was only intellectual and there was nothing spiritual there, they introduced as a separate activity, the Liberal Catholic Church, and connected it with the Roman Church by tracing some missing link in the tradition. But since no religion which is not divinely inspired will take root in this world long enough, it is a question if this Movement will really meet with success. When there is a difficulty even for something real to take root in this world, what chance is there for imitation?

Another activity was started by the members of the Society which is called 'The Order of the Star', to prepare the way for the coming Teacher. But he must rise only from within the horizon of this institution, introduced to the world by the high authority of the Theosophical Society, or else he must descend directly from the sky, performing miracles. Such a thing has never been possible, nor will it ever be. As the communities in the past have waited until he came and went, and they are still waiting, the same old course is followed in the present generation by the most enthusiastic followers of the Order of the Star.

There has always been a struggle between a living Church and a dead Church; it was the coming of a prophet of God with a Divine Message from time to time at the need of humanity who represented the living Church; but the previously existing Church which struggled for existence being threatened by the influence of the newly coming prophet, proved to be a dead Church. It is most interesting to watch the struggle that has taken place in the past, how the Jewish religious authorities tried to avoid the influence of Jesus Christ being felt among their Churches and communities. They said to their people, 'The promised Messiah of the Kabbala tradition will come, but at the end of the world,' so that all the time between might be theirs; the Roman Church afterwards, by virtue of the new life brought by the prophet of Nazareth, evolved and spread its influence throughout the world. But the conception that was given to the people in answer to the question, as to the promise of Christ to come again, was that the promise was fulfilled by the descent of the Holy Ghost upon the twelve Apostles, and that there was nothing afterwards to look forward to. Then came the influence of Islam rushing with its material and spiritual force into the Western world; the existing Church was able to resist its material power by putting out the invaders from their territories, nevertheless, the spirit remained, bursting out later in the form of the Reformation which became the Protestant Church. No doubt this was a building made upon another foundation, and there was always a desire in the minds of the followers of this newly formed Church, an expectation of seeing their long adhered to Master, and the authorities of the Church have always tried to give an answer, which satisfied but for a moment.

I once met a Swiss Protestant in a train, and in conversation asked him, 'Do you expect the Master to come again?' In answer to this he said, 'Yes, certainly we do!' I said, 'When?' He replied, 'We know not when.' I said, 'How will you recognize him, if he ever comes on earth?' He said, 'It will not be difficult to recognize him, for he will follow the coming of the antichrist.' I asked, 'How would you recognize the antichrist?' He said, 'He will be almost as great as to be taken for Christ, but it is not he who will be the real Master; the Master will follow him.' I was very amused at the cleverness of this idea, that one who would not be able to show himself to be as great in glory as the Master of the past, he naturally would not be accepted, but one who succeeded in proving in some way or other almost as great, he will be considered the antichrist, so that in both cases he may not have a chance to enter their Church.

Muslims have closed the doors of the mosque by saying that Muhammad was the seal of *Risalat* which they interpret as the last of the prophets. They do not seem to realize that it does not mean at all that he was the last prophet to come, it only means that he was the last of claimants of prophecy; and that according to the nature and character of humanity after his time it would not be advisable for his successor to make an open claim, for it would be against the rule of the time. There is no seal that cannot be opened, though it must not be opened by everyone, but only by the one who has the right to open it.

The Theosophical Society tried to supply to the students of Theosophy the conception of different Masters which gave satisfaction to some for a time, and yet did not answer the continual longing of the souls to see the Master in the flesh walking on earth, sympathizing in their pain and trouble, casting upon them his glance of compassion, stretching over their heads his hands in blessing, telling them in words that may be audible to their physical ears, of the life here and in the hereafter, inspiring them with the conviction – if not all at least some – to know and to believe in something and someone who is real. This need necessitated a Movement such as 'The Star in the East', to comfort the hopeful and maintain their belief; everything has been done, is being done and will be done, and yet who can answer this demand? He alone who is sent from above, who is appointed by God to deliver His Message, who is empowered by the Almighty to stand by them in their struggles, and who is made compassionate by the most Merciful to heal their wounds. Man wants something he cannot get, man wishes to believe in something he cannot understand, man wishes to touch something he cannot reach. It is the continual struggle for the unattainable that blinds man, and he forms such high ideas even of the prophet who is only a Messenger, a human being, one like everyone else, and who is subject to death and destruction and all the limitations of life, that the prophet does not seem to come up to man's ideal until he has left the world, leaving behind the memory which again rises as a resurrection of the prophet, spreading the influence of all he brought to the world and pouring from above that blessing which arose as vapour and came back from above as a rainfall.

Anthroposophy is another offshoot of Theosophy, which has sprung up in the West as a result of a conflict between two great workers of the Theosophical Movement: Mrs. Besant and Dr. Steiner. In order to distinguish this Movement as different from the Theosophical Society the founder had to build another building on the same foundation, leaving out all Eastern colours and designs which exist in Theosophy. Every effort has been made by its founder to impress his followers with the idea that Eastern wisdom is different from the Western, and the way of the West is different from the way of the East, and what is called in Buddhism 'Nirvana', annihilation, is not the thought of Christ; Christ's teaching is the eternal and ever progressing individuality, by which he means to say that it is not God alone Who lives forever, but every individual entity, as a distinct and separate entity, is eternal and is gradually progressing to the fullness of its own individuality. In this way he divides one truth into two thoughts opposing each other, the oneness of the whole being on the part of the Eastern thought; and individuality of every being as the Western thought. It is a pity if a thinker, in order to distinguish one special doctrine which is his own conception, goes as far as cutting into two parts the truth which in reality is one. No doubt, this idea answers the Western mentality, for to many the idea of annihilation as expressed in Eastern terminology is awful, although it is a transitory state. The day is not far off when, if not through religion then by science, the people in the West will realize the oneness of the whole being, and that individuals are nothing more than bubbles in the sea.

Some followers of the Protestant religion, realizing the truth of the Theosophical ideas and startled by its rapid spread in the world, loosened a little the strict bonds of simple belief and called the old thought which always existed a new thought. Some of them went a step further, and called it a new life, the life which is always the same and everlasting, contrary to the words of Solomon, who says there is nothing new under the sun. There sprung another branch in the same Movement, they named themselves 'Higher Thought', which suggests that, compared to theirs, every other thought is a lower thought.

If there has been any religious Movement which has really done some good, it is the Christian Science Movement, which has fought against materialism which is productive of pessimism and is destructive in all forms according to the psychical point of view. If there is a Sufi idea in the realm of a Western religion, it is in Christian Science. I was surprised to read in the Christian Science books so much which is known to the Sufis and believed by the people of the East. And on making further inquiry I came to learn that there had been a simple man who had got the Sufi thought from the Persian source, and this came into the hands of Mrs. Eddy Baker, who was gifted enough to interpret it in Biblical terms, by which she was able to give a new coat of colour to Christianity, which had been fading away for many years. However, the conception of Christian Science is directed only to one side of religion, that is to combat illness which is evil, and it denies the existence of matter, which is mocked at especially by the materialistic world and very often, at the death of different patients, the practitioner of Christian Science is taken to the police court. Since the development of material science in the West the number of diseases has increased, and it is to the credit of Christian Science that many have been kept back from going to the clinics, which in the lives of many become as slaughterhouses. Many whom the physician gives up, the Christian Scientist takes up, and many are cured who have been disappointed by medicine. No doubt, the followers of this faith are taught to find the truth only in their own Churches, also some refuse medicine in all cases and prefer death to medical treatment, whereas a Sufi uses the same faith, in believing that God heals through the air, through the food or drink, drug or herb, through all things, since God is all, and all is God.

The greatest curse of the age today is the rapid spread of what is called Spiritualism. It is the lack of the spiritual ideal in the Protestant religion which has given rise to this Movement. The war which has caused so many to moan over their dear ones has helped the furtherance of this Movement. Also the Spiritualist says his Movement is in conflict with the materialism of the day, which he rightly says has caused the recent great war. But his reason is wrongly founded; by combat materialism is strengthened. No-one in this world wishes to feel that he is wrong, and by telling him so, one makes him still firmer in his idea. They think spiritual phenomena will make man believe in the soul and in the hereafter, which today is not believed in by many. But this love of phenomena gives scope to many who wish to deceive the world by a spiritualistic fad, and once a person knows its falsehood even the believer would turn into an unbeliever. Nothing can give belief in God, the soul, or the hereafter; it must grow in the child with the growth of his body and develop in him with the development of his mind. Belief in God is in a person and it comes by itself when the moment arrives, one need not force it. What one can do is to make a way for it to rise. Spirit phenomena, wonder-working, only stimulate curiosity and strengthen antagonism in one's nature. How can the Movement of Spiritualism ever be useful to humanity and successful in the world, since after a thorough examination most of the spiritualistic activities prove not to be genuine? It is a pity that well-known men like Sir Oliver Lodge, the great scientist, and Sir Conan Doyle, by taking interest in such objects, give reason for the simple ones to grope in superstitions. Love of Spiritualism begins by a little play, which is getting spirit messages in automatic writing. Then it grows to spirit-communication, this develops one naturally to mediumship. In order to communicate with the dead, one must become practically as dead, one must become absent to the world around one in order to touch the world of the dead. Furthermore, one finds those inclined to mediumship lack health or balance, and most of those who continue in the spiritualistic practices grow more and more nervous and unbalanced, until they arrive at a state in which both their mind and body become unsound. Besides, most of the Spiritualists seem to be simple-minded believers in superstitions and after spirit-communication rather than in the pursuit of God or Truth. Spiritualism cannot be a religion, although it professes to be so, for the main object of religion is to lead to unity by the God-ideal, not to variety by trying to communicate with all those passed from this earth.

Seeing the different Movements awakened in the educational world of the Occident a revolution came, and the idea of modern psychology was brought forward which every day is being developed and is coming to the fore. Yet compared to the ancient psychology this is quite an infant idea although the educational world of this day takes to it more readily than to anything ancient. For it is simple and easy to grasp, and given in the form of scientific terminology; it becomes enormously useful in medical science, and it is now being used as hypnotism, mesmerism, and psychoanalysis. However, the mental cult can be most dangerous when morals are not cultivated, and it is a question if without moral culture the modern psychology will really prove beneficial. The tendency of the modern science is to attribute most of the mental disorders to sex and to see in sex the cause of all natural faculties. This idea, no doubt, mars the morals and drowns the spiritual ideal. Material science has led the mind of the world mostly to destruction. Now when mental science and modern psychology will lead humanity further yet in the pursuit of matter instead of spirit, what could be the result? The most valuable saying of Christ seems to be the only right way to follow: 'Seek ye first the Kingdom of God and all things will be added unto you.'

In the spirit of democracy which is to be found in the Western world, I saw more of the socialistic spirit, to complete it. There are two sides to socialism, a wrong side and a right side. The right side is its practice as consideration to others, and the wrong side is its practice owing to self-pity, as it produces envy, jealousy, rivalry, competition and all manner of bitterness. In the constitutional system, which is becoming every day more the foundation of every activity in the modern world, in spite of all the advantages of self-expression that it gives to many, there is something missing and that lack is caused by the one-sidedness of the system. There will come a day when humanity will come to realize that aristocracy and democracy develop one from the other as a natural course of evolution, and yet one is incomplete without the other. This whole manifestation has in it both aristocracy working from above, and democracy from below. And when, according to this natural scheme of life, humanity will build its reconstruction, that will be the ideal civilization.

For some time, there have been Eastern missions working in the West, among them Babism, which began in America and changed in time into Bahaism. Bahaism is an offspring of Sufism, its object being the bringing of nations and followers of different religions into closer touch, void of inner cult. Baha Ullah, after whom this sect has been named, had been kept a prisoner in the East because of his proclamation of prophetship. After him his son, Abdul Baha, carried on his mission. I had the pleasure of meeting Abdul Baha when he was in Paris, who showed great interest in my music and with whom I had an interesting talk about our experiences in the Western world. During the conversation we had he exclaimed, 'There should be no secret, you must speak; either you know, or you do not know.' I answered, 'The whole nature of things and beings has a secret; each thing and each being has a secret which reveals its nature and character, and the life itself has its secret, and it is the uncovering of its secret which is the purpose of life. Speaking out aloud does not prove a person to be the knower of the secret. Neither every occasion is a suitable occasion, nor is every person a person fitted for the truth to be spoken to.' 'You are also preaching the brotherhood of nations?' I said, 'I am not preaching brotherhood, but sowing the seed of *Tawhid*, the unity of God, that from the plant of Sufism may spring up fruits and flowers of brotherhood.'

At the world exhibition of Chicago in 1893 where people of different religions had gathered, Vedanta philosophy was represented in America by Swami Vivekananda, the delegate who was sent to the West from the Ramakrishna mission – the mission which had been organized by Swami Ramakrishna, who had visited the West. However, for Swami Vivekananda it was the best opportunity to represent Vedanta at the World Fair. It was something strikingly new and interesting to the intellectual minds of the West, something to appeal to their reasoning faculty which had been whetted by modern progress and had been starved by the lack of a religion of intellect. A simple religion of faith was not sufficient for the minds so rapidly progressing in all directions of life. The voice of Swami Vivekananda echoed throughout the States. As he was the pioneer of Yoga, the first to represent it to the people of the West, he made a great impression upon all who met him. Later in America everybody knew the name of Yoga and began to search for it as one does for every drug or herb, seeking if they can buy it somewhere. There were many equipped with business faculties who soon after Swami Vivekananda's departure from America founded institutions for teaching Yoga philosophy, and books were published of which it was said that by reading them Yoga could be learned in ten days.

After Swami Vivekananda various exponents of Vedanta philosophy came from India, among them Baba Bharati, who preached the love of Krishna, and after fifteen years good trial went to the East and never returned. I had met him in America; he was sorry for me, for the work I had undertaken to accomplish. Yet nothing could discourage me or move me from my firm determination.

Swami Abhedananda, who is told to be a pupil of Vivekananda, came and established a Vedanta Society in New York and an *ashrama*, a place for retreat, was made for the members of the Society to go into retirement for a certain period. This Society is still existing, having been through a great many floods and storms, which is astonishing to many. It always becomes convenient for the opponents of the Eastern cult to demolish the character of its exponent, however self-sacrificing the person may be.

I saw to my great surprise in San Francisco a Hindu temple built in the Indian style, founded by Swami Trigunatita. He struck a note in me, a thought which I have had all my life, that East and West both have their particularities; either need the other and both together make the world complete. And it is not the political or commercial interest which will unite them for their mutual benefit so much as a marriage between them, for a true marriage means unity between souls. The Swami was very gentle and tender-hearted, but to keep on his work was a constant struggle. If it had not been for his constant enthusiasm he would long ago have left San Francisco. I heard to my great distress that the Swami had been assassinated while giving a public lecture.

I have also heard of a Vedanta Society existing in Boston, established by Swami Paramananda, a young exponent of Hindu philosophy, and many talk about his gentle personality. He has held his institution firm against winds which came to sweep it away. However, to think that Vedanta philosophy will become a religion of the Occident is absurd. In the first place Vedanta is not a religion, it is a philosophy, and it will only appeal to those interested in the wisdom of the East from an intellectual point of view, who care little for religion. Yes, Yogism has a great attraction for many, but the renunciation, sacrifice, patience and perseverance which Yoga demands, make it almost impossible for a person whose life is absorbed in a thousand responsibilities of life, and the surroundings that he has to live in in the West to undertake and to accomplish it satisfactorily.

A good many years past the Brahmo Samaj of India, the Movement which was founded by Devendranath Tagore, was introduced in England by its exponent Keshoba Chandra Sen. After a lapse of time, some little fragment of it is still to be found, kept alive by his son who has been for some time in England. Mr. Gupta started in England a side issue of this Movement, 'East and West', which kept dimly lit like a lamp without oil.

Rabindranath Tagore's tour through the West has been the one which met with great success. His command of English and his poetry saturated with the Eastern fluid, has no doubt made a great impression upon the Western mind. His ideas on the present problem have been liked by some, and some call them pacifism by which is meant peace at any cost, which many are not eager to hear of just now. There is no doubt the works of Tagore have brought real credit to India. Some people think his poetry is weak. No doubt, it is those who are not accustomed to fineness.

I also have read the three works of Kahlil Gibran, *The Madman*, *The Forerunner*, and *The Prophet*. In this he has shown the great wit of the East, proving his to be a dancing soul. He writes with a great command of English and with deep insight in life. He seems to be a complete artist who draws beautiful pictures of life, in lines and in words.

An Islamic mission has been started some time ago in England by Khwaja Kamaluddin, the Imam of the mosque at Woking, which is under the control of the India Office. It is supposed to have made a great many converts to Islam, among them Lord Headly. The Imam made a pilgrimage to Mecca, just before the Sherif changed his policy. There is little tendency seen among people in the West to follow Islam, especially among the intellectual classes, on account of the wrong impression spread in the West by political and religious sources. There is another Muslim Mission called Ahmadia, which is working in England, seeming to stand apart from this main Mission of Khwaja Kamaluddin, working hard to make up a good long list of converts every year, upon which solely depends their success. These Missions could not exist in the West were they not provided for by the hopeful Muslims of Islam, who out of their good faith in the furtherance of Islam try to give a part of the only loaf of bread they have.

Organization

There has been no end to my difficulties in the organization. Many I found willing to follow the Message, but not to belong to an organization, and I throughout my life had constantly to answer on that question to every newcomer, agitated against the idea of an organization. It is natural that people who would be attracted to my ideas should not necessarily be attracted to the organization. Besides many organizations have failed, and many have brought discredit upon the members, and many organizations are in competition with one another, ignorant of the idea for which the organization stood. It is true that in time the idea becomes lost and the organization remains as a body without a soul. But the consequence is that after seeing dead bodies, many become afraid of the living body, thinking that it also may be an apparition of the dead.

I had to answer them that an organization is like a ship which is built for a purpose: to carry the people and things from one port to another. If there was no organization, the home could not exist, there would be no defence for the country, in all works of life organizations are necessary to make things easy and life convenient. Many who disapprove of an organization, are ready to take the benefit that comes out of it. For them to say, 'We do not care for an organization' is like saying, 'I like to eat, but I do not think about the kitchen.'

Then many thought that they could tolerate me as the head of an organization, but not anyone else, who was different. It was like accepting the head and rejecting the body, which cannot be detached one from the other so long as life connects them both. And I had to tell them that I could not make of myself many, and if I could ever make myself into many parts, still each part of myself must be different, and the lesson that they had to learn was tolerance. Many said they could tolerate me, but I told them that it was not sufficient, they must tolerate others too, who are given a certain work to perform in the organization. Human nature always proves like a child, especially in the working of the organization, which is not necessarily spiritual. It gives them a worldly impulse and once it is aroused, the spiritual ideal for which the organization stands, is forgotten.

In the administration of the work I had no end of trouble and difficulty, caused by some of my helpers, who for some reason or other worked for the Cause without my point of view and my outlook on life. They very often through the lack of patience left their work and made things disagreeable, which thing one sees in all different activities. And yet I found that without the organization it was impossible to carry the work through, and especially in the West. For in the beginning I had tried to do so, on the same principle as in the East, but could not succeed. Many became interested in the idea, in the Message, most drawn to it, but in absence of organization there was nothing to keep them together; so, disappointed many dropped away and became scattered. You cannot collect flowers without a basket, so is the organization for the ideal. For me, who was born with a tendency to be away from all worldly activities, and who grew every day more apart from all worldly things, to have an organization to make, to control, and to carry out has been a great trial, and any disturbance in carrying it out made my position very difficult, and my spirit disturbed. If it had not been for the Cause, which is worth every sacrifice in life, I would not for one moment have troubled about the organization.

My great difficulty has been to find sufficient workers to answer the demand of the Cause. Some good ones seemed to lack the enthusiasm for going forward and standing for the Cause, and some who had the same, wanted tact and the wider point of view, that all embracing spirit which is the key to all success.

Some had not enough confidence in themselves, some did not endure sufficiently the difficulties which come as a natural course of the affair, some owing to their strong likes and dislikes did not get on very well with their fellow-workers; in some perhaps without their knowledge, remained a grain of nationalism or a spark of religious bigotry; in the heart of some a shadow of racial feeling; and in some the thought of their kind. Some mureeds whose help I anticipated to further the Cause, said 'My people are not yet ready for your Message', which I interpreted as meaning that they themselves were not yet ready to work for the Message, the Message which is to the whole world. Some said, on my requesting them to work for the Cause, 'Murshid, you yourself are your best propaganda', which did not flatter me, it only showed me that they would rather have me work than trouble themselves.

Some came to me with goodwill and every desire to help, but with their own ideas and plan of working. They wanted me immediately to change the whole organization, by taking away the different works which have been given to certain mureeds who voluntarily rendered service, out of their devotion to the Cause. They wanted to change, according to their plan, everything which I had made after the work and experience of years. It seemed to me like a person coming and seeing a new building made, and offering his service to complete it, but on condition that the whole foundation must first be dug out. Not only that, but the one who was working alone in making the foundation of the building and those who came to help when there was no-one else to assist, must be told to go out from there when most of the foundation is completed, because someone else more capable wishes to assist. My very sense of reason could not find out justice in it. Often when this question was raised before me it dumbfounded me, I had no words then to discuss the matter. When the gulf is too vast between two ideas it is difficult to meet, and to my very great disappointment I had to refuse their offer of service.

On my part a continual conscientiousness to consider everybody's feeling, and on the part of some of my co-workers' disregard of this principle, made me at times feel so sensitive as if a peeling had come off from my heart.

Some workers came to me promising me aid most eagerly, not because they wanted to help the Sufi Movement, only that they wanted to do something; if it was not to be the Sufi Movement, they would have chosen something else to do. I sometimes accepted their help, though not often. It has never proved to be satisfactory, for the reason that it is not their devotion for the Sufi Message that prompts them to work, it is their restless spirit which cannot remain still; they want to be doing something all the time.

Many wished to be benefitted by the Sufi teachings and my help on the path, but would not be willing to sacrifice for this what they consider their best principle, and that is to join nothing, for they were afraid they would become limited, but they did not know that they limited themselves by their own principle by not being able to join, for they were not free. This showed the injustice of human nature, even of those seeking after Truth, the most precious thing that could be sought. Even in the search of Truth they are not ready to sacrifice their little principle.

Some did not want to label themselves with the name of a certain organization and they refused to join the Order in spite of their keen interest. But the true reason of their refusal always is that they are not yet free from some label they have put upon themselves, of which they themselves are unaware. For once a soul is free, it is also free to join anything it likes, nothing binds it. For a free soul shows openness to all things.

Some workers complained about the difficulties in working, and brought before me as news something which I have always known, the solution of which difficulties could be found in themselves, nothing else would answer. Some workers said, 'People say this or that against the Murshid, or workers or the way it is worked out, or against the teaching.' I found that the worker was not yet wakened to find the answer and was affected by what was said to him and he only wanted a force to strengthen his belief against what has been said. Some critical souls put all that came through their mind as said by someone else, as something told by someone else, and in this way they got relief by giving an outlet to it. My adversaries always took advantage of a mureed's weakness of faith, a worker's feebleness of mind, and tried to do so either by showing sympathy with the work or the person and through sympathy saying, 'What a great pity it is so badly done', or by frightening them, making a *bhau* either of my person or of my work, saying, 'It is political, there may be some danger behind it', or that it is anti-religious, or something to bring a slur upon my life. Those who could not resist long enough gave in to such influences and suddenly left me and my work. Those wanting to create a discord among mureeds and workers found it easy to accomplish their aim (even with most devoted mureeds), and succeeded in doing so in influencing the most devoted workers and mureeds by appealing to them, touching their religious, national, or racial pride. And it was interesting for me to notice how this produced a barrier immediately in their minds, without them knowing.

I was thrown into the same battle unavoidably, which many others seek eagerly. Some think it does not matter if they are against Murshid, as long as they work for the Cause. But they forget that Murshid is the first Cause.

Some came to me, telling me, 'I like your ideas, but not the religious form of it.' Some said, 'I would like an initiation, but no discipline.' Some said, 'It must be all impersonal, it must not be anything personal.' Some said, 'The spiritual personality is the only thing that gives me the proof of the Truth you have brought, though I care little for the Order.' Some said, 'The idea of brotherhood appeals to me very much, but I cannot believe in any mysticism.' Some said, 'In mysticism I am quite interested, but I do not care at all for the religious part of it.' Some said, 'It is the most beautiful thing I have ever heard, but I wonder if it is Christian?' Some said, 'It is an Eastern idea, which is foreign to the Western mind.' Some said, 'It is not unfamiliar to us Western people. We know our religion, what we would like to know is something of the East.' Some said, 'I can join if only I knew that you believed in the doctrine of karma and reincarnation, which has been the basis of my knowledge.' Some asked if the learning of wisdom that Sufism teaches would take away their faith in their own religion. Imagine if faith, a thing which belongs to oneself, which no one in the world has power to touch, would be affected by the light of wisdom; and if the light of wisdom ever affected their faith it would only light it up!

In order to answer the question what people want and what they do not want, dogma, form, priesthood, creed, if one summed it all together, the sum total would be zero.

This certainly caused more or less difficulties, which added to the troubles already existing in my work. But I took it as a natural course of things and tried not to mind, except when I happened to have a worker whose tendency was to hold the Movement by its neck, who was thankful to have had that chance given to him and who held the Movement back by the power of his office from letting it flourish. It has not happened once, but many times, and has not only showed the tyranny of human nature, but the absurdity of trying to tread a spiritual path and yet feeding that egotism as a thorn in one's soul. I pitied them more than I despaired over my affairs. I found some working in the Movement who extended their social influence among mureeds of value and importance, in order to make an impression upon me that it is they who are holding the members, and that, if I did not agree with them, they would make all those in their influence disagree with me. The troubles which came to me from friends and helpers were sometimes harder to bear than the difficulties caused by my opponents.

It is the work of the organization that made me realize a side of human nature which I did not expect in a spiritual cause. I was amazed beyond words to find some workers who would either be my friends if I followed their advice, or otherwise they would act as my adversaries. It is like saying, 'Either we will be your friends, or we will be your foes, nothing between.' That made me feel sore, yet I pitied them for their loss in their fruitless effort more than myself.

Many, not only strangers, but also friends, mureeds and workers, told me that they were afraid that this, our Sufi Movement, might become in time a creed; and some of them did not feel inclined to further the Cause for the same reason. I quite see their point of view, as clearly as they themselves see it, but yet I dare say that a creed which holds a divine Message freshly given, works like the heart that circulates the blood throughout the body, which is the world. It is the creeds which have lost that magnetism after having finished their period of mission in the world, that live in this world just like dead blood cells in the body. The one who sees it rightly need not compare the heart with the dead blood cells. Besides, it is like telling the Creator God, 'Make not a physical body for the soul which is divine; this body will be passionate, will make man material, will make him lose his way, will make him forget God, will cause him to shed blood. These bodies will fight and quarrel and create floods of blood in the world, and all sorts of sins these bodies will commit. There is so much disadvantage in creating these bodies.' And the Creator would give one answer, that 'You see the disadvantages, and I see the advantage beyond them all. You know not, who criticize; I know, it is my affair.'

There is sometimes a tendency of mureeds, especially of workers, who are capable of interesting themselves more on things of organization, thinking that Murshid is from the East, and therefore unaccustomed to Western way of organization, taking this as a good excuse for their discontent, which caused more trouble and confusion than necessary in an organization which is neither economical nor political.

One thing I observed everywhere I went, and it amused me every time. My friends in the East and West both spoke to me as to a child, in regard of my work; in spite of knowing that I had already worked and had some experience I always heard from them: 'The character of our people is different from that of every other people.' It was like saying: 'The sky of our country is quite different from the sky of all the rest of the world, where our own sun shines, and a particular moon beams.' However, I learned from this how everybody, being conscious of his own particular section of humanity, ignores the common principle of human nature working in all places in the same way under many and varied forms.

There has always been the financial problem before me to solve, and it still remains unsolved. If it had been a religion that made a certain creed proud of its spread, or if it had been a patriotic Movement which made a race or a nation interested in its furtherance, I would have had no end of help from all sides, but this being something which was neither in the interest of a particular creed, nor did it bring success or credit to any nation in particular but was in the interest of the whole humanity, naturally no particular section of humanity took any special interest in the Movement, though many admired its object; and therefore it always suffered financially. And now I got so accustomed to this condition that I feel it is natural for it to be so. But nothing in the world would discourage me. If there were not one single coin towards carrying on the work, if there was not one soul standing by my side to assist me in my work, I would still work to my last breath. For my entire strength comes from that Source, whose Message it is, which I am destined to give. My only satisfaction, therefore, is in having done my best, and it does not matter under what circumstances.

East and West

I found among the different classes in the West three divisible parts: the upper class or 'society'; the middle class or the intellectual; and the working class, and found the middle class to be the most interesting and promising, good in their morals, energetic, enthusiastic, and all-round in their knowledge. The upper class, with all its fineness and culture, seemed to be on the decline. The working class most eager to advance, impatient to mount to the top, most powerful owing to their organized unions, and desperate in bettering their position through life.

In the West I found a storm rising, disturbing in all different classes, which culminated in the war and upset so many nations and is continuing its disastrous effects still now. The present method of progress in the Occident seems to me quite contrary to what it ought to be. Instead of efforts being made by the people who are more evolved to raise the people who are not yet evolved much, the efforts are continually made by the latter to pull down to their own level the former. When the head is too proud to greet the feet, the feet rise in the place of the head and use the head in the place of the feet. Today the picture of the world is just like a marketplace, where every seller is pulling the customers by their garments, more so than it has ever been before; for civilization is known to be a commercial and industrial development. The tradesman just now has his eyes on the face of his customer and his heart in his purse. Profession in the West, in spite of all the development and culture, is mainly directed to earning money, which naturally destroys the brotherly love for mankind, taking away at the same time the nobility of spirit in the professional world. It is an ever-increasing cupidity from every side, which is no fault of the people, but is owing to the modern education. There must be something to live for; if it is no high ideal, then the earth becomes the only ideal in life, the ideal which is too poor in itself with all its riches and yet full of limitation.

Once they thought the religious magic of the Church took away all that people had, but now the temptation that the industrial and commercial activities offer, attracts the fancy of men, and women especially, to the ever-changing fashions, thus making life harder and harder every day. Besides, all the means of frivolity and gaiety that the theatres and hotels supply for the merriment for the people remind me of the Rajas in the East, whose downfall was caused by such things. But in the East, only some few could afford to experience that life which now in the Western world is within the means of almost all.

It is the artificiality of life which has caused a general misery in the West. The people in the West have outgrown simplicity, and now it is hard for them even to imagine life any other than the life they know, which mostly is the cause of the misery of woman in the world. Man, having so much to do in the world, becomes less inclined to home life. Thereby life in general suffers. However, the progress in the Western world is mostly due to the work of man and woman hand in hand, and the lack of the same is the reason of the backwardness of the East.

There is much to be said about woman in the West. She is courageous, patient, efficient, and capable, not only of home duties but of doing all work in life. Yes, she is less concerned with home, as compared to an Eastern woman, but her duties are divided, she has a part of duty to perform outside. Woman is idealized in the East, but in the West her vanity is sustained. A lover in the West knows how to woo; a lover in the East knows how to long. Woman's life in the West I found nearly as hard as in the East, perhaps harder, for in the East woman is more protected by man. In the West she stands responsible for herself, at home and outside the home, and it is that which makes her strong in every way. Nevertheless, this blunts her feminine qualities and develops male qualities. Some women are inclined to cut their hair short, and some to smoke cigarettes. Some are inclined to rough games and crude ways of recreation. Woman thinks by this she stands equal to man, ignorant of the fact that she becomes less attractive to him, who completes her life. Whereas in the East, under the shelter of man, the feminine qualities of woman develop freely, and her womanly charm is maintained. Woman by nature is spiritually inclined, in the East or West. But especially in the West, where the life of man is mostly absorbed in business and politics, it is woman who interests herself in religion, even in philosophy and all works pertaining to God and humanity. The spirit of the Western woman with which she fights her battle all along through life, is most splendid.

There is no line of work or study which woman in the West does not undertake and does not accomplish as well as man. Even in social and political activities, in religion, in spiritual ideas, she indeed excels man. The charitable organizations existing in different parts of the West, are mostly supported by the women, and I see as clear as daylight that the hour is coming when woman will lead humanity to a higher evolution.

The country which is commercially developed is alone considered to be civilized. Moral or spiritual progress has no recognized standard. The chivalry of the knights is now a story of the past, personality is not observed, but authority. I was very amused once to hear a so-called democrat commit himself to the opinion that: 'It is the moneyed people who must have the charge of money, for only they know how to make use of it to its best advantage.'

Besides business there is education, which consists of science, but that also is held by commerce, which holds in one hand science and in the other hand art. The modern reform which has sprung out of the abandonment of the Church, is the cause why an intelligent person in the West, as a rule, discards anything spiritual. Not only in a man engaged in commerce and industry, but even in an artist, a scientist, a musician, and a literary man it is seen. He seems to guard himself and his profession from a spiritual stain, as one would guard his beautiful clothes from getting spotted by something undesirable. I do not mean all, but many; whereas in the East a poet or musician apart, even a business man, an industrial person desires to link up his life and work with religion and spirituality. Therefore, even in the folklore of India a spiritual re-echo is perceived.

Art and literature suffer in the East, owing to the lack of support. People in the East are accustomed to think that an art is a gift of God, painting, poetry, or music, any art; and art is its own reward. They praise it, but seldom think how the artist must live. Whereas, in the West, commercialism, in spite of all its disadvantages, has taught them how to give and take. Art, poetry and music, therefore, in the West, are more or less maintained, but in the East, are starved and neglected.

The West may be waking to the beauty of Eastern poetry, but it will take years for the West to waken to the beauty of India's music; but I am afraid by that time India will have lost its song.

The Western music represents Western life; in the orchestra many instruments play together, in a social gathering many people speak together, whereas in the East one person sings at a time or plays his instrument singly, and in their gatherings one talks and others listen silently.

It amused me very much in my country to see how readily friends requested me to sing a song, giving them an example of something in a moment which took years to practise. And it amused me still more in the West when friends said so easily: 'But tell me, how does one arrive at spirituality?' As if it was something I could count on my fingers and tell them instantly.

Politics, which were once based upon morals and spiritual ideals, have now commercialism as their central theme. Alliance between nations exists for the interest of each; therefore those who are friends in one situation turn enemies on another occasion. For there is no moral ideal to hold humanity together in a bond, except the treaties made for the protection of their own interest. And the East to the West politically is like a milch-cow to the husbandman, a point of view which is supported by Darwin's theory that the world is the survival of the fittest.

As many courts there are, so many more lawyers, and as many prisons are made, so many more criminals, ready to occupy them. A time has come when the word of man has much less value than a sixpenny stamp. Divorce is getting easier, if not by law, without law. Marriage is becoming a private business affair. A love affair today is considered less than a friendship, for man loves with his head, rather than with his heart. And the cause of all this degeneration is the absence of the spiritual ideal which keeps hearts shallow and souls in obscurity.

The Western man in the spiritual path wishes to know first 'What will it lead to? Where will be the resting place? And what will be the destination? What profit shall I get by the enterprise? And how long will it take?' As the spiritual path is inexplicable in the words of the human tongue, which is only made to express things of the external life, his exacting faculty remains unsatisfied. In the East the traveller in the spiritual path knows already what path it is, and it is his love for that path which makes him seek the guide. Therefore the guide need not try to create the interest for it in his heart. In the West before a person chooses a path he wants to know if that path is an authorized one, a recognized one, if others also tread that path, otherwise he cannot very well have faith in it. In the East a man takes whatever path he thinks best for him; if everybody in the world says to him, 'That is not the path', he will still say, 'That is my path.' *Pir-i-man khas ast i'tiqad-i-man bas ast.* (If my Pir-Guide is worth a straw, my faith in him is sufficient.)

What I remarked especially in the West is the absence of the tolerance of the East toward the life of a faqir. No man in the East, especially in India, with some sense would ever dare judge a sage. For he knows that every person has his right or wrong peculiar to him and no one has a right to weigh the action of another, especially that of a sage, who, owing to his spiritual growth is entitled to more freedom than the average man. For freedom is a sign of evolution. The child is not free to do what his elders can, so a soul who is not yet evolved has certain laws to follow strictly, whereas the evolved souls are at their evolved stage beyond the ordinary standard of law. Today man understands this with regard to worldly power, position or rank, but not with regard to spiritual evolution. In the West man thinks less of a spiritual person than in the East, but asks more of him.

If a Western person looks up to someone as his spiritual ideal, as a rule he expects his ideal to live up to the picture he has made of him; and the moment he finds that his ideal has not shown in life the picture made by his own imagination, he becomes disappointed and his ideal breaks. Whereas when an Eastern person considers someone as his spiritual ideal he is always willing to take him as he is, and before judging him he tries to understand him. So in the former case the ideal must follow the devotee, in the latter the devotee follows his ideal. In the East, if a man is so evolved that he has the realization of a saint, everything that he does unfolds his soul; and in everything the vision of God is revealed to him; yet he still goes on in the religious path in the same humble attitude as his fellowmen, so that he may not spoil the faith of those who have the journey yet to accomplish.

Since the time of the Reformation a wave has come in the West causing every soul to think that he has advanced further than his forefathers did in the past, and this is so in all walks of life, and he has sufficient reasons for believing it. However, in the question of the spiritual path the same attitude can never be profitable, and even if it may seem profitable in the case of one individual, it certainly must prove disadvantageous in the lives of many. When a man thinks, 'I have outgrown my religion or a certain standard of morals', even if he has outgrown it, still by saying so and by acting differently, he must surely confuse those who are walking with him on the same path and yet have not reached the distance to which he has reached.

Individualistic progress is so far allowed as a man's inner advancement is concerned; but as to the outward actions uniformity is needed, which is not at all difficult for a Western man, for Western civilization shows uniformity in all walks of life, yet sometimes fails to bring this light to bear upon religion.

The Western young man looks back upon his ancestors as on a lower level of evolution than he is now at present. On the contrary in the East a person considers his ancestors much better than himself, higher in evolution, greater in their principles. While the former wants to reject their ways and terms it a revolution, the latter wants to follow their footsteps calling it idealization. It is difficult to judge these two opposite tendencies as both seem to have their advantages and disadvantages. The wrong of either of the parties is that one depreciates the past, the other the present.

It seems to be in the character of some people in the West that they may show a great appreciation to religion, more so to their forefathers' belief, and yet one cannot say when they will have a revolt against it, as it comes like a fit. Some keep it back in order to maintain their religious belief. It seems to be a result of the impression upon the Western mentality made by the Reformation, of which the generality is unconscious. Whereas in the East it is quite the contrary. They get a fit of revolt against material life which is now to be seen in the Indian mentality.

The remarkable tendency one sees in the East and West is that, however small a person in the East, his desire is to be or act like a king, and however great a person in the West, even if he be a king, he tries to act like a workman. The Kaiser who often used to cut wood as a recreation, was not an exception among the royalties of Europe. A millionaire in America does not mind in the least running on the platform to catch a train, with a leather bag in his hand. Whereas in the East a nobleman who will be starving in his house would always avoid walking among the crowd.

I very often remember, newspaper reporters in the United States used to come and would speak with me on different subjects and would be very much impressed by the ideas, and next day a very ugly article would appear in the paper. I had great hopes after their response. One day I saw a reporter after having seen his article. I said, 'I had a great hope, in you I found such an understanding.' He said, 'You are quite right. I was very interested, and I am still interested. (That is why I came to you.) But when I took it before my superior officer he said, 'It is too sweet, it is too good for the man in the street. Even the President must read this paper. That is why we want to keep every man on the lowest level.' And it is a great pity. For instance, a young writer develops a sense of beauty in his writing. He takes it to the agent who sends the writing to the magazines. He looks at it and the first thing he says, 'It will not take.' That means: it is very nice. He has no fault to find with it, only it will not take. He is looking at it from the point of view of the mind that will read it. He wants to bring that great gift to the penny paper level. This shows that mankind is always dragging back. The soul's progress toward spirituality is always dragged back from every side. And the one who will make progress in the path of beauty will have to make a great many sacrifices in order to keep to his point of view.

At the present time the world is becoming very commercial, even to such an extent that, absorbed in commercialism, it overlooks the sense of beauty. In other words, the sense of beauty is being sacrificed to commercialism. But at the same time in commercialism there is no purpose of life accomplished. That which accomplishes the purpose of the soul is in its wakening to beauty in all aspects.

In ancient civilization people had other faults, but this is the fault of the present time. In Rome I met the editor of a paper. I was telling him about the question how much a newspaper can help because today the paper is a medium between the thinking people and those who would follow the thought. And it would be such a great thing if the newspaper world would take up in their mind as their sacred mission to elevate humanity. 'Yes,' he said, 'that is quite right. But do you know what our education is just now? When we learn to be editors we have to write so many words in such a short time, that is where we begin; and if we do not write as much we cannot pass our examination. And if we write so many words as that, we cannot think, we have no time to think. The only time for us to think is when we are writing.' I quite admitted the fact, but at the same time that does not take us any further.

I was once very amused: in Boston a reporter of a newspaper came to me and his first question was: which hall was it where I was going to lecture? I thought the first important question he would have asked would have been, what was the subject that I was going to lecture on? But his most important point was the hall in which I was to lecture. And as unfortunately the hall was not so large as he had anticipated, all the conversation with him and every impression he had, it turned out to be nothing, because the hall was not large enough for the editor to admit the article.

It has been inconceivable to me to see to what extent some people in the Western world could be outspoken. I often wondered if it was to be called honesty. If it was honesty I could not think for a moment that it could be wisdom.

What I found missing in the West is the tendency to keep veiled all that is beautiful, which one finds in the East. In the West every seeking soul wishes to know all in plain words, which makes the idea cut and dry, taking away the beauty of its curve, which in the terms of the Sufi poets is called, 'the curls

Photograph 50. New York, USA. December 1925

of the beloved'. No sooner does a student read something than he is eager to discuss it, he is ready to judge before pondering upon the subject by himself; before touching the depth of an idea, he wishes to justify it by weighing it in the scale of his own reason, however sacred the idea be.

Progress to a Western person is going forward and he understands going forward by passing things, leaving them behind and stepping forward into new experiences. The spiritual progress is made on a path quite opposite to the path of the world. It is progress towards one's self, plainly speaking within oneself, and no new experience does one meet with on the way, but one finds all that is known and has been forgotten by one's soul; and in this pursuit in the beginning one does not feel one is progressing, for one finds nothing new.

The thing which greatly amazed me was to see the tenacity in a person in the West. He may be spiritually inclined and may have risen to value the things of the world less, yet he seems to say without saying that, 'I know of this physical existence; the other existence of which I know not but of which I am told, with all my desire to attain it I would not purchase it at the cost of what I have. It is so contrary to the idea that Shams Tabriz, the great soul of Persia says: 'You desire God and the world both; it is a difficult thing, almost impossible.'

A Western seeker takes up the inner cult as a study rather than as a religion. He considers the idea he has as his own and the idea of another foreign, whereas in reality every idea is one's own when possessed by one's mind and every idea is foreign before it is accepted. No idea has ever come from one's soul; all ideas have come from others; but it is human nature to feel the idea one holds in mind to be one's own, and the idea which he has not yet held to be foreign. No idea in reality belongs to anybody.

The religious laws given to the people of the West by the Christian Church have made their moral conception rigid. For the moral principles are given to them cut and dry. Those incapable of following such morals depart from religion; those who follow these principles advance no further than their dry principles of moral, in which there is no beauty nor tenderness to be found. Their virtues may be likened to solid rocks. Whereas in the East, especially among Hindus, there is a science of conscience developed. Their moral conceptions are not like rocks, but like water running in a stream, springing from the heights of the mountains and falling into the arms of the ocean.

The symbolical form of Oriental teaching seems too subtle and vague to the Western mind. The Western person says, 'Please speak in plain words.' One day a lady was very much annoyed with me, and said to me, 'Here I have been attending your lectures for six months and have heard all you have said. It enters in one of my ears and passes out through the other. It all seems to be in a mist; there seems to be nothing to grasp, nothing to hold on to.' Once an amusing thought came to me, I thought I would take some good square cut bricks and write upon them 'Mystery', and if one asked for an intelligible mystery I would give in their hands one brick, to hold in the hand and tell them: 'That is the most intelligible mystery, hold it fast, don't let it drop!' That is the reason why the teachers in the ancient times when they were constantly asked: 'But show me where God is', made idols out of rock and placed them in shrines, and with a heavy heart they themselves also had to bow before the handmade idols.

That is the reason why Sufism is less known to the West than Vedanta. Though Vedanta is deep, it is plainly put in words. But when a person reads Hafiz or any other Sufi poet of Persia, it takes him to a beautiful garden, where they hear nightingales, and find the glass of wine, and the vain beloved, and nothing else. They cannot imagine that it ever can be a religion or a philosophy. Many think it is a beautiful imagery. In reality it is the same Vedanta which is given in Sanskrit more in scientific terms; by the Sufis the same is expressed artistically. For poetry does not mean simply words, poetry is an expression of inner beauty. Many asked me, 'What did Omar Khayyam mean by wine and beloved in his Rubayat? Did he really mean it or was it something else?' But it was funny enough for me to see in the West some drinking clubs who were named 'Omar Khayyam Club' and taverns named after him.

Many Eastern ideas seem severe in the Western mind. Western nature is self-assertive and demanding. That is why spiritual attainment becomes difficult for the people in the West, as it is only attained by self-effacement and self-denial. The idea of crushing the 'I', to become selfless, to become indifferent to the life around one, to become strong enough to endure different natures around one, to feel that there can never be a judgement in the hereafter, to feel that one must lose oneself in God and to think that this individuality is an illusion and to imagine it to be four days[39], these things frighten many from a deeper understanding of the philosophical thought of the East. Therefore those who have worked in the West in spreading the spiritual thought have to keep back many deep ideas of philosophy in order to cope with the people. Even the Bible had to be so many times revised and modified to suit the present generation in the West. On the other side there are many facilities which I found in the West which I could not have found in the East. People in the West are as a rule not bigoted in their faith, and therefore there are many who are ready to receive truth from whatever source it may come. They do not always meet with violence a spiritual reformer, be he a moral, political or religious one. What they cannot understand they simply turn their back on. What they like nobody can keep them from, their relations, clergy or friends. They follow it of their free will, except some who are somewhat conscious of the opinion of the society around them. They welcome and respect all the representatives of knowledge, open their door to them to welcome them and invite them to their table. Wisdom being a human inheritance, it is neither Eastern nor Western, and therefore wise and foolish are to be found every-

---

39. Indian expression signifying long period

where, in the East or West; only the difference is that in the East, especially in India, much more importance has been given to the spiritual ideal, to inner life, which is real, whereas in the West, for centuries the progress has been made in the outer direction of life. Having gone opposite ways, it is natural that there should seem to be a difference in their ways.

Man in the East is satisfied with the subjective. The great quality that a man from the West shows, is that he tries to bring all he can from the subjective to the objective. It is in this that he surpasses the Eastern mentality and proves his success in his inventive genius.

In order to unite the people in the West, you must raise a common enemy. In order to unite people in the East, you must have a prophet come.

However, the seeking of every soul, either Eastern or Western, is for the Truth, which I have found among many sincere seekers after Truth in the West. Many among my mureeds, have shown a great devotion, an openness of heart, a unity without barrier, a friendship which is constant, a spirit of discipleship, which is worthy of regard, and an outlook on life from a mystical point of view. I must admit I have friends in the West whom I consider closer than my own friends and relations in the East, and some with complete confidence in me, which makes me trust them forever. This, in spite of all differences between the East and West, has convinced me that a good and true person, a thoughtful and wise soul, is the same everywhere, in the East or West.

Photograph 51. London, UK. June 1919

Music

I found that the Eastern and Western music are vastly different in spite of one and the same basic principle and in spite of the well-known belief that music is the language of the universe.

It became difficult for me to uphold the superiority of Indian music any longer, even in my own sight, for comparison became impossible. In certain things I found Indian music no doubt much more advanced in some respects, but the Western music seemed to have advanced much further than a musician of India can ever imagine. Nevertheless, it seemed easy to convince an Indian artist of that truth by showing tangible examples, but I found it most difficult to prove the superiority of Indian music to the Western person, for the reason that the direction in which the music of India has evolved is in the abstract, obscure to the perception of every person. The chief difference which I found between the music of India and that of the West was that the Indian music was more individualistic, with scope for creation, more psychological, more an art rather than mechanically constructed, appealing to the heart and productive of peace.

The remarks that every Western person made about Eastern music was that it is weird, melancholy, sad. And a musician will say, it is mostly in a minor key and it consists of many repetitions. And a question that was constantly asked was, 'Why is there no harmony in Indian music?' This it embarrassed me most to say, for it would need the giving of a whole lecture on philosophy and music to tell anyone fully why we have no harmony. The word harmony, which is the soul of music, is used in Western terms also for a system of playing various notes together. And in order to say 'No, we have not such a system', I had to use the words, 'We have no harmony', which in the true sense means, 'We have no soul in our music.'

The ragas in India upon which the art of Indian music is built are characteristic of the nature of the Hindus, whose religion consists of mythology and whose divine ideals, Gods and Goddesses, are the pictures of certain characters of life. So the ragas represent certain characters and we find ourselves intimate with the ragas as we are with our friends. A raga is a natural thing, as character is natural, and ragas even exist in the West. The Western people unconsciously compose and enjoy ragas, but as they do not distinguish their ragas they are not bound to keep in the region of any particular raga, as we are in India. The music of the East and that of the West cannot be judged by an intellectual comparison, but only by its effect upon one. For it is the nature of the soul to enjoy better what it has once already enjoyed. Every pleasing sensation, so to speak, makes a line upon one's soul and retouching the same line, next time redoubles the sensation. It is therefore that the music of every country is liked by its inhabitants more than the music of other lands. The Swiss air, *Ranz des Vaches*, was never allowed to be played in the hearing of the Swiss guard of the French kings, because to hear that air made them long to return to their own country. Also, in order to enjoy the music of any country one must know something about it.

To every person music appeals according to his grade of evolution, for every person there is a certain music which can appeal to him. But no one from the East or West of the world can deny that the Western music has an effect of rousing passion or emotion, whereas Indian music has a tendency to produce calm and peace. An Indian artist lives for his art, in the West an artist cannot afford to do so, the demands of life force him to submit his art to the commercial realm of people's demand. The artist in India is the composer at the same time. Even an amateur in India begins his first step in art with a creative attitude. However great a singer or player in the West, he must subject himself first to the composer whose music he sings or plays. His creative faculty therefore has very little opportunity to play a part.

By the kind invitation of Monsieur Dalcroze I had the great pleasure of seeing some of the demonstrations given by his pupils under his personal direction. In Dalcroze I saw someone in the West who has such a great tendency to improvise and, in spite of some crude and most exaggerated gestures which he first teaches to his pupils, he seems to be advancing to the same goal which is continually sought by an artist of Hindustan.

With all the richness of voice possessed by a Western singer, the intricacies of Indian art of singing are such that he cannot easily render it. Nor can a singer of India with his flexibility of voice and with its silky texture make his voice audible to the large audience in the Grand Opera House.

After seeing the Western operas, where one hears the splendour of Occidental vocal culture, I was much impressed to see to what extent the art of singing has been developed. This was a wonder to me. No doubt, it has always been difficult to accustom my ears to enjoy singing accompanied by so many different instruments and different voices. At the same time, I saw what facility it gives to a singer to be so supported by the whole orchestra and by other voices so that he may have time to breathe and to give a better expression to his voice. And I saw how much more difficult the task of an Eastern singer was when the whole performance depended upon his one voice, accompanied by nothing but the tambura, which gives one chord to help him keep the keynote. This I found one of the reasons why the voice of the Eastern singers is not so large in volume and so widely audible to a crowd as that of an Occidental singer. However, I noticed the quality to be different. The quality of a Western singer's voice is not such that could produce with facility what an Eastern singer could, whose voice is more flexible. But at

Photograph 52. Jena, Germany. October 1921

the same time the Western singer excels in the volume of his voice, which is considered in the West as a mark of his development.

In the stories of operas, I found also the difference of the Eastern and Western taste. To the Eastern mind the touch of vairagya, which is renunciation, makes the greatest appeal. Therefore in every drama the plot has something of it. If the same idea was produced in the West, it would perhaps be interesting, but not appealing. What mostly touches the Western mind is heroism, although it is the quality of heart which makes the greatest impression on man, whether he be of the East or West.

The European voice is classified in different voices such as tenor, baritone, bass, soprano. But in India there is no classification of voices for the very reason that there is no choral singing, which gives the Indian singer a great freedom of expression and an individual pitch, peculiar to himself. Therefore each singer has his natural pitch of voice which is peculiar to himself. In India what particularly appeals to an audience is the sympathetic quality of a singer's voice, instead of a large volume of voice. If there is anything which is common to India and the West in singing, it is what they call in the West *oratorio*. And there is a reason for this. It is religious music and it has its origin in the East. No doubt, one thing is remarkable in comparing the music of the East and West. That is that the compositions of the great Western musicians which are called in the West classical, are of a similar character, but in quite a different form, as *dhrupad* and *khayal* of India.

However Indian music represented in Oriental style in an Eastern voice, even to my own ears appeared poor, as a whistle before the noise of drums. The very ideal is different from that of the West. Indian music is for a few people sitting in solitude, having all the time in the world[40] to tune their instruments and to sing, even if it were the whole night, as suits that climate, where in the middle of the night music has more influence than at other times. In the West if a man practises in his flat after eleven o'clock at night he will soon hear from his landlady. To an average Western person that music falls beneath his standard, and a thoughtful person takes it in another way, often out of politeness. He says, 'Your music is something which we cannot understand.' But I saw some people in the West, most of them sympathetic to the East and its thought, who were more deeply struck by Indian music, which seemed to appeal to them even more than the music of their own land. Some I have seen in the West who felt on hearing our music that this was the music that they thought was something that their soul had longed for all through their life, as if their spirit knew it already. Some called it not music but magic, but such people were seldom to be found.

In whatever form Indian music was presented, I now and then met with people who became fascinated with the music I had to represent, and I met with some who even grasped the idea which was hidden beneath my music.

---

40. First edition has Dutch rendering: 'all their time their own'

Several became so bewildered after having a conversation with me, thinking: how can a musician have such ideas? It was an unusual thing to them. They thought that it was religion I was representing in my music. They thought that it was making a stage a temple, and a concert hall a church. Some saw that a moral and spiritual Message of reform I was giving from every place where I was allowed to stand, and they marvelled at the idea of someone doing that depending upon his own work for his livelihood, without any support from anywhere and yet not wanting to convert people to any particular religion, only fulfilling his life's mission by showing those who came across his way the straight path that leads to the destination of life.

Anecdotes

Pir-o-Murshid was one day travelling in the train and there came some gay young people, boys and girls, who were making all sorts of jokes among themselves. Looking at the appearance of the Murshid and thinking he is a foreigner, he will not know the language, they fully joked and laughed, and made all sorts of funny remarks which Murshid also enjoyed very much. In order to know whether Murshid knew the language one of them spoke to him in English, but as Murshid answered in Hindustani they found the platform free for jokes. After some time suddenly Murshid took off his hat to rest his head back freely, and looked at the two people sitting in the corner, and the girl gently spoke to her boy. She said, 'It is the head of Christ', and the boy seriously said, 'Right you are.' A third person said, 'Heaven knows who this man is; is he an Indian, or a Greek, or a Romanian?' His girl said, 'Whoever he is, he seems to be a thoroughly good man.' This remark changed the atmosphere of the whole compartment. Their joking mood turned to the mood of admiration, and as each moment passed, they felt more and more weighing on them some presence which perhaps throughout their life they had never realized, and in time it became so heavy that gaiety did not seem to exist in the sphere. The girls became absorbed in looking at Pir-o-Murshid in perfect bewilderment and the boys entirely speechless and spellbound. In this way their spirit, soul and body were held in suspense until the station of Murshid's destination arrived, when he left them all with a bow.

One day, Murshid arrived in a town at an unexpected hour, and found nobody at the station to receive him. No lights were to be found in the streets, during the time of war, nor was a vehicle to be found. Murshid was left alone with all his things to carry, his hands full of bags and his instrument. He walked along the road, expecting to find someone who could show him the way. He saw at a distance men coming. As he approached he found that they had all drunk and were at the moment of their greatest glory. They were laughing aloud. Shouting, fighting and dancing, they came near to the Murshid where he was standing, loaded with all his bags in the dark. As they approached, one saw Murshid and said, 'Oh, who is that?' And in answer to this came out from everyone a bursting laughter. And Murshid's glance fell on them as a lightning and it seemed as if all their intoxication and feeling of gaiety vanished in a moment. Then he asked them for the place he was searching after and they said, 'We will take you to the place.'

One man took Murshid's bag, a second another bag and a third one also something, but Murshid would not give anyone his vina, but two took it away from him with all the force they had and walked on the way so quietly as if they were on their sacred duty. There was not the slightest sign of intoxication left. Every one of them seemed to have been controlled by some impression within him, which he himself did not realize till the moment they escorted the Murshid.

A Catholic priest met Murshid in a park and asked him if he was Catholic. 'Yes,' said Murshid, 'by religion, not by the Church.'

A civil officer asked Murshid, 'What are you doing in the West?' Murshid said, 'Working.' He asked, 'Working for what, for money?' Murshid said, 'No, working for God.' 'Is your work materially profitable', asked the civilian. Murshid said, 'If I had material profit in view I had taken something else in life to do.' The civilian said jokingly, 'Yes, you will be paid your wages in the hereafter.' Murshid said, 'No, I don't work for returns, either here or in the hereafter. I work for the sake of the work itself.' 'Have you no family?' asked the civilian. 'Yes, a large one,' said Murshid. 'What will become of them after you have passed?' asked the civilian. Murshid said, 'I beg your pardon, Sir, will you tell me what will become of your family after you have passed?' He said, 'My family will get a pension from the Government.' 'So will my children from that great government to whose service my life has been dedicated.'

Someone asked, 'Murshid, do you also work for the coming of the Master?' 'Yes,' said Murshid. 'We all work for him.' 'But will you tell me, when is the world teacher coming?' asked the person. Pir-o-Murshid said, 'You will get that information from the Order of the Star, for they are supposed to get the telegram of his arrival.'

Somebody questioned Murshid: 'What do you think of Christ?' 'Which one, the historic Christ or the Christ of the ideal? As to the historic Christ even the different traditions say different things, so how are we to know and have a common conception of Christ? And as to the ideal Christ, it depends upon every man's ideal and one man's ideal cannot be the other man's ideal also. Besides, ideal is something that we make ourselves and is always too sacred to put into words!'

Someone said to Murshid, 'Take some of our Christian religion to the East.' Murshid replied, 'It has already come from the East, sir.'

Someone asked Murshid, 'What difference is there between Theosophy and Sufism? Is it not one?' 'Yes,' said Murshid, 'these are only two doors of one puzzle; one to enter and one to exit.' The questioner asked, 'But which is which?' The Murshid said, 'it is left to you to find out for yourself.'

Someone said to Murshid, seeing him to be a religious man from the East, that it is Christianity which is the cause of all the progress that the Western world has made, and it is the absence of Christianity which is the root of the downfall of the East. The Murshid answered, 'No; it is the Christ spirit in the East which is keeping us back from material progress and it is the lack of Christianity in the West which has helped you to progress so materially.'

Someone asked Murshid, 'If you believe that all is just, and all is good, and all is well, then why do you work to change conditions in the world?' Said Murshid, 'It is the human in me that is working its way towards divine perfection.'

A materialistic Italian, a young man, said to Murshid, 'I believe in the eternity of matter.' And to his surprise the Murshid replied, 'My belief is not much different from yours, only that which you call eternal matter, I call spirit.'

A lady came to see Murshid and said to Murshid, 'Now look here, Murshid, I want to speak with you on an important subject, for it is a question of faith. Now I believe that Jesus Christ was the Son of God, and our Redeemer and that his religion must be taught to the heathen world. And I hear that you consider all the prophets equal. Now, that I cannot understand.' Murshid answered, 'I have never said that all prophets are equal. I only say that I do not feel equal to judge them, following the words of Christ: 'Judge ye not'. So I simply bow my head to all in humility.'

A Dutch poet asked Murshid at a dinner table: 'Don't you think, Murshid, that the poet must love God, but admire Satan also?' Murshid answered: 'I do not separate God from Satan.' He said, 'but God Himself has separated.' Murshid said, 'that is His own affair.'

A bigoted Christian asked Murshid, 'How could you ever connect the name of Muhammad with our Lord Jesus Christ?' 'I beg your pardon,' said Murshid. 'I did not mean Muhammad whom you know through your clergy, I meant the Prophet known to the faithful followers of Islam.'

When Murshid was travelling in America a child saw him and said to his mother, 'Ma (pointing to the Murshid), God.' The mother said, 'No, priest.' The child answered, 'Will he pray for Pa?' When in the train the lady met Murshid, she told him what the child had said, and his desire that his long-suffering father might be helped. It touched Murshid very much and he readily promised to pray for the child's father.

A child, after coming to a lecture with his mother, went next day to his school and said to his schoolmates with great enthusiasm, 'I have seen the best man in the world!' His mother having heard about it, came with the news to Murshid, asking him to bless her child who had proclaimed him thus before all his friends.

Someone from the audience asked Murshid after his lecture: 'And what do you think of the coming of Christ?' 'He has never gone for me,' said Murshid.

One day, Murshid was travelling and had spent every penny in his pocket. No money was left to give the porter, and he so much wished that some of his load would be carried by someone. After wishing that, he did not walk perhaps twenty steps, that a young soldier happened to come near, and he said, 'Shall I take some of your load?' Murshid said, 'Thank you', and thought in his mind, 'How truly needs are answered if only one really needed. Verily a deep-felt need is a prayer in itself.'

Someone asked Murshid, 'Are you the head of the Sufi Order?' 'No, God,' he said. 'And you?' asked the man. 'The foot,' said he.

One day a visitor came to have an interview with Pir-o-Murshid. He was a lawyer, materialist and atheist, besides was greatly opposed to all those who did not belong to his nation, and had been turned against the work of Murshid by somebody. Therefore he began his conversation, expressing with vigour his attitude. But as he got answers, so it seemed as if the fire of opposition met with water, and as he went along in his dispute, he, instead of getting hotter became cooler. He had expected to hear from the Murshid spiritual beliefs that he could argue upon and to tear them to pieces, but he found Murshid's belief not very different from what he himself believed. He found no effort on the part of Murshid to force his ideas upon anybody. He saw in Murshid the tendency to appreciate every kind of idea, for in every idea there is a good side and he felt that the tendency was to be sympathetic rather than antagonistic. He saw that there was nothing that Murshid stood for, but only believed that the truth was in every heart and no-one else can give it to another unless it rose up from the heart of a person as a spring of water from the mountain. He became so softened in his tone and in his manner after an hour's conversation that he parted quite a different man from what he had come. He shook hands with Pir-o-Murshid and said, 'We shall always be friends' and Murshid thought that it was not a small achievement.

Someone said to Murshid, 'In your writings I read two things which contradict each other.' Murshid said, 'Take one of those two things with which you are in agreement and forget the other.'

Photograph 53. Haarlem, Netherlands. 10ᵗʰ September 1921

Someone asked Murshid, 'Are you a pessimist?' He said, 'No, an optimist, but with open eyes.'

Someone said to Murshid, 'I heard them talk against you.' 'Did they?' said he. 'Have you also heard anyone speak kindly of me?' 'Yes,' the person exclaimed. 'Then,' said Murshid, 'that is what is the light and shade to life's picture, making the picture complete.'

A pupil said to Murshid, 'But you also make mistakes.' 'Yes,' replied Murshid, 'if I had not made mistakes I would not be able to teach you.'

Somebody asked, 'Have you any faults, Murshid?' 'Yes, many more than you may think.'

A friend said to Murshid, 'Somebody told me bad things about you.' 'What?' asked Murshid. 'He told me so and so and so.' 'Is that all?' said Murshid. 'I can be much worse than that.'

A person seeing a ring on Murshid's finger asked, 'What mystical signification does your ring convey?' 'It says that those whose hearts are not yet open to the ever-revealing life around them, they look for mystery in me.'

A woman said to Murshid, on hearing his lecture on faith, 'Murshid, I have lost everything I had by having faith in an unworthy person.' 'But you have not lost your faith, I suppose,' asked Murshid. The woman said, 'Yes, I have lost faith.' 'If you had lost all save faith, it would be worth as much as the price you had to pay for it, and even more than that,' Murshid replied.

'Murshid, when I come to you I come with a thousand complaints to make. Why is it that the power of your presence disarms me?' Murshid: 'Because I have disarmed myself.'

'You have nicely said to us, Murshid, how Sufism is one with all religions. Now please tell us, what is the difference between Sufism and other religions.' The Murshid says, 'The difference is that it casts away all differences.'

A Theosophical mureed asked: 'Do you consider the doctrine of reincarnation right or wrong?' Murshid: 'Right in fact, and wrong in truth.'

Someone asked Inayat Khan, knowing that once he was a great singer: 'It is a great pity you gave up your singing.' He replied: 'If the world was not deaf, I would have still continued to sing.'

A lady asked Inayat Khan in a ballroom: 'Do you ever take interest in such a frivolous thing as dancing?' Inayat Khan said: 'Yes, I too feel inclined to dance when I am with little children.'

In my German visit to Munich, while introducing me, Dr. Steindamm said that: 'The mysticism of Pir-o-Murshid Inayat Khan is practical mysticism, pertaining to the life of today. For one might think that a mystic would remain in his visions and dreams, but our Murshid drives his own car.'

In all stages of his evolution, progress and work, one thing never left Inayat Khan through all joys and sorrows, and it was a sense of mirth, and he mostly used this sense of mirth in his everyday life, in speaking and writing, but frequently by psychic power, he played and amused himself.

One day a young man came to him, a son of a mureed and said his mother had sent him, for he was in a great despair, thinking that Murshid will give him some advice; and Murshid asked him what was the reason of his despair. He answered: he had loved a girl who first showed him a great love, but now she is beginning to get detached, because she seems to be getting interested in some other young man. Murshid seemed amused at hearing this from quite a young man. He said, 'Then what do you wish to do?' The young man said, 'I want her to love me or else life has no interest for me any longer.' Murshid laughed and said, 'Oh, life is always interesting. If not in one object, in another object, one finds interest. It is perhaps your momentary spell that makes you so depressed. Let her alone, if she loves someone else, you go and love somebody else too.' The young man made a face of disappointment and looked at Murshid who asked, 'What do you want?' 'I want her to love me.' Murshid said, 'Go just now and she will be alright.' He went immediately from there to her and found her, to his great surprise, entirely changed, as amiable, sympathetic and agreeable as ever. The young man was so pleased that he left a note of thanks to the house of the Murshid. When next day he went she was quite indifferent and did not care for him and he again was very unhappy. For two or three days he was too depressed and then came again to Murshid and said, 'The time when you sent me she was loving and good, but after that she is treating me in the same manner as before. Now I do not know what to do.' But Murshid said, 'What do you want?' He said, 'I want her to be good to me.' As Murshid said, 'Go just now, she will be good to you', and when he went there she was very kind to him, very loving, but only that day, next day she again turned. He came again home and was very disappointed and came to Murshid to give the report of her behaviour. Murshid was very amused and said to him, 'Now look here, my son, I showed you what power is latent in man. But at the same time this power is not to destroy anybody's freedom. As you wish your freedom in life, so she must have her freedom to choose whom she must love. Although it is a bitter experience to you, after some days you will be most thankful to think that you did not induce someone to love you by force who was not in reality your lover. I would be all my life without someone's love who did not care to love me and would be quite content. You are young, you have life before you waiting. You do not know what is in store for you. It is just a matter of patience. Therefore be cheerful and go and all will be well.'

One day Murshid was walking in the street and saw a soldier walking stiff and straight. He seemed as stiff as a log of wood, no movement, no bend in his walk. Murshid was very amused at it and as Murshid walked immediately behind him, he thought, he must make this log move. First he felt irritation in his neck and gave a slap on his neck and began to rub his neck. Murshid was very amused, but thought it is not enough, he must twist a little and he felt uncomfortable in his waist and he began to twist both sides. Murshid thought that is not enough, he must look back. Something came in his brain, giving him a feeling that somebody was calling him from behind and he looked back. This made this man turn and twist which provided for Murshid a good amusement.

One day Murshid was travelling in a train. After the whole day's work, in the evening Murshid was so tired that he really desired quiet, but those sitting with him in the compartment were all busy talking among themselves, which was to Murshid rather a nuisance. Therefore Murshid thought, 'Now I must get them all to sleep. That is the only way of getting quiet.' He looked at the person who was sitting just before him, an old man, who was smoking, which was a double nuisance, and dropped his head down, and the old man began to nod. His cigarette fell down from his hand, and in one moment he began to snore. Then Murshid looked at a young man, who was talking so much with his girl and dropped his head down, and the girl dropped her head on the breast of the man, and the man dropped his head on the head of his girl and both fell fast asleep. Murshid looked at the man who was sitting at his side who was looking in a book and mumbling to himself and no sooner was the glance cast on him, then he began to yawn, raising his book against his mouth. He once stretched and twisted and turned and stretched his body on the legs of the old man and went to sleep. Murshid was very amused and had all the quiet he wanted all through his journey, for all of them were so fast asleep that the porter at the station had to waken them after Murshid had left the compartment.

While talking on the character of the English, Murshid said, 'The Englishman is just, fair in his dealings, moderate, gentle, straightforward, sociable, businesslike and many-sided, and when a friend, always to be depended upon.' The person to whom he spoke said, 'But you have not told his faults.' Murshid said, 'That you must ask of someone else.'

After hearing 'the Sufi Message' a lady came and said how very much she enjoyed the lecture and asked, 'What have you to say about the coming of the World Messenger?' Murshid: 'The World Message is here, but I do not know where the Messenger has gone.'

A lady came after 'the Message' was given, very much impressed by it, and thought that certainly, if ever a Master came, he would speak something in this manner, and she came to shake hands with Murshid and said, 'I am sure next time you will come here on earth as a Master.' 'Thank you, I am highly honoured,' said Murshid.

Someone asked Murshid, 'Is it true that the people in the East believe that woman possesses no soul?' Murshid said, 'Yes, true, they have every reason for it, for they know that woman is soul itself.'

Somebody asked Murshid, 'Are women better than men?' Murshid answered, 'Men say that women are better, and women say that men are better. Everyone considers that better which he lacks in himself. Really speaking they are both complements to one another.'

Someone from the audience asked Murshid after his lecture on the power of the word, 'Which is the best word?' Murshid replied: 'Silence.'

A good natured, plump lady, while busy eating, asked Murshid at table, 'Tell me please, is it spiritual to fast?' Murshid answered smilingly, 'It is as spiritual to fast as it is to enjoy a delicious dinner.' The lady was happy to get this answer.

Someone asked Murshid, 'Of what Church are you a minister?' 'Of God,' said Murshid.

Someone asked Murshid, how Sufism works upon him once a person has studied Theosophy. 'As a disinfectant,' said Murshid.

A pupil said, 'Murshid, it is since I met you that I have lost my faith.' 'Did you lose your faith, how wonderful.' Pupil: 'Wonderful! Why, it is most dreadful Murshid!' 'It is just as well that you have lost a faith which was so easy to lose. But I am afraid if you are not careful, next you may lose yourself.'

A materialistic young man after a public lecture came to Murshid and said, 'What you said was most beautiful and fine, but it seems to be all somewhere in the air.' Murshid said: 'Yes, it is in the air, because you are all on the earth.'

Once, walking through the city of New York with a friend, the friend asked:

'Murshid, I have read your Sufi ideas, but they are not broad enough for me.' 'Certainly, they are not as broad,' said Murshid, 'as the Broadway of New York.'

Epilogue

After the Summer School at Suresnes in 1926 Pir-o-Murshid travelled to India, his beloved homeland, and was accompanied by his mureed and secretary Kismet Stam. After a few very busy months of travelling and lecturing, he passed away after a short illness in Delhi on the 5th of February 1927.

Illustrations

List of Illustrations

1. Maharaja Sayaji Rao Gaekwar of Baroda   251
2. Sampat Rao Gaekwar of Baroda   252
3. Maula Bakhsh   253
4. Rahmat Khan   254
5. Mehr Bakhshe in the centre of a group (Gayanshala, Baroda)   255
6. Murtaza Khan   256
7. Alaoddin Khan (Dr. A.M. Pathan)   257
8. Maula Bakhsh, standing far left.   258
9. Ramyar in a group   259
10. Ali Khan   260
11. Maheboob Khan   261
12. Musharaff Khan   262
13. Ruth **St. Denis**   263
14. Mrs. Ada **Martin** (Murshida Rabia)   264
15. Mrs. E.M. **Morrison**   265
16. Amina Begum **Inayat Khan** née Ora Ray Baker   266
17. Dr. A. **King**   267
18. Miss Beatrice **Irwin**   268
19. Monsieur E. **Bailly**   269
20. The Royal Musicians of Hindustan; from left to right: Ramaswami, Ali Khan, Musharaff Khan, Maheboob Khan, third row: Inayat Khan   270
21. Claude **Debussy**   271
22. Monsieur Albert I. **Caillet**   272
23. Ali Khan (picture taken in Moscow in 1913)   273
24. Musharaff Khan (picture taken in Moscow in 1913)   274
25. Princess E. Sirtolov **Lavrovsky**   275
26. Monsieur H. **Balakin**   276
27. Olga **Tucki**   277
28. The Royal Musicians of Hindustan; from left to right: Ali Khan, Inayat Khan, Musharaff Khan, Maheboob Khan   278
29. Miss Mary **Williams** (Zohra)   279
30. Miss L. **Goodenough** (Murshida Sharifa)   280
31. Miss Janette **Steer**   281
32. Miss Mabel **Thomson**   282
33. Miss Rose **Benton**   283

34. Miss **Shirley** sitting second at Pir-o-Murshid's left side,
    Miss I.P. Young (Khatidja) first lady standing in the third row,
    Herr E. Glaser Crohas, third person standing in third row
    (London 1918) 284
35. Mrs. H. **Sheaf** (Hanifa) and her daughter 285
36. Mr. C. **Best** (Sheikh Shahbaz) 286
37. Dr. O.C. **Gruner** (Khalif) 287
38. Mr. Edward **Carpenter** 288
39. Madame Emma **Nevada** 289
40. Mignon **Nevada** 290
41. Khankah, 86 Ladbroke Road, London 291
42. Madame Gabriella **Strauss** 292
43. Dr. A.B. **Scott** (Khalif) 293
44. Miss J.E. **Dowland** (Khalifa Nargis) 294
45. Miss **Wiseman** 295
46. Miss **E.M. Saintsbury-Green** (Murshida Sophia) 296
47. 15 rue Neuve, Wissou, France where Pir-o-Murshid lived
    for some time in 1921 297
48. Prof. Ir. E.L. **Selleger** and family 298
49. Mr. and Mrs. **Hart van Sautter** 299
50. E. Baron von **Graffenried** 300
51. Group photograph Viladat Day 1923. Miss N. **Mitchell**,
    back row, second person, standing and touching tree with hand 301
52. Mevrouw Agathe Baronesse van **Hogendorp-van Notten** (Mahtab) 302
53. Madame M.C. la Baronne **d'Eichthal** (Sheikha) 303
54. H. P. Baron **van Tuyll van Serooskerken** (Sheikh Sirdar),
    Mevrouw H. Baronesse **van Tuyll van Serooskerken-Willebeek le Mair** (Saida) 304
55. Mejuffrouw J.E.D. **Furnée** (Khalifa Sakina,
    later named Nekbakht) with Khairunnisa Khan 305
56. De Heer C.A. **Wegelin** and family 306
57. Madame **Héris** 307
58. Madame H. **Graeffe-van Gorckum** 308
59. Miss Nancy **Oliver** 309
60. Monsieur E. **Dussaq** (Khalif Talewar) 310
61. Comtesse M.L. **Pieri née Dussaq** (Shadman) 311
62. Monsieur E. **de Cruzat Zanetti** (Sheikh) 312
63. Mrs. Rebecca C. **Miller** (Khalifa) 313
64. De Heer J. **Willebeek le Mair** 314
65. Mr. Luther **Burbank** with Pir-o-Murshid Inayat Khan 315
66. Mr. E. **Connaughton** (Khalif) 316
67. Mrs. Marya **Cushing** (Sheikha Khushi) 317
68. Mr. E. **Engle** (Sheikh Fatha), Mrs. Martin, centre,
    and Mrs. Miller, left, in a Universal Worship service 318

69. Pir-o-Murshid Inayat Khan, Amina Begum and their four children with Maheboob Khan and Musharaff Khan   319
70. Fazal Manzil, Suresnes, France   320
71. Mevrouw N. **Egeling-Grol** (Murshida Fazal Mai)   321
72. Fräulein M. **Burkhardt**   322
73. Frau H. Meyer **de Reutercrona** (Sheikha)   323
74. Marchesa **Farinola-de Tanfani** (Zebunnisa)   324
75. Herr B.R. **Baur**   325
76. De Heer A. van **Stolk** (Sheikh Sirkar)   326
77. Mr. R.A.L. **Armstrong** (Sheikh Mumtaz) and Mrs. P. **Armstrong** née van **Hogendorp** (Lakmé)   327
78. Mrs. L. **Hoeber** (Sheikha)   328
79. Fröken Susanna **Kjøsterud** (Sheikha)   329
80. Mejuffrouw A. van **Braam** (Salima)   330
81. Mevrouw J. van **Ingen-Jelgersma** (Zuleikha)   331
82. Mevrouw G. **Eggink-van Stolk** (Bhakti)   332
83. Mejuffrouw D. **Stam** (Kismet)   333
84. Miss Angela **Alt**   334
85. Mrs. G. **Craig** (Munira)   335
86. Sufi Garden in Suresnes with Fazal Manzil in the background   336
87. Luncheon for Church Unity, New York, 29th May 1926   337
88. Miss Gladys I. **Lloyd** (Sheikha Kefayat)   338
89. Moulana Syed Muhammad Hashmi   339

The Nekbakht Foundation regrets that in the first edition of the Biography (1979) a picture on page 406 of that edition was erroneously identified as the murshid of Pir-o-Murshid Hazrat Inayat Khan, Sayyed Muhammad Abu Hashim Madani. We are grateful to Khursheed Ali of Hyderabad for informing us that it was in fact a picture of Moulana Syed Muhammad Hashmi, who taught Pir-o-Murshid Persian and Arabic literature, as detailed on page 72 of the original edition and page 66 of this edition. The Nekbakht Foundation apologizes sincerely for this error and is happy to be able to make the correction.

1. Maharaja Sayaji Rao Gaekwar of Baroda

2. Sampat Rao Gaekwar of Baroda

3. Maula Bakhsh, grandfather of Hazrat Inayat Khan

4. Rahmat Khan, father of Hazrat Inayat Khan

5. Mehr Bakhshe in the centre of a group (Gayanshala, Baroda)

6. Murtaza Khan

7. Alaoddin Khan (Dr. A.M. Pathan) uncle of Hazrat Inayat Khan

8. Maula Bakhsh, standing far left

9. Ramyar in a group

10. Ali Khan

11. Maheboob Khan

12. Musharaff Khan

13. Ruth St. Denis

14. Mrs. Ada Martin (Murshida Rabia)

15. Mrs. E.M. Morrison

16. Amina Begum Inayat Khan née Ora Ray Baker, wife of Hazrat Inayat Khan

17. Dr. A. King

18. Miss Beatrice Irwin

19. Monsieur E Bailly

20. The Royal Musicians of Hindustan; from left to right: Ramaswami, Ali Khan, Musharaff Khan, Maheboob Khan, centre back: Inayat Khan

21. Claude Debussy

22. Monsieur Albert I. Caillet

23. Ali Khan (picture taken in Moscow in 1913)

24. Musharaff Khan

25. Princess E. Sirtolov Lavrovsky

26. Monsieur H. Balakin

27. Olga Tucki

28. The Royal Musicians of Hindustan. Left to right: Ali Khan, Inayat Khan, Musharaff Khan, Maheboob Khan

29. Miss Mary Williams (Zohra)

30. Miss L. Goodenough (Murshida Sharifa)

31. Miss Janette Steer

32. Miss Mabel Thomson

33. Miss Rose Benton

34. Miss Shirley sitting second at Pir-O-Murshid's left side, Miss I.P. Young (Khatidja) first lady standing in the third row, Herr E. Glaser Crohas, third person standing in third row, London 1918

35. Mrs. H. Sheaf (Hanifa) and her daughter

36. Mr. C. Best (Sheikh Shahbaz)

37. Dr. O.C. Gruner (Khalif)

38. Mr. Edward Carpenter

39. Madame Emma Nevada

40. Mignon Nevada as Lakme in Delibes' opera-comique, in a costume which is claimed to be historically correct.

41. Khankah, 86 Ladbroke Road, London

42. Madame Gabriella Strauss.

43. Dr. A.B. Scott (Khalif)

44. Miss J.E. Dowland (Khalifa Nargis)

45. Miss Wiseman

46. Miss E.M. Saintsbury-Green (Murshida Sophia)

47. 15 rue Neuve, Wissou, France where Pir-o-Murshid lived for some time in 1921

48. Prof. Ir. E.L. Selleger and family

49. Mr. and Mrs. Hart van Sautter

50. E. Baron von Graffenried

51. Group Viladat Day 1923.
Miss N. Mitchell back row, second person standing and touching tree with hand

52. Mevrouw Agathe Baronesse van Hogendorp-van Notten (Mahtab)

53. Madame M.C. la Baronne d'Eichthal (Sheikha)

54. H.P. Baron van Tuyll van Serooskerken (Sheikh Sirdar) and
Mevrouw H. Baronesse van Tuyll van Seerooskerken-Willebeek Le Mair
(Saida)

55. Mejuffrouw J.E.D. Furnée (Khalifa Sakina, later Nekbakht) with Khairunnisa

56. De Heer C.A. Wegelin and family

57. Madame Héris

58. Madame H. Graeffe-van Gorckum

59. Miss Nancy Oliver

60. Monsieur E. Dussaq (Khalif Talewar)

61. Comtesse M.L .Pieri née Dussaq (Shadman)

62. Monsieur E. de Cruzat Zanetti (Sheikh)

63. Mrs. Rebecca C. Miller (Khalifa)

64. De Heer J. Willebeek le Mair

65. Mr. Luther Burbank with Pir-o-Murshid Inayat Khan

66. Mr. E. Connaughton (Khalif)

67. Mrs. Marya Cushing (Sheikha Khushi)

68. Mr. E. Engle (Sheikh Fatha) with Mrs. Martin and Mrs. Miller performing the Universal Worship in the early years

69. Pir-o-Murshid Inayat Khan, Amina Begum and their four children with Maheboob Khan and Musharaff Khan

70. Fazal Manzil, Suresnes, France

71. Mevrouw N. Egeling-Grol (Murshida Fazal Mai)

72. Fräulein M. Burkhardt

73. Frau H. Meyer de Reutercrona (Sheikha)

74. Marchesa Farinola-de Tanfani (Zebunnisa)

75. Herr B.R. Baur

76. De Heer A. van Stolk (Sheikh Sirkar)

77. Mr. R.A.L. Armstrong (Sheikh Mumtaz) and
    Mrs P. Armstrong née van Hogendorp (Lakmé)

78. Mrs. L. Hoeber (Sheikha)

79. Fröken Susanna Kjøsterud (Sheikha)

80. Mejuffrouw A. van Braam (Salima)

81. Mevrouw J. van Ingen-Jelgersma (Zuleikha)

82. Mevrouw G. Eggink-van Stolk (Bhakti)

83. Mejuffrouw D. Stam (Kismet)

84. Miss Angela Alt

85. Mrs. G. Craig (Munira)

86. Sufi Garden at Suresnes with Fazal Manzil in the background

87. Luncheon for Church Unity (New York, 29th May 1926)

88. Miss Gladys I. Lloyd (Sheikha Kefayat) at the window of the Lecture Hall, Sufi Garden

89. Moulana Syed Muhammad Hashmi

*Biographical sketches
of
principal workers*

List of Sketches

Mr. Ahsan ul Haq (Sheikh)
Miss Angela Alt
Mr. R.A.L. Armstrong (Khalif Mumtaz)
Mr. George Baum (Sheikh)
Mr. Bryn Beorse (Shamcher)
Mr. Cecil Eric Britten Best (Sheikh Shahbaz)
Fräulein Martha Bürkhardt
Mr. Edward P.A. Connaughton (Khalif)
Mr. David Craig (Sheikh)
Mrs. Marya Cushing (Sheikha Khushi)
Miss J.E. Dowland (Khalifa Nargis)
Monsieur E. Dussaq (Khalif Talewar).
Mevrouw N. Egeling (Murshida Fazal Mai)
Madame M.C. la Baronne d'Eichthal (Sheikha)
Mr. E. Engle (Sheikh Fatha)
Mejuffrouw J.E.D. Furnée (Khalifa Sakina, later named Nekbakht)
Miss L. Goodenough (Murshida Sharifa)
Madame H. Graeffe-van Gorckum
Miss E.M. Saintsbury-Green (Murshida Sophia)
Mrs. D.A. Gregory (Sheikha)
Dr. O.C. Gruner (Khalif)
Colonel Guillon
Mrs. Laura Hoeber (Sheikha)
Mr. Maheboob Khan (Khalif)
Fröken Susanna Kjøsterud (Sheikha)
Mrs. Gladys I. Lloyd (Sheikha Kefayat)
Mrs. A. Martin (Murshida Rabia)
Frau Hilda Meyer-von Reutercrona (Sheikha Sarferaz)
Miss Rebecca C. Hepburn-Miller (Khalifa Mushtari)
Comtesse M.L. Pieri née Dussaq (Shadman)
Dr. A.B. Scott (Sheikh)
Mr. E. Shaughnessy (Sheikh)
Mejuffrouw D. Stam (Kismet)
Herr Dr. Steindamm (Sheikh)
De Heer A. van Stolk (Sheikh Sirkar)
H. P. Baron van Tuyll van Serooskerken (Sheikh Sirdar)
Monsieur E. de Cruzat Zanetti (Sheikh Birbal)

About Sheikh Ahsan ul Haq

He was present at the International Headquarters of the Sufi Movement, Geneva, at the International Council meeting and at the Esoteric Council meeting, held in September 1925.

In his speech on Viladat Day 1925 at Suresnes, Pir-o-Murshid mentioned him and said: 'We hear that Sheikh Ahsan ul Haq has commenced Sufi activities in Delhi by editing a Sufi Magazine, which gives us hope of the Message spreading throughout India.'

From the archives of the
Nekbakht Foundation.

Biographical sketch of Miss Angela Alt (Ill. 84)

She encountered Pir-o-Murshid Inayat Khan in London and was initiated by him. After Murshid's first visit to Italy in 1923, Miss Alt conducted the group of new mureeds there. Then she was given the charge of the Movement in Italy.

In his speech on Viladat Day 1925 at Suresnes, Pir-o-Murshid spoke about her in the following appreciative words: 'The first person who began the work in Italy was Miss Angela Alt, to whom the credit of introducing the Message there will always be due. The delicacy and tact with which the Italian people must be met, were ready in her nature. She has never made them think her an outsider . . .'

At the Summer Schools at Suresnes, after the interviews, Angela Alt gave a short explanation of the exercises to mureeds to whom practices or additional exercises had been given at those interviews. She did this on Murshid's request.

Some of the older mureeds, present at the Summer School at Suresnes in those days, remember her at the piano composing music for the sayings about incense from the Gayan.

The biographical sketch about Murshida Sophia Green, also to be found in this Biography, was written by Angela Alt.

From the archives of the
Nekbakht Foundation.

Biographical sketch of Mr. R. A. L. Armstrong (Khalif Mumtaz) (Ill.77)

I was born in England in 1892 and educated at St. Paul's School and Oxford University.

The first time I came in contact with Pir-o-Murshid Inayat Khan was in Switzerland in 1921, after a long study of the Persian Sufism. I joined the Sufi Order and was initiated by Pir-o-Murshid in 1921. That same year I was appointed Murshid's private Financial Secretary. Then I became a member of the first Executive Committee of the Sufi Movement and was therefore signatory of the Constitution of the Movement when it was legalized in October 1923 at Geneva. In that same month I was ordained a Cherag,

Then I went to South America, lectured on Sufism in Argentine and held the first Service of Universal Worship in South America in November 1924.

In March I was appointed by Murshid to be the Editor of the newly founded magazine *The Sufi Quarterly* and I was made Secretary to the Press Bureau.

In 1925 and 1926 Murshid initiated me as a Sheikh and a Khalif and in 1925 I was made the National Representative for South America.

On 20th September 1926 Murshid consecrated my marriage to Lakmé van Hogendorp at Geneva.

From data sent by him to Sakina Furnée
at Pir-o-Murshid Inayat Khan's request.

Mr. George Baum (Sheikh)

The only data about him which could be found in the archives of the Nekbakht Foundation are that in 1923 Pir-o-Murshid Inayat Khan made him a Sheikh and ordained him a Cherag.

Biographical sketch of Bryn Beorse (Björset) (Shamcher)

In October 1923 when I was 27 years old and had travelled all over India looking for a teacher of Yoga, which I had studied from when eight years old, Sirkar van Stolk telephoned to me in Oslo: would I translate a lecture to be given at the Oslo University by the world's greatest mystic? 'We know that you have travelled in India . . .'

A Theosophist friend insisted on going to the Grand Hotel together, where Inayat Khan was staying. I was irritated: this friend, too talkative, would ball up my serious interview about how to proceed with the translation – sentence by sentence or a script? Wondering how I would be able to get in my practical questions amid the heavy spiritual artillery fire I expected from my friend, I entered the room, a worried man. Inayat Khan looked up at us with laughing eyes. 'Shall we have silence?' The gentle, sincere, almost apologetic tone of his voice contrasted the startling sense of his words. With a graceful bow he asked us to sit down. We seated ourselves in opposite corners of a sofa and he sat down between us and closed his eyes. So did we . . . I woke up, refreshed, when a bell rang. The interview was over, not a word was exchanged.

Next evening Inayat Khan gave his lecture and I translated it, after it had been given in full, without taking notes. People said I did not miss a word. I don't know how.

I told him I liked his Message but I was already a member of the Theosophical Society and the Order of the Star in the East, so of course I could not join him. 'No, of course not.' Four days later he came back from a trip. I said: 'I think my membership in those other organizations was a preparation for something to come. I believe this may have come now. May I join you?' 'With great pleasure.' Then he gave me practices and initiated me in a railway compartment. The people around us seemed unaware of what was going on.

I had played with God as a lusty playmate from early childhood, so could never be quite as serious and awed as some other mureeds, and once, in the middle of the first Summer School in Paris, I suggested to Inayat Khan that perhaps I was not really fit for this life. He reassured me smilingly that I was, and protected me against assaults by other mureeds, in very subtle ways. Murshida Green had asked us 'What does Murshid mean to you?' 'Well,' said I, 'a friend, an example.' 'Oh you don't understand at all. Murshid is so much more than all that.' That same evening Murshid gave a talk but before he started he looked thoughtful, then said: 'Before I start my talk I want to mention that sometimes a teacher's best friends become his worst enemies – by lifting him up onto a pedestal and making of him an inhuman monster instead of what he is and wants to be: just a friend, an example . . .' Nevertheless, I want to ask forgiveness for my lack of respect. I even once asked Inayat whether we could give up the 'Sufi' name on the Message since people misunderstood it for some Muslim sect. He said: 'It could happen. But for the time being the name seems right to me, and if we did not put a name on ourselves, others would put a name on us and it might be worse.'

More important is that Inayat pushed into my mind worlds of impulses that will take me eons to unravel and use.

When mureeds asked if Sufis should not be pacifists, Inayat replied: 'If people of goodwill lay down their arms today, they will still fight: they will be forced to fight, and not in defence of their ideals any longer, but against them.'

In September 1926 I saw Inayat for the last time. I said: 'I look forward to seeing you next summer.' 'From now on,' he replied, 'you will meet me in your intuition.' Then, during the first days of February 1927 I had a strange urge to travel to Suresnes, a three to four day trip by boat and rail from Norway.

When I arrived others had had the same urge. Early on fifth February came the answer to why we had come. Now the Message was with *us*.

Inayat Khan often said 'Mureeds who have never met me, never seen me, will often be closer to me than you, who know me as a person'. I am meeting such mureeds, closer to him, every day.

Berkeley, CA. U.S.A. From Shamcher's autobiographical data.
27th July 1977.

Biographical sketch of Cecil Eric Britten Best (Sheikh Shahbaz) (Ill.36)

Cecil Eric Britten Best was born in Leytonstone, England, in 1882, one of a family of 13, educated at Ardingley College and trained as a banker. By the end of World War I he had had a chequered career both in England and overseas as banker, merchant, miner, soldier, editor and semi-professional singer.

A free thinker from early adolescence, it was while serving as Syllabus Secretary in the Theosophical Society in 1916 that he met both his future wife and the Sufi Master Inayat Khan. The encounter with the latter had a profound influence on his life. Pir-o-Murshid Inayat Khan gave him the name 'Shahbaz', literally meaning 'royal falcon' but in his case meaning 'carrier of the Message', and for the next 30 years Shahbaz strove to advance the Sufi Cause in Brazil, to which country he returned as a Bank official.

His first book: *Genesis Revised*, was written after eleven years' study of Fabre D'Olivet's *The Hebraic Tongue Restored*. *The Drama of the Soul* followed. It was the crowning piece of a life of deep thought and reflection.

Shahbaz Best returned to live in England in 1952 and died in Southampton in his 92nd year.

This information was sent to the Nekbakht Foundation on its request by Sheikh Shahbaz's eldest daughter, Joyce Best.

Some biographical data on Martha Bürkhardt (Ill. 72)

She was born on 30th April 1874 at Aarau, Switzerland. She studied painting in Paris and Munich, and from the age of 20 was interested in religion. In 1911 and 1912 she travelled in the Far East, visiting many prominent sacred places in India, China and Japan. Then she returned to her mother at Rapperswil, wrote books and articles about the different religions and founded several charitable Societies. She had her spiritual rebirth on 29th April 1922 and entered the Order of the Sufis in 1923.

From data sent by her at
Pir-o-Murshid Inayat Khan's
request to Sakina Furnée.

Biographical sketch of Edward Patrick Augustine Connaughton (Khalif) (Ill.66)

I was born in 1887 at Manorhamilton in Ireland as the youngest son of John Connaughton, District Inspector of the Royal Irish Constabulary, and Hannah McFadden. I was educated at public schools and in 1904 entered the Ulster Bank Ltd. in Belfast. Four years later I resigned and associated with Messrs. Elders & Fyffes, Santa Cruz de Tenerife, Canary Islands. I was brought up a Catholic but at the age of 21 became interested in psychic research and spent some years attending seances, lectures and reading about the subject; this lead to the study of comparative religion. In 1912 I left Messrs. Elders & Fyffes and in that same year married Ethel Marian Pritchard Davies and we had one son. During the World War I, I assisted in military hospitals and worked in the British Consular Service. More and more the need was felt for self-development and direction and early in 1915, I read about Sufism and called at the Sufi rooms in London, but Murshid was away in the country. In September 1915 we left for California and in 1918, I was initiated into Sufism by Murshida Martin at San Francisco. During a visit to England in the summer of 1919, I was initiated as Khalif by Pir-o-Murshid. My wife died in 1921 and two years later I married Angela Theresa Sieys in San Francisco. When Murshid came to New York in 1923, I went there to meet him. Between 1919 and 1925 I studied landscape painting and opened a rare bookshop in Santa Barbara, California. A few years later I opened an art studio and entered real estate business.

From Khalif Connaughton's
autobiographical data.

Some biographical data about Mr. David Craig (Sheikh)

He was an Englishman living in Rome where he was working for British Airways. In November 1923 he met Pir-o-Murshid Inayat Khan in Italy and was initiated by him. In August 1924 he came to the Summer School at Suresnes and was ordained a Cherag. One year later, during the Summer School, Murshid made him a Sheikh.

In his speech on Viladat Day 1925 at Suresnes, Pir-o-Murshid said: '... Later on Mr. and Mrs. Craig joined forces and arranged my visit to Rome most successfully (February 1925). They are now carrying out admirably the work of the Message there in Rome.'

From the archives of the
Nekbakht Foundation.

About Mrs. Marya Cushing (Sheikha Khushi)(Ill.67)

This American mureed came to the first Summer School held at Suresnes in 1922 where she was initiated by Pir-o-Murshid Inayat Khan. During Murshid's second visit to the United States from the end of February to the beginning of June 1923 she helped to organize his lecture tour, especially in New York. Khushi then took down many of Murshid's lectures in shorthand.

She was made a Sheikha and Murshid asked her to form a group in New York. In a letter to Pir-o-Murshid of 25th June 1923, she wrote: 'I confess I have not much inspiration just now as to how the work can be made to grow in New York but feel certain that as it is God's work He will send out the call to the hearts ready and waiting for it, and show me how to reach them. The most important thing is that we all here, particularly myself, shall become illuminated by the Divine Wisdom so as to be proper channels for the Message. For this I pray every day.'

From the archives of the
Nekbakht Foundation.

Biographical sketch of Miss Jessie Eliza Dowland (Khalifa Nargis) (Ill.44)

Khalifa Nargis Dowland was the head of the Polygon House Hotel in Southampton, England, and seems to have been an efficient and capable manager. In 1919 Pir-o-Murshid Inayat Khan initiated her and then she put this same efficiency also into the work for the Sufi Order and Movement in England. Her help and assistance to Pir-o-Murshid at the time when this was most needed, during the troublesome period following World War I, were invaluable. All sorts of difficulties were accumulating and threatened the newly started work for the Sufi Message in England. Nargis became National Representative of England in 1921, which function she held until 1933.

Besides her capacity of organization and of handling practical affairs, she developed an extraordinary sensitivity[41] and had outstanding heart qualities. This enabled her to become an excellent sounding board for the Sufi Message. She understood the inner meaning of Murshid's words, even received Murshid's thoughts often and wrote them down in her own language as 'Murshid's inner Teachings as received in the Silence and rendered by Nargis'. (These are words directly inspired by Pir-o-Murshid.) Her sympathy for other mureeds was deep and touching and her desire to be helpful to Pir-o-Murshid was boundless. In a letter to Murshid of 1st November 1920 she wrote: 'I am very well and in spite of all the difficulties feel quite happy and peaceful, except that I do not know how you are situated and whether you are needing anything. Will you give me your confidence and tell me which way I can help most . . . My earnest desire is to do whatever will help to spread the Message in the way you wish most, even if this means that you have to be away from us. Of course I miss you dreadfully and it is a great disappointment to miss your classes this winter. While life lasts I shall never be able to show my gratitude for all you have done for me and can only hope to show it in some small measure by service. I am afraid you are having a terrible time still, all the forces of evil seem trying to stop the work and upon you alone the burden falls.'

She wrote three books: *Between the Desert and the Sown*, *At the Gate of Discipleship* and *The Lifted Veil*. In her own words these books are meant to be 'some practical teachings for aspirants to discipleship, inscribed by Nargis'. Moreover she founded the Sufi Book Depot (a publishing company) at Southampton.

Throughout the Second World War she continued to live in Southampton and once wrote to Miss Angela Alt: 'The Wisemans' shop has been demolished entirely, in fact the whole town has almost. They are trying to get a place in Portswood near here. There was no fire fortunately, so they have salvaged a good deal, although everything is covered with dust and dirt. The odd thing is that the very first things which were found are my books and later some of

---

41. First edition had 'sensitiveness'

Murshid's and all these are only dusty; I have them all here now...'

In another letter to Angela Alt she wrote: 'I am sure the seeds he broadcasted are taking root. Everywhere I can see it . . . Much more will be seen after the war has ended and the beginning of the New Age starts. You have done a great deal, don't feel worried if you have to stop any definite Sufi work. The real Message Murshid brought will be given in quite a different form from the Sufi Order as we know it, of that I feel sure.'

She continued to gather around her the mureeds until her passing away at Southampton on the 29th December 1953.

From Miss Dowland's letters to
Pir-o-Murshid Inayat Khan and from
the archives of the Nekbakht Foundation.

Biographical sketch of Emilien Dussaq (Khalif Talewar)(Ill.60)

He was born in Havana, Cuba in 1882, the son of Maurice C. Dussaq and Maria Luisa Fischer. In 1905 he married in Paris and had four children. In 1921 he divorced in Vevey, Switzerland. He became a member of the Sufi Order in 1921 and was initiated by Pir-o-Murshid Inayat Khan. In October 1922 he was given the charge of General Secretary of the Sufi Movement at Geneva. From 1922 to 1924 he was Acting National Representative for Switzerland of the Sufi Movement. In October 1923 Pir-o-Murshid ordained him a Cherag. He also participated in other activities of the Sufi Movement.

He married a second time in January 1924 in Geneva (Marie Isabelle Lussy), and the religious ceremony was performed by Murshid at the Hague two days later at the residence of Mr. H. P. Baron van Tuyll van Serooskerken, the National Representative of the Sufi Movement in Holland. On this same day Talewar became a Khalif at the hands of Pir-o-Murshid and three months later Murshid ordained him a Siraj in Bern, Switzerland. In his speech on Viladat Day 1925 at Suresnes Pir-o-Murshid said: 'It is a great consolation to feel that the General Secretary of our Movement, Khalif Dussaq, has worked through all difficulties and has won our confidence and trust every day more and more, in conjunction with his worthy sister Countess Pieri.'

From data sent at
Pir-o-Murshid Inayat Khan's
request to Sakina Furnée and
from the archives of the
Nekbakht Foundation.

Biographical sketch of Mevrouw N. Egeling-Grol (Murshida Fazal Mai) (Ill.71)

I was born on 27th March 1861 in the Netherlands. {Murshida Fazal Mai first describes her childhood and youth which were happy – in spite of the early loss of her loving parents – and her equally happy married life. She got a Christian orthodox education and later on became a member of the Theosophical Lodge.}

After my husband had passed away I went to Switzerland to live near Lausanne with friends. One day I received a letter from a friend, telling me that he had been elected as the secretary of Murshid Inayat Khan and that he accompanied Murshid, who was travelling in Switzerland to give a series of lectures, and who intended to give a lecture at Lausanne. My friend asked me to assist and so it happened that I was among the audience when Murshid came on the platform. Instantly the revelation came to me: 'That is the Master I have been waiting for and whom I have hoped fervently to have the privilege to see one day.'

It was this revelation that decided my further life, for there was for me but one step to take to become a mureed and to devote my life to the Master and his work.

When Murshid, on his next visit to Switzerland, proposed to me to come and live with him and his family, I did not hesitate for a single moment and answered: 'Yes Murshid, I will come and live with you.' Then I arranged everything for moving to Suresnes, where I arrived mid-April 1922 and was received by Begum and the children, Murshid and the brothers being in Holland. We liked one another from the beginning and when Murshid and the brothers arrived, we were instantly aware that we were of one spirit and that we had one Ideal: to devote our life to the great Cause of humanity. The day of my arrival at Suresnes, Begum had given me a letter from Murshid in which he told me that my Sufi name would be 'Fazal Mai' meaning 'Blessed Mother' and that our house would be called 'Fazal Manzil', meaning 'Blessed House'.

A blessed time for me and the few mureeds who were in Suresnes were the Summer classes in the garden of Fazal Manzil that first year, when we were sitting in a circle under the trees listening to the lectures Murshid gave us. Then during the next two years the summer classes were given in the same way only with more mureeds.

On the morning of Viladat Day (5th July) 1922 I received my ordination as a Cheraga and on Christmas day of the same year Murshid made me a Siraja.

At the beginning of December 1922 I started the first Sunday service in Fazal Manzil, which I have officiated from that time on, every Sunday at 4.30 in the afternoon.

On Viladat Day 1923 I became a Shefayat and later on Kefayat and started once a week a private healing group.

These two services in their simplicity and at the same time in their deep meaning, have become most precious to my heart. To me as a whole they are a meditation, an upliftment, a revelation to a greater consciousness, to a higher state of being. The Supreme Lord, the Illuminated Souls, whose words I pass on to the audience, are a reality to me and I know that I am cooperating with them and that they surround me when I am officiating.

On the morning of Christmas Day 1923 Murshid made me a Murshida and from that date on, every morning, a Blessing goes out from Fazal Manzil to the workers and the mureeds of every country. Beginning with the Messenger I bless with 'Fazal' first those of India and America, then Belgium, Holland, England, Norway, Sweden, Denmark, Germany, Austria, Italy, Switzerland, France, to end with Fazal Manzil, embracing them all together in one love-chord. I look at them all as to my children, sending them my loving thoughts, being happy when they are happy, praying for them in their illnesses and troubles. More and more I realize the privilege to be trusted by my Murshid with this precious trust, working in the inner planes to help to uplift mankind, to bring heaven nearer to earth and to bless my fellowmen, whenever I feel inclined to do so.

Last summer I had a glorious vision of Murshid as the Buddha. I saw him as he used to sit before us in the silence. At both sides of him there were the mureeds in the shape of long rays of light. Around and above Murshid was a splendid coloured light crowded with beautiful beings, who were radiating just as Murshid, and at his feet the whole humanity looking up at him. A big light came from above and shone upon the whole in different colours: golden, silvery and purple, at the bottom in a darker shade.

There is not much to say about the many difficulties I have had in my life; for when troubles have passed we look at them in a different way; then they are only important in so far as we know that we have gained wisdom by these very difficulties. Every sorrow, as well as every pleasure, has its value as a teacher. It is all given to find in the end our own self, to find the Christ within our own heart.

'Soli Deo Gloria'
'Fazal'
to every living being.

27 March 1926   From Murshida Fazal Mai's autobiographical sketch.

Murshida Fazal Mai passed away on 27th December 1939, at Arnhem, the Netherlands, at the age of 79.

From the archives of the
Nekbakht Foundation.

Biographical data on Madame M. C. la Baronne d' Eichthal (Sheikha) (Ill.53)

As far as we can ascertain, Madame d'Eichthal became a mureed of Pir-o-Murshid Inayat Khan in or even before 1921. In 1923 she was made a Sheikha and in 1925 a Siraja. From 1924 to 1929 she was the National Representative for France of the Sufi Movement, and from 1926 to 1929 she was the Editor of the Magazine *Soufisme*. She passed away in April 1929. In her apartment in Paris she gathered mureeds and friends and Murshid has often given lectures there.

In his speech on Viladat Day 1925 at Suresnes Pir-o-Murshid said the following appreciative words about her: 'We are thankful for our venerated friend and esteemed collaborator Baroness d'Eichthal who has been the backbone of the Movement in France. Had it not been for her unceasing efforts to hold fast and further the Cause in France, where should we have been? She has not only been a great help in bringing out Sufi literature in French, but she has also generously shaped our new establishment of the Summer School.'

From the archives of the
Nekbakht Foundation.

Biographical sketch of Fatha Earl Engle (Ill.68)

Fatha Earl Engle was born in central Indiana, U.S.A. in 1888, orphaned at the age of five years, and reared by an Indiana farmer, a hard and thorough task-master. He received vigorous and intensive training from the age of six years through twenty-nine in every kind of work entailed in agricultural life. After graduating from high school, and being of a studious nature, he continued his education in studies of scientific farming, psychology, philosophy and English. Due to hard work and exposure, his health became impaired and he went to Colorado where he regained his health, and for the first time experienced the freedom from a life of enslavement and domination. From the age of twenty-nine to thirty-five Fatha travelled and gained valuable experience of human life and nature, as well as some understanding of business and industry, and human relationships.

At the age of thirty-one, following a profound religious experience, he became deeply interested in religion and philosophy, their inner significance and their real meaning in human life. Fatha then studied for one and a half years with Murshida Rabia Martin and became a disciple of Pir-o-Murshid Inayat Khan, under whose personal guidance he again spent one and a half years.

Early in 1923 Pir-o-Murshid Inayat Khan arrived in America for a lecture tour of the large cities. He was due to arrive in San Francisco and Murshida Martin and her pupils were filled with a great joy and expectancy. On his first day in San Francisco Murshida had arranged for each of her pupils to have a private interview with Pir-o-Murshid. Fatha's appointment at the hotel was for 10 a.m. As he was riding, joyfully riding on the cable-car on the way downtown, a wonderful experience of illumination took place. It seemed to him that the streets, the houses, the cable-car, everything was of shining gold; he seemed to be riding on a golden car through golden streets of a golden city; and the illumination continued right up to the hotel entrance. When he was ushered into the presence of Murshid, Fatha was still experiencing a most exalted state of consciousness. Afterwards, he remembered that by a few simple questions about himself, Murshid had gently brought him down to earth and enabled him to get on with the interview which was a never-to-be-forgotten event. Together with some other pupils of Murshida's, Fatha was initiated into the Sufi Order by Pir-o-Murshid during that month of March 1923. He attended all of Murshid's lectures, hung on every word he spoke and had several private interviews.

Then, one day, he asked Fatha if he would like to return with him to his home in Suresnes, France, for a year and be his pupil there. Without a moment's hesitation the answer was 'yes'. The instruction and guidance of Murshida Martin had served to orient Fatha's mind to philosophical, religious and mystical terminology and had made him acquainted with the fact that many persons, in the past and in the present, had had similar experiences. He had learned something of the significance of his own inner experiences; and now, under the guidance of Pir-o-Murshid Inayat Khan he was to learn the science and art of attaining the Realization of God, how to purify and discipline the body, mind and heart in order to reflect the inner Love, Light and Life.

On the 10th of May 1923 Fatha was to join Pir-o-Murshid in New York City and on June 9th they sailed for Europe on the SS Olympic, one of the largest liners then afloat. Some mureeds and friends thought it inexcusable that Inayat should be travelling in a second-class cabin; but Inayat remarked to Fatha: 'they do not understand that we are dervishes and it makes no difference to us!'

Immediately on arrival at Suresnes they launched into preparations of the Summer School which was to begin there in a few days. Fatha was assigned many duties to be performed in connection with the activities of the Summer School and with Murshid's household. Within a few weeks he found his activities to consist of the following: helping to find accommodations for mureeds and friends visiting the Summer School, and getting them settled in their respective places on arrival. Taking care of and driving the new automobile which Murshid had purchased for the use of himself and his family; taking care of the walled-in garden surrounding Murshid's home; importing the Sufi books from England and handling the sale of them during the Summer School; going with Inayat Khan's youngest brother, Musharaff, to the public market on Tuesdays and Fridays to buy provisions for the large household; going to Paris with messages for Murshid and to do shopping errands; taking Murshid and/or other members of the family to places when and where they wanted to go.

In connection with the inner workings of the Summer School itself, Fatha had complete charge of all interviews that anyone was to have with Murshid – except his secretaries and the members of his family. It was a strict rule that, in order to see Pir-o-Murshid, everyone must make an appointment with Fatha; that rule was in force through the two Summer School sessions he was there. He had also to be on hand during the hours of the interviews, to usher the visitors in and out. It was a most interesting and most valuable experience. It meant the forming of close acquaintance with everyone who attended the Summer School. It afforded Fatha the opportunity of observing how Murshid received each visitor and how he terminated each interview. It became a most sacred and illuminating privilege. The hours for interviews each day were divided into five, ten, fifteen and twenty minute periods; seldom ever did an interview last over twenty minutes. There were seventy to eighty people attending at any one time, their stay ranging from a day or two up to the whole three months. The length of interviews was regulated according to suggestions made by Murshid. It was quite a task for one person to handle all the details of so many interviews of varied lengths each week and keep everyone pacified, consoled or satisfied.

At that time the classes and lectures were held outside in the garden on nice days and inside Murshid's house on rainy days; there was a gravel walk leading from the entrance at the lower end of the garden up to the house and it was a rule strictly enforced that no one was to make any noise or to walk up the gravel walk to join the circle after Murshid had begun to speak; he spoke entirely from a high source of inspiration and did not wish the flow of inspiration to be interrupted. Fatha never wished to miss a word of Murshid's teaching; but one day he was late in returning from doing some errands in Paris and the mureeds were assembled and were already listening. He came quietly inside the garden and laid down on a cot in a room beside the garage, feeling a bit unhappy that he would miss hearing the words of his Murshid that day. But as he laid there meditating, he became aware that he was hearing every word of the talk, then being given, distinctly in his heart; it was as if Murshid's voice was sounding clearly, as from a radio receiver, right there in his own heart. It was a most remarkable case of a mureed's heart being perfectly attuned to the heart of his Murshid.

After his preparation for the Work, Fatha was assigned to New York City where for fifteen years he conducted the Centre there. In 1942 he moved to Cleveland, Ohio, with his family and established a Centre there. Over these years he initiated hundreds of mureeds, delivering numerous lectures and consoling, counselling, uplifting and inspiring . . .

Fatha answered the Call of Return on 28th February 1955.

> From biographical data, received
> from Fatha's wife, Bhakti Engle
> and his daughter Jalelah Fraley.

Biographical sketch of Miss J.E.D. Furnée (Khalifa Sakina, later Nekbakht) (Ill.55)

Kinna (as she was called in the family circle) Furnée was born at The Hague in 1896, where she got her education at a girls' school. Her parents had engaged an English nurse for the children, so she learned English in an easy way. Later on she was sent to a College at Vevey, Switzerland, to learn French fluently. In Holland again, she went to a horticultural College and obtained her final examinations there. She had a liking for welfare work and was engaged for some time by a glass factory at Leerdam to work among the labourers. Her character was rather uncommunicative and even as a child she kept to herself. She was a good pianist, a pupil of the well-known Netherlands musician and composer Willem Andriessen, and she practised regularly and for hours together. For some time she was a member of a Movement, called 'Practical Idealism'. She tried to live a vegetarian life but had to give up, as she got undernourished.

Her first contact with Sufism was through Mrs. Fontijn Tuinhout at Vierhouten, when asked by this lady to lay out her garden.

In 1921 she became Pir-o-Murshid Inayat Khan's secretary and began to take down his lectures. Sakina's father strongly objected to the way of life she had chosen but in later years reconciled himself to it.

Sakina then learned shorthand and a great deal of Murshid's lectures have been taken down and transcribed by her. Due to her devotion to Murshid and the Sufi Message, and also to her accuracy, many of Murshid's words have been preserved exactly as they were pronounced. In 1922 Murshid made her Peshkar, head of the Brotherhood activity of the Sufi Movement. She accompanied Murshid on a journey to Vienna and to Belgium where she was made acting National Representative in December 1923. Towards the end of 1924 she bought the house at 34 Rue de la Tuilerie, opposite Fazal Manzil at Suresnes. Murshid insisted on accompanying Sakina when she went to sign the sale's contract and he added his signature to it.

Between summer 1922 and autumn 1925 Murshid dictated many parts of his Biography to her. Murshid created the Biographical Department and made Sakina the keeper of it. She was set the task to gather all Murshid's words and everything connected with Sufism and the Sufi Message and to keep all these documents and objects most carefully. In her own handwriting she describes this in the following way: '...Murshid handed me several objects and papers. Each time there was again something which Murshid liked to add to one of these collections, Murshid handed it to me, simply saying: 'Keep it, for the Biographical Department'. And I kept it...' She continued to do this work for nearly fifty years, in a very unassuming way, living a solitary and retired life in her little house at Suresnes, setting an inspiring example of faithfulness to Murshid and to the Sufi Message, not only for those who had the privilege to contact her now and then, but also for the future generations of Sufis who will be benefitted by her patient and most valuable work.

Her Sufi name 'Sakina' later on was changed by Murshid into 'Nekbakht'. In 1950 she established the foundation 'Nekbakht Stichting', intended to ensure the continuation of the work which Murshid had entrusted to her.

> From the archives of the Nekbakht Foundation
> and data received from her sister
> Mrs. E.D. Fuchs-Furnée and from Kismet Stam.

Biographical sketch of Miss Lucy M. Goodenough (Murshida Sharifa) (Ill.30)

We know very little about the first period of Lucy Marian Goodenough's life. She was born on 25th August 1876, in London, second daughter of Colonel W. H. Goodenough (afterwards Lt. General Sir William Goodenough K.C.B.) and of Mrs. (afterwards Lady) Goodenough, née Countess Kinsky.

She travelled quite a lot, 'was a fearless rider', 'a very delicate child, but inclined to take the lead over her sisters'. Later on, during her Vienna period, she became a leader in fashion for a season or two . . . At the same time she was master of German and French and well versed in Italian. She even knew by heart Dante's *Divine Comedy*.

Her social and rather mundane life suddenly came to an end when she came in contact with Pir-o-Murshid Inayat Khan in London during the First World War (probably in 1916). From this time onward her entire life became devoted to Pir-o-Murshid and settled upon Sufism.

Through her deep interest in Sufism, her staunch devotion to Murshid and her swift progress along the spiritual path, Murshid made her Khalifa, then Murshida, and finally she became the Silsila Sufiya of the Sufi Order, which means the link, necessary for the transmission of initiation in the Sufi Orders. Pir-o-Murshid had a seal made, after his own drawing, and gave this to her as a token of this greater responsibility.

Except for her work for the Sufi Cause, she was then inclined to be remote, exclusive and lonely.

The death of the Master was a very severe shock to her. No doubt it has been so for many faithful mureeds. But on her this event seemed to work as a devastating earthquake and it affected her whole being. She fell seriously ill and had to live in seclusion for months together. She emerged from this period as a different person. Formerly she used to be shy; now by her mere presence, one could perceive a sort of mastery over herself and over others. She used to be exclusive; now she was ready to welcome each and all with a patience, a meekness and kindness, at times more than human. One would breathe, in her presence, that peace, that tranquillity of mind which made one feel one's truer self.

After the passing away of Baroness d'Eichthal she became the National Representative for France and gathered around her a group of mureeds with a lively interest in the Sufi teachings. Some among them had known Pir-o-Murshid and had been in contact with him, such as Mesdames Yvonne Detraux, Yvonne Guillaume (both artists) and Marie-Madeleine Frère; and others were newcomers: Madame Antoinette Schamhart and Miss Adriana van der Scheer (Feizi). The former became a very close friend to Murshida, the latter a devoted attendant at the time of Murshida's ill health and overworking. A few other mureeds of Pir-o-Murshid, also attracted by that mind of rare insight and the utter purity of that soul, were Sheikh Sirkar van Stolk, the poetess Zebunnisa (Marchesa Farinola de Tanfani), Shahnawaz van Spengler, the philosopher Louis Hoyack and Wazir van Essen. All recognized in Murshida Sharifa a quality that was unique and found in her the reflection of the Master for whom they had such a great admiration and for whom they were longing so much.

All the above mentioned persons have been valuable workers in the Cause, each according to his talents and field of activity.

From 1930 to 1936 Murshida Sharifa gave lectures in Paris and in Vienna and held Sufi classes at Suresnes and in Paris. Her lectures were attended by a distinguished public and more members joined the Movement. About two hundred of her lectures were taken down in shorthand by Mademoiselle Jelila Guérineau and in 1962 a first volume, *Soufisme d'Occident*, was issued, including ten lectures, giving a sample of Sufi thoughts. More of her lectures are to be found in the French Sufi magazine *La Pensée Soufie*. Murshida Sharifa also promoted the regular publication of *Le Message* from 1932 to 1937, mostly at the expense of her own meagre income.

But alas! Her life and health were waning. And she deeply felt the inner strains and outer splits in the Sufi Movement, as if they were inflicted on her own body and heart. And it must be said here that the constant trust and confidence that the Master had shown to her during his lifetime now seemed to arouse prejudice, jealousy and distrust from several sides, now that he was no more there in person to keep things in balance and to help keep each and all in harmony. Therefore she, the Silsila Sufiya, had to experience harshness and friends turning their backs upon her.

And so she passed away on the 8th of March 1937. In the house of a stranger, but on the land of Suresnes, dying in poverty, but rich in a hope and a faith which could not be overborne. With her pupils and friends and with all those who so immensely admired her she left the lasting influence of a living spirit and the true fragrance of holiness, as the memorial of a perfected mureed.

Suresnes, August 1977

By one of her pupils,
Michel Guillaume

About Madame E. Graeffe-van Gorckum (Ill.58)

She helped to form a group of the Sufi Order in Brussels, Belgium, when Pir-o-Murshid Inayat Khan first visited this country in 1921. She seems to have been the National Representative for Belgium in those years.

From the archives of the
Nekbakht Foundation.

Biographical sketch of Sophia Saintsbury-Green (Murshida)(Ill.46)

Sophia Saintsbury-Green came of an old family and was reared in an atmosphere of tradition and good taste. One of her grandfathers had been High Sheriff of Berkshire; one was a boon companion of the Prince Regent and ran through three fortunes, which necessitated his son, Sophia's father, entering a profession (the first in the family to do so).

A born poet and writer of exquisite English prose, Sophia passed through a vivid girlhood of study and mental attainment. She was never taught her letters but at the age of three read aloud from a page of The Times. She was always drawn towards ancient philosophies and cultures, and at the age of five (while playing with toys upon the floor) broke into the conversation of two startled elders with her own original comment upon a two-thousand-year-old heresy which they were discussing!

In May 1921 Pir-o-Murshid Inayat Khan founded in London the Universal Worship as an exoteric activity of the Sufi Movement. He ordained Sophia Green the first Cheraga, an office she held alone for fifteen months, conducting the services regularly. On becoming a Siraja, further Cherags and Sirajs were ordained and Universal Worship spread to other countries. In 1921 she had been given the initiation of Khalifa (a position on the esoteric side of the Sufi Movement) and in 1923 she was created a Murshida.

She continued until her death to interpret the Message, and although never in good health valiantly declined to consider her personal comforts, up to the last year, rising above physical limitations to work undeterred for the welfare of others. The deep and esoteric side of the Message was part of her very being, but she joyed in the exoteric activity of Universal Worship; and symbolism also, as a world language, appealed to her strongly, covering as it does in one sense, yet suggesting and revealing to those who can see, the hidden mysteries of life. In the later years of her mission, in order to meet the requirements of listeners who were not at home in the English language (or else unfamiliar with esoteric lore) she altered her former methods and adopted a more simple and direct manner when speaking or lecturing. Perhaps in later years it was only the few who were privileged to listen when she was untrammelled by circumstances, and could freely rise and carry them to heights where momentarily, under her inspiration, they could view something of that heaven of wisdom which she longed to share with others.

Of her personality and temperament it is difficult to speak. She was not understood by many. But to some of those who knew her intimately the memory of certain characteristics shone out vividly: exquisite sensitiveness and refinement together with stoic courage; a habit of bearing misrepresentation and detraction silently; lightening quickness of perception and insight into human nature, and utter forgetfulness of self. Blessed be her memory.

Two of her books published by the Sufi Movement, reveal something of what the Messenger and the Message meant to Murshida Sophia. Their titles are: *Memories of Hazrat Inayat Khan* (London) and *Wings of the World* (London and Deventer).

Angela Alt.

Murshida Green passed away on the 2nd of March 1939.

From the archives of the
Nekbakht Foundation.

Some biographical data about Mrs. D.A. Gregory (Sheikha)

An American mureed from Detroit, Michigan (U.S.A.). She was made a Sheikha in 1925 and in June 1926, just before leaving the United States from New York, Pir-o-Murshid Inayat Khan ordained her a Cheraga.

From the archives of the
Nekbakht Foundation.

Biographical sketch of Dr. O.C. Gruner (Khalif) (Ill.37)

I was born in Altrincham in Cheshire, England, in 1877. At the age of eleven I first thought of following the science of Medicine. The choice of this career was determined by my guardian on the ground of my having displayed an undue interest in microscopic natural history and a certain facility in learning physiology which happened to be for one term a part of the instruction given in the private school to which I had been sent. In 1896 I left the Manchester Grammar School with a Scholarship for Owens College (University), Manchester, and began my medical studies. The study of drugs necessary for the Intermediate Examination of Medicine led to my distinction of First Class Honours in Materia Medica and Pharmacology in 1898. The latter part of the medical curriculum was spent at the University College Hospital in London. After qualification in 1901 an appointment was at once obtained as house physician at the Leeds General Infirmary. A year later I graduated at the London University and returned to Leeds, with residential appointments at the General Infirmary and Dispensary. In 1904 I became Pathologist at the Infirmary and Demonstrator of Pathology at the University. In 1908 I obtained the degree of M.D. at the University of London, being awarded the Gold Medal in Pathology. Then followed in 1910 the appointment of Ass. Professor in Pathology at McGill University, Montreal, Canada. In 1913 my first work entitled *The Biology of the Blood Cells* was published and well-received by the late Professor Pappenheim of Berlin, who invited me to be included in his staff of collaborators for 'Referate' to 'Folia Haematologica' which I accepted. During the First World War I found myself back in England, in military service till 1919. Then I resumed clinical work for a time – again at Leeds – and was in charge of the Tropical Diseases and Nephritis sections of the East Leeds War Hospital till the closure of the hospital, From 1920-1924 private practice in pathology was undertaken, in Leeds.

During this period the privilege of meeting with Pir-o-Murshid Inayat Khan led to a recasting of my outlook. He introduced me to the Canon of Medicine (Qanun) of Avicenna, the study of which has occupied my attention from then till now, in the light of the interpretations which he suggested to me. The first impression of that study was published in the *Annals of Medical History* (New York) in a paper entitled *The Interpretation of Avicenna*. In 1924, partly to come into closer touch with clinical medicine of a form which would help the study of Avicenna, I started general practice in a country place in Kent, not far from London.

Since 1926 I entered into a semi-retirement, for the purpose of obtaining sufficient leisure to develop an adequate interpreted translation of the work in question, and acquire some knowledge of those Eastern languages which are necessary before the original texts can be appreciated. Residence in London itself thus became necessary.

At that time I was received into the Catholic Church and followed with my wife and children the practices of that religion. I completed the translation of Avicenna's *Canon of Medicine Vol. I* and Messrs. Luzac & Co. published it. My eldest son having married in Montreal, Canada and the other having died after an accident in Australia, we took the advice of the elder one and went to Canada, settling near Montreal in 1931. The following year I was appointed to take up Cancer Research at McGill University, Montreal and in 1933 I attended the 1st International Cancer Congress in Madrid and gave a brief communication. As my degrees from London were not recognized in Canada, it became necessary to enter for medical examinations for the second time. After having obtained the Licence for Canada, the Cancer Research Fund was renewed and I was persuaded to resume the work on a larger scale. The results were published in a Medical Exhibition in 1938 and were awarded a Gold Medal. I continued this work together with the Chief

Surgeon of the Royal Victoria Hospital in Montreal, Dr. E. W. Archibald, and a staff of eleven, till my retirement in 1945. By that time I had reached a conclusion about the nature and cause of cancer, but it was not accepted by the various 'authorities'. I continued working as research worker in cancer at the St. Mary Hospital in Montreal. After this my work attracted the attention of a doctor who founded the Hett Cancer Treatment and Research Foundation under Government auspices. While working with him I prepared a *Guidebook for the Diagnosis of Cancer by Microscopical Study*, an expansion of the monograph published in 1942 by the Archibald Cancer Research Fund, and based on several thousand cases. In 1950 I attended the International Congress on Cancer in Paris and spoke of my 'test' with remarkable effects with the Hett-serum. Since 1955, however, I have almost completely retired from professional work, because utilization of any of my suggestions for cancer treatment apart from X-rays and radium, was refused and the use of the blood test for cancer was not considered of any real value. So I submitted resignation.

One day I met the head of the Jinnah Hospital in Pakistan, Dr. Shah, He had been trying to 'modernize' Avicenna and had prepared a translation from the Urdu, He wanted me to go through his manuscript as his English was not too good. Months later a doctor who had spent years in Bahrain, asked me to write an article on Avicenna. Dr. Shah's request 'woke up' all my Sufi thought which had filled me all the time I was doing my 'Treatise'. But subconscious development gave me the urge to develop the teaching even further. So I accepted the new offer and the article was published at the beginning of 1957. I then took out from the Osler Library at McGill University my very full notes on Avicenna's book Vol. II, about the medicines, deposited there with all my manuscripts in 1940, and re-wrote the opening section, as far as where the medicines are described in detail, and put the revised version back in the Library.

These experiences certainly revived the time of the days when Murshid inspired me to start all that work, and to bring his teaching again to the forefront in my daily round. For some months I have returned to the art of weaving, which I left in 1932 because of the scientific work to be done. It provides a means of meditation more intensively with a Sufi background.

July 1927, July 1957 and October 1965, Montreal.	From Dr. O.C. Gruner's autobiographical data.

In England after the First World War Dr. Gruner was in close contact with Murshid, by correspondence and by meeting Murshid regularly at Leeds or sometimes in London. He started the Leeds Lodge of the Sufi Order, took down in shorthand numerous lectures of Murshid, then transcribed them and published them in book form under the name *In an Eastern Rosegarden* (London 1921). From Dr. Gruner's letters to Murshid appears how great was the influence of the Sufi teachings which he underwent and of his deep pondering upon them. This worked on in his whole scientific career, as seen from the following quotation from his letter dated New Year's Day 1919: 'The reflection upon the emotional cause of a particular piece of music gave me the proof that certain vibration-characters underlie both music and biology.'

From Dr. Gruner's letters to
Pir-o-Murshid Inayat Khan.

In addition to his professional interests Dr. Gruner was an accomplished musician, artist and linguist. He passed away in Montreal at the age of 95.

From the archives of the
Nekbakht Foundation.

Biographical sketch of Colonel Guillon

He was born in 1871 and reared by his widowed mother with her two unmarried sisters. He sought and found the religious discipline in the Catholic Church, under the guidance of the Jesuits at the age of sixteen and was interested in literature, poetry, history, geography and politics.

When over forty years of age, he thought his life to be finished, especially after the death of his mother. A good friend, however, brought back his interest in life by drawing Colonel Guillon's attention to the book *Le Traitement Mental* by Caillet, which was a revelation to him. In one of his letters to Pir-o-Murshid Inayat Khan he wrote: 'I gave up my narrow conception of God, and understood that God is not a personality as I believed till then, but the everywhere pervading spirit. I became an adept of Indian philosophy, believing in God the All-mighty and All-pervading Spirit, without attachments to any Church and independent of my narrow observances.'

Then he discovered the books containing Pir-o-Murshid Inayat Khan's lectures and writes: 'The Sufism is a super religion, above all sects. I found in it what I had missed hitherto – the feeling of perfect Love.' He became a mureed and later on was appointed by Pir-o-Murshid to be the president of the Sufi Order in France.

From Colonel Guillon's letters to
Pir-o-Murshid Inayat Khan.

Some biographical data about Mrs. Laura Hoeber (Sheikha) (Ill. 78)

She visited Suresnes in 1923 and was ordained a Cheraga at the end of the Summer School. In October 1924 Pir-o-Murshid put her in charge of the Sufi Centre at Munich, Germany, where she was the Esoteric Leader, Leader of Healing and of the Church of All and also Brotherhood Representative for a period of three months. In 1925 Murshid made her a Sheikha.

In his speech on Viladat Day 1925 at Suresnes, Pir-o-Murshid said the following about her: 'Mrs. Hoeber was the first volunteer in rendering some help in establishing a branch of the Movement in Munich, and the way in which she stood through all difficulties there, winning in the end the admiration of some thoughtful mureeds, is most splendid.'

From the archives of the
Nekbakht Foundation.

Biographical sketch of Mir Pyarumiyan Maheboob Khan (Khalif)(Ill.11)

During his early years Maheboob Khan (Baroda 1887-The Hague 1948) was sent to Bombay for a musical test and examination by a visiting European expert. The German professor not only found him to have absolute hearing for both tone and rhythm, he moreover noted with astonishment that this boy from Baroda possessed the most extraordinary musical sense and talent he had ever been able to observe.

However, giving expression to whatever was intensely alive within himself, be it music or mysticism, to Maheboob Khan always was something of a sacrifice. Rich talent and conscientiousness in him were matched by a shyness that in growing up matured into utter unpretentious modesty and self-abnegation on the one hand, and a deep sense of dignity, honour and style on the other. These in turn concealed an immense sensitivity and subtlety of perception and insight.

For years Maheboob Khan had delighted his elder brother with his compositions, adapting Indian songs to Western harmony. Yet his humility prevented him from presenting – in 1925 – to his deeply revered brother his first own composition to one of Pir-o-Murshid Inayat Khan's English texts written that same year: *Thy Wish*. The one such song composed during Pir-o-Murshid's lifetime (being followed by the majestic *Before you judge* in 1927) thus remained unheard by him.

Yet again, alongside these qualities of extreme consideration and self-effacement Maheboob very fully shared his brother's 'dancing soul', his intense warmth of feeling, combined with that particular brightness and radiance of spirit and alertness, and with the resultant ability to evoke, attune and inspire. For those lucky enough to belong to the circle of his intimates, he was the brilliant representative and commentator of the person and teachings of

Pir-o-Murshid Inayat Khan, his 'ocean of wisdom' that wholly absorbed him.

After having received the initiation of Khalif, Maheboob Khan was additionally made a Sheikh during the Suresnes years and after the passing away of Pir-o-Murshid Inayat Khan he succeeded as Sheikh-ul-Mashaikh to the leadership of the Sufi Movement.

Pre-war mureeds continued to remember with emotion his Summer School readings of Pir-o-Murshid Inayat Khan's lectures, which seemed inimitably to revive them, the personal affinity and profound meditation on them reproducing something of the freshness of their first impact. Such preparatory secluded absorption in the Master's words was in addition to Sheikh-ul-Mashaikh's regular and lifelong three periods of spiritual exercise and meditation, commencing daily at ten a.m. and four-thirty and nine p.m. But apart from, and despite all spiritual expansion and transmission, this was the hardest of successions, calling for the greatest endurance, tact and vision not only at the outset and during the first phase of consolidation but throughout. Pir-o-Murshid's spiritual heritage was accompanied by an inheritance of principles of communal, organizational and administrative leadership, laid down and strongly reconfirmed by him in 1925. Their implementation called for entire dedication, and this whole Sufi commitment involved further personal sacrifice.

In 1910 the alternatives open to Maheboob Khan had been eventually to become the senior Maula Bakhsh heir of his generation as successor to Dr. Pathan, with all the independence, honour and security that would entail; or to abandon secular primacy and henceforth continue in a secondary capacity to Pir-o-Murshid Inayat Khan. The choice was made unhesitatingly, even though further involving a separation, become permanent by her death from grief, of his newly-wed wife Sabirabiy, who well deserved her name of 'the patient one' (in God), as the projected few years' tour lengthened into permanency. In 1924, Pir-o-Murshid gave his benediction to Maheboob Khan's second marriage in Holland to Miss Shadbiy van Goens, who became the mother of his daughter and son.

In the course of time Sheikh-ul-Mashaikh was obliged to a large extent to sacrifice what both he himself and the Sufis generally felt, would be his most essential and abiding personal contribution to the future of the Sufi Message: his composition of music to Pir-o-Murshid Inayat Khan's Gayan, Vadan, Nirtan poetry, in addition to Indian songs preserving the Maulabakhshi and Gayanshala répertoires. Nevertheless, some twenty-five songs remain in the former category alone, expressions of a creative process both musical and meditative. By well-qualified rendering in appropriate 'sama' conditions, these compositions may add a further dimension to Sufi experience, as Murshid Ali Khan's wonderful singing of them so often proved. For they evoke within the compass of one song the ultimate perspective of all mysticism.

September 1977.   From biographical data,
                                             rendered by his son Mahmood.

Biographical sketch of Fröken Susanna Kjøsterud (Sheikha) (Ill.79)

I am born in Drammen, Norway, in 1864, as the eldest of seven children. My father was a physically strong, clever businessman but did not have a strong character. My mother, who died when I was only nine-and-a-half years old, was a very fine, religious person. So, already as a young child I had the responsibility for my six younger sisters and brothers. We were brought up by different housekeepers, and in often unstable and hard circumstances.

When I was seventeen years old my father married my mother's housekeeper, and I left home becoming a governess, and after that taking up several other jobs. At twenty-five I left for America where I stayed two-and-a-half years. Then I went back to Norway where my father made me start a business in spring 1893 which, although I found it rather hard as I had always been longing for spiritual work, I continued for thirty-three years.

During my long life I have travelled a great deal, seen many countries, come in contact with all kinds of people and have a lot of friends all over the world.

In 1919 my youngest sister died; I then adopted her two children, a girl and a boy, as my own; they are at present both in America. Being now the oldest of the whole family, I know that my relations are looking to me as kind of a mother for them all. It is very nice but at the same time it takes a great deal of my precious time. My health has never been good neither as a child nor later, until I was sixty years old. I have gone through many sicknesses and suffered a great deal in every way.

I think I may say that I always had a religious longing; I have been seeking and have tried different things without finding satisfaction, until at sixty I met my destiny. In November 1924 Pir-o-Murshid Inayat Khan came to Norway. Only by seeing his picture I had the feeling that through him I would find what I had been seeking for years. I was then made a mureed and also National Representative for the Sufi Movement in Norway. Since then my whole life seems to have changed. I am another being, always healthy, happy and busy all day long, trying to do my beloved Master's work as far as I am able.

In the Summer of 1925 I went to the Summer School at Suresnes, where I stayed from the first to the last day. Murshid made me a Siraja in June and Sheikha a few weeks later, blessings beyond my comprehension! I sincerely hope and pray that I never may feel differently toward this blessed work, which I so unworthy have been chosen to lead for my country, that I may be growing in strength and faith from day to day knowing God will accomplish the rest, because the work is His.

Oslo, April 26th 1926.

In his speech on Viladat Day 1925 at Suresnes Pir-o-Murshid Inayat Khan said: 'I found in my tour through Scandinavia a precious soul like Aladdin found his lantern: Miss Susanna Kjøsterud, a soul who belonged to us. I only had to go to find her. Her devotion to the Cause gives us a hope that one day our Movement will be established in Norway.'

>From her autobiographical sketch
and from the archives of the
Nekbakht Foundation.

Biographical sketch of Kefayat Lloyd (Sheikha) (Ill.88)

Mrs. Gladys I. Lloyd was born in England to a Christian aristocratic family. After her husband's death in 1921 she dedicated her life to the work of the Sufi Message and offered her service to Pir-o-Murshid Inayat Khan, 'whether it be for healing or anything else'. She offered her house – 35 Tregunter Road, London SW10 – to Murshid for his interviews and lectures. Murshida Green also lived in her house for some time. In this same house was held the very first Service of the Church of All, in the upper room, in May 1921.

From 1921 on she was conducting a healing group in her house after having been initiated by Murshid as Shefayat. In her, Murshid found the person with whom he could discuss the possibility of creating Spiritual Healing as one of the activities of the Sufi Movement and later on Murshid made her the head of the Spiritual Healing. Murshid told her that healing of sickness of the soul would be more her work: comforting and helping those who are sad and perplexed and lost. She felt also much drawn to that branch of the work but at the same time welcomed whoever came to her.

She always kept a room in the house (the 'Prophet's Chamber') ready for Murshid to stay there whenever he would come to London.

She reported Murshid's lecture *The Message* (1921 in London) and Murshid told Miss Green that he was pleased with the way she took it down. Kefayat felt that there could be no greater honour than to be the reporter of inspired words. It was at the Summer School at Suresnes in 1923 that among others, also Kefayat Lloyd was allowed to write the lectures down while Murshid was speaking in the garden of Fazal Manzil. In the evening Mrs. Lloyd, Miss Green and Mr. van Tuyll compared their notes and it always showed that Mrs. Lloyd was the only one who had hardly missed a word. At the Summer School of 1924, besides Murshid's secretaries, only Mrs. Lloyd was authorized to take down the lectures. From these lectures she selected sentences which were so beautiful that the idea came to her to make a collection of sayings. She showed those selections every week to Murshid, and Murshid was very pleased. This encouraged her and she used to say that the mureeds in England sometimes called her 'the stringer of beads' as she often restrung their rosaries when broken, and she added: 'now I am the stringer of beads for Murshid, as I am stringing together his precious sayings like beads on a thread.'

Later on those selections from Murshid's lectures, made by Kefayat, were published by Mr. Armstrong in *The Sufi Quarterly* (December 1927 to June 1929) and were called Aphorisms.

Compiled from data in the archives
of the Nekbakht Foundation
and from recollections of
Kefayat Lloyd by Gawery Voûte.

Autobiographical sketch of Mrs. A. Martin (Murshida Rabia) (Ill.14)

Jan. 2-14,

Blessed Murshad[42]:

This represents a short biography of my life.

My parents were born in Russia, came to California in 1850, and were pioneers. They married in San Francisco, and I was born here in 1871. I was reared and educated here and graduated from the public schools.

I was always (as a child) deeply fond of older people, and wanted ever to converse with them. My folks had a difficult time of it I guess, because when I played with children I wanted to lead them, and they had to follow, or there was no play for me. My sense of Justice in my world of play was so marked, they did not understand me, and consequently my family felt I was too positive and all sorts of advice was unheeded. Of course you know, I could not accept less than the ideals of my childish heart, and somehow as I grew older I felt quite alone within the family circle.

I married at nineteen – my dear daughter was born a year later; this was real happiness, to train her in the principles of morality, *justice* and patience, and then the blessed music.

In my 28th year a deep grief came to me, and for four years I suffered much, and the problem compelled me to search deeper for the questions I asked of God – for the reasons demanded an explanation and in this storm and tumult of a problem too sad for words, I was led into spiritual teachings and freed myself from pain and heart sorrow, and *tested* these principles and universal laws, and stayed here in this form. After certain realizations came in the secret place of my own heart, I gave all to Allah and studied, served, prayed ever to realize His laws, love, mercy and justice. This period of my life I call the reconciliation and spiritual regeneration, all praises to Allah.

---

42. Old way of rendering the word Murshid

I was not satisfied with the Western teachings, so made an independent study of comparative religions, and prayed Allah to lead me to the source, as thus far it was only drinking from a brook instead of the Ocean of Reality. Lecturers, teachers and advanced students here, I met always, but none touched my heart's longing, they all represented more or less the circumference. I longed for the centre. Then Allah sent my blessed Murshad, spiritually, and later in form. These mystical and blessed experiences I cannot give to the world – to me they are too sacred – this may be selfishness, I cannot share them. My blessed Murshad's Murshad too – may Allah glorify you both – came to me and it can never be told in words, realizations which belong only to the Rabia not of this world, and so all I care for in this life is to worship Allah, love and serve Him – and Murshad and all Murshads in chain. May Allah keep my heart pure and my spirit humble (Amen).

Humbly – (signed) Rabia.
(Ada Martin)

Please Note:
We have an artist, and also a Rabbi Priest in our family. Also I have almost a passion for the study of philosophy and in New York I found there were others (men) of my family branch who likewise gave a lifetime to this study.

Murshida Martin passed away in San Francisco in 1947.

From the archives of the
Nekbakht Foundation.

Autobiographical sketch of Frau Hilda Meyer-von Reutercrona (Sheikha Sarferaz) (Ill.73)

I am born in Sweden in 1863 at a place very high in the North and called, literally translated, *the Valley of Light*. One of nine children I learned early to take care of myself and of the younger ones. We all got a good education and were sent to excellent schools. Studies interested me very much, and my facility to learn by heart has been a precious gift which became most useful in a later period of my life. So I remember a great many quotations from the Holy Bible, learned in my early youth, especially by the help and religious teaching of our clergyman. When I was 18 years old I gave lessons to children and young girls to help my father with his big family. At 28 I left for South America and there married a widower. He had been married to a cousin of mine and had four children to whom I tried to be a good mother. I got one daughter of my own and this child gave me much satisfaction and filled my life. After 13 years we left Buenos Aires and went to live in Brussels. It was

Spring 1904. My health was delicate and I had to undergo a dangerous operation. Catholic sisters nursed me and became my friends. All religious and philosophical subjects interested me and I always felt that somewhere there was the Truth to be found but did not succeed in finding it. So I clung to the dogmas and rites of the Lutheran Religion in which I had been brought up. At the time of the First World War, however, all my religious constructions tumbled down. My husband could not understand my inner life – he never cared for unseen things – my daughter married and went to Manila, so I became very lonely. During the war (1914-1918) we stayed in our country house in Switzerland and we are still living there now. In these years my seeking after God had become more intensive, I sought in many and different religious Movements but was not satisfied. I always came to a wall and then could not advance any further. Then the cry of my heart became desperate: Where art Thou, O God?

The answer came: I met Pir-o-Murshid Inayat Khan. It was in the winter of 1922/1923 in Brussels. My health was not good, life had little interest for me. In the house of friends I saw a picture of Pir-o-Murshid and his glance brought about a change in me. I then went to listen to a lecture he gave in the little hall of Le Cinquantenaire in Brussels. The first impression was not determinant for my life; it was the second time that I heard Pir-o-Murshid, two days later in a private house. I can still see and hear him there, standing near a grand piano and holding a silence with us before lecturing. And out of this silence came his voice, singing the Prayer of Invocation . . . My soul was caught by this music, which seemed to me coming from another sphere. I don't remember the lecture. I only heard the song.

Coming back to Switzerland I heard that Pir-o-Murshid was lecturing there and I went to see him. He came to my home where I always feel his presence after that. He helped me to recover physically and spiritually. I was his pupil forever.

In Bern 1923 Pir-o-Murshid entrusted me with the representation of the Sufi Movement for the whole of Switzerland. He initiated me as a Sheikha in the Sufi Order in 1924 and in that same year he made me a Siraja,

He has been my helper, my Saviour. He is for me the Messenger who brought me the Divine Message for which my soul was longing. My only wish now is to be a humble worker in the Sufi Movement, to help in spreading the Message and to show the Path to God to other seekers.

November 1925.

Biographical sketch of Mrs. Rebecca C. Hepburn-Miller
(Khalifa Mushtari) (Ill.63)

Our beloved Pir-o-Murshid Inayat Khan has often told his mureeds that they are pioneers in the great work of spreading his Message of Love, Harmony and Beauty.

That Khalifa Mushtari Rebecca C. Hepburn-Miller should be a pioneer in some field is but natural as her great-grandfather, William Hepburn, came from Scotland to America in 1769 when this land was largely unexplored wilderness. He settled in Pennsylvania, becoming a farmer and magistrate and founding the City of Williamsburg. Also her grandfather and father in their turn braved the dangers and hardships of the unexplored and the unknown, meeting their share of both good and ill fortune.

Rebecca was born in California in 1865, educated in the public schools and she grew to womanhood in a home atmosphere of liberal thought and high moral and spiritual ideals. Then followed marriage, motherhood and widowhood and in 1912, through Murshida Rabia A. Martin, she came to know the teachings of Sufism. In that same year Murshida Martin gave Mrs. Miller the blessing of Bayat (initiation) and in April 1923 blessed Murshid Inayat Khan himself bestowed upon her the yellow robe of Khalifa after having been ordained Cheraga by Murshid, and in March 1926 she received from him her Sufi name of Mushtari. In February 1927 she was initiated as Leader of the Healing Service by Kefayat G.I. Lloyd, who then was travelling through the United States of America.

Being the first mureed of Murshida Martin, Khalifa Miller has been through the tests and trials of helping to introduce a new point of view on life and to spread the Message of Sufism as expounded by Pir-o-Murshid Inayat Khan,

From her autobiographical sketch.

Biographical sketch of Comtesse M.L. Pieri née Dussaq (Shadman) (Ill.61)

She was born in Havana, Cuba in 1879, daughter of Maurice C. Dussaq and Maria Luisa Fischer. On the 3rd of July 1901 she was married in New York to Count Pompeo Luciano Pieri.

In 1921 she became a member of the Sufi Order and received Bayat at the hands of Pir-o-Murshid Inayat Khan. She was ordained a Cheraga by Pir-o-Murshid in 1923 and participated in various other functions of the Sufi Movement. After having assisted the General Secretary of the Sufi Movement in Geneva in October 1922 she was given the charge of General Treasurer one year later.

> From data sent at Pir-o-Murshid Inayat Khan's request to Sakina Furnée.

About Dr. Arthur Bodley Scott (Sheikh) (Ill.43)

Born in 1885. He joined the Sufi Movement in 1921.

He was made a Khalif in the esoteric side of the Order by Pir-o-Murshid Inayat Khan in August 1923 during the Summer School at Suresnes.

In 1926 he was made a Cherag of the Universal Worship.

Author of *The Soul of the Universe*, published in London by Rider & Co. In writing this book Dr. Scott feels, as he says in the Preface, that it fulfils a profound trust placed in him by Inayat Khan, a trust (to use, largely, his own words) to interpret and explain his Message after the manner of thought and in the more scientific language of the Western world; that thus, in a meeting of the mentalities of the East and West, his Message might have that certain setting and reach that would cause, in time, much that lay hidden in its depths to stand revealed . . .

This book contains many quotations from the Gayan and other sayings of Pir-o-Murshid Inayat Khan,

In his speech on Viladat Day 1925 at Suresnes Pir-o-Murshid remembered him and said: 'Khalif Dr. Scott has splendidly worked for the Cause in Bournemouth, England.'

> From data sent at Pir-o-Murshid Inayat Khan's request to Sakina Furnée by Dr. Scott himself and from the archives of the Nekbakht Foundation.

About Mr. E. Shaughnessy (Sheikh)

An American mureed, mentioned twice by Pir-o-Murshid Inayat Khan in his Biography.

He met Murshid in the United States in 1923 and in 1925/1926. He was made a Sheikh and worked in New York as a Siraj.

From the archives of the
Nekbakht Foundation.

Autobiographical sketch of Mejuffrouw D. Stam (Kismet) (Ill.83)

Father being an officer in the Dutch Marine, I was born in Indonesia, in Batavia which is now called Djakarta, in October 1893. Mother was a Furnée, born in The Hague. And my parents decided to settle there, so that the greatest part of my youth was spent in that town. I first went to the Girls' College and later became a student at the University of Leiden, where I received my degree as a teacher in Dutch Colleges, in the French language. This has been very precious later on, as I have been able to translate Murshid's lectures into French, standing beside Him on the platforms before Murshid's always crowded audiences.

I met Murshid in The Hague in the spring of 1923. Murshid then asked me to come to the Summer School in Suresnes. I was initiated there, that summer. My first year Murshid asked me to live in Geneva. I learned shorthand and typewriting at the School of Aimé, Paris, and I took violin lessons with Joseph Szigeti. Every evening there was a silence class at International Headquarters on the Quai des Eaux Vives (now Quai Gustave Ador) under the leadership of Talewar Dussaq, the General Secretary. My second year Murshid asked me to stay with Baronne d'Eichtal at her summerhouse in Sèvres, Ville d'Avray, and to help her with the Sufi work at the Avenue Emmanuel III in Paris. Also Murshid asked me to print Gathekas. So I bought a Gestetner machine, and I printed Gathekas, sending them to all the Sufi Centres existing.

During a lecture tour Murshid made in Holland, I acted as a reporter for different Dutch newspapers. And my task has been, later on, to send articles to newspapers of all the principal cities of Europe and America. In the spring of 1925 Murshid made me prepare lecture tours, first in Nice, France, and then in Munich, Germany.

While in Suresnes I prepared with Murshid's help the first edition of *Vadan*; and later on *Nirtan*.

After the Summer School of 1925 I accompanied Murshid, as his secretary, on the steamship Volendam, from Cherbourg to New York. Sirkar van

Stolk joined Murshid there, but did not accompany Him on His lecture tour throughout America. In New York and surroundings, the car of Mrs. Shaokat Frey was at Murshid's disposal. In California the car of Saladin Reps took Murshid from San Francisco via Los Angeles and Santa Barbara to La Jolla and San Diego. Murshid and I were invited to fly in an open aeroplane over the Bay of Mexico. One could smell the perfumes of the flowers from the earth, while flying. On the trip back to New York via Colorado Springs, Kansas City and Denver, we visited the Grand Canyon, where photos were taken on 'ablack' horses, the American-Indian horses, white, black and brown.

Throughout Murshid's travels it has been my task to help Murshid with the correspondence, and to explain the exercises Murshid gave to all those who have become mureeds in the different countries where Murshid lectured.

On 28th September 1926 I accompanied Murshid on His last journey to India. Murshid took an Italian boat which started in Venice, and arrived in India at Karachi. It made a stop of some days in Massawa (Erithrea), where Murshid said what I mentioned in the book *Rays*: 'Even the rocks have been burnt black here.'

After Murshid's passing away, I lived for ten years in the house of my cousin Nekbakht Furnée in Suresnes. I worked out all the shorthand notes of Murshid's American lecture tour 1926. And I wrote three Sufi books: *Fragrance from a Sufi's Garden*, *Sufi Lore and Lyrics*, and *Musings from a Sufi*, which received their English copyright through Luzac & Co. in London.

Everything that has occurred in the long life that has been vouchsafed to me after Murshid's passing away, has been based on what Murshid has taught me and has endowed me with. I shall remember this forever, with unutterable gratitude.

(signed:) Kismet Dorothea Stam
Palma de Mallorca, May 1977

Some biographical data of Dr. Steindamm (Sheikh)

I was born in Berlin, in 1880. First I studied Protestant Theology, then Political Science, Technology and Public Finance and Administration. I am working in Berlin as a syndic for Economic Affairs. My literary interest has mostly been for economics and politics, and my main activity has been in the field of Department Stores and Publicity. In several Universities I gave lectures and Courses about Publicity.

From a letter to Sakina Furnée,
dated Berlin, 28th April 1926

In the autumn of 1924 Dr. Steindamm met Pir-o-Murshid Inayat Khan in Berlin and became his mureed. In 1925 Murshid made him a Sheikh and he accompanied Murshid on his tour through Germany that year and helped to organize the lectures to be held in different cities. Murshid appointed him National Representative for Germany.

In his speech on Viladat Day 1925 at Suresnes, Murshid said: 'The great zeal for the Cause shown by Dr. Steindamm we value and appreciate very much.'

From the archives of the
Nekbakht Foundation.

Biographical sketch of Sirkar van Stolk (Sheikh) (Ill.76)

Apjar van Stolk (Sirkar) was born the 27th March 1894 as the eldest son of a well-to-do grain merchant in Rotterdam in the Netherlands. His father was a big businessman with a keen interest in art and education. The family possessed a country house at Wassenaar where Pir-o-Murshid Inayat Khan and his family stayed several times. Already in his youth Sirkar was introduced to the great Indian sacred Scriptures by his teacher in English, Mrs. Esser, who also gave him his first meditation practices. In his early twenties Sirkar passed sometime in the United States working in the family business, but then developed tuberculosis and returned to Europe, where he had to stay three and a half years in a Swiss sanatorium. During this period in the Swiss mountains Sirkar read many Theosophical and mystical books. His health, however, did not improve.

In 1922 a Dutch friend wrote to him about an Indian mystic, philosopher and musician, named Inayat Khan, who at that time was lecturing in different countries of Europe. Sirkar read a number of these lectures, published in the book *In an Eastern Rosegarden*, and was deeply impressed by them. When in December 1922 Sirkar met Pir-o-Murshid Inayat Khan for the first time, the latter offered to accept him as his mureed. Sirkar told Murshid that he had to go to London for medical treatment first and then would contact Murshid again. In spring 1923 Sirkar met Murshid in London and received initiation. From that moment Murshid became the inspiration in his life. Murshid healed him from his illness by giving him daily treatments and since that time Sirkar helped Murshid with the work for the Sufi Movement. In 1923 and 1924 Sirkar attended the Summer School at Suresnes and was made a Sheikh by Murshid. In spring 1925 Murshid asked him to take upon him the organization of the Summer School, which he did for many years in a most effective way. It was also with Sirkar's help that the mureeds house (behind Fazal Manzil at Suresnes) and the Sufi land were purchased. From September 1924 till September 1926 Sirkar was Murshid's constant assistant and accompanied Murshid on many journeys through Europe and the United States.

After Murshid's passing away Sirkar became the leader of a Sufi Centre at The Hague in 1930, and performed other functions in the Sufi Movement until 1951. In South Africa, to which country Sirkar emigrated in 1951, he founded several Sufi Centres, together with Wazir van Essen, his able and devoted co-worker in Holland and Suresnes, during the years 1925 to 1950. In 1960 he started writing his *Memories of a Sufi Sage*, which was completed by his secretary Mrs. Daphne Dunlop and was published in 1967. This book has been translated in various languages.

Sirkar van Stolk passed away in Cape Town in 1963. He has initiated many mureeds, given numerous public lectures and by his charming personality has attracted many people to the Sufi Message.

By one of his pupils, Ameen Carp.

Biographical sketch of Hubertus Paulus Baron van Tuyll van Serooskerken (Sheikh Sirdar) (Ill.54)

Sirdar van Tuyll was born on 26th September 1883. When Pir-o-Murshid Inayat Khan visited the Netherlands for the first time in January 1921, accommodation in Arnhem had been found for him with Sirdar van Tuyll, who was waiting for him to arrive one evening at dusk at the railway station. Among the many people, Sirdar's eyes were searching for an Eastern, and all of a sudden a voice came to him, saying: 'How are you?' Murshid had found Sirdar by himself! The impression which this first contact made upon Sirdar was such that he said to have completely refound in one moment's time the faith in God which he had as a child. A few months later, on 13th April 1921, Sirdar was initiated in England. He was present at the first Universal Worship held in London on 7th May 1921.

In that same year the first Summer School was held in France, in a small village south of Paris, called Wissous. Just before the Summer School Sirdar accompanied Murshid as his secretary on a trip through Switzerland. After a second visit to Holland in September/October 1921, Murshid went to Germany for the first time and Sirdar went with him as his secretary.

On 2nd February 1922 Sirdar married Henriette[43] Willebeek Le Mair (Saida). In May 1922 Sirdar and Saida settled down at Katwijk in a spacious villa at the seaside, in which was held the Summer School in September 1922. Murshid had appointed Sirdar as the National Representative for the Netherlands.

On 26th September 1922 Sirdar became a Cherag, the first Cherag in Holland. The ultimately accepted rituals for the various Services and ceremonials were dictated by Murshid to Sirdar in 1922 at Katwijk aan Zee and in 1924 at The Hague.

43. First edition has Hendrika

About 1923 Sirdar and Saida went to live at The Hague, where they had the old tramway station building transformed into a house (besides the Peace Palace). This house, Anna Paulownastraat 78, became a Sufi Centre and there, in 1928/1929 Sirdar had the Sufi Church built from his own funds, as an annex to his house. On 18th January 1929 took place the consecration of the Church. Till his last illness Sirdar gave a sermon in the Universal Worship in this Church every Sunday. These talks have been recorded, first on wire and later on tape, and gradually from these texts books were made and published: *Groter Christendom I* about the Old Testament, *Groter Christendom II* about the New Testament; after that came out *Het Heilige Boek der Natuur* (The Holy Book of Nature) and *De Karavaan naar de Eeuwigheid* (The Caravan towards Eternity). Another book *Gebed, Meditatie en Stilte* (Prayer, Meditation and Silence) has now been published. At The Hague as well as in many other cities Sirdar gave numerous lectures on the unity of religions, brotherhood and mysticism. Also in Berlin, Germany, Sweden, Denmark, Norway and in India he has spread the ideals of the Sufi Message by giving sermons and lectures and by making contacts.

Besides his Sufi activities Sirdar was one of the pillars of horse-racing and thoroughbred-breeding in the Netherlands. For many years he possessed a large racing stable and a stud of his own. His love and knowledge of the thoroughbred are worth mentioning.

On 16th August 1958 Sirdar passed away at The Hague. Every year during his lifetime his birthday was celebrated by his mureeds and is still commemorated today as it was Murshid's wish that it should be for the first Cherag, the pioneer of the Message in his country.

> From data received by the
> Nekbakht Foundation from
> Sirdar van Tuyll's former secretary
> and devoted pupil Miss An C. Spirlet.

Biographical sketch of Enrique de Cruzat Zanetti (Sheikh Birbal) (Ill.62)

He was born at Matanzas, Cuba, in 1875, the son of Domingo S. Zanetti and Irene de Cruzat. When ten years old he was taken to Portland, Maine, where he frequented the public Grammar School. At the age of fourteen he went to Boston, Mass., residing with the family of the Rev. Eduard Everett Hale, a distinguished divine and man of letters. There he frequented the Roxbury Latin School from which he graduated in 1893. In that same year he entered Harvard College in Cambridge, Mass., where he studied principally Literature and History and graduated with the degree of Baccalaurei in Artibus in 1897. During 1897-1898 he studied International Law and Sociology at the University of Geneva, Switzerland and then entered the Harvard Law School where he graduated in 1901. In that year he joined the Law Offices of Page & Conant in New York City, having been admitted to practise at the Bar of the State of New York, specializing in Corporation and International Law. He was married in 1904 to Esperanza Conill of Havana, Cuba, where was born his only son Enrique Carlos Zanetti. He was divorced in 1912 and from then on has travelled extensively in the pursuit of study, mainly of the art of painting. During 1917-1918 he was unofficially in the service of the American Embassy at Madrid. In 1923 he joined the Sufi Movement which he has served principally as Executive Supervisor and for this purpose in 1925 he took residence in Geneva.

In his speech on Viladat Day 1925 at Suresnes Pir-o-Murshid Inayat Khan mentioned him with the following words: 'The coming of Mr. Zanetti into the Sufi Movement has released me from many responsibilities connected with the working of the administrative part of the Movement, for which I am most thankful.'

> From his autobiographical sketch and data from the archives of the Nekbakht Foundation.

Family Tree

FAMILY TREE A

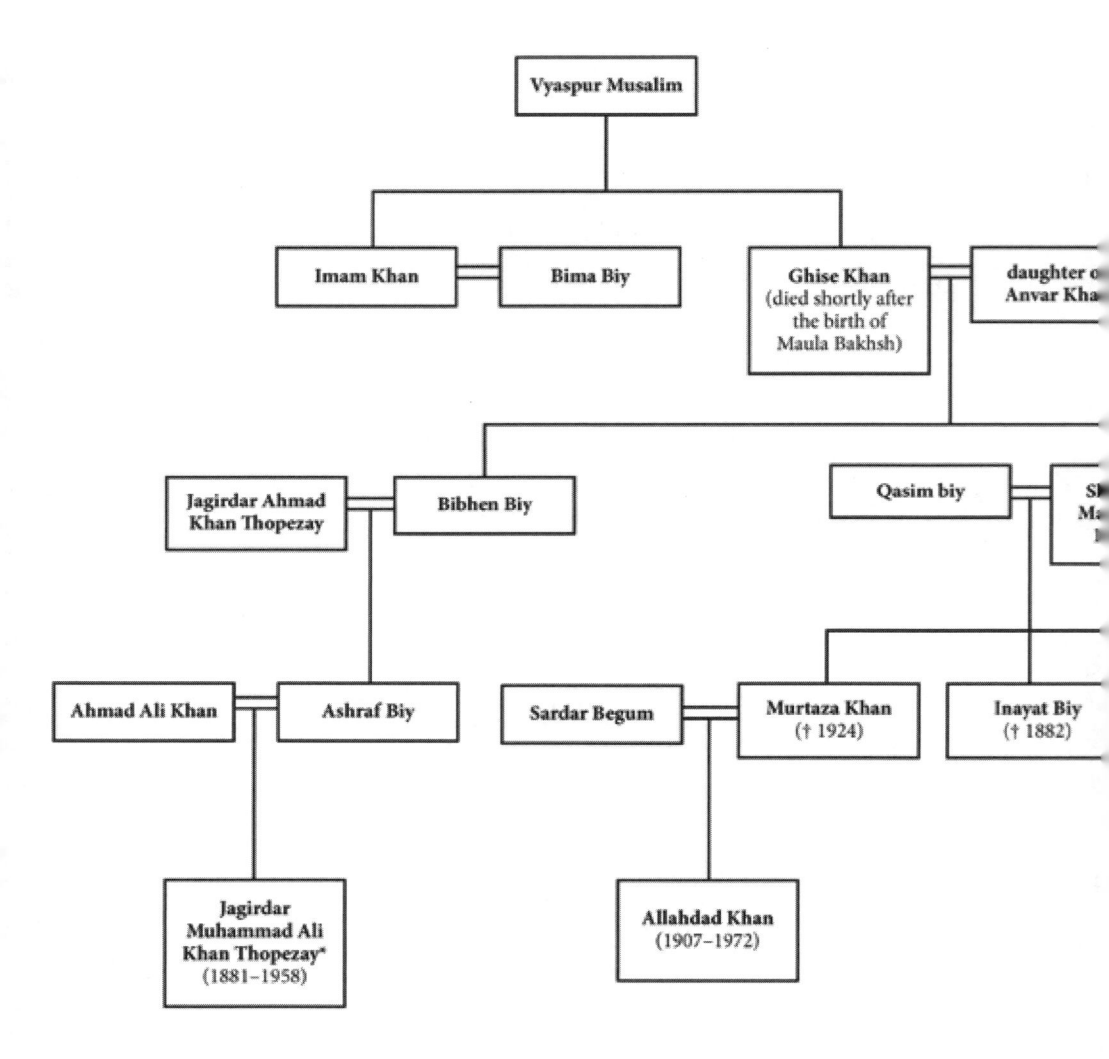

```
                        Vyaspur Musalim
                              |
         ┌────────────────────┴──────────────────┐
    Imam Khan — Bima Biy              Ghise Khan — daughter of
                                   (died shortly after   Anvar Kha...
                                    the birth of
                                    Maula Bakhsh)
                              |
         ┌────────────────────┴────────────────────┐
  Jagirdar Ahmad — Bibhen Biy          Qasim biy — S...
  Khan Thopezay                                     Ma...
         |                                     |
  Ahmad Ali Khan — Ashraf Biy    Sardar Begum — Murtaza Khan    Inayat Biy
                                                  († 1924)        († 1882)
         |                                     |
    Jagirdar                              Allahdad Khan
    Muhammad Ali                          (1907–1972)
    Khan Thopezay*
    (1881–1958)
```

* cousin/brother of Hazrat Inayat Khan who travelled with him to USA in 1910

Family Tree A

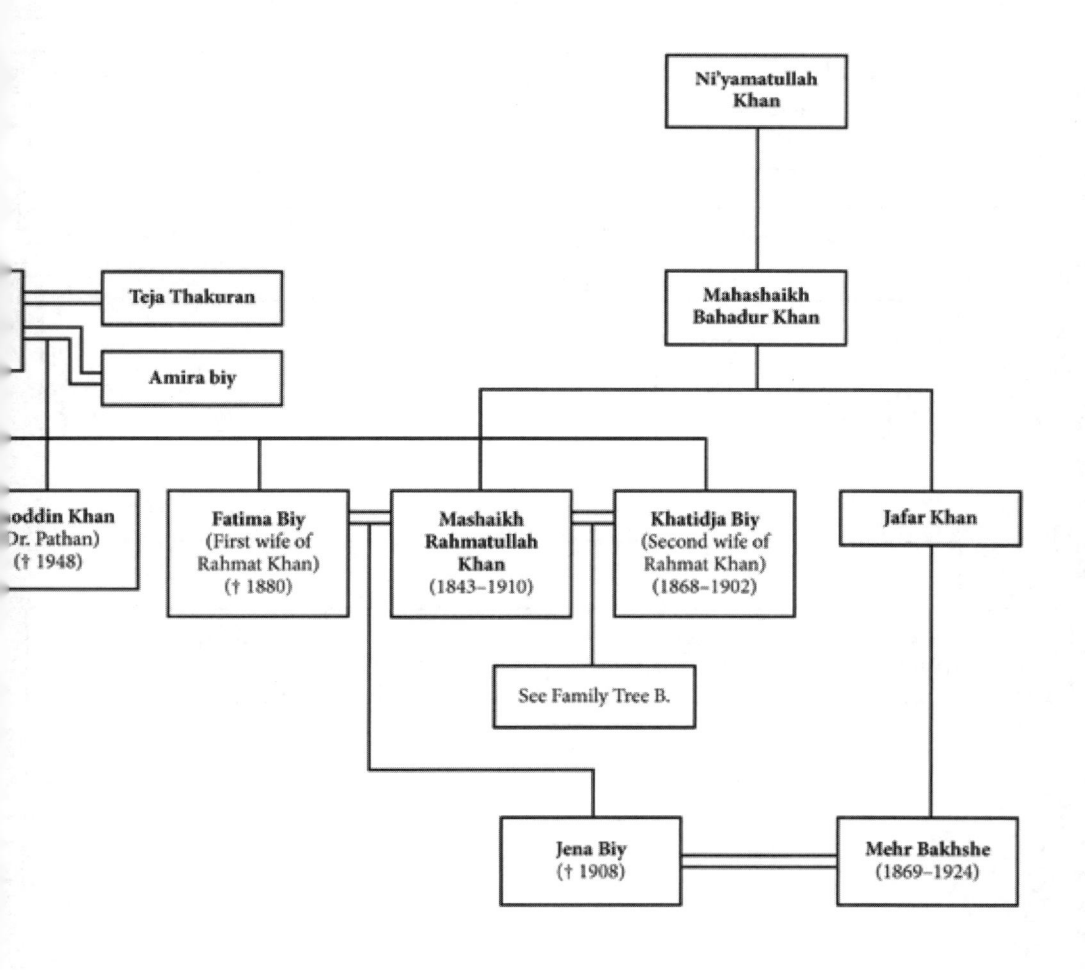

- Ni'yamatullah Khan
  - Mahashaikh Bahadur Khan
    - Fatima Biy (First wife of Rahmat Khan) († 1880)
    - Mashaikh Rahmatullah Khan (1843–1910)
    - Khatidja Biy (Second wife of Rahmat Khan) (1868–1902)
    - Jafar Khan

- Teja Thakuran
- Amira biy
- ...oddin Khan (...r. Pathan) († 1948)

See Family Tree B.

- Jena Biy († 1908) — Mehr Bakhshe (1869–1924)

382　FAMILY TREE B

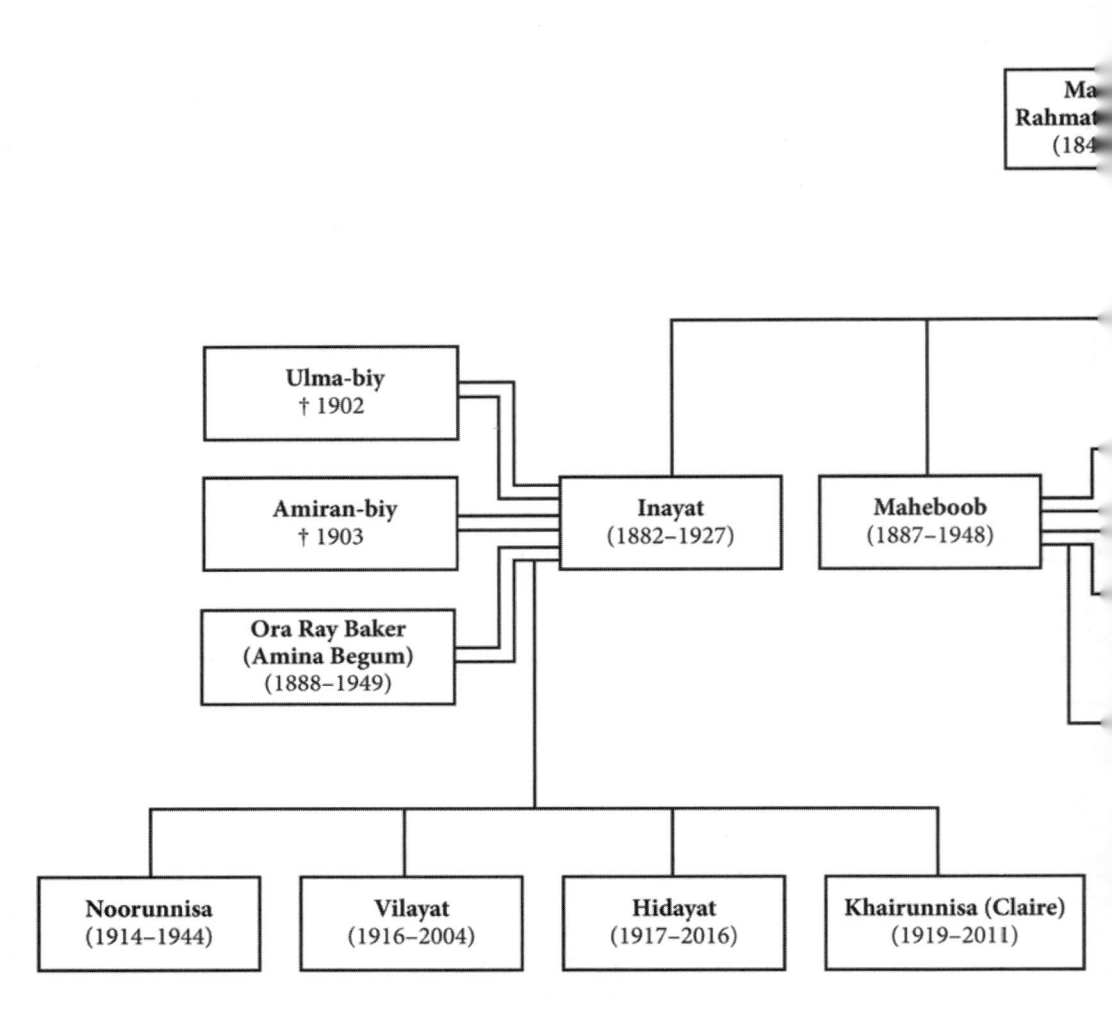

Ma...
Rahmat
(184...

Ulma-biy
† 1902

Amiran-biy
† 1903

Ora Ray Baker
(Amina Begum)
(1888–1949)

Inayat
(1882–1927)

Maheboob
(1887–1948)

Noorunnisa
(1914–1944)

Vilayat
(1916–2004)

Hidayat
(1917–2016)

Khairunnisa (Claire)
(1919–2011)

Family Tree B

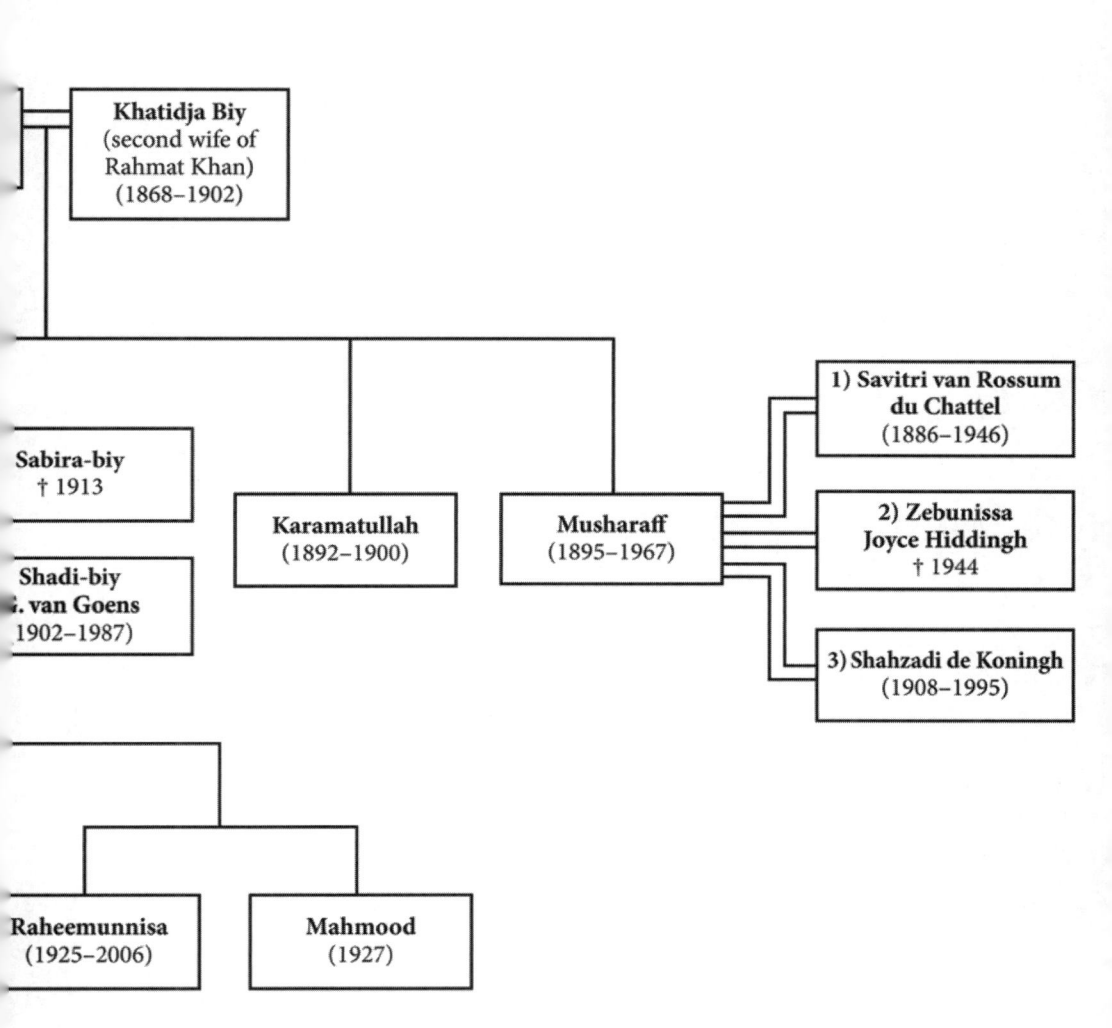

- **Khatidja Biy** (second wife of Rahmat Khan) (1868–1902)
  - **Sabira-biy** † 1913
  - **Shadi-biy** . van Goens (1902–1987)
  - **Karamatullah** (1892–1900)
  - **Musharaff** (1895–1967)
    - 1) **Savitri van Rossum du Chattel** (1886–1946)
    - 2) **Zebunissa Joyce Hiddingh** † 1944
      - **Raheemunnisa** (1925–2006)
      - **Mahmood** (1927)
    - 3) **Shahzadi de Koningh** (1908–1995)

This family tree ends with the generation of the children of Pir-o-Murshid Inayat Khan.

Maps

RUSSIA

CHINA

AFGHANISTAN

KASHMIR

BELUCHISTAN

PANJAB

TIBET

• 22

• 12

RAJASTHAN • 1 UTHAR NEPAL
• 17 • 23 • 20
• 19 • 2 15 PRADESH
• 26 • 5 ASSAM
• 31 BIHAR • 34
GUJARAT • 27 • 11
• 4 • 40 BENGAL
MADYA PRADESH • 7 MYANMAR
I N D I A
MAHARASTRA ORISSA
• 6
• 33
• 14 • 16
ANDHRA
PRADESH BAY OF
MYSORE BENGAL
• 3
• 24
• 28
• 9 MADRAS • 32
• 37 • 21 • 29
• 8 • 13 36
KERALA 35
• 25
• 38 • 39
SRI LANKA
• 10 • 18
30

INDIAN   OCEAN

INDIA
1. Agra
2. Ajmer
3. Bangalore
4. Baroda
5. Benares
6. Bombay
7. Calcutta
8. Cochin
9. Coimbatore
10. Colombo
11. Dacca
12. Delhi
13. Ernakulam
14. Gulbarga
15. Gwalior
16. Hyderabad
17. Jaipur
18. Kandy
19. Karachi
20. Katmandu
21. Kumbakonam
22. Lahore
23. Lucknow
24. Madras
25. Madura
26. Marwar
27. Murshidabad
28. Mysore
29. Negapatam
30. Nuwara Elya
31. Patan
32. Rangoon
33. Secunderabad
34. Sylhet
35. Tanjore
36. Trichinapoli
37. Trichur
38. Trivandrum
39. Tuticorin
40. Ujjain

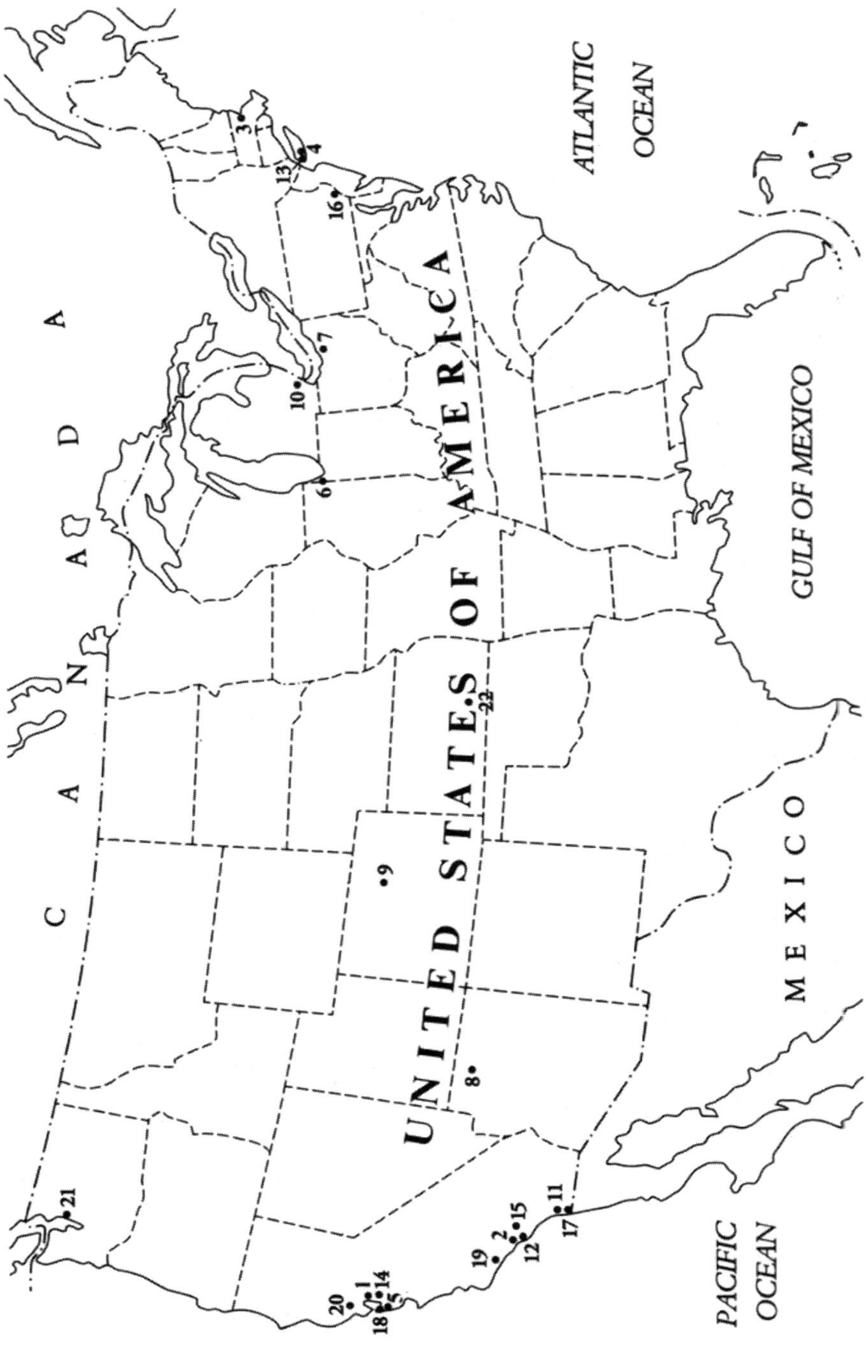
C A N A D A
UNITED STATES OF AMERICA
ATLANTIC OCEAN
GULF OF MEXICO
M E X I C O
PACIFIC OCEAN
1
2
3
4
5
6
7
8
9
10
11
12
13
14
15
16
17
18
19
20
21
22

UNITED STATES OF AMERICA
1 Berkeley
2 Beverly Hills
3 Boston
4 Brooklyn
5 Burlingame
6 Chicago
7 Cleveland
8 Grand Canyon
9 Denver
10 Detroit
11 La Jolla
12 Los Angeles
13 New York
14 Oakland
15 Pasadena
16 Philadelphia
17 San Diego
18 San Francisco
19 Santa Barbara
20 Santa Rosa
21 Seattle
22 Wichita

390

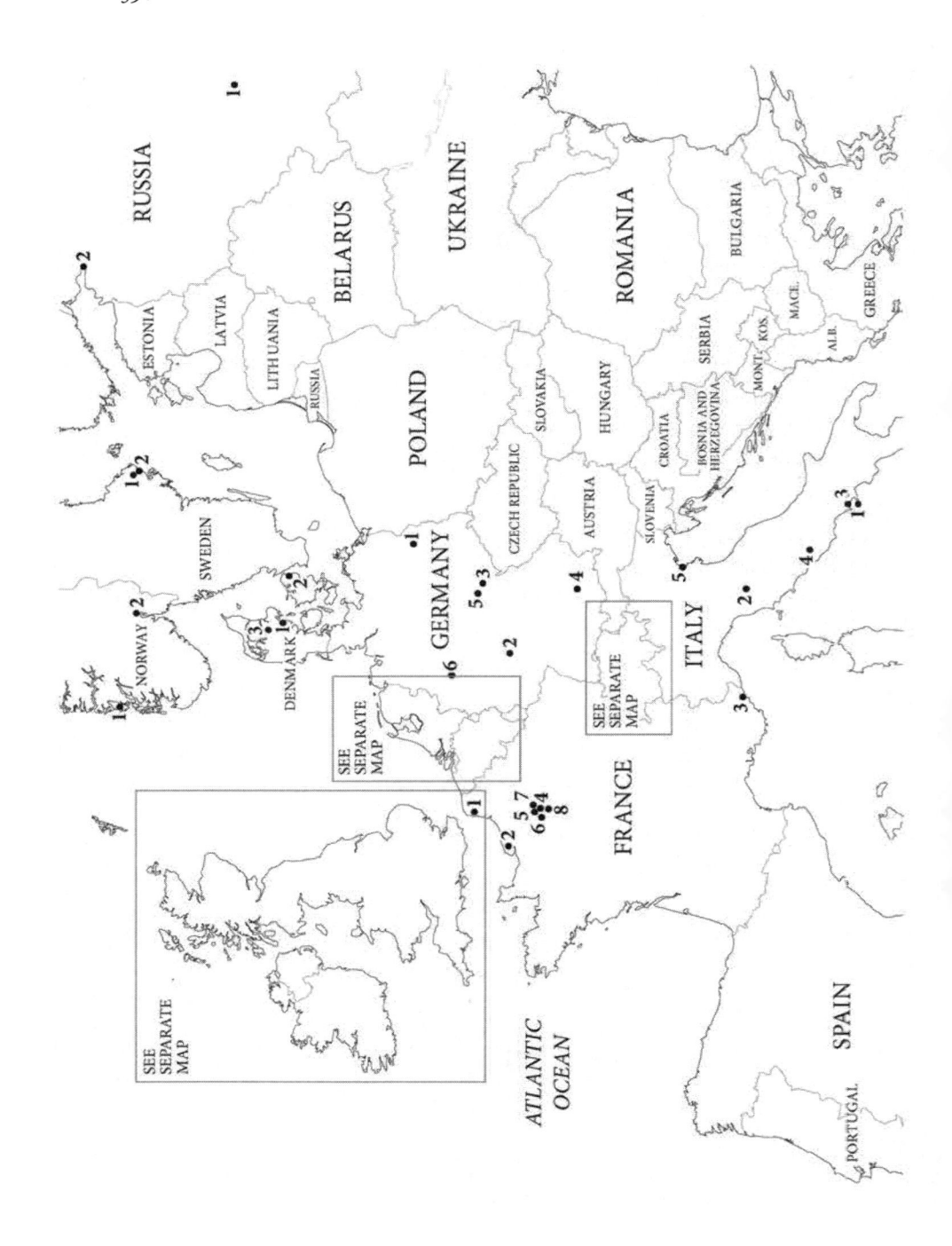

DENMARK
1 Arhus
2 Copenhagen
3 Randers

FRANCE
1 Boulogne
2 Etretat
3 Nice
4 Paris
5 Puteaux
6 Tremblaye
7 Suresnes
8 Wissous

GERMANY
1 Berlin
2 Darmstadt
3 Jena
4 Munich
5 Weimar
6 Hagen

ITALY
1 Capri
2 Florence
3 Naples
4 Rome
5 Venice

NORWAY
1 Bergen
2 Kristiania (Oslo)

RUSSIA
1 Moscow
2 St. Petersburg (Leningrad)

SWEDEN
1 Sigtuna
2 Stockholm

392

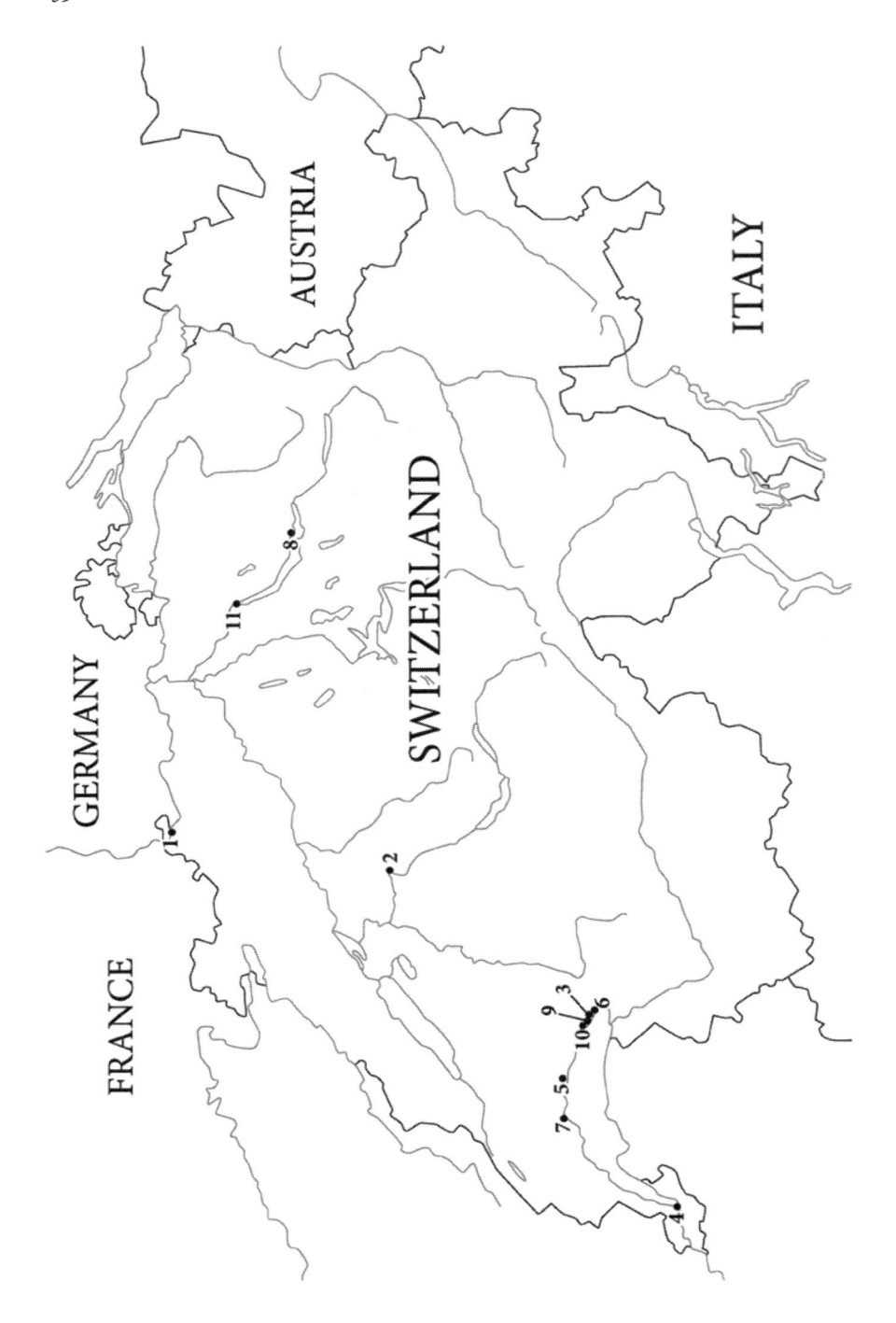

SWITZERLAND
1. Basel
2. Bern
3. Clarens
4. Geneva
5. Lausanne
6. Montreux
7. Morges
8. Rapperswil
9. La Tour de Peilz
10. Vevey
11. Zurich

394

UNITED KINGDOM
1. Bournemouth
2. Brighton
3. Cheltenham
4. Dundee
5. Edinburgh
6. Glasgow
7. Harrogate
8. Leeds
9. Letchworth
10. Leytonstone
11. London
12. New Milton
13. Nottingham
14. Sheffield
15. Southampton
16. Southsea
17. Stockton on Tees
18. Upper Edmonton
19. Woolwich

NORTH SEA

THE NETHERLANDS

GERMANY

BELGIUM

FRANCE

LUXEMBOURG

BELGIUM
1 Antwerp
2 Brussels
3 Liège

THE NETHERLANDS
1 Amersfoort
2 Amsterdam
3 Arnhem
4 Bergen
5 Bloemendaal
6 Deventer
7 Haarlem
8 The Hague
9 Hilversum
10 Katwijk
11 Leiden
12 Nijmegen
13 Rotterdam
14 Wassenaar

Notes and Glossary

Notes and Glossary

Although Indian custom is to list by first name, in this glossary the name taken as surname in the west has been used, ie Murshid Ali Khan, is listed under Khan, rather than Ali

Abhanga	– unbroken, continuous. Poem without stanzas. Marathi devotional song.
Abhedananda, Swami	– one of the disciples of Shri Ramakrishna, who renounced the worldly life sometime after the Master's passing away. He worked at the Vedanta Society in New York where he gave many lectures afterwards published as books e.g. *Why a Hindu accepts Christ and rejects Churchianity*.
Abrams, Dr. Albert	– American physician (1863-1924) who published *New Concepts in Diagnosis and Treatment* in 1916, which holds that disease is disharmony of electric oscillations in the body.
Advaita	– School of Vedantic philosophy, doctrine of non-dualism, which teaches the oneness of God, the soul and the universe, the exponent of which is Shankaracharya (8th or 9th century).
Afsar	– officer. Afsar-ul-Mulk (Aide de Camp).
Ahl-i-Hadith	– literally: the people of the Tradition. A modernist neo-orthodox sect or trend of thought existing already in the 10th century A.D. (4th century of the Hegira). Advocating a return to the pure sources of Islam, especially the Traditions about the Prophet, it condemns all later innovation or acknowledgement of non-Muslim beliefs and reasserts Islam, over and against Hindu (Arya Samaj), Christian and Ahmadia missionary efforts.
Ahmad Qadiani, Mirza Ghulam Hussein	– (1835-1908) founder of the Ahmadia Movement.
Ahmadia Movement	– a Muslim sect founded in 1880 by Mirza Ghulam Ahmad Hussein Qadiani (Qadian is a district of the Punjab province in India), who wrote *Barahin-i-Ahmadiya* – the arguments of the Ahmadiya. At the time of Pir-o-Murshid Inayat Khan's birth and Mehr Bakhshe's student days in his native Punjab, Ghulam Ahmad was still well regarded by Muslims, amongst other things for

his reaction against the propaganda of Christian missionaries. Later, however, acceptance of British rule, claims of prophethood and fanatic views led to the Ahmadia's virtual rejection from the main body of Islam.

Akbar — the greatest of the Moghul emperors (1542-1605). He made his Court a centre of culture and favoured religious tolerance; he discussed religious matters with Hindus, Muslims, Christians and Zoroastrians. After 1582 he formulated his *din-e-ilahi*, a monotheistic religion.

al Maari, Abu al Ala Ahmad — Arabic poet (973-1057) who wrote on morals and philosophy.

Ali — literally: eminent, noble.

Ali, Hazrat — Cousin and son-in-law of the Prophet Muhammad and fourth Khalif in succession to him, head of most of the Sufi Orders.

Aligarh College — Anglo-Oriental College founded in 1875 by Sayyed Ahmed Khan. It was originally intended to give education to children and later became a Muslim University, also attended by many Hindus.

Alt, Miss Angela — see biographical sketches.

Amir, Emir — commander.

Anjuman — assembly, meeting, society. A nomination used by a great many Muslim associations.

Anthroposophy — created in 1913 by Rudolf Steiner (1861-1925) as the result of his break with the Theosophical Society. He put Christianity above the Eastern religions and gave ample scope to science. For Rudolf Steiner science is the knowledge of reality not limited by senses and intellect. He also created a pedagogic philosophy and founded the Waldorf School in Stuttgart.

Arbabi nishat — Arabic words meaning 'masters of entertainment', dancers and musicians.

Arjuna — friend and disciple of Shri Krishna, one of the heroes of the Mahabharata. He hesitated to fight his own kinsmen and this was the occasion of the delivery by Lord Krishna of the best known Hindu text, the *Bhagavad Gita*.

Armstrong, Mr. R.A.L. (Khalif Mumtaz) — see biographical sketches.

Arnold, Sir Edwin	– English poet (1833-1904), Principal of the Sanskrit College in Puna. His poetry was influenced by the Orient and inspired by Oriental themes and legends, e.g. *The Light of Asia*. He translated the *Gīta Govinda: The Indian Song of Songs*, love songs of Krishna and Radha.
Arya Samaj	– literally: Aryans' Society. An orthodox religious association of Hindu Vedic revivalism founded in 1875 by Swami Dayananda Saraswati (1824-1883).
Aryan	– name applied to the Indo-European language family.
Ashrafi	– originally a gold coin worth about 16 rupees.
Assagioli, Dott. Roberto	– emphasised the necessity of making one's conscious personality strong enough to cope with all that psychoanalysis reveals. He wished to teach the patient 'the harmonious co-ordination of the subconscious with the higher elements or the soul-qualities of the personality'. The patient then draws on his own spiritual resources. Among his works are: *Denaro e Vita Spirituale* (Rome 1937), (Money and Spiritual Life), *Il Mistero dell'Io* (Florence 1954), (The Mystery of the Ego).
Assam	– a State in the north-east of India.
Astal	– first section of a Hindustani melody.
Augener & Co.	– publishing company in London.
Baba	– Father, old man, faqir.
Babism	– see Baha'ism.
Babu	– a title of respect, like Sir.
Baha, Abdul	– see Baha'ism.
Bahadur	– Persian word for hero, also used as a title.
Baha'ism	– in 1844 Mirza Ali Muhammad proclaimed himself 'Bab' (the door) and tried to reform the Islamic institutions. He was executed in 1850 in Persia and a revolt of his adherents was cruelly suppressed. The Movement was continued by Baha Ullah who passed forty years in prison. He preached a world religion, recognizing the eternal truth of the essence of all the previous God-revelations and he strove towards a world federation in which all men would be free and equal. His son Abdul Baha succeeded him in 1892 and spread Baha'ism in the Western world.

Bailly, Edmond	– French author of many books on music and sound e.g. *Du Merveilleux dans la Musique et de la Thérapeutique Musicale* (On the Marvellous in Music and on Healing by Music) and *Les Vibrations du Son et la Vie Universelle* (The Vibrations of Sound and the Universal Life). Pir-o-Murshid Inayat Khan wrote in the magazine *Sufi* of November 1916: 'In memoriam – This modest and quiet gentleman with his childlike simplicity was a most enthusiastic and earnest student of Eastern music and philosophy.'
Baker, Mrs. Mary Eddy	– American (1821-1910) who founded Christian Science in 1902. Author of *Science and Health* based on interpretation of texts from the Bible.
Bala Sabha	– children's association.
Bala sangit mala	– a garland of music for girls.
Banda Nawaz Sayyed Muhammad Gesu Daraz	– Indian Sufi Saint of the Chishti Order and healer (1320-1422), writer of a great many books on Sufism and on Islamic doctrine. His tomb is situated just outside Gulbarga (Deccan) and is a well-known place of pilgrimage.
Bandagi	– Persian word for slavery, service, humility.
Baum, Mr. G. (Sheikh)	– see biographical sketches.
Becharagi, be charegi	– Persian word, meaning: being without remedy, helplessness, poverty.
Beecham, Sir Thomas	– internationally acclaimed English conductor (1879-1961) who founded the British National Opera Company and the London Philharmonic Orchestra.
Belgachia	– a place west of Calcutta also called Bargachia, whose Maharaja was Saraswati Chendra Bahadur.
Bengal	– a region in the north-east of India.
Benton, Miss Rose	– one of Pir-o-Murshid Inayat Khan's early mureeds in London. About her Pir-o-Murshid wrote in the magazine *Sufi* of January 1919 that her interest in the beauty and harmony of Oriental music and dance had taken up her life in the cultivation of beauty in body, mind and soul.
Besant, Mrs. Annie	– Englishwoman (1847-1934) who became President of the Theosophical Society in India. She contributed much to the foundation of an Order of Freemasonry open to both men and women, which originated in France under the name of *Le Droit Humain* (Human Rights) in 1899 and

404 NOTES AND GLOSSARY

spread rapidly. With Mr. Leadbeater, she founded The Order of the Star in the East (Benares/Varansi 1911), with the object of preparing humanity to receive the coming world-teacher. The Order was dissolved in 1929. She also established the Liberal Catholic Church.

Best, Mr. Cecil E.B. (Sheikh Shahbaz) — see biographical sketches.

Bhagavad Gita — *The Song of the Lord.* Sacred Scripture of the Hindus in which Shri Krishna gives spiritual instruction to Arjuna before the great battle.

Bhajia, bhujiya — fried balls made of flour and vegetables.

Bharati, Baba Premanand — author of *Shri Krishna, the Lord of Love.*

Bhatkhande, Mr. — could be Pandit Vidvan N.V. Bhatkhande, who patronized the All-India Academy of Music from 1916 and strove to develop Indian music, collecting and preserving the best classical compositions and trying to arrange the ragas according to a uniform method.

Bhau — fear, dread, terror.

Bhau, bhav — sentiment, relationship.

Bibhen Biy — Biy Behen Bi(bi): her ladyship sister. The use of proper names especially of elder respectable ladies is considered in the East to be rather impolite.

Bibi — see Biy.

Biblioteca filosofica — centres for the study of philosophy, founded in Florence, Italy, in 1907. Courses and lectures on the main philosophical and religious problems were arranged and then published.

Bilgrami, Sayyad Hassan — born in 1844, professor of Arabic at the College of Lucknow, India, director of education to H.E.H. the Nizam, appointed as his private secretary in 1911.

Bima Biy — Biy Ma Bi(bi): her ladyship mother.

Biy, bi — Lady. When not contracted the word '*bibi*' ('*biwi*': lady of the house, wife) is often associated with the married state, seniority or special reverence and affection.

Bjerregaard, Carl H.A. — lecturer and author of many books on mysticism and inner life. Before writing *Sufism, Omar Khayyam & E. Fitzgerald* (London 1915), he had written *A Sufi Interpretation of the quatrains of Omar Khayyam* (New York 1902). Pir-o-Murshid

Inayat Khan wrote about him in the magazine *Sufi* of November 1915: 'He has explained how the conventional phraseology of Sufi poets has been so often misinterpreted by writers who have only been linguists, not mystics.'

Björset, Mr. B. — see biographical sketches.

Blavatski, Mrs. Elena Petrovska — (1831-1891) co-founder with Colonel Henry Steel Olcott of the Theosophical Society and author of *The Secret Doctrine* which she said was inspired by great Masters from Tibet and the Himalayas and which contains her main teachings.

Bloch, Regina Miriam — first sub editor of the quarterly magazine Sufi produced in London 1915-1920, author of *The Confessions of Inayat Khan* (London 1915) and *The Book of Strange Loves* (London 1918) and other books.

Bois, Jules — French author of novels, plays and poems, well-known in Paris before the 1914-1918 war. He was particularly interested in esotericism and feminism. During the Congress of Religions held on the occasion of the Universal Exposition in Paris in 1900, he received Vivekananda in his house.

Brahman — Hindu caste of priests.

Brahmo Samaj — a liberal religious Hindu Movement founded by Raja Ram Mohan Roy and Devendranath Tagore in 1830. It broke with the ritualism and the clericalism of orthodox Hinduism. In England it was introduced by Keshoba Chandra Sen.

Breteuil, François Marquis de — made an arrangement for the theatre of *The Light of Asia*, adapted from Sir Edward Arnold's poem.

Bridges, Sir Robert — English poet (1844-1930), poet laureate from 1913 until his death. He published T*he Testament of Beauty*, a philosophical poem, on his 85th birthday.

Brown, Bishop William Montgomery — was unfrocked by the Protestant Episcopal Church for heresy because of his book *Communism and Christianity*. His defence was presented with mocking insolence.

Burbank, Luther — American plant cultivator (1849-1926) who developed over 800 new varieties of flowers, fruits and vegetables by taking advantage of a plant's heredity and by influencing its surroundings.

Bürkhardt, Fraulein Martha — see biographical sketches.

Burma	– part of the Indian Empire until 1937. Forming a natural geographical entity in Southern Asia. Throughout its history it has been inward looking; its capital was called 'the centre of the universe'. Now known as Myanmar.
Caillet, Albert	– French author of several books e.g. *Hymnaire de ma Parèdre* (Paris 1922) where he mentions his initiation in the Sufi Order. He founded the Société Unitive which aimed at teaching the practice of the science of life in order to attain to individual and collective harmony. Pir-o-Murshid Inayat Khan was an honorary member of the Société Unitive and several of his early lectures are published in its review, *Bulletin Mensuel*.
Calvinism	– a Christian doctrine centering in the Sovereignty of God and the predestination of every human being, either to a state of bliss in God's presence or to eternal perdition.
Carpenter, Edward	– English writer (1844-1929) revolting against the social and religious conventions of his time, became a travelling lecturer for the instruction of persons unable to attend universities. He wrote on the relation of art to life.
Carrel, Alexis	– French-American surgeon (1873-1944) who was awarded the Nobel Prize in medicine in 1912 for his development of a new technique for sewing up blood-vessels end to end. He joined the Rockefeller Institute, New York, for medical research in 1906 and there mainly studied the transplantation of organs. Author of *Man, the Unknown* (1935) and other works.
Chaliapin, Feodor Ivanovitch	– famous Russian bass-singer (1873-1938), interpreter of *Boris Godunov* (opera by Moussorgski). He introduced the treasures of Slavonic music in Paris.
Chamar, chamur	– a baton of honour. One of the old distinctions used by Maharaja Krishnaraj of Mysore.
Charanam	– melody consisting of a number of parts.
Chatri	– gold canopy or umbrella. One of the old distinctions used by Maharaja Krishnaraj of Mysore.
Cherag(a)	– literally: lamp, light. Denoting a function in the Universal Worship of the Sufi Movement.

Chhanda	– sacred hymn, a measure in music.
Chicago	– Universal Exhibition of Chicago 1893, held to celebrate the 400th anniversary of the discovery of America by Christopher Columbus. Its main purpose was to show the progress of civilization and simultaneously a Parliament of Religions was organized.
Chishti Order	– founded by Khwaja Abu Ishaq of Syria, who migrated from Asia Minor and settled in Chisht (now called Shaqalan) in the Persian province of Khorasan. He was a disciple of Mimshad Ali Dinwari. Hazrat Khwaja Muinuddin Chishti, born in Persia in 113 A.D. and brought up in Sanjar was a spiritual descendant of Khwaja Abu Ishaq, eighth in the line of succession. He completed his religious education in Samarkand and Bukhara and was initiated in the Chishti Order by Khwaja Uthman Haruni in 1156. He met the great Abdu-l-Qadir Jilani, the founder of the Qadiri Order and also Abu-n-Najib Suhrawardi, the renowned Saint of the Suhrawardi Order. At Tabriz he met the spiritual Teacher of Mawlana Jalaluddin Rumi: Shams Tabrizi. In 1191/1192 he came to Ajmer (Rajasthan, India) and established the centre of the Order there. After having appointed Khwaja Qutub Sahib as his spiritual successor, he passed away in 1229. His tomb in Ajmer is visited by Muslims from all over India and Pakistan and is a well-known place of pilgrimage for Indians and people from many other countries of the world, of different religions and beliefs. The main idea of the Chishti Order which is one of the most important Sufi Orders in India, is the concept of the Unity of Being. Conversion to Islam was no pre-requisite to initiation in this Order. Besides special practices, the efficacy of music to attune the heart to the Infinite, is emphasized.
Chitti, Babu Naidu	– author of *A Key to Hindu Music*.
Cholas	– name of Muslims in Malabar.
Christian Science	– created by Mrs. M. Eddy Baker. Denying the reality of matter, it strives toward the deliverance from error by a right understanding of God and man, which will cause all egoism, fear and illness to disappear.

408   NOTES AND GLOSSARY

Chromatics, International College of	– see International College of Chromatics.
Cingalese, Sinhalese	– largest ethnic group in Sri Lanka (Ceylon).
City College	– a publicly controlled co-educational institution in New York City.
Columbia University	– a private, non-sectarian university in New York City. It dates from 1754 when it was granted its charter as King's College by King George II of England.
Congress of Paris 1914, Musical	– see Ecorcheville.
Connaughton, Mr. E. (Khalif)	– see biographical sketches
Coomaraswamy, Ananda K.	– (1877 Colombo-1947 Boston). Leading Indian Art Historian. Keeper of the Indian, Persian and Muhammadan Art Section of the Boston Museum of Fine Arts from 1917-1947. Author of approx. 500 books and articles on Indian Art, such as: 'The Dance of Siva (1912); Myths of Hindus and Buddhists (1914); Buddha and the Gospel of Buddhism (1916); History of Indian and Indonesian Art (1927); Yaksas (1931); The Transformation of Nature in Art (1934); Am I my Brother's Keeper (1943)', etc.
Coué, Émile	– French psychotherapist (1857-1926), invented a curative method by self-suggestion. Patients were instructed to repeat to themselves phrases such as Every day in every way I am getting better and better.
Craig, Mr. D. (Sheikh)	– see biographical sketches.
Cushing, Mrs. Marya (Sheikha Khushi)	– see biographical sketches.
Cynosure	– centre of attraction.
Dadra	– a Hindustani melody – a syncopated tala (time measure), especially used with the dadra class of song.
Dadu	– Indian Saint/poet (1544-1603), devotee of Shiva. The ideas expressed in his poetry are much like Kabir's.
Dalcroze, Emil Jaques	– Swiss composer (1865-1950). He taught eurythmics aiming at blending intellectual, emotional and muscular functions by means of music.
Darbar (durbar)	– Court.

NOTES AND GLOSSARY 409

Darwin, Charles	– British naturalist and physiologist (1809-1882) who stated that all living beings follow the same line of evolution; they have not been created individually but have evolved by natural selection from more primitive species. His theory of evolution is called Darwinism.
Dasei, festival of	– see Dassera.
Dayananda Saraswati	– (1825-1883) founder of Arya Samaj
Debussy, Claude	– French composer (1862-1918). He enlarged the scope of musical composition by introducing the use of exotic gamuts thus including Oriental musical characteristics in Western music. He also endeavoured to preserve improvisation in music.
Detraux, Yvonne	– French painter and disciple of Pir-o-Murshid Inayat Khan. She painted mainly landscapes and still life.
Dervish	– see Faqir.
Devendranath Tagore	– see Tagore.
Dewan, diwan	– Prime Minister of the Governor of a State in India. Collection of poems.
Dharma	– socially approved conduct in relation to one's fellowmen and other living beings or superhuman powers. Law, morality and most of what we ordinarily mean by religion. Righteous way of living, as enjoined by the Sacred Scriptures.
Dholuk, dholak	– a kind of drum, used in Northern India. It is cylindrical in shape, made of wood bored out of the solid and played with sticks or struck by the palm of the hand.
Dhrupad, dhurpad	– popular form of the Sanskrit word Dhruvapada, meaning an outstanding category of melodies in use in Northern and Southern India, a solemn religious song (see also Pallavi).
Dikshitar, dikshitr	– literally: one who has received initiation.
Dikshitar, Muttuswami	– Indian musician, contemporary of Tyagaraja (1776-1835). He invented a new system of Indian notation and composed a well-known hymn to Shri Ganesh in the *raga hamsadhvani*.
Din Dayal, Raja	– appointed painter to the Court of H.H. Mir Maheboob Ali Khan, the Nizam of Hyderabad.
Dowland, Miss J.E. (Khalifa Nargis)	– see biographical sketches.
Doyle, Sir A. Conan	– English physician born in Edinburgh (1859-1930), author of the Sherlock Holmes detective stories.

	He was honorary President of the International Spiritualist Federation and proprietor of The Psychic Bookshop in London.
Dulac, Edmond	– French born English artist (1882-1953), illustrator of fairy tales and also of the *Rubaiyat* of Omar Khayyam (1909) and of *The Arabian Nights* (1907).
Duncan, Isadora	– American dancer (1878-1925) whose movements were inspired by her observation of nature; she was the precursor of the modern free-dance school and created schools in Germany, France and Russia. Author of *Dancing in Relation to Religion and Love* (New York 1927), *My Life* (New York 1927) and other works.
Duncan Westbrook, Jessie	– Englishwoman who rendered the *Diwan of Inayat Khan* into English and helped Pir-o-Murshid to translate other poems from the Urdu, Hindi and Persian. In 1913 her translation of the *Diwan of Zeb-un-Nisa* was published.
Dussaq, Monsieur E. (Khalif Talewar)	– see biographical sketches.
East and West	– a Movement founded in England by Mr. Gupta, son of Keshoba Chandra Sen. See also Brahmo Samaj.
Ecorcheville, Dr. Jules	– French music-lover (1872-1915) who contributed much to the bringing together of the different Music Societies in Europe. In June 1914 he organized the Congress of Music for the *Société Internationale de Musique* in Paris and he was the editor of the Magazine of this Society, to which many famous musicians contributed.
Egeling, Mrs. N. (Murshida Fazal Mai)	– see biographical sketches.
Eichthal, Madame M.C. la Baronne d' (Sheikha)	– see biographical sketches
Ellis Island	– island in Upper New York Bay. In 1892 it became the site of the chief immigration station in the United States of America.
Engle, Mr. E. (Sheikh Fatha)	– see biographical sketches.
Ethnographical Museum	– Several Russian newspapers (among which the Russian Newspaper and News of 5th, 7th March, 17th, 20th, 27th and 30th April and 3rd May 1914) write about Pir-o-Murshid Inayat Khan's lectures with musical

illustrations, organized by the Ethnographical Section of the Imperial Society of Amateurs in Physics. The lectures given in April and May were organized by the Russian Theosophical Society in Moscow. All these lectures were held in the old auditorium of the Politechnical Museum in Moscow.

Eucken, Professor Rudolf — German philosopher, promoter of *Idealistic Thought*. He attached great importance to the inner life of man in whom nature and spirit meet. In 1908 he was awarded the Nobel Prize for literature. Author of *Der Sinn und Wert des Lebens* (The Meaning and Value of Life) (1908) *Können wir noch Christen sein* (Can we still be Christians) (1911) and *Rudolf Eucken, his Life, Work and Travels by himself* (1922).

Faqir — poor before God. Particularly the one who follows the path of contemplation; equivalent of the Persian *dervish*.

Farinola de Tanfani, Marchesa — under the Sufi name of Zeb-un-Nisa she wrote many poems and mystery plays, e.g. *Pierrot, Trois Mystères Franciscains, l'Art Universel*.

Fazal Manzil — literally: Blessed Abode; name of the house in Suresnes, France where Pir-o-Murshid Inayat Khan lived from 1922 to 1926.

Ford, Henry — American automobile manufacturer (1863-1947) who revolutionized industry by his assembly methods. Author of *My Life and Work* (1922) and *To-day and To-morrow* (1926).

Freemasonry — an international fraternal Order of men, evolved from the medieval guilds of stonemasons. Members are bound to secrecy by an oath. It teaches spiritual morality and charity using the mason's working tools as symbols (see also Besant, Mrs. Annie).

Frossard, Henri, Jean — Professor of vocal technics, author of various books on the culture of the voice, e.g. *La Science et l'Arte de la Voix* (The Science and Art of the Voice), Paris 1927, and a complete handbook for the singer explaining how to form sounds and giving rules for correct breathing as well as for a hygienic life (diet, clothing, sleeping). To the purchaser of his book a free singing-lesson or voice-consultation was offered.

Furnée, Miss J. E. D. (Khalifa Sakina, later named Nekbakht)	– see biographical sketches.
Gaekwar	– name of a dynasty of the Marathi kings.
Gaekwar, Maharaja Sayaji Rao of Baroda	– a great Indian reformer in the State of Baroda (1862-1939). Pir-o-Murshid Inayat Khan wrote about him in the magazine *Sufi* of October 1920 that he was a patriot but at the same time appreciated many points of Western civilization, considering neither East nor West superior. Every reform had his full attention. He started mills and model farms, was interested in cattle breeding and introduced all sorts of crafts. He was also a pioneer of thought, philosophy and art, and the first school of comparative religion was founded in his Kingdom. In the following words some of his ideas find expression: *We ignorantly often take the form for the ideal. There is only one spirit of Truth, there is only one Truth behind all ideals.'*
Gaekwar Shrimant Sampat Rao	– Barrister-at-Law, brother of the Maharaja Sayaji Rao Gaekwar of Baroda. He collected a private library of over 3,000 books in Gujerati and Marathi language, which he offered as a gift to the Central Library of Baroda, together with an adequate budget to enrich the stock.
Gandhi, Mahatma Mohandas Karamchand	– (1869-1948). Social reformer, philosopher and politician, leader of the Indian nationalist Movement, 'The Father of modern India'.
Ganesh, Shri	– elephant-headed Hindu God. He is the remover of obstacles and is the first God invoked on beginning a new enterprise.
Garba	– special song sung in the days of the festival of Shri Krishna.
Garbawali	– containing garbas, a book of garbas.
Garthawali, Granthwali	– containing the *Granth* (sacred book of Sikh religion), a book with parts of the *Granth*.
Gasparri, Cardinal	– Italian Roman Catholic Canon. During World War I (1914-1918) he tried to end the hostilities and to aid the war-victims through diplomatic channels.
Gayan	– singing, song.
Gayanshala	– abode of singing, Academy of Music.

Ghada	– a musical instrument.
Ghazal, gazal	– Hindustani melody, usually a love lyric.
Gibran, Kahlil	– poet, painter and philosopher (1883-1931). He was born in Syria, spent twenty years of his life in Lebanon and in 1912 made New York his permanent home. Among his many books are *The Prophet* (1923) and *Jesus the Son of Man* (1928). His books, illustrated by himself, were translated in thirty languages.
Goodenough, Miss L. (Murshida Sharifa)	– see biographical sketches.
Graeffe-van Gorckum, Madame E.	– see biographical sketches.
Grainger, Percy Aldridge	– Australian-American composer and pianist (1882-1961). He was interested in the collecting and the notation of English folk-songs.
Granth	– sacred book of the Sikhs.
Green, Miss Saintsbury (Murshida Sophia)	– see biographical sketches.
Gregory, Mrs. D.A. (Sheikha)	– see biographical sketches.
Gruner, Dr. O.C. (Khalif)	– see biographical sketches.
Guillon, Colonel	– see biographical sketches.
Guimet, Musée	– museum of religions in Paris having a remarkable collection of art from Japan, China and India. It was founded by Emile Guimet, a French scholar and industrialist (1836-1918).
Gujerat, Gujarat	– Province in Western India.
Gujerati	– language spoken in Gujerat.
Guni	– talented; also used as a title.
Guru	– spiritual Teacher, Murshid.
Gwalior	– city in the north of the Indian Province of Madhya Pradesh, native town of Tan Sen, famous singer at Akbar's Court, whose mausoleum at Gwalior attracts many visitors from India and abroad.
Hafiz, Khwaja Shamsud-Din Muhammad	– Persian poet (2nd half 14th century) known for his piety and learning. It is told that when he died some of his verses were considered too heretical by the Muslim divines to allow him to be buried with the Muslim funeral prayers. In order to settle the dispute that followed, a child was directed to pick a couplet of Hafiz' verse. It said: *Do not retire from Hafiz' bait* (meaning: abode and couplet),

NOTES AND GLOSSARY

for though he was a sinful man he goes to Paradise. The prayers were then read over his body. His poetry is remarkable for its beauty and sincerity. Among other works he wrote his *Diwan*, a collection of poems.

Hal	– condition, ecstasy.
Hamsa	– a bird which can discard the water and drink the milk from a mixture of milk and water. It absorbs the essence and leaves what is of minor importance, i.e. it distinguishes between Heaven and earth.
Harding, W.G.	– 29th President of the United States of America elected in 1920. In 1921 he called the Washington Conference, where the governments of the big nations agreed to a certain limitation of armament.
Harish, Chandra	– legendary king, famous for his benevolence and loyalty. This theme is dealt with in the *Markandeya Purana* and is taken up by Rawachandra in a well-known play.
Hazrat	– from the Arabic, a title which may be used for any great man or woman out of respect.
Hedemann, Prof. Wilhelm	– German professor in Law at the University of Jena, born in 1878. Author of books on Law.
Hidayat Inayat Khan	– see Inayat Khan.
Hindi	– the official language of North India, containing many words of Sanskrit origin.
Hindustan, Hindusthan	– a Persian word meaning India; properly restricted to the Northern provinces.
Hindustani	– belonging to India. The language of Hindustan.
Hoeber, Mrs. L. (Sheikha)	– see biographical sketches.
Hori	– a song of the Holi festival in Northern India.
Hoyack, Louis	– Dutch scholar. One of Pir-o-Murshid Inayat Khan's early mureeds much inspired by his teachings. He wrote many books covering a vast field of thought. His personality as well as his work is well rendered by the following poem written by his friend, the Dutch editor Nico Kluwer, for Hoyack's 60th Birthday:

Louis Hoyack   Ik bouwde mij een kant en klaar systeem,
Waaraan Inayat's leer ten grondslag ligt,
Toch is door mij iets nieuws en groots verricht,
Waarop van Hoyack prijkt het trots embleem.

Aan 's Meesters Boodschap gaf 'k mijn commentaar,
Voor 't Westen deed ik open de Koran,
In Galilea liet 'k een man opstaan,
Ge vindt het in mijn werken al te gaar.

Nog daaglijks vijl ik aan mijn eigen leer,
Waarin 'k als spin in 't web gevangen zit.
Ik gaf mijn kijk op de verveling weer.

Maar 't allerdiepste, onbewuste bidt:
Bevrijd me van systeem en leer, o Heer,
Dit is mijn zielsverlangen en mijn wit.

Translation: I built myself a system ready made
Louis Hoyack   Which has Inayat's teaching as its base,
Yet something new and great was wrought by me,
On which Hoyack's proud emblem shines.

On the Master's Message I gave my own comment,
To Western minds I opened the Qur'an,
In Galilea I brought to life a man,
You'll find it all in my works' contents.

Still my own doctrine daily I amend,
In which I'm caught as a spider in its web,
My view on boredom I expressed.

And yet my deep unconscious self implores:
Deliver me, oh Lord, from system and doctrine,
This is my soul's true yearning and my aim.

The books referred to in the poem are: *De Boodschap van Inayat Khan* (The Message of Inayat Khan), *De onbekende Koran* (The Unknown Qur'an), *Een Man stond op in Galilea* (A Man arose in Galilea) and *De Philosophie van de Verveling* (The Philosophy of Boredom).

Huzur	– presence of a superior authority, Highness.
Hyderabad	– capital of the Indian province of Madya Pradesh. From the Arabic word *hyder* meaning lion, and the Persian word *abad* meaning inhabited, populated, city, town. It was the capital of the Nizams (see Nizam) and was founded in 1591.
Hypnotism, hypnosis	– a sleep like state during which the subject is submitted to suggestions; also used for therapeutic purposes.
Imam	– literally: one who is followed or imitated; guide, leader, head of a religion (especially of Islam), leader of prayers in a mosque.
Inayat Khan, Hidayat Murshid Zade	– (1917-2016) Pir-o-Murshid's youngest son, who composed several musical works, e.g. *Nous vous invitons a la Prière, La Monotonia* and *The Message Symphony*.
Inayat Khan, Khairunnisa Pir Zadi (later Claire Ray Harper)	– (1919-2011) Pir-o-Murshid's youngest daughter, trained as a pianist and a nurse; worked in Dr. Heatley's penicillin laboratory during WW II; moved to USA after her mother's death, returned to Suresnes, France 1970's
Inayat Khan, Noorunnisa Pir Zadi	– (1914-1944) Pir-o-Murshid Inayat Khan's eldest daughter, who wrote stories for children, e.g. *Twenty Jataka Tales* (London 1939, The Hague 1975).
Inayat Khan, Vilayat Pir Zade	– (1916-2004) Pir-o-Murshid's eldest son, who wrote *The Light of Truth* (a play, 1932), *Stufen einer Meditation* (1962), *Towards the One, Samadhi with Open Eyes* (1977) and many other works.
International College of Chromatics	– founded in London, for the study of the science of colour. It gave instruction in the use of colour in architecture, archaeology, costumes, ethnology, etc.
Irwin, Beatrice	– author of *The Gates of Light*, a record of progress in the engineering of colour and light (London 1930) and a collection of poems called *The Pagan Trinity* (London & New York 1912).
Ivanov, Viatoslav	– leading Russian poet of the Russian Symbolist Movement (1866-1949). He lived in St. Petersburg where he gathered the important Russian literary world. His chief poetical work is *Cor Ardens* (1911).

Jalatarang	– music played on a number of cups containing various quantities of water. By dipping the fingers in the water and rubbing them around the rims of the cups, 18 notes in two octaves can be produced.
Jami, Maulan Nur-ud-Din	– Persian scholar, mystic and poet (1414-1492) author of *The Seven Thrones*, a poetical work including the story of Yusuf and Zuleikha, and other works.
Jilani, Abdu'l Qadir	– Sufi lecturer and mystic (1077-1166) with many disciples all over Iraq, who lived in Baghdad and gave his name to the Sufi Order of the Qadiris. In some parts of India the Qadiris celebrate the Urs of their founder with a ceremony in which a large green flag is carried in procession. With torches and music the standard is then put up.
Jinn, djinn, genius	– generally explained in the Qur'an as a spirit or an invisible, or hidden force, created from a flame of fire. In *The Soul, whence and whither* Pir-o-Murshid Inayat Khan says: 'The genius is an entity with a mind, but not such a mind as that of man; a mind more pure, more clear, which is illuminated by the light of intelligence.'
Ka'aba	– Muslim sanctuary in Mecca, built by Abraham.
Kabbala	– Hebrew tradition, esoteric Jewish mysticism claiming secret knowledge of the unwritten Torah, which God communicated to Moses.
Kabir	– Indian mystic poet (1440-1518). His poems were translated by Rabindranath Tagore. Hindus and Muslims both claim him as their Saint. He taught ardent personal devotion instead of ritual and formalism.
Kaiser	– Kaiser Wilhelm (William) II (1859-1941), Emperor of Germany from 1888 to 1918, when he was forced to abdicate towards the end of World War I. He took refuge in the Netherlands where he lived a retired life.
Kala Bhawan	– temple of art. A centre for dance, drama, music and plastic art.
Kalaggai, Kalagi	– ornament on the turban: a gold circlet with a plume. One of the old distinctions used by Maharaja Krishnaraj of Mysore.

Karma	– the law of action and the consequences it produces in the present or in a future birth.
Karnatak	– from *Karnat* in the South of India. The Karnatic race are Dravidians and the Karnatic music is their music produced in Southern India.
Kathiawar	– peninsula on the West coast of India, in the State of Gujerat.
Kavi	– literally: poet and sage.
Keshoba (Keshab), Chandra Sen Babu	– one of the leaders of the Brahmo Samaj.
Keyserling, Count Graf Hermann	– German philosopher (1880-1946) deeply interested in Oriental philosophy. At Darmstadt he established the School of Wisdom, which sought to blend the best of Eastern and Western thought. Author of *Reisetagbuch eines Philosophen* (Travel Diary of a Philosopher) published in 1919.
Khalif(a)	– esoteric title conferred by Pir-o-Murshid Inayat Khan upon some of his mureeds.
Khan, Maheboob	– see biographical sketches
Khan, Musharaff Moulamia	– (1895-1967) youngest brother of Pir-o-Murshid Inayat Khan, author of *Pages in the Life of a Sufi* (London 1932, 1971) containing memories of his youth. One of the Royal Musicians of Hindustan.
Khan, Murshid Ali	– (1881-1958) cousin of Pir-o-Murshid Inayat Khan, musician and healer, one of the Royal Musicians of Hindustan.
Khan, Sayyad Ahmad	– (1817-1897), founder of the Aligarh College, India, and author of a series of essays on the life of Muhammad, representing Islam as the most tolerant religion.
Khandan	– family, lineage, dynasty.
Khankah	– word of Persian origin. A convent for Sufi recluses; a convent, a monastery.
Khatidja, Khadija	– originally with 'd', but in India generally pronounced as a 't'. First wife of the Prophet Muhammed.
Khayal, khyal	– style of classical music of Northern India, developed in the 17th and 18th century. It is a short melody, like the *dhrupad*, lengthened by repetitions and variations; a light melodic air.
Khayyam, Omar	– His real name was Giyasuddin Abulfath Omar ibn Ibrahim al Khayyami, a famous Persian mathematician, astronomer, free-thinker and poet. In his own days he was best known as a scientist, now in the West as a poet. Among other things

NOTES AND GLOSSARY   419

	he wrote the *Rubaiyat*. He died at Nishapur in 1123.
Khilafet Movement	– a Movement in favour of the Sultan of Turkey, recognized by the Indian Muslims as their Khalif and as suzerain of the Holy City (Mecca). After the peace treaty of 1918 his position was greatly weakened in spite of allied promises to the contrary. This was considered humiliating and against the honour of Islam. In March 1920 the cause of the Khalifat was pleaded in London by several representatives of India but in vain. Thereupon the All India Muslim League joined the non-cooperation Movement of Mahatma Gandhi.
Khusru, Amir	– Indian poet, singer and musician. He was probably the first to introduce the sitar and among the first to use the Urdu language for his literary work. A disciple of Nizamuddin Auliya of Delhi, he died shortly after his Murshid and was buried close to him.
Kismet	– literally: destiny, fate. A play in three acts by Edward Knoblauch after an Arabic tale. The Royal Musicians of Hindustan were engaged to perform their music as an intermezzo in a bazaar scene.
Kjøsterud Miss S. (Sheikha)	– see biographical sketches.
Krishna, Shri	– Divine incarnation of Vishnu, whose teachings are given in the *Bhagavad Gita*.
Kshatriya, kshatra	– belonging to the second or military caste of the Hindus.
Lakmé	– opera by Léo Delibes, first performed in Paris in 1883. The play is set in India and in order to introduce some touches of realism the Royal Musicians of Hindustan were invited to perform their music in a bazaar scene. The contrast between the Western idea of orientalism in Delibes' music and the genuine Indian art was obvious.
de László, Philip Alexius	– English painter (1869-1937) born in Hungary, who gained international fame for his portraits of eminent men.
Laya, lay	– style of expression in rhythm, time movement. Tune.
League of Nations	– international organisation established in Geneva by the peace treaties ending World War I. It functioned from 1920 till 1946.

Léon, Professor Henri M.	– born in Paris in 1856, he was professor in English literature and in geology at the Imperial Ottoman University. In 1912 he went to England where he was appointed General Secretary of the *Société Internationale de Philologie, Sciences et Beaux Arts*.
Lewis, Samuel L.	– (1896-1971), American mureed of Mda. Rabia Martin. He studied Oriental philosophy and was received in several Oriental esoteric schools such as Zen, Yoga and Sufi schools. He believed in speaking openly about his experiences and initiations, and in bringing peace through the dance. He created numerous dances (partly inspired by Ruth St. Denis) which were representative of all religions. Author of *Toward Spiritual Brotherhood* (San Francisco 1972), mystical poems, and other works.
Liberal Catholic Church	– see Besant, Mrs. Annie.
Lincoln, Abraham	– 16th President of the U.S.A., elected in 1860. In 1863 he issued the emancipation proclamation abolishing slavery.
Lloyd, Mrs. Gladys I. (Sheikha Kefayat)	– see biographical sketches.
Lodge, Sir Oliver	– English physicist (1851-1940). He was the first to suggest that the sun might be a source of radio waves. After 1910 he became prominent in psychic research.
L.R.A.M.	– Licentiate of the Royal Academy of Music.
Madani, Sayyad Abu Hashim	– Pir-o-Murshid Inayat Khan's Murshid, a Sufi of the Chishti-line. In 1923 after her journey through India Murshida Rabia Martin wrote: 'The blessed Murshid of our Murshid Inayat Khan was Sayyad Abu Hashim Madani, who was born in Madras. He was one of the most profound and blessed of sages. His sacred remains are near the Puran Pul (old bridge) in the compound of Mian Paisa Dargah at Hyderabad. There are three tombs there in a row. This man was of a very gentle disposition, soft and kindly, yet inwardly powerful. He had an almost hypnotic ability to purify the minds and hearts of all he contacted through his inner purity and perfection of personality.'
Madar-ul-Maham	– the centre of affairs, the minister. A title given by Pir-o-Murshid Inayat Khan to the Secretary of the Esoteric School.

Mahajan Mandal	– society of the bankers' caste; caste of the Mahajani; society of great people. A magazine published in Baroda, in which an article about Maula Bakhsh by his grandson Inayat Khan, appeared in 1896 in Gujerati.
Maharaja	– a Sanskrit word meaning: great king. A title given to ruling chiefs of the States of India, sometimes applied to persons of high rank and to holy men.
Mahatma	– large-minded, noble, eminent, one of great, divine soul.
Majzub	– one whom God has drawn to Himself, one absorbed in God. Pir-o-Murshid Inayat Khan says: 'The majzub is the lover of God, who does everything to hide his love of God before his fellowmen, so that it confuses them and he is called by them foolish or insane. He does not care, he is a harmless person and his love of God gives him a great power.'
Mala	– garland.
Malayali	– a Dravidian language spoken in the South of India.
Marathi	– an Indo-Aryan language spoken in Maharashtra (south of Gujerat in the west-central part of India, including Bombay). Marathi literature begins in the 13th century with a number of poets drawing their inspiration from the worship of Vishnu.
Martin, Mrs. A. (Murshida Rabia)	– see biographical sketches.
Mashal	– torch. One of the old distinctions of Maharaja Krishnaraj of Mysore.
Masnavi, Mathnavi	– main poetical work of Jelal-ud-Din Rumi.
Masonry	– see Freemasonry.
Maula Bakhsh	– Inayat Khan's grandfather. An article written by Pir-o-Murshid Inayat Khan about him, was published in the magazine *Sufi* of September 1915. The name means 'God-gifted' (Maula-lord, master; Bakhsh-a Persian word meaning giving, giver.)
Maulana	– a title given to learned persons.
Maulavi	– lordship.
Maya	– making, art, conveying at the same time the sense of illusion. As a vedic term it is used for the cosmic illusion which makes the Only Being appear as a multitude of beings.

422 NOTES AND GLOSSARY

Maya civilization	– one of the great civilizations of Mexico and Central America. The Maya were famous for their astronomers and mathematicians.
Mehr Bakhshe	– brother-in-law of Pir-o-Murshid Inayat Khan.
Mesmerism	– was for a long time the term for what is now called hypnosis.
Meyer von Reutercrona, Mrs. H. (Sheikha)	– see biographical sketches.
Miller, Mrs. R. C. (Khalifa Mushtari)	– see biographical sketches.
Minqar-e-Musiqar	– a book on music in Hindustani, written by Inayat Khan about 1903 and issued in 1912 by the Indian Press, Allahobad. Literally: the beak of the sound-bird, the phoenix of music.
Mir Maheboob Ali	– H.E.H. (His Exalted Highness) the Nizam of Hyderabad. He succeeded in 1869 at the age of three as the ninth Nizam and was invested with full powers in 1884.
Miran Datar/Ditta	– a Sufi Saint at whose tomb in Ujjain in Central India possessed people are often healed. His name has the meaning of great healer.
Mitchell, Edgar Austin (Shahbaz)	– (1877-1939). He was a journalist and leader writer of the Southern Daily Echo, Southampton and wrote under the nom de plume of Townsman. For over 20 years 'Mike' as his many friends used to call him, was an active member of the Sufi Movement after he met Pir-o-Murshid Inayat Khan in London during the war (1914-1918). He worked both as a preacher, a lecturer and a literary worker to spread the Sufi ideals. He wrote a book: *Southampton Notes*, which has become a collector's item.
Moghul, Mughal	– dynasty of Mongol rulers of India, founded in 1526 by Babar, a descendant of Tamerlane. Under Akbar the Great, the Moghul Empire embraced Central and Northern India. Bahadur Shah II was the last of the Moghul Emperors and was deposed by the British in 1857.
Morax, René	– Swiss author of poems and of plays for puppet theatre.
Muhur, muhr	– a gold coin of the value of 16 rupees, the same as an ashrafi.
Muinuddin Chishti	– see Chishti Order.

Mukti	– liberation from the bondage of the world, the goal of spiritual practices.
Müller, Friedrich Max	– German orientalist (1823-1900) who settled in Oxford, England, in 1848, specialized in Sanskrit. He translated many Sanskrit and Pali texts and wrote among other things *Essays on Hindi Philosophy*.
Munsif	– magistrate.
Mureed	– from the Arabic, meaning desirous, willing, a follower, called *chela* among the Hindus.
Murshid	– from the Arabic, meaning guide, a spiritual teacher, head of a religious Order, called *Guru* among the Hindus and *Starets* in the Russian Church.
Mutiny	– 1857, India, also known as the Sepoy Mutiny, when the different Sepoy regiments, mainly consisting of Hindus, rebelled against the British rulers who ignored their hereditary customs. Probably some foreign countries took advantage of this situation and by stirring up the national feelings of the Indian people, the existing dissatisfaction developed into a fierce and widespread mutiny.
Nanak, Guru	– founder of Sikhism (1469-1539), a religious movement which has its roots in Hinduism. The Sikhs follow the idea of joining the Hindus and Muslims in love and devotion to God, and service to man. Their sacred Scripture, the *Adi Grantha Sahab*, is a compilation of teachings and songs of Guru Nanak and his successors and of the Saints in the Sikh Movement.
Naqib	– a leader, an adjutant. A title given by Pir-o-Murshid Inayat Khan to some of his mureeds, which at that time was translated as 'herald'
Narayan, Shri Guru	– born in Malabar in 1854, he was first a wandering monk and became later a famous spiritual leader in South India and Ceylon. As a spiritual and social reformer he showed that the principles of Vedanta could be applied. His message was one of all-embracing unity: 'One God, one Religion, one Caste. There being only one Eternal Reality, dedicated service to That is the true religion; and since all men are capable of that service, and since all people, all life and all things move and have their existence by that One, all separateness and

NOTES AND GLOSSARY

	division into race, caste, colour and creed are nothing but illusion foisted on the minds of men by ignorance and forgetfulness of this sole Universal Reality.'
Narsiji, Narsingi	– a Maharashtrian Hindu Saint living in the 16th century, by whom Mahatma Gandhi was influenced.
Narsiji, Narsingi	– the name of the hereditary Guru of the (Mandir) Hindu temple in Baroda.
Navarat	– name of a festival in India, meaning nine nights.
Nawab	– title of a provincial governor of the Moghul Empire. Vicegerent, deputy, lord.
Nazar	– gift.
Nepal	– Kingdom North of India in the Himalaya region. Its capital is Kathmandu.
Newbolt, Sir Henry	– English poet (1862-1938) best known for his patriotic verse. He also edited anthologies of English poetry.
Nirvana	– literally: no difference. Extinction, annihilation, eternal bliss. Realization of the soul's freedom.
Nizam	– from the Arabic meaning order, arrangement, governor, composer. A title originally conferred by the Moghul Emperors upon the ruler of the State of Hyderabad, in the Deccan, India, and held by his descendants.
Nizam-ul-Mulk	– Governor of the kingdom.
Noorunnisa Inayat Khan	– see Inayat Khan, Noorunnisa.
Nuralja	– Nurvara Eliya of Ceylon.
Olcott, Colonel Henry Steel	– co-founder with Helena Petrovna Blavatski of the Theosophical Society.
Oratorio	– musical composition for chorus, orchestra and solo voices on a sacred subject, first introduced in the 16th century in Europe, in the Church in Rome.
Order of the Star in the East	– see Besant, Mrs. Annie.
Oudh	– the old Ayodhya, a holy place of the Hindus, the birth place of Ram, in the North-West of India.
Paderewski, Ignace Jean	– Polish composer and pianist (1860-1941). He interrupted his musical career to work for the re-establishment of an independent Polish State after World War I and became its first President in 1919.

Pakhawaj	– a sort of drum with two heads covered with parchment.
Pallavi	– a section of *dhrupad*, as it is known in Southern India, which contains the main subject and usually possesses a well-defined rhythm. A chorus.
Panama Canal World Fair	– a Congress of religious philosophy at the Panama Pacific International Exposition, San Francisco 29th-31st July 1915. The honorary President was Rabindranath Tagore. There was a Christian day, a Hindu day and an Oriental day. Murshida Rabia Martin spoke on the latter about Sufi Philosophy (published in the magazine *Sufi* of November 1915).
Pandit (pundit)	– learned man.
Panjab (Punjab)	– five waters or rivers; a province in the North-West of India.
Pariah, paria	– a person of the lowest Hindu caste formerly known as 'untouchables' but named *Harijans* (children of God) by Mahatma Gandhi.
Parsi	– a follower of Zarathushtra, especially found in the West of India.
Pathan	– name of Iranian tribes in what is nowadays the North West of Pakistan and Afghanistan and of their descendants who immigrated to India in the 15th century. There they formed a dynasty that ruled in Delhi, and also groups of landowners and martial tribes. During the British rule the frontier Pathans were the only people of the subcontinent who were never wholly subjugated. Due to this record of independence Pathans have enjoyed the reputation of being a knightly and war-waging class among the Indo-Islamic community. Dr. Pathan (Alaoddin Khan) adopted this name when in England when he needed a surname, and Inayat Khan adopted the same name during his musical tour.
Paul, Saint	– great Apostle of Christianity. Very little is certain about the historical person of St. Paul. Of the letters ascribed to him, which are known to be anterior to the Gospels, a certain number is also attributed to several other authors. Equally little is known about the origin of the Gospels, which have come down to us in their actual form only about or after the year 200. A study of this epoch

Peshkar — reveals very scarce and contradicting data of the facts and of the spiritual climate in which Gospels and Letters were written. It might therefore be interesting and important to take Pir-o-Murshid Inayat Khan's view on the matter into consideration.

Peshkar — a word used by Pir-o-Murshid Inayat Khan to indicate the head of the Brotherhood (an activity of the Sufi Movement). The word in Urdu means: assistant, deputy, manager.

Pickthal, Marmaduke — English Muslim who translated the Qur'an: *The meaning of the Glorious Koran, an Explanatory Translation*, published in London in 1930 and reprinted in 1948.

Pieri, Comtesse M. L. — see biographical sketches.

Pillay, T. Lakshmana — author of *Travancore Music and Musicians* (Trivandrum 1918.)

Pir — Persian word, meaning old, the oldest, a holy man. A spiritual guide, the founder or head of a religious Order, the one who helps individuals towards the unfoldment of the soul.

Pir-o-Murshid — see Pir and Murshid.

Pool, Rev. John J. — Principal of the International College of Chromatics, author of *Colour and Health* (London 1919).

Prabhandha — ancient name of a musical composition (song), used in the 13th century.

Purana(s) — belonging to ancient times. Sacred Scriptures supposed to have been compiled by the poet Vyasa and containing Hindu theology and mythology.

Pyaru miyan — Urdu translation of the Arabic 'Maheboob Khan': Pyara – Maheboob (beloved), miyan – Khan (a title).

Qur'an — the sacred Scripture of the Muslims, containing the divine revelations as received by the Prophet Muhammad and faithfully and promptly taken down by his followers.

Rabia — a renowned woman Sufi-Saint of Basra (Iraq) who lived in the 8th century A.D. and about whose ascetic saintly life many stories and anecdotes are known.

Raga	– a pattern of music designed in a certain pitch of the scale, which is improvised upon by the artist. Literally: passion; from ancient times each raga has been associated with particular passions and emotions.
Raga Hamsadhwani	– a South Indian raga.
Ragtime	– syncopated music.
Rahusen, Miss (Murad)	– painter and illustrator of, among other things, children's books.
Railway Institute	– erected buildings for the Railway Companies in India for the benefit of their employees, equipped with a reading room and a central hall which could be hired for performances.
Raja	– a title of hereditary princes of the Hindus.
Raja Yoga	– the king of yoga. The yoga of control of the mind. Pir-o-Murshid Inayat Khan calls it the yoga of the path of learning from life's experiences.
Rajbar	– royal garden.
Ram Das	– Marathi Saint-poet (2nd half 17th century). He was also a religious leader and founder of a sect. In his *Verses to the Mind* (Manache Shlok) he gives much advice for a wise way of living.
Rama, Shri, Shri Ram	– seventh incarnation of Vishnu, whose story is told in the Ramayana, the famous Sanskrit epic poem.
Ramakrishna, Shri	– a God-realized sage (1834-1886) who lived an ascetic life in Dakshineswar (Calcutta) and attracted many disciples. He considered the different religions as one.
Ramyar	– a friend and admirer of Inayat Khan in Hyderabad (Deccan), India (Ill.8). In a letter dated 10th December 1926 he wrote to Pir-o-Murshid Inayat Khan : 'You will be pleased to learn that during your absence the Government of India have been pleased to confer upon me the title of Khansaheb in 1916 and on the first of January 1926 I got the distinction of Khan Bahadur. At present I am a special Bench Magistrate Honorary of Secunderabad.'
Ranz des Vaches	– Ranz from the German word *Reie* meaning row, range, series and in this case probably flock; originally a melody without words, a kind of improvisation used by shepherds to gather their flock.
Ratnavali	– necklace of gems. Album of songs by Inayat Khan (c.1903).

Reformation	– religious revolution, going on simultaneously in several countries of Europe, which led to the formation of the Protestant Church in the 16th century.
Reps, Paul (Saladin)	– an American mureed of Pir-o-Murshid Inayat Khan, author of *Zen Flesh, Zen Bones* (Tokyo 1958) and *Zen Telegrams* (Tokyo 1959).
Risalat	– Persian word from arabic origin, meaning: Message, Apostleship. Muhammad was the seal of *Risalat*. The discussion centres on *Khatim al Mursalin* (Seal of the Apostles), used in Indian Sufism to combine the finality and supremacy of the prophethood and religious law of Muhammad as *Khatim al Nabiyyin* (Seal of the prophets) with the continuity of inspired spiritual experience, one of the oldest problems in Islam. *Rasul* thus primarily becomes the highest initiatic stage and esoteric degree rather than a socio-religious apostleship: *His words, the law; his message, the wisdom; his being, that peace*. Inayat Khan contributes a further concept of the aspects of the role of the messenger: 'those of message-bearing and prophethood have been terminated; now only that of teacher remains' (*Unity of Religious Ideals*, first ed., p 282-283). The *Risalat* concept is fused with the gnostic *Nur-Muhammadi* (Spirit of Guidance) hence 'the light of *Risalat* shines before him' (i.e. the Sufi mystic) 'in every being and thing in the universe'; *Shahada*, the final revelation, implies that 'every soul has the source of the divine message within itself'. Further, it is 'the prophets' words' that are 'the seals upon the secret of God'; hence, the *kamal* (perfect) mystic may become entitled to open them as long as spiritual perception and transmission remain 'without claim', i.e. of modifying revelations and religious law.
Robe	– garment, conferred by Pir-o-Murshid Inayat Khan upon certain of his mureeds, chosen for a certain function.
Rockefeller Foundation, Institute	– philanthropic organization, founded in 1901 by the American industrialist John Davison Rockefeller (1839-1937) for the promotion of knowledge throughout the world.

Roshan chauki	– illuminated platform, the place where musicians play and sing.
Rosing, Vladimir	– Russian tenor singer. He was a member of the Imperial Opera in Moscow, then a concert singer in London. He organized the opera season in London in 1915.
Roy, Ram Mohan	– founder of Brahmo Samaj.
Royal Academy of Music	– established in London in 1823.
Royal Musicians of Hindustan	– as Inayat Khan, his two brothers, his cousin and Rama Swami called themselves. They also called themselves 'The servants of the Sufi Order'. The Indian Magazine wrote about them: 'The Royal Musicians of Hindustan have persevered in establishing the Order of Sufism by touring throughout the world. They appeared in strange lands, wearing their native dress and playing their own instruments, regardless of the response, people or place. They expressed Sufism in the realm of music and have devoted their profession to the Order as a means of support. With lectures and concerts they have attracted the prepared minds to the Truth of Sufism.'
Rubayat	– a quatrain, a poem by Omar Khayyam.
Rumi, Jelaluddin	– a Sufi mystic poet (1207-1273): born in Balkh (Afghanistan) he lived in Konya and other places in Asia Minor. In 1244 he met his spiritual guide, the wandering dervish Shams Tabriz. He founded the Order of the Maulawi dervishes (Mevlevis). Rumi's famous works are the *Masnavi* and the *Discourses (Fihi ma fihi)*.
Rummel, Walter	– a virtuoso, conductor and composer (1887-1953), well-known in Paris in the period before World War I (1914-1918), a friend of Debussy and of Isadora Duncan.
Russell, Edmund	– American scholar of Oriental art and philosophy, poet and portrait painter. He painted many famous people in America and Europe. He visited India several times. The Royal Musicians of Hindustan played at his renowned studio receptions, both in New York and in Paris.

Sa'adi, Muslihuddin	– Persian Sufi poet (13th century A.D.) born in Shiraz. He received instruction from Abdul Qadir Jilani and Suhrawardi. He called his books *Bustan* (place of fragrance) and *Gulistan* (rose garden), and Pir-o-Murshid Inayat Khan said about Sa'adi that in simple language, without mystification, he has tried to give man a helping hand towards the development of his personality, explaining how the heart can be turned into a flower. His poetry is full of wit and intelligence.
Sabha, shabha	– public hall, meeting-place, council.
Sahib	– lord, master, sir.
St. Denis, Ruth	– founded the Ruth St. Denis School of Dancing and its Related Arts in Los Angeles after having made two tours from coast to coast in the U.S.A and given performances in Paris, London, Vienna and Berlin. Among the subjects of her repertoire were: *Radha; the Cobras; the Yogi; the Incense;* and Egyptian and Japanese productions. Author of *Lotus Light*, a collection of poems (New York 1932) and *An Unfinished Life*, an autobiography (New York and London 1939). The Royal Musicians of Hindustan toured with her in 1911.
Salar Jung, Sir (Jang)	– was appointed Minister of the State of Hyderabad in 1853 and was regent during the minority of H.E.H. the Nizam Mir Maheboob Ali Khan. He was an efficient and hard-working man whose ambition it was to prove the independence of the State. He reorganized the entire system of government.
Sama, sema	– literally: hearing, ear; a term applied to a special musical gathering of Sufis, in which the hearing of harmonious sounds moves the heart and kindles the fire of love for God.
Samadhi	– state of consciousness in which the mind becomes identified with the object of meditation. Sufis call it *hahut*.
Samaj	– meeting, assembly, society.
Sammelan	– assembly, meeting.
Sangit Sammilani	– musical society.
Sa, ra, gam	– like do, re, mi, the notation of a melody on which the musician improvises.
Saraswati, Swami Dayananda	– (1824-1883) founder of Arya Samaj.

Sarpachi	– chaplet of pearls for the turban. One of the old distinctions of Maharaja Krishnaraj of Mysore.
Sauvrezis, Alice	– composer and pianist. She organized artistic evenings consisting partly of authentic Oriental music and partly of Occidental music inspired by the Orient.
Sayaji Garbawali	– name of a book of songs composed by Inayat Khan and dedicated to the Maharaja of Baroda whose name is Sayaji.
Sayyad, Sayyed	– a descendant of the Prophet Muhammad, a title, lord, chief.
Scott, Dr. A.B. (Khalif)	– see biographical sketches.
Scott, Cecil	– should probably be Cyril Scott, a friend of Percy Grainger, composer, and author of books on occult subjects.
Scriabin, Alexander Nicolajevitch	– Russian composer and pianist (1871-1915). He had a religious and mystical conception of art and believed in the redeeming nature of music. He was interested in Oriental philosophy which inspired his compositions *Poem of Ecstasy; Divine Poem* and others. He consecrated the last years of his life to a work that united music, poetry, dance, light-show and perfume, culminating in the ecstatic return of the cosmos to the Only Being.
Shake	– vibrato on the instrument, thrill.
Shakuntala	– a poetic work by Kalidasa (in verse).
Shams-e-Tabrez, Tabriz	– a dervish Sufi mystic and poet who became the spiritual guide of Jelaluddin Rumi. The latter dedicated *The Diwan of Shams-e-Tabriz* to his Murshid.
Shankaracharya	– one of the greatest philosophers of India, exponent of the *Advaita Vedanta* (8th or 9th century A.D.).
Shastra	– scripture, science.
Shastri	– a learned man.
Shaughnessy, Mr. E. (Sheikh)	– see biographical sketches.
Shishya	– disciple, mureed.
Shiva	– the disintegrating or destroying and reproducing Deity who is the third God of the Hindu Trinity. Literally the name means: 'in whom all things lie'.
Shuhud	– visible. The vision of the God of Truth seen by Himself. Pir-o-Murshid Inayat Khan says in Manifestation: 'the fourth step of the consciousness, viz. its conscious experience of life from the depth to its utmost height.'

432   NOTES AND GLOSSARY

Sikh	– follower of the religion taught by Guru Nanak.
Sirkar, Sarkar	– chief, master, Your Honour.
Sirkar Ali	– Your Eminent Honour.
Sitar	– a stringed instrument, smaller and without the curved neck and gourd of the vina and with a single bridge. The strings are made of steel and brass. The Karnatic sitar is somewhat different from the sitar used in Northern India.
Skrine, F.H.	– wrote *The Heart of Asia* in collaboration with E.D. Ross.
Société Unitive	– organisation founded by Albert Caillet.
Söderblom, Nathan	– Swedish Lutheran theologian. In 1914 he became archbishop of Uppsala, and in 1930 he was awarded the Nobel Prize for Peace. He promoted unity among the Christian Churches and was a propagator of the Ecumenical Movement.
Sorbonne	– Paris University, founded by Robert de Sorbon (1201-1274) as an establishment for poor students to study Theology. In 1554 the Sorbonne became the official meeting place of the faculty of Theology. In 1808 its buildings were given to the Paris University.
Spiritualism	– doctrine of the existence of the spirit as a substantial reality; also belief in spirit-communication. It spread from the U.S.A to several countries in Europe.
Stam, Miss D. (Kismet)	– see biographical sketches.
Statue of Liberty	– name of a colossal statue in New York harbour, originally called *Liberty enlightening the World*. It was a gift from France to the U.S.A. in 1886 and was conceived by the sculptor Bartholdi. Pir-o-Murshid Inayat Khan wrote a poem about this statue.
Steer, Janette	– English actress and popular lecturer, who wrote articles about the Woman's Part in the Life of the British Nation.
Steindamm, Dr.	– see biographical sketches.
Steiner, Dr. Rudolf	– (1861-1925) founder of Anthroposophy.
Stolk, Mr. A. van (Sheikh Sirkar)	– see biographical sketches.
Strangways, Arthur Henry Fox	– author of *The Music of Hindostan* with illustrations and musical notes (Oxford 1914).
Subedar	– chief of a province. Collector of taxes. A title.
Sudra, shudra	– a man of the fourth or servile caste of the Hindus.

Sufism	– 'Sufism is the religious philosophy of love, harmony and beauty. It is the essence of religions.' As a school its descent and tradition go back to the earliest times, and can be traced from Egypt, through the Hebrew prophets, spreading later to Persia and throughout the East. The Sufi Message descends from this School and yet is new. 'It can only be explained as a certain light thrown upon life. It is the process by which this light, the divine inheritance of man, is unveiled.' (The quoted words are from Pir-o-Murshid Inayat Khan.)
Summer School	– also called *Urs* by Pir-o-Murshid Inayat Khan. The idea of holding a Summer School was first carried out in 1921, when Pir-o-Murshid gathered a small group of mureeds from different countries at Wissous, near Paris, where he was then living. From 1922 on, the Summer Schools took place at Suresnes, France and more and more mureeds attended. A letter was sent out explaining the object of the Summer School as being 'a meeting of a sacred character which takes place at the time when Pir-o-Murshid is taking a time of tranquillity after all the months spent in spreading his ideas throughout the world. During this season Murshid gives a part of his time to talks, meditation and interviews with his mureeds...'
Sundar	– Indian Saint, poet.
Svarga	– going to, or being in Heaven. Heaven.
Swiss Guards	– Swiss troops forming part of the military house of Charles VIII, king of France (1496) and his successors. From the 15th to the 19th century numerous Swiss soldiers served in foreign armies, especially in France. Today there still exists a corps of Pontifical Swiss guards at the Vatican, Italy.
Tabarruk	– sacred relics, sacred gift, looking for a blessing by partaking of rose petals or food which has been exposed on the tombs of saints or other holy places. In Hindi: *prasad*.
Tagore, Devendranath	– (1817-1905), founder of the Brahmo Samaj with Raja Ram Mohan Roy in 1830, father of Rabindranath Tagore.

Tagore, Rabindranath	– (1861-1941), Bengali poet and mystic who won the Nobel Prize for literature in 1913. He founded a school where he tried to blend the best of Indian and Western literature.
Tagore, Surendra Mohan	– (second half 19th century) Bengali Pandit, author of important works on music, e.g. *Universal History of Music*, a compendium of musical knowledge.
Tambura	– a stringed instrument without which no Indian orchestra is complete. Its varieties are numberless. In shape it is something like the vina, without the extra gourd and without the elaborate headpiece.
Tanasukh	– transformation, transmigration, reincarnation.
Tansen, Tan Sen	– famous musician and composer (second half 16th century), born and buried at Gwalior. He was summoned to the Court of the Emperor Akbar. Homage is still paid at his tomb. Pir-o-Murshid Inayat Khan wrote a play about Tansen, published in the magazine *Sufi* of April 1916.
Tanzih	– the first three steps towards manifestation. The identification of the Only Being by negation: 'He is not this ... not that.'
Tappa	– a typical Muslim song with very rich melody, consisting as a rule of two movements only; usually a love song.
Tashbih	– the last three steps towards manifestation. The identification of the Only Being by the way of comparison: 'He is like this ... like that.'
Tawhid	– being single or alone, declaring God to be One alone.
Theosophical Society	– founded in 1875 in the United States of America by Helena Petrovna Blavatski and Colonel Henry Steel Olcott. The latter became its first President and at his death in 1906, Mrs. Annie Besant succeeded him. In 1882 the headquarters were established in India, first at Benares and then at Adyar (Madras). The objects of the Theosophical Society are to form a nucleus of the Universal Brotherhood of Humanity without distinction of race, creed, sex, caste or colour; to encourage the study of comparative religion, philosophy and science; and to investigate the unexplained laws of nature and the powers latent in man. The Theosophists consider that belief should be the result of individual study or intuition and should rest on knowledge.

Ticca gharry, tikka gari	– horse-cab.
Todi	– one of the most common of the Karnatic ragas.
Traz, Robert de	– French-Swiss writer, born in Paris in 1884, author of novels and essays. He founded *La Revue de Genève*.
Trigunatita, Swami	– head of the Hindu temple and Teacher of the Vedanta Society in San Francisco, USA, disciple of Shri Ramakrishna.
Tripech	– mark of honour. One of the old distinctions used by Maharaja Krishnaraj of Mysore.
Tukaram	– Mararthi Saint-poet (1598-1649). Unsuccessful in his business as a grain dealer, he became a wandering ascetic and devoted his life to spiritual exercises and to the composing of religious songs. His *abhangas* are among the most famous of Indian poems.
Tuyll van Serooskerken, H. P. Baron van (Sheikh Sirdar)	– see biographical sketches.
Tuyll van Serooskerken, H. Baronesse van (Saida)	– see Willebeek le Mair, Henriette.
Tyaga Raja, Swami (Tyagaiya)	– a well-known Karnatic musician, great singer and poet (1759-1847) who lived and died at Tanjore, Southern India. He wrote over 800 songs and found the source of his inspiration in his worship of Ram. He gathered around himself a group of disciples who have continued his tradition. He was a creative musical genius and his compositions mark a definite advance in the musical development of Southern India.
Universel, The	– the Sufi Temple which was to be built at Suresnes. Pir-o-Murshid Inayat Khan gave the outline for its construction and further indications. It is meant to be a place for Universal Worship and a centre for art, study and meditation.
Urdu	– literally: army, camp. The Hindustani language spoken by the Muslims of India. It contains Hindi, Arabic and Persian words.
Urs	– wedding festivity, generally indicating the anniversary of the death of a Saint. It may refer to the union with the Divine Beloved, attained by him/her and completed at the time of his/her death. Pir-o-Murshid Inayat Khan also used to term the Summer School at Suresnes *Urs*.

Ustad	– master, teacher.
Ustadi	– superior.
Vainic	– relating to the Vina.
Vairagya	– a Sanskrit word meaning indifference. Pir-o-Murshid Inayat Khan explains it in the following words: 'Renunciation of the desires of the senses, Vairagya means satisfaction, the feeling that there is no desire more to be satisfied, that there is nothing on earth that is desired.'
Vajad Ali Shah (Wajad...)	– last Nawab of Oudh, a great patron and innovator of Indian dance.
Vakil, Wakil	– advocate, lawyer, administrator.
Vallabhacharya	– born in 1479. Devotee of Shri Krishna; a celebrated Vaishnava teacher and founder of a Vaishnava Sect, a poet and philosopher. At an early age he began travelling throughout India to propagate his doctrine and finally settled down at Benares where he composed seventeen works the most important of which were his commentaries on the *Vedanta* and on the *Bhagavata-Purana*. He taught a non-ascetical view of religion.
Vedanta	– the explanation of the creed of the Hindus, called *Vedanta* either as teaching the ultimate scope of the *Veda* or simply as explained in the *Upanishads* which come at the end of the *Veda*, *Vedanta* meaning: the end of the *Vedas*.
Vidurniti	– a book on morals and politics of State during the reign of Shri Krishna written by Vidura.
Viladat	– birth. Viladat Day, the 5th of July, being the birthday of Pir-o-Murshid Inayat Khan, still celebrated by his mureeds.
Vina	– a stringed instrument having a large wooden hollow bowl on one side and a detachable gourd on the other side near the neck. Besides the main strings (4) stretched over the body of the instrument, it has a number of side strings on a separate bridge (3), which is fastened to the main bridge and to the wooden bowl. It is played either with the fingernails or with a plectrum.
Vinayak	– Vina player. The suffix 'ak' expresses action, a name of Vishnu.

Vishnu	– literally: immanent spirit, the God who preserves. One of the Hindu Trinity of Gods, the other two being Brahma, the Creator, and Shiva, the Destroyer.
Vivekananda, Swami	– (1863-1902), disciple of Shri Ramakrishna. Founder of the monastic Order of Ramakrishna and of the Vedanta Society in New York, USA in 1896.
Vodyer, Bahadur Krishna Rajindra	– Maharaja of Mysore, whose dynasty dates from the beginning of the 15th century.
Waiz	– preacher.
Wajad	– ecstasy, rapture.
Walaja	– dignitary.
Walsh, Walter	– leader of the Free Religious Movement, who wrote *The Free Religious Movement Explained* (London 1925) and *My Spiritual Pilgrimage from Sectarianism to Free Religion*.
Willebeek le Mair, Henriette (Saida)	– (1889-1966), illustrator of many books for children, among others *Little songs of Long Ago* and *Christmas Carols for young children*. Between 1911 and 1917 she published her popular books of illustrated nursery rhymes. Besides this she decorated a children's chapel in a church and a children's ward in a hospital in the Netherlands. Apart from her many drawings, paintings and designs, she made water colour pictures of various episodes in Pir-o-Murshid Inayat Khan's life (see *The Flower Garden of Inayat Khan*, 1978) When on a visit to India she made a drawing of Khwaja Moinuddin Chishti's tomb in Ajmer. Her artistic temperament found also expression in dancing and playing the vina. She married Mr. H.P. Baron van Tuyll van Serooskerken.
Wise, Rabbi Dr. S.S.	– from the New York Herald, European edition, Paris 26th December 1925: '... Rabbi Wise's announcement in a sermon earlier in the week that the Jews must acknowledge the teachings of Jesus as that of a great Jewish scholar, created a storm in Jewry throughout the country.'
Wujud	– existence, manifestation. Inayat Khan calls it in Manifestation: 'the third step of the consciousness, viz. the creation of vehicles such as mind and body.'

Yoga	– yoking, setting to work, effort, concentration of the mind, meditation, contemplation, a discipline aiming at the obtaining of the union of the individual soul with the Universal Soul.
Yogi, yogin	– one who practises yoga.
Zamindar	– landlord, landowner.
Zanetti, Mr. E. de Cruzat (Sheikh)	– see biographical sketches.
Zikr, Dhikr	– remembrance, recital of the praise and names of God; a Sufi practice.

Index

As noted in the Editor's Note and before the Notes and Glossary, in India surnames, family names are not used in the same way as in Europe. For this reason in creating this Index, Indian individual are listed by their first name, ie Maheboob Khan is found under M and not K, Sayyed Mohammed Abu Hashim Madani is found under M (Sayyed being a title and not a name); Noorunissa Inayat Khan under N and not either I or K, etc. There are two entries for Pir o Murshid's wife, one under Amina Begum, the title she was known by, and one under her maiden name, Baker; titles of books are listed in italics.

A

Aarhus, Denmark 391
Abdul Baha 208, 402
Abdul Qadir, Maulavi 65, 75, 430
Abhedananda, Swami 209, 400
Abrams, Dr. Albert 192, 400
Abu'l-Ala
 – Arabian poet 78
Academy of Music
 – of Baroda 25, 29, 41, 44, 45, 47, 113, 404, 412
Advaita 76, 400, 431
Adyar 201, 434
Afsar-ul-Mulk 64, 400
Ahl-i-Hadith 197, 400
Ahmad Khan, Sir Sayyed 17, 131
Ahmadia Movement 17, 400
Ahsan ul Haq, Sheikh 343
Ajmer 10, 77, 387, 407, 437
Akbar 65, 66, 401, 413, 422, 434
Akdanta, Mount 56
Alaoddin Khan, Dr. (Dr. Pathan) 10, 45, 46, 58, 60, 102-104, 257, 365, 425
Alchemy of Happiness, The 133
Alexandra, Queen 129
Alhigazi, Mr. Fouad Selim Bey 136

Ali Hussain 23
Ali Khan, Murshid 13, 46, 101, 104, 109, 129, 260, 270, 273, 278, 365, 418
Ali, Hazrat 401
Alias, Saint 28
Aligarh College 17, 401, 418
Allahdad Bakhsh Khan 44, 380
Alt, Miss Angela 176, 184, 334, 343, 349, 350, 360
America, United States of 10, 178, 371, 389, 410, 414, 454
Amina Begum, Ora Ray 164, 165, 266, 319
Amsterdam, Netherlands 141, 182, 397
Anandacharlu, Right Hon Mr. 59
Anjuman Islam 89
Anthroposophy 205, 401, 432
Antichrist 204
Antwerp, Belgium 141, 397
Anvar Khan 19
Apostles, the twelve 204
arbab-i nishat 25, 401
Arcot, the Prince of 81
Aristocracy and democracy 208
Arjuna 43, 401, 404

440 INDEX

Armstrong, Mr. RAL
– Sheikh Mumtaz 178, 327, 344, 368, 401
Arnhem, Netherlands 141, 352, 376, 397
Arnold, Sir Edwin 198
Art in the East and West 25, 219
Artificiality of life in the West 218
Arya Samaj 17, 400, 402, 409, 430
Aryans, the 89, 402
ashrafi 65, 402, 422
Assagioli, Dott. 176, 402
Assam 100, 402
Astor Library 111
At the Gate of Discipleship 133, 349
Attar 9

B

Baba Bharati 111, 209
Babism 208, 402
Bacciocchi, Contessa 174
Bagley, Mr. 155
Baha Ullah 208, 402
Bahadur Hadi Pasha Khan 59
Bahadur Khan 28
Bahadur Walji Lalji Khan 59
Bahaism 136, 208
Bahujangi Raja 57
Bailly, Edmond 114, 269, 403
Baker, Judge 165
Baker, Mrs Eddy 166, 206, 403
Baker, Ora Ray (Amina Begum) 164, 165, 266, 319
Bala Sabha 47, 403
Balakin, Henry 119, 276
Balasangitmala 53
Bandanawaz 74, 76, 77
Bangalore 83, 85, 387
Barany, Baron and Baronin von 178, 184
Barnes, Dr. 154
Baroda 10, 18, 22-27, 29, 33, 34, 44-48, 51, 53, 54, 58-60, 70, 73, 77, 80, 99, 102-104, 131, 167, 251, 252, 255, 364, 387, 412, 421, 424, 431
Baroda College 18

Bartram, Mrs. 136
Basel, Switzerland 173, 178, 184, 393
Baum, Mr. George 154, 344, 403
Baur, Herr 176, 182, 325
Beecham, Sir Thomas 129, 403
Belgachia, Dewan Hiran Maya of 47, 403
Belgium 141, 143, 167, 176, 182, 352, 356, 359, 397
Benares, India
– now Varanasi 17, 54, 201, 387, 404
Bengal, India 93, 99, 100, 403, 434
Bennetts, Missses 155
Benton, Miss Rose (Bahar) 127, 283, 403
Bergen, Norway 180, 391
Berkeley, USA 110, 191, 346, 389
Berkley, Lady 131
Berlin, Germany 143, 148, 178, 180, 184, 361, 374, 375, 377, 391, 430
Bern, Switzerland 176, 184, 350, 370, 393
Besant, Mrs. Annie 133, 190, 200-202, 205, 403, 411, 420, 424, 434
Best, Mr. Cecil E.B. (Sheikh Shahbaz) 127, 286, 346, 404
Best, Mr. Clifford 127
Between the Desert and the Sown
– by Nargis Dowland 133, 349
Bevere, Monsieur de 141
Bey Beg 121
Bhagavad Gita 43, 401, 404, 419
Bharati, Baba 111, 209, 404
Bhartiji 48
Bhatkhande, Pandit 62, 404
Bhim Shamsher of Nepal, Maharaja 54, 57
Bible, the 78, 190, 197, 198, 225, 369, 403
Bima Biy 404
Biographical Department 356
Bjerregaard, Mr. C.H.A. 111, 125, 404
Björset, Herr Bryn (Beorse) 180, 344, 405
Blavatsky, Mrs. E.P. 201, 202
Bloch, Miss Regina Miriam 10, 125, 405
Bloomfield, Lady 136
Bodmer, Mr. and Mrs. 131
Bois, Jules 114, 405

INDEX

Bombay, India
– now Mumbai 60-62, 364, 387, 421
Bommer, Dr. 141, 176
Boston, USA 154, 209, 222, 377, 389, 408
Bournemouth, UK 184, 372, 395
Bowl of Saki 133
Braam, Mejuffrouw A. van (Salima) 182, 330
Brahmo Samaj 17, 210, 405, 410, 418, 429, 433
Brazil 127, 346
Brémond, Comtesse de 143
Breteuil, Marquis de 138, 405
Bridges, Sir Robert 131, 405
Brotherton, Mrs. 127
Brown, Bishop William 190, 405
Brussels, Belgium 141, 176, 359, 370, 397
Buddha 91, 352, 408
Burbank, Luther 154, 315, 405
Burkhardt, Fraulein M. 173, 322
Burma
– now Myanmar 10, 90, 406

C

Caillet, Monsieur A.I. 114, 272, 363, 406, 432
Calcutta
– now Kolkata 10, 24, 93, 95, 97, 99, 103, 387, 403, 427
California, USA 154, 192, 347, 368, 371, 374
Callow, Miss 123
Carpenter, Mr. Edward 129, 288, 406
Carrel, Dr. Alexis 190, 191, 406
Cascia, Monsignore 174
Caste distinctions 74, 85
Celibacy 196
Ceylon
– now Sri Lanka 10, 90, 408, 423, 424
Chaliapin, Feodor Ivanovitch 119, 406
Chandra Vikram Shah, Prince 57
Chappel, Mrs. 127
Chicago, USA 46, 154, 155, 165, 209, 389, 407
China 141, 157, 347, 413

Chishti(s) 19, 63, 71, 77, 403, 407, 420, 422, 437
Chitti Babu 81
Cholia 85, 87, 407
Choumitzky, Monsieur 138
Christ, Jesus 157, 161, 197, 204, 237
Christian Church 195-199, 224, 432
Christian Science 166, 206, 403, 407
Christiania, Norway
– now Oslo 180
Christianity 17, 161, 206, 237, 401, 405, 425
Christowsky, Madame 138
Chromatics, International College of 131, 408, 416, 426
Church of All
– aka Universal Worship 133, 178, 318, 344, 359, 364, 367, 372, 376, 377, 406, 435
Churchill, Lady 114
Clain, L'Abbé 196
Cochin, India 89, 387
Coimbatore, India 89, 387
Collins, Miss 111
Colombo, Sri Lanka 61, 90, 387, 408
commercialism 43, 61, 115, 161, 199, 219, 222
Conan Doyle, Sir A. 207
Confessions of Inayat Khan, the 10, 125, 405
Congress of World Religions
– San Francisco, USA 111
Congress, Musical
– Paris, France 123, 408, 410
Connaughton, Mr. E.P.A. (Khalif) 155, 316, 347, 408
Conrow, Mr. Edgar 155
Conservatory of Music, Imperial
– Moscow, Russia 119
Conservatory of Music,
– London 113
Coomaraswami, Dr. A.C. 154
Coon, Mrs. Sitara 157
Copenhagen, Denmark 180, 391
Corsh, Professor 121
Cosgrave, Mr. 186

Cossimbazar, Maharaja of 99
Cotton, Mr. and Mrs. 46
Coué, Emile 158, 408
Craig, Mr. and Mrs. 184, 335, 348, 408
Crowley, Mr. Chase 157, 186, 190
Cunard, Lady 129
Cushing, Mrs. Marya (Sheika Khushi) 150, 157 191, 317, 348, 408

D

Dadu 17, 43, 202, 408
Dalcroze 230, 408
Darmstadt, Germany 143, 391, 418
Das Banerji, Sir Guru 95
Dasei 81, 409
Dayananda Saraswati 17, 43, 202, 402, 409
Debussy, Claude 114, 271, 409
Decca, Nawab of 100
Delhi Darbar 27
Democracy and aristocracy 208
Denmark 180, 352, 377, 391
Dervish 10, 19, 42, 78, 79, 85, 95, 104, 165, 200, 354, 409, 411, 429, 431
Detraux, Madame 138, 358, 409
Detroit, USA 154, 155, 191, 360, 389
Devendranath Tagore 17, 202, 210, 405, 433
dharma 52, 409
Dhiraja of Nepal, Maharaja 55
Dholuk 79, 409
dhrupad 29, 232, 409, 418, 425
Dickson, Mr. 127
Dietrich, Herr 143
Dikshitar 21, 51, 409
Din Dayal, Raja 62, 409
Dinajpur, Maharaja of 100
Diwan of Inayat Khan 125, 410
Dowland, Miss J.E. (Khalifa Nargis) 131, 133, 167, 294, 349, 350, 409
Duffy, Mr. and Mrs. 154
Dulac, Edmond 131, 410
Duncan Westbrook, Mrs. Jessie 125, 410
Duncan, Isadora 114, 410, 429

Dunsany, Lord 113
Durand, Mrs. 155
Dussaq, Monsieur E. (Khalif Talewar) 136, 144, 182, 310, 350, 373, 410

E

East and West 11, 101, 110, 161, 209, 210, 215, 217, 221, 226, 232, 372, 410
East, Inayat Khan's longing for 165
Eastern Rose Garden, In a 127
Ecorcheville, Professor Jules 123, 408, 410
Education 17, 18, 25, 26, 37, 51, 53, 60, 87, 356, 369, 375, 401, 404, 407
Egeling, Mevrouw N. (Murshida Fazal Mai) 169, 321, 351, 410
Eggink-van Stolk, Mevrouw G. (Bhakti) 155, 182, 332
Eichthal, Madame M.C. la Baronne d' 138, 182, 303, 353, 357, 373, 410
Ektadarul Huq, Maulana 95
Elder, Paul 154, 191
Eldering, Mrs. 111, 154
Ellis Island 150, 410
Emerald ring 65
England 10, 45, 46, 58, 113, 123, 125, 127, 129, 131, 133, 154, 162, 167, 176, 184, 210, 344, 346, 347, 349, 352, 354, 360-362, 367, 372, 376, 405, 408, 410, 420, 423, 425
Engle, Mr. E (Sheikh Fatha) 157, 173, 191, 318, 353, 410
Ernakulam 89, 387
Eucken, Professor Rudolf 143, 411
Europe 13, 18, 45, 58, 102, 112, 150, 157, 158, 178, 201, 354, 373, 375
Exhibition
– of Chicago 46, 209, 407

F

Faqir 42, 57, 67, 68, 77, 95, 104, 220, 402, 411
Farinola, Marchesa (Zebunnisa) 324, 358, 411
Farwerck, Herr 141

Fate and free will
- a dialogue between 42
Fatima Bibi 29, 30
Fazal Manzil 320, 336, 351, 352, 356, 367, 375, 411
Fitz Simon, Mrs. 131
Fizl Rubbee
- the Dewan 99
Fletcher, Miss Aileen 127
Florence, Italy 173, 174, 176, 184, 391, 402, 404
Ford, Mr. Henry 191, 411
Formichi, Professor 176
France 10, 45, 114, 115, 131, 133, 138, 200, 352-354, 357, 363, 373, 376, 391, 403, 410, 411, 416, 432, 433
Frankfurt, Germay 143
Frankowska, Madame 138
French, Lord 129
Frey, Mr. and Mrs. 191, 374
Frossard, Professor Henri Jean 131, 411
Furnée, Miss J.E.D. (Khalifa Sakina)
- later Nekbakht 10, 11, 141, 176, 182, 305, 356, 357, 412

G

Gandhi, Mahatma 162, 412, 419, 424, 425
Ganesh 50, 51, 409, 412
Ganges, the 54
Gasparri, Cardinal 174, 412
Gayanshala 41, 44, 47, 255, 365, 412
Gélis Didot, Madame and Mademoiselle 138
Geneva, Switzerland 131, 133, 136, 144, 159, 162, 173, 176, 178, 186, 343, 344, 350, 372, 373, 377, 393, 419
Germany 45, 123, 143-145, 147, 148, 178, 180, 184, 231, 352, 364, 373, 375-377, 391, 410, 417
Ghasit Khan 19-21
Ginkel, Herr and Mevrouw van 141
Giuliani, Signorina 174
Glaser, Herr 173, 284
Gold medals
- loss of 97, 100
Goodenough, Miss L.
(Murshida Sharifa) 10, 11, 125, 136, 144, 162, 173, 174, 182, 280, 357, 413
Gopika Ramon Roy, the Raja of Sylhet 100
Görcke, Professor 180
Government, British 17
Govind Vishnu Dev 42
Graeffe-van Gorckum, Madame E. 141, 176, 308, 359, 413
Graffenried, Baron von 136, 300
Grainger, Percy 113, 413, 431
Gregory, Mrs. D.A. (Sheikha) 360, 413
Gruner, Dr. O.C. (Khalif) 127, 287, 360, 362, 363, 413
Grünewaldt, Baronin A. von 178
Gubbins, Mr. and Mrs. 131
Guillon, Colonel 131, 138, 363, 413
Gujerat, India 19, 33, 412, 413, 418, 421
Gulbarga, India 65, 74, 76, 387, 403
Guni Jan Khana, Jeypur 25
Gupta, Mr. 210, 410
Gupta, Sir 131
Gwalior, India 54, 387, 413, 434

H

Haarlem, Netherlands 141, 239, 397
Habib-ud-Din, Maulawi 65, 81
Hackett, Philip 154
Hadu
- the eminent singer 54
Hafiz Khan 66
Hafiz, Khwaha Shamsuddin 9, 78, 79, 203, 225, 413
Hagen, Germany 143, 391
Haglund, Fröken 178
Hague, The, Netherlands 141, 182, 350, 356, 364, 373, 376, 377, 397, 416
hal
- ecstasy 72
Hamsa 110, 414
Hamsadhvani, raga 51, 409
Hamsasvarupa, Swami 49
Harding, Lady 129

Harding, President 113
Harish Chandra
  – the play 38, 414
Harmony 62, 65, 79, 100, 101, 123, 229, 358, 364, 371, 400, 403, 406, 433
Harrogate, UK 127, 395
Hart van Sautter, Mr. and Mrs. 133, 299
Hashimi, Maulana 66
Hassan Bilgrami, Maulawi Sayyed 65, 404
Hasu Khan 54
Havens, Mrs. Frank 154, 191
Headly, Lord 210
Headquarters
  – of the Sufi Movement 11, 133, 136, 144, 178, 182, 243, 343
Hedemann, Professor 143, 414
Hengstenberg, Herr and Fräulein 143
Hepburn, Miss D. 154
Héris, Madame 141, 307
Hermund, Herr 180
Hessen, Herzog von 143
Hidayat Inayat Khan 165, 416
Hierarchy, spiritual 115, 200, 201
High School
  – of Baroda 53
Higher Thought 206
Higher Thought Centre 123
Himalaya 57, 201, 405, 424
Hindi 59, 109, 410, 414, 423, 433, 435
Hindu literature 202
Hindu morals 42, 436
Hindu music 46, 407
Hindu mythology 110
Hindu philosophy 209
Hindu poets 202
Hindu temple 110, 209, 424, 435
Hinduism 49, 405, 423
Hindustani language 435
Hindustani Lyrics 125
Hiran Maya, Babu 97
Hobart, Mr. and Mrs. 155
Hoeber, Mrs. L (Sheikha) 178, 186, 328, 364, 414

Hogendorp, Jonkvrouwe P. van (Lakme) 178, 327, 344
Hogendorp, Mevrouw A. Baronesse van (Mahtab) 136, 176, 182, 302
Holland (the Netherlands) 141, 167, 176, 178, 182, 350-352, 356, 365, 373, 376
Holmes, Mr. August 113
Honour 19, 21, 23, 25, 38, 43, 48, 50, 52, 71, 91, 97, 170, 364, 365, 367, 406, 419, 432, 435
Hope, Miss 123
House, Colonel 190
Howen, Baron von 184
Hoyack, de Heer L. (Salamat) 182, 358, 414, 415
Human Personality 133
Hurst, Mrs. 155, 191
Hydari, Mr. A 66
Hyderabad, India 13, 23, 24, 26, 60, 62, 64-68, 70, 73, 250, 387, 409, 416, 420, 422, 424, 427, 430

I

Idar, Kathiawar, Gujarat, India 49
Imad-ul-Mulk, Nawab 65
Imperial School of Opera and Ballet
  – Russia 119
Inayat Bibi 33
India
  homesick for – 165
India in 1882 17
Ingen-Jelgersma, Mevrouw J. van (Zuleikha) 182, 331
Inleiding tot het Soefisme 141
Inner Life 133
Irwin, Miss Beatrice 113, 268, 416
Isaachsen, Fru 180
Islam
  – and mosque at Woking, UK 210
  – and Protestantism 197
  – and Qur'an 78, 197, 198, 415, 417, 426
  – and the Prophet 9, 31, 40, 49, 56, 66, 78, 197, 204, 205, 208, 226, 237, 367, 400, 401, 413, 418, 426, 428, 431
  prejudice against – 161, 198, 200

Italy 45, 173, 176, 184, 343, 348, 352, 391, 404, 433
Ivanov, Mr. 119, 123, 416

J
Jafar Khan 28
Jaipur, India 25, 48, 387
Jalatarang 80, 417
Jami 79, 417
Japan 110, 112, 136, 157, 347, 413, 430
Jemat Ali Shah, Pir 83
Jena Bibi 30, 35
Jena, Germany 143, 391, 414
Jenssen, Herr 180
Jews 70, 198, 437
Jilani, Khwaja Abdul Qadir 75, 407, 417, 430
Jinn 48, 417
Jinsi Wali 38
Jorys, Mademoiselle 114
Jotindra Mohan Tagore, Maharaja 24

K
Kabbala 204, 417
Kabir 17, 26, 43, 202, 408, 417
Kahlil Gibran 210, 413
Kahn, Mrs. Otto 190
Kaiser Wilhelm II 221, 417
Kala Bhawan 18, 417
Kamaluddin, Khwaja 210
Kandy, Sri Lanka 90, 387
Kanhai 23
Karamat Khan 30, 383
Karma 76, 202, 203, 214, 418
Karnatic
  the music of the - 21, 23, 24, 47, 60, 85, 87, 418, 432, 435
Kashmir, Maharaja of 28
Kathiawar, Gujerat 49, 418
Kathmandu, Nepal 56, 57, 424
Kaushik Ram, Professor 47
Kavi Ratnakar 43, 418
Kerdijk, Mejuffrouw 141
Keshoba Chandra Sen 202, 210, 405, 410, 418

Kesri Singh, Raja 49
Keyserling, Graf 143, 418
Khadim Hussain 23
Khair-ul-Mubin, Maulana 68
Khairunnisa Inayat Khan (Claire) 166, 305, 416
Khan, Alaoddin (Dr. Pathan) 25, 45, 46, 58, 60, 102-104, 257, 425
Khan, Captain Baker Ali 81
Khan, Murshid Ali 13, 46, 101, 104, 109, 129, 260, 270, 273, 278, 365, 418
Khanda Rao, Maharaja 22, 24, 26
Khankah, London 129, 131, 291, 418
Khankah, San Francisco 192, 418
Khatidja Bibi
  – (mother of Inayat Khan) 29-31, 58
Khayal 54, 232, 418
Khayyam, Omar 111, 125, 225, 404, 410, 418, 429
Khilafet Movement 162, 419
King, Dr.
  – of Brighton 113, 267
King, Mr.
  – of Harrogate 127
Kishan Gar, Maharaja of Rampur 131
Kishan Pershad, Maharaja of Hyderabad 63, 73
Kismet
  – a play 114, 419
Kjösterud, Fröken Susanna (Sheika) 180, 186, 329, 366
Knights of Purity 9
Krishna Raja Vodyer, Maharaja of Mysore 59
Krishna, Shri 401, 404, 412, 436
Kumar Swami, Mrs. 114
Kumbakonam, India 85, 387

L
La Jolla, USA 192, 374, 389
Laheri, Babu 95
Laka, Comte and Comtesse de 143
Lakmé
  – an opera 129, 290, 419

Laszlo de Lombos, Mr. 131, 419
Lausanne, Switzerland 136, 173, 176, 178, 184, 351, 393
Lavanchy, Madame 136
Lavrovsky, Princess Sirtolov 119, 275
laya 23, 419
Leadbeater, Mr. 201, 404
League of Nations 136, 138, 419
Leeds, UK 127, 361, 362, 395
Lenox Theatre, New York 191
Léon, Professor Henri M. 131, 420
Leverkus, Frau Arens 143
Leverkus, Fräulein Latifa 143
Lewis, Mr. Samuel 154, 420
Liberal Catholic Church 203, 404, 420
Liège, Belgium 182, 397
Life after Death 125
Lincoln, Abraham 112, 420
Lloyd, Mrs. Gladys I. (Sheikha Kefayat) 338, 367, 371, 420
Lodge, Sir Oliver 207, 420
Logan, Mr. 150
Logan, Mrs. 111, 154
London, UK 10, 25, 45, 113, 125, 131,162, 167, 343, 347, 357, 359, 359-362, 367, 372, 374-376, 395, 402-405, 410, 416, 419, 429
Long, Mrs. 154
Los Angeles, USA 110, 154, 155, 192, 374, 389, 430
Love Human and Divine 125
Lowe, Mr. and Mrs. 155
Ludwig, Dr. Arthur 178
Lukman ud Dawlah 62
Lybeck, Dr. E.W. 119

M

Macarthy, Miss Maud 113
Mackenzie, Lady Muir 125
Madar ul Maham 63, 144, 420
Madhari Rao, Sir T. 18, 25
Madras, India 59, 81, 82, 387, 420, 434
Madura 87, 387
Mahajan Mandal 43, 421
Mahamudalyar Bhandara Nayak 90

Mahatma 58, 68, 99, 412, 419, 421, 424
Maheboob Ali Khan, H.H.Mir, the Nizam of Hyderabad 62, 409, 430
Maheboob Khan 101, 102, 109, 186, 261, 270, 278, 319, 364, 365, 418, 426
Maheboob Yar Jung 65
Mahmad Casim Barucha 93
Mahmud Arif 95
Majzub 40, 95, 97, 421
Malabar 21, 89, 407, 423
Malhar Rao, Maharaja of Baroda 24, 25
Manacharsha 95
Manchester, Duke of 129
Manek Prabhu, the temple of 74, 75
Manekpur, India 74
Marathi language 37, 43, 59, 400, 412, 421, 427
Marcks, Madame 141
Markar, Haji Muhammad Macan 90
Markia, Jelaluddin 90
Markias, the 90
Martin, Mrs. Ada (Murshida Rabia) 110, 111, 150, 154, 155, 191, 192, 264, 318, 347, 353, 354, 368, 369, 371, 420, 421, 425
Martin, Pasteur Charles 136
Masiti 91, 93
Masnavi 109, 421, 429
Masonry
  – freemasonry 200, 403, 411, 421
Maula Bakhsh 19-27, 29, 30, 33, 41, 42, 44-46, 48, 49, 53, 54, 60, 95, 102-104, 253, 258, 365, 421
Maula, Mount of 62
Mayan philosophy 191
Meerwijk, de Heer en Mevrouw van 141,
Mehr Bakhshe 10, 29, 30, 255, 400, 422
mehter 112
Meyer de Reutercrona, Frau Hilda (Sheikha) 184, 323, 369, 422
Miller, Mrs. Rebecca C. 154, 313, 371, 422
Minqar-e-Musiqar 62, 422
Miran Datar 77, 422
Mirza Abbas Ali Beg, Sir 131
Mirza Assad Ullah, Mr. 155

INDEX 447

Mirza Ghulam Hussein Qadiani 17, 400
Missionaries 17, 201, 401
missionary 44, 46, 115, 161, 201, 400
Mitchell, Miss Nina 136, 301
Mitchell, Mr. (Sheffield) 129
Mitchell, Mr. Edgar Austin
  (Southampton) 133, 422
Moghul(s) 21, 22, 57, 401, 422, 424
Mohendra Nath Chaterji 95
Moinuddin Chishti 77, 437
Moore, Mr. A. Harry 190
Morax, Monsieur René 173, 422
Morges, Switzerland 173, 393
Morrison, Mrs. 111, 265
Morsi Manoher, Raja 65
Moscow, Russia 115, 121, 122, 273, 391,
  411, 429
Muhammad Abu Hashim Madani,
  Sayyed 10, 13, 70, 71, 420
Muhammad, Nawab Sayyed 81
Muhammad, the Prophet 9, 30, 31, 49,
  69, 204, 237, 401, 418, 426, 428, 431
Muhidin, Sultan of Habibuddin 81
Mukti 76, 202, 423
Müller, Professor Max 198, 423
Munawar Khan 99
Munich, Germany 143, 178, 184, 241, 347,
  364, 373, 391
Murshidabad, India 99, 387
Murtaza Khan 26, 43, 44, 48, 60, 256
Musée Guimet, Paris 138, 182, 413
Musharaff Khan 30, 102, 103, 109, 262,
  270, 274, 278, 319, 418
Mustapha Khan Bahadur, Sayyed 87
Mysticism of Sound, The 133

N

Nagore, India 87
Nanak, Guru 17, 26, 43, 202, 423, 432
Narayan, Swami 17, 202, 423
Nardar 63
Narsiji 42, 424
Narsiji, temple of 53, 424
Nasir Khan 23, 24

Nationalism 157, 199, 212
Natore, Maharaja of 95
Navarat, festival of 59, 424

Nawab Bahadu
  the Dewan of H.H. the - 99
Nawn, Miss Genie 111, 154
nazar 64, 424
Negapatam, India 87, 387
Negroes 112
Nekbakht Foundation 11, 13, 250, 357
Nepal 46, 54-58, 89, 424
Netobi, Dr. 136
Nevada, Madame Emma 129, 289
Nevada, Mignon 129, 290
New Testament 198, 377
New York, USA 107, 109, 111, 150, 154,
  157, 186, 190, 191, 209, 243, 244, 347, 348,
  354, 355, 360, 369, 372-374, 378, 389,
  400, 406, 408, 410, 413, 432, 437
Newbolt, Sir Henry 113, 424
Nice, France 184, 373, 391
Nietzsche, Frau Förster 143
Nizam of Hyderabad 62, 409, 422
Nizami 9
Noorunnisa Inayat Khan 165, 416, 424
Norway 180, 345, 352, 366, 367, 377, 391
Notation, system of 24, 27, 409, 413, 430
Notes of the Unstruck Music 133
Nuralja, Sri Lanka 90, 424
Nyamat Khan 28
Nyrop, Herr 178

O

Oakland, USA 191, 389
Olcott, Colonel 201, 405, 424, 434
Old Testament 198, 377
Oliver, Miss 143, 178, 184, 309
Order of the Star in the East, the 345, 404
Organization 211-216
Oslo, (Christiania), Norway 180, 344,
  366, 391
Otlet, Monsieur P. 143

P

Paderewski, Ignacy Jan 173, 424
pakhawaj 23, 425
Pallavi 60, 409, 425
Panama Canal World Fair 111, 425
Paramananda, Swami 110, 209
Paris, France 10, 46, 114, 123, 131, 138, 176, 182, 184, 196, 208, 345, 347, 350, 353-355, 358, 362, 373, 376, 391, 405, 406, 408, 410, 411, 413, 419, 420, 429, 430, 433, 435, 437
Parsi 61, 66, 70, 425
Pasadena, USA 192, 389
Patan, Baroda State, India 48, 387
Path to God, the 133
Pathan, Dr. A.M.
  – see also Alaoddin Khan 10, 45, 46, 60, 257, 365
Patriotism 161, 199
Pattabhirame Ran 89
Paul, Saint 196, 198
Peak, Miss (later Frau Triebel) 143, 178, 184
Pearls from the Ocean Unseen 125
Perish, Ralph 111
Petersburg, Russia 123, 391, 416
Phenomenon of the Soul, the 125
Philadelphia, USA 157, 389
Pickthall, Mr. Marmaduke 131
Pieri, Comtesse M.L. (nee Dussaq) 136, 144, 182, 311, 350, 372
Poetry – Inayat's interest in 38, 42, 43, 107
Pool, Rev. Dr. John 131, 426
Portier, Madame Slatov 131
Press – the, USA 11, 158, 186, 190-192
Press, the 158, 178, 344, 422
Probha Shankar Patni, Sir, 131
Protestant religion 196-198, 200, 204-206
Prozor, Comte and Comtesse 184
Psychology 24, 109, 111, 143, 207, 208, 353
Punjab, India 28, 29, 57, 400, 425

Q

Qur'an 78, 197, 198, 415, 417, 426
Qutbuddin 87

R

Rabia, of Basra 111, 426
Rabindranath Tagore 95, 113, 210, 417, 425, 433
Ragas 29, 60, 62, 66, 114, 229, 404, 435
Rahmat Khan
  – father of Inayat Khan 28-30, 54, 254
Rahusen, Mejuffrouw Hayat 176
Rahusen, Mejuffrouw Morad 180, 427
Raja Kopal Chari
  – the Dewan 89
Raja of Lalgola 99
Raja Yoga 203, 427
Ram Das 43, 202, 427
Ram Singh, Maharaja 25
Ramakrishna, Swami 209
Rampur, Prince of 131
Ramyar 66, 259, 427
Rangoon, Burma 90, 91, 93, 387
Rapperswil, Switzerland 173, 178, 184, 347, 393
Rasponi, Contessa Spaletti 176
Reebner, Professor C.
  – Head of Music, Columbia University 109, 154
Reelfs, Mr. 133
Reformation, the 197, 199, 204, 220, 221, 428
Reincarnation 21, 76, 192, 202, 203, 214, 240, 434
Reps, Saladin 192, 374, 428
Reutercrona, Dr. von 178
Reutern Barteneff, Madame de 114
Richardson, Lady Constance Stewart 131
Risalat 204, 428
Rockefeller Institute, the 190, 406, 428
Roibul, Monsieur de 138
Rome, Italy 174, 176, 184, 196, 198, 222, 348, 391, 424
roshan chauki 74, 429

Rosing, Mr. 129, 429
Ross, Mr.
 – Principal, Madras College 99
Rotterdam, Netherlands 182, 375, 397
Royal Academy of Music, London 25, 45, 113, 420, 429
Royal Asiatic Society 123
Royal Musicians of Hindustan, the 270, 278, 418, 419, 429, 430
Rubaiyat of Omar Khayyam 125, 410, 419
Rumi, Jelaludin 9, 62, 79, 109, 407, 421, 429, 431
Rummel, Walter 114, 429
Russell, Mr. Edmund 109, 429
Russia 114, 115, 119, 121-123, 129, 174, 199, 201, 368, 391, 410

S

Saʻadi 9, 43, 430
Saintsbury-Green, Miss
 (Murshida Sophia) 10, 296, 343, 359, 413
Salar Jung, Sir 23, 430
Samacharan Dutt, Babu 95
Samadhi 100, 416, 430
San Diego, USA 192, 374, 389
San Francisco, USA 110, 111, 154, 191, 209, 347, 353, 369, 374, 389, 425, 435
Sangit Sammilani 95, 430
Sanskrit 21, 23, 47, 123, 225, 409, 414, 421, 423, 427, 436
Sanskrit College 111, 402
Santa Barbara, USA 155, 192, 347, 374, 389
Santa Rosa, USA 154, 389
Satan, God and 237
Sauvrezis, Mlle. de 138, 431
Sayaji Garbawali 59, 431
Sayaji Rao Gaekwar,
 – Maharaja of Baroda 18, 25, 51, 131, 251, 412
Scandinavia 178, 367
Scherman, Professor 143, 144
Schroeder, Frau 136
Scott, Cecil 113, 431
Scott, Dr. A. B. 131, 293, 372, 431

Scott, Lady Sybil 174
Scriabin, Alexander Nicolajevitch 123, 431
Seattle, USA 110, 389
Secunderabad, India 66-68, 387, 427
Selleger, Professor Ing E. 133, 298
Sen, Mr. 131
Shahzade Aftab Ahmad Khan 131
Shaishanna 60
Shamanna 60
Shams Tabriz 9, 79, 224, 407, 429, 431
Shankaracharya 17, 400, 431
shastra 21, 62, 431
Shastri 47, 431
Shaughnessy, Mr. E. (Sheikh) 157, 186, 373, 431
Sheaf, Mrs. Hanifa 10, 127, 174, 184, 285
Sheffield, UK 127, 129, 395
Sheilds, Miss Wentworth 133
Shewan, Mrs. 191
Shirley, Miss 127, 284
Shiva 123, 408, 431, 437
Shivaji Rao, Raja 87
Shivaraj Bahadur, Raja 65
shudras – castes 85, 112
shuhud 69, 431
Sigoli, India 54
Sikhs 17, 413, 423
Sinha, Lord S.P. 95
Sirdar Dastur Hoshang 66
Sitar 79, 419, 432
Skinner, Miss Margaret 127
Skrine, Mr. F.H. 131, 432
Slavery 81, 112, 403, 420
Smit, Mevrouw Corrie 141
Smith, Mr. 113
Smith, Sir Frederick 131
Social classes in the West 217
Socialism 162, 208
Société Internationale de Philologie, Sciences et Beaux Arts 131, 420
Société Unitive 10, 406, 432
Söderblom, Archbishop Nathan 180, 432
Soefi Boodschap van Geestelijke Vrijheid 141

Songs of India 125
Sorbonne, La (University) 123, 182, 184, 432
Soul Whence and Whither, the 133, 417
South Africa 131, 376
Southampton, UK 127, 184, 346, 349, 350, 395, 422
Spengler, Jonkheer G. van (Shahnawaz) 182, 358
Spiritual Liberty, A Sufi Message of 10, 114, 119
Spiritual path
 – in East and West 68, 214, 220, 357
Spiritualism 206, 207, 432
Springmann, Frau 143
Srinivasa Raghava Ayangar, Dewan 58
St. Denis, Miss Ruth 109, 110, 263, 420, 430
Stam, Mejuffrouw D. (Kismet) 11, 12, 182, 184, 245, 333, 357, 373, 374, 432
Star Movement 141
State Musical Department, Baroda 60
Statue of Liberty 107, 432
Steer, Miss Janette 127, 281, 432
Steindamm, Dr. (Sheikh) 180, 184, 241, 374, 375, 432
Steiner, Dr. Rudolf 205, 401, 432
Steven, Fru Paula 180
Stockholm, Sweden 178, 180, 391
Stolk, de Heer A. van (Sheikh Sirkar) 176, 178, 184, 186, 326, 344, 358, 374-376, 432
Strangways, Mr. Fox 113, 114, 432
Strauss, Herr Ernest 143
Strauss, Madame Gabrielle 131, 173, 292
Strecker, Mr. 113
Stürler, Madame de 141
Subanna 60
Subedar of Gulbarga 65, 432
Subramani Ayar 21, 47
Sufi Book Depot 133, 349
Sufi Magazine 125, 343, 358
Sufi Publishing Society 125, 133
Sufi Trust 131

Sufism and Omar Khayyam 111
Sufism, magazine 11, 133
Sultan-ul-Mulk, Nawab 65
Sumatra, India 87
Summer School 10, 159, 178, 184, 186, 245, 343, 345, 348, 353-355, 364-367, 372, 373, 375, 376, 433, 435
Sundar 17, 26, 43, 202, 433
Surendra Mohan Tagore 24
Suresnes, France 10, 12-14, 144, 157, 159, 169, 178, 245, 343, 345, 348, 350, 351, 353, 354, 356, 358, 364-367, 372-376, 378, 391, 411, 416, 433, 435
Sweden 178, 352, 369, 377, 391
Switalovsky, Madame 119
Switzerland 133, 136-138, 141, 162, 167, 173, 182, 197, 344, 347, 350-352, 356, 370, 376, 377, 393

T
Tagore, Devendranath 17, 202, 210, 405, 409, 433
tahajjud 77
tambura 83, 230, 434
tanasukh 76, 434
Tanjore, India 87, 387, 435
Tanras Khan 54
Tansen 54, 65, 434
tanzih 69, 434
Taraway of Indore, Princess 131
Tartars 121
tashbih 69, 434
Theosophical Publishing Society 119
Theosophical Society, the 17, 89, 127, 141, 180, 190, 201-203, 205, 345, 346, 401, 403, 405, 411, 424, 434
Thistle, Fröken 180
Thomson, Miss Mabel 127, 282
Thurburn, Mr. M.H. 114
Thursby, Emma 109
Tingley, Mrs. 192
Tiruswam Hayra Naidu 81
Toeman, de Heer 141
Tolstoy, Count Serge 119, 123

Towbridge, Lady 131
Travancore, India 89, 426
Traz, Monsieur de 136, 435
Trichinapoli, India 87, 387
Trichur, India 89, 387
Triebel, Herr and Frau (nee Peake) 143, 178, 184
Trigunatita, Swami 110, 209, 435
Trikuti Kavel Krishna Ayar 81, 85
Trotter, Dr. 113
Tucki, Olga 123, 277
Tukaram 43, 202, 435
Tumbara 63
Turkey, Consul for 90
Turner, Dr. 190
Tuticorin, India 90, 387
Tuyll van Serooskerken, H.P. Baron van (Sheikh Sirdar) 141, 144, 176, 182, 186, 304, 350, 367, 376, 435, 437
Tyagaraja 21, 60, 409

U

Umar, Maulawi 67
Unity of Religious Ideals, the 428
Universel 159, 186, 435
University, Berkeley 110
University, Columbia 109, 408
University, Los Angeles 110
University, San Francisco 110
Urdu 30, 59, 362, 410, 419, 426, 435
Urs 157, 417, 433, 435
ustad 66, 436

V

vairagya 50, 51, 70, 232, 436
Vajad Ali Shah 25, 436
Vallabha Charya, Guru 48, 436
Vandernaillen, Mr. 191
Vatican, the 174, 433
Vedanta 76, 157, 209, 210, 225, 423, 431, 436
Vedanta Society 209, 400, 435, 437
Venable, Mrs. 155, 191
Vevey, Switzerland 136, 350, 356, 393

Vidurniti 42, 436
Vilayat Inayat Khan 165, 416
Vina 23, 26, 58, 81, 99, 104, 114, 165, 236, 432, 436, 437
Vinayak 43, 436
Vishnu 42, 43, 419, 421, 427, 436, 437
Vivekananda, Swami 209, 405, 437
Voice of Inayat, the 125

W

Waldorf Astoria Hotel, the 186
Wallace, Dr. 127
Walsh, Rev. Dr. Walter 131, 437
Warr, Lady de la 123
Watson, Dr. 191
Way of Illumination, the 127
Wazir Jung, Nawab 65
Wegelin, de Heer C.A. 141, 306
Weimar, Germany 143, 391
Whitehouse, Mr. 157
Willebeek Le Mair, Mejuffrouw (later Baronesse van Tuyll van Serooskerken) 141, 304, 376, 435, 437
Williams, Miss Mary (Zohra) 125, 127, 279
Wise, Rabbi 190, 437
Wiseman, the Misses 133, 295
Woking, UK 210
Wolff, Mr. and Mrs. 154, 155
Women
  valuable service to Cause by – 150
Women,
  admitted to order of the Masons 200
Women, in the East 243
Women, in the West 218
Women's rights 47
Women's education 26, 53
World Teacher
  the coming of the – 190, 201, 236
World War I 123, 346, 347, 349, 357, 361, 370, 412, 417, 419, 424, 429
Wounded Indian soldiers 125
wujud 69, 437
Wurmbrandt, Graf and Gräfin 174

Y

Yoga 209, 210, 344, 420, 427, 438
Yogis 40
Young, Miss Khatidja 10, 127, 284
Yusuf Ali Subedar, Maulawi 65

Z

Zamindars 19
Zanetti, Monsieur E. de Cruzat 144, 159, 182, 184, 186, 312, 377, 378, 438
Zikr 73, 438
Zoroastrians 66, 401
Zürich, Switzerland 173, 178, 184, 393